CAMBRIDGE STUDIES IN
INTERNATIONAL AND COMPARATIVE LAW

*General Editor:*
SIR ROBERT Y. JENNINGS
Judge of the International Court of Justice,
Former Whewell Professor of International Law
University of Cambridge

# JUDICIAL REVIEW IN COMPARATIVE LAW

CAMBRIDGE STUDIES IN
INTERNATIONAL AND COMPARATIVE LAW
NEW SERIES

Tortious liability for unintentional harm in the Common law
and the Civil law: Volume 1, Text; Volume 2, Materials
F.H. LAWSON AND B.S. MARKESINIS

The application of the rule of exhaustion of local remedies in
international law: its rationale in the international protection
of individual rights
A.A. CANÇADO TRINDADE

The legal regime of foreign private investment in the Sudan and
Saudi Arabia: a case study of developing countries
FATH EL RAHMAN ABDALLA EL SHEIKH

Non-appearance before the International Court of Justice
H.W.A. THIRLWAY

Conflict of Laws
J.G. COLLIER

# JUDICIAL REVIEW IN COMPARATIVE LAW

ALLAN R. BREWER-CARÍAS
Professor in the Central University of Venezuela
Simón Bolívar Professor in the University of Cambridge, 1985/6
Past Fellow of Trinity College, Cambridge

with editorial assistance of D.F. Bur

The right of the
University of Cambridge
to print and sell
all manner of books
was granted by
Henry VIII in 1534.
The University has printed
and published continuously
since 1584.

CAMBRIDGE UNIVERSITY PRESS
CAMBRIDGE
NEW YORK PORT CHESTER
MELBOURNE SYDNEY

Published by the Press Syndicate of the University of Cambridge
The Pitt Building, Trumpington Street, Cambridge CB2 1RP
40 West 20th Street, New York, NY 10011, USA
10 Stamford Road, Oakleigh, Melbourne 3166, Australia

First published 1989

Printed in Great Britain at the University Press, Cambridge

British Library cataloguing in publication data
Brewer-Carías, Allan R.
Judicial review in comparative law –
(Cambridge studies in international and comparative law).
1. Capital punishment. Judicial review –
Comparative studies
I. Title
342.71

Library of Congress cataloguing in publication data
Brewer-Carías, Allan Randolph.
Judicial review in comparative law / Allan R., Brewer-Carías.
p. cm. – (Cambridge studies in international and comparative law. New series)
ISBN 0–521–33387–3
1. Judicial review.    I. Title.    II. Series.
K3175,B74 1989
347–dc 19
[342.7] 88–21085 CIP

ISBN 0 521 33387 3

DQ

# CONTENTS

## Contents

# *Contents*

# Contents

## Contents

## Contents

# Contents

# FOREWORD

When he accepted appointment as Simón Bolívar Professor of Latin American Studies at Cambridge for the year 1985–86, Professor Allan R. Brewer-Carías also accepted assignment to the University's Faculty of Law and agreed to deliver a course of lectures in the Faculty's LL.M. programme for that year. The subject he chose was 'Judicial Review in Comparative Law', and this book contains the substance of his lectures, corrected and revised for publication.

The good fortune of the Faculty in having Professor Brewer-Carías as one of its members for the year will be apparent to all who read this book. The lectures themselves were prepared by the author in English, which is not even his second but his third language, and though some linguistic correction was necessary before publication, the book is not a translation from the author's native Spanish. The effort that this cost him can only be imagined, but there can be no doubt of the value to the reader that no translator is interposed between the author and himself. What is more, while the constitutionalisation of the 'Etat de droit' – a phrase for which there is no adequate English translation – is a central theme and is a process which has only been discussed but never undertaken in this country, Professor Brewer-Carías is, or made himself, more than well enough informed about the peculiarities of English law to be able not only to deal fully with its relevant aspects at an early stage, but to present the whole of his material in a way calculated to make it readily understood by an English lawyer with little or no prior knowledge of other systems.

This does not mean that this is one of those comparative works which starts from a basis of English law. On the contrary, although 'judicial review' has come into the language of English law thanks to Order 53 of the Rules of the Supreme Court, and although Professor Brewer certainly could have written a book about administrative law, he has not done so here. His principal, if not his exclusive, concern in this book is judicial review of legislation and that, of course, we do not have.

Most lawyers in the United Kingdom have by now become accustomed to discussion of the question whether we should introduce a 'Bill of Rights' or otherwise subject parliamentary legislation to judicial control of some kind within our own domestic legal systems. Nevertheless, most of them still seem to believe that the time-hallowed and still prevailing rule in this country about the supremacy of Parliament is in some sense 'natural': the legislation of Parliament can only be interpreted by the judges, never held to be without effect, still less formally annulled. To this elementary principle of democracy, it still seems to be thought by many, only the United States and perhaps some other federal countries with more than one legislature, need create an exception because otherwise they could not maintain the federal division of legislative competence dictated by the Constitution. The fact is, however, that in continuing to exclude judicial control of parliamentary legislation in any form, the United Kingdom finds itself in a tiny minority of developed countries outside the socialist part of the world. Even France, which formerly rejected such control notwithstanding the existence of a written Constitution, and which may be thought therefore to have made even more of Parliamentary supremacy than we do, has now developed through the *Conseil Constitutionnel* its own kind of *a priori* judicial review and two of the socialist countries – Czechoslovakia and Yugoslavia – have actually established constitutional courts. This book should, at least, provide an invaluable corrective to the insularity of our thinking.

It is no part of the business of a Foreword to summarise the contents of the book which follows. It must be said, however, that there is gathered here, probably for the first time and certainly for the first time in English, a wealth of information about the theoretical background and the variety of methods adopted in numerous different countries throughout the world for implementing the subjection of the state, including its legislative arm, to the law. It must also be said that it would be difficult to find anyone better qualified than Professor Brewer-Carías to undertake the mammoth task which the preparation of the original lectures and then this book required. Some of his work, it is true, has been devoted exclusively to the law and its administration in his own country Venezuela, where he has been a Substitute Senator, an Alternate Magistrate of the Supreme Court and President of a Presidential Commission on Public Administration as well as a practising and prolific academic lawyer. His interest in comparative public law, his research and his writings have, however, taken him far beyond the limits of Latin America into North America, Continental Europe and elsewhere. His reputation in those countries which English lawyers tend to lump together as countries of the 'civil law' has for many years been well established. His period as Simón Bolívar Professor in Cambridge and the publication of this book will guarantee that his international renown extends to this country as well. It is not only comparative lawyers but all those who care for the future of law and liberty in this country who owe him a debt of gratitude for the production of this book.

November 1987                                                    J.A. Jolowicz

# PREFACE

This book is an abridged and revised version of a course of lectures I wrote and gave during my tenure as Simón Bolívar Professor of the University of Cambridge, in the academic year 1985–86. The original version, written between September 1985 and May 1986, was the result of the progressive preparation of the forty-hour course of lectures which I gave, as Paper No. 20, on Judicial Review in Comparative Law, in the Degree of Master of Law (LL.M.) course at the Faculty of Law.

Of course, for its publication, the original version of the work needed to be revised, reduced and simplified, not only because of its original lecturing purpose, but mainly because it was written directly in English, which is not even my second language. To carry out this work, the Press suggested Mr Donald F. Bur, a graduate student in Cambridge, who did an excellent job.

I wish to thank Mr Derick Holmes, of the Studio Language Course in Cambridge, for his patient assistance in reviewing with me the original manuscript of my lectures, day by day, before they were delivered. Also, my thanks are due to Mrs Ana Gray, Secretary to the Simón Bolívar professors, who bore the brunt of typing the original version of my lectures and on whose skill I have greatly relied.

My love and appreciation to my wife, Beatriz, whose permanent support allowed me to cope with the intensive work of preparing and writing the lectures.

Finally, my gratitude to the Master and Fellows of Trinity College for the welcome and hospitality I received as a Fellow of the College, and particularly to my friend of many years, Professor J.A. Jolowicz who asked me to give the course of lectures on Judicial Review in Comparative Law that made this book possible. I remain most grateful for his foreword.

A.R.B.C.

# INTRODUCTION

Judicial review, in its original North American sense, is the power of courts to decide upon the constitutionality of legislative acts; in other words, the judicial control of the constitutionality of legislation.

It has been said that judicial review is the most distinctive feature of the constitutional system of the United States of America,[1] and it must be added that it is, in fact, the most distinctive feature of almost all constitutional systems in the world today. All over the world, with or without similarities to the North American system of judicial review, special constitutional courts or ordinary courts have the power to declare a law unconstitutional by declaring it null and void or by annulling it, and as a result refusing to enforce it.

This judicial review of the constitutionality of legislation, in other words of laws and other legislative acts, requires at least three conditions for it to function in a given constitutional system: in the first place, it requires the existence of a written Constitution, conceived as a superior and fundamental law with clear supremacy over all other laws; secondly, such a Constitution must be of a rigid character, which implies that the amendments or reforms that may be introduced can only be put into practice by means of a particular and special process, preventing the ordinary legislator from doing so; and thirdly, the establishment in that same written and rigid Constitution of the judicial means for guaranteeing the supremacy of the Constitution over legislative acts.

By contrast, the system in the United Kingdom is quite different as the main feature that distinguishes the British constitutional system is precisely the lack of judicial review of legislation. Thus, Professor D.G.T. Williams has said that 'most British judges and the vast majority of British lawyers must have had little or no contact with the problems and workings of judicial review'.[2] This substantial difference between the constitutional system of the United Kingdom and, in general, the other constitutional systems in the world, derives from a feature unique to the

British Constitution: the principle of the sovereignty of Parliament. This principle has been described by Dicey as the 'secret source of strength of the British Constitution' or the 'element of power which has been the true source of its life and growth'.[3]

This sovereignty of Parliament, with all its importance in constitutional law in Great Britain, is at the same time, the most powerful obstacle to judicial review of the constitutionality of legislation. It implies that, even if it is true that the British courts are the ultimate guarantors of the rule of law, they are bound to apply an Act of Parliament irrespective of the view the judges take of its morality or justice, or of its effects on important individual liberties or human rights.[4]

This situation was described by Lord Wilberforce in the House of Lords decision of *British Railways Board* v. *Picken* (1974). In that case, it was stated:

> The idea that an Act of Parliament, public or private or a provision in an Act of Parliament, could be declared invalid or ineffective in the courts on account of some irregularity in Parliamentary procedure, or on the ground that Parliament in passing it was misled, or on the ground that it was obtained by deception or fraud, has been decisively repudiated by authorities of the highest standing from 1842 onwards. The remedy for a Parliamentary wrong, if one has been committed, must be sought from Parliament, and cannot be gained from courts.[5]

The sovereignty of the British Parliament continues because of the absence of a written constitution, with an entrenched declaration of fundamental rights and liberties.

Therefore, this book naturally need not describe the British constitutional system, except perhaps for comparative purposes, but rather certain important constitutional systems where actions can be brought before the courts by individuals to obtain control of legislation. This description will include those actions which can be brought before the courts by individuals for the defence and protection of their fundamental freedoms and rights as established in the Constitution. The book will therefore be divided into six parts.

The first part will examine the concept of what is called, in European and Latin American law, *état de droit*, *estado de derecho*, *stato di diritto* or *Rechtsstaat*: – terms that do not have an exact equivalent in English law although the expressions 'legal state' or 'state according to law', or to the 'rule of law' attempt to express a similar idea.

In this first part, the main characteristics will be examined. In particular, the consequences of the limitation and distribution of state powers; the principle of legality, as a basic concept more related to the idea of the English concept of the rule of law; and the establishment of entrenched fundamental liberties and rights. These topics will be related to the process of the constitutionalization of the *état de droit*, which will be referred to in the second part with particular historical references to the process of constitutionalization or constitutionalism in the United States, France and Latin America in the late eighteenth and early nineteenth centuries. This concept of the state according to the law, old and new, is the one that leads us, in the non-British contemporary constitutional systems, to the possibility of a judicial review of the constitutionality of all state acts, including legislative acts. The other four parts of the book will concentrate on the judicial review of the constitutionality of legislation.

Although judicial review of legislation has been considered one of the main contributions which the constitutional system of the United States gave to the political and constitutional sciences,[6] this American or diffuse system of judicial review is not the only one that exists in present constitutional law. There is also the Austrian or concentrated system of judicial review, originally established in the 1920 Austrian Constitution and the mixed systems, mainly Latin American, with the main features of both the American and Austrian systems.

The distinction between the American and the Austrian systems of judicial review is based on the judicial organs that can exercise the power of constitutional control. The American system entrusts that power to all the courts of a given country and it is for this reason that the system is considered to be a decentralised or diffused one. On the contrary, the Austrian system entrusts the power of control of the constitutionality of laws either to one existing court or to a special court, and it is therefore considered a centralized or concentrated control system.

Both of these main systems will be examined, and that examination will include, within the 'American system' an analysis of the constitutional system of the United States as well as some of those systems that have been influenced by it, including various Latin American systems. Within this structure, other constitutional systems that have developed in many of Britain's former colonies will be examined.

Within the Austrian system certain continental European systems of constitutional courts or tribunals will be examined, including the French Constitutional Council system even though it is an incompletely centralized system.

3

There are also systems of control of the constitutionality of legislation which combine the decentralized system with the features of the centralized system. Certain examples of this mixed system will be analysed individually and comparatively.

Finally, particular aspects of the control of constitutionality related to fundamental liberties and rights will be examined. As one of the main characteristics of the process of constitutionalization of the *état de droit* has been the formal establishment of an entrenched declaration of fundamental liberties and human rights, in many instances there are judicial means for the protection of such liberties and rights.

Apart from the classic writ of *habeas corpus*, there is the special 'action for protection' (*amparo*) of Mexico, and the recently developed equivalent recourse for protection in continental Europe, particularly in Germany and Spain. I will refer to all those institutions as a means for judicial review of legislation.

Part I

# THE MODERN STATE SUBMITTED TO THE RULE OF LAW (*ÉTAT DE DROIT*)

# 1

## THE MODERN *ÉTAT DE DROIT*

The subject of judicial review or judicial control over the exercise of power is, undoubtedly, one of the basic and most characteristic elements of all contemporary states. Due to the submission of the state to the rule of law, all states have some system of judicial control or review over activities resulting from the exercise of public powers. This concept of judicial review is essentially related to the classical but current concept of what in English terminology is known as the state according to law or the state according to the rule of law, equivalent to the German *Rechtstaat*, the French *état de droit*, the Spanish *estado de derecho* and the Italian *stato di diritto*. Therefore, the *état de droit* will be treated as the rule of law; law understood in this sense to mean the normative acts which make up the legal order of the state.

This concept of the state according to law is based on the principle that not only must all power of the public bodies forming the state stem from the law, or be established by law, but that this power is limited by law. According to this concept, the law becomes, as far as the state is concerned, not only the instrument whereby attributions of its bodies and officials are established, but also the instrument limiting the exercise of those functions. Consequently, the *état de droit*, or state according to the rule of law, is essentially a state with limited powers and subject to some form of judicial control. This, obviously, has numerous connotations in the evolution of the modern state and also presents characteristics peculiar to each of the major contemporary legal systems.

Seen from this standpoint, the *état de droit* as a state with powers regulated and limited by the law and other legal instruments, is the opposite of any form of absolute or totalitarian state or any state possessing unlimited power, and can be characterized by a combination of the following fundamental principles.

In its classical sense, state power has been limited by its division into the legislative, executive and judicial branches. This is an attempt to guarantee liberty and to curb possible abuse of one power in relation to

7

another; and the consecration of the necessary autonomy of the judiciary so as to ensure submission of the state to the law.

In its most common sense, this may refer to the subjection of the state, not only to formal law, but also to all the sources of the legal order of a given state. This implies, therefore, that all state bodies are required to obey the law of the state, and particularly the law as enacted by Parliament. This has given rise to the 'principle of legality' applied to government or administrative actions, according to which the administration must act in accordance with the law and can be controlled judicially to that end. A series of procedures has been established for the purpose of controlling administrative action and in order to control the constitutionality of laws as a protection against despotism on the part of the legislative power.

These principles have led to others inherent in the *état de droit*; the primacy of the legislation regulating all state activity, including that of the executive and of the judiciary. This has led to the establishment of a hierarchical system of the legal order and consequently of the various rules comprised therein. This system classifies the different rules in various ranks, according to their respective sphere of validity, usually in relation to a supreme or higher law, which is the Constitution.

More recently, the *état de droit* refers to the recognition and establishment of fundamental rights and liberties as a formal guarantee contained in constitutional texts so as to provide for their effective enjoyment as well as for the political and judicial means to ensure such enjoyment.

# 2

## THE LIMITATION OF POWER
## AS A GUARANTEE OF LIBERTY

The first feature of the 'state according to law' is the existence of a division or separation of powers. This means that Parliament, or some other legislative power, creates the legal rules while the administrative and judicial bodies are responsible for enforcing, interpreting and applying them. This system of separation of powers operates so as to guarantee to the citizens that only those individuals who have been elected as legislators will be permitted to create laws. Thus, the law will exist as a product of the representatives of the people. As a consequence, the executive bodies, despite the normative faculties with which they are endowed, cannot be permitted the power of legislators, in the sense of being able to create laws binding on the population. In this way the ability of the executive to limit individual rights and guarantees is itself limited.

Furthermore, this system of separation of powers ensures that no person holding a legislative or an executive office can hold a judicial office as well. As a consequence, the autonomy and independence of judges is ensured and this serves as a minimum guarantee of individual rights.

However, even in a system which recognizes the rule of law, the system of separation of powers is not absolute and rigid. There are numerous interrelations between the various state bodies and it is through these that mutual control and limitation is ensured. This is referred to as the system of weight and counterweight or checks and balances according to which the power of the legislature, for example, is balanced by another power. Under this system, the legislative power, which operates as a check on its historical antecedent, the executive power, becomes supreme. But the primacy of the legislator is not necessarily tantamount to sovereignty, and to avoid absolutism on the part of the legislator, an 'elected dictatorship',[1] the legislative power is necessarily subjected to the Constitution. Thus, since the legislator is limited by the Constitution, a system must be set up to control the constitutionality of his acts, either by ordinary courts or by special courts.

9

In this system of separation of powers the independence of the judiciary *vis-à-vis* the legislator and the executive is a fundamental element of the *état de droit*. Naturally this requires that procedural guarantees exist so as to avoid abuse of authority on the part of the judges.

The principle of the separation of powers is at the very origin of the *état de droit* as it was conceived by the theoreticians of absolutism – Locke, Montesquieu and Rousseau.

### (a) Theoretical background

John Locke, in his *Two Treatises of Government* (1690), became the first ideologist in the reaction against absolutism when he advocated the limitation of the Monarch's political power. He based his proposal on the consideration of man's natural condition and the social contract of the society which gave birth to the state. In Locke's opinion, the reason why men enter into a social contract is to preserve their lives, liberties and possessions, the three basic assets which he regarded, in general, as 'property'. It is this 'property' that gives men political status. In Locke's own words: 'for liberty is to be free from the restraint and violence from others which cannot be, where there is no Law: But freedom is not, as we are told, a liberty to dispose, and order, as he wishes his person, action, possessions and his whole Property.'[2]

As this social contract altered man's natural condition, it must have given rise to the formation of a government which was designed for the purpose of preserving the property of mankind. An absolute government could, therefore, not be considered as legitimate as a civil government which protected this property. If the state failed to emerge as a protector of natural rights, which could not have been transferred to the state, man was therefore justified in resisting this abuse of state power.[3]

Within the measures designed to rationalize and limit power, Locke developed his classical distribution of state functions, some of which he regarded as powers. In paragraph 131 of *Two Treatises of Government*, Locke said the following:

and so whoever has the legislative or supreme power of any Commonwealth, is bound to govern by established standing Laws, promulgated and known to the people and not by Extemporary Decrees; by Indifferent and upright Judges, who are to decide Controversies by those Laws and to employ the force of the Community at home only in the Execution of such Laws, or abroad to prevent or redress Foreign Injuries, and secure the Community from Inroads and Invasions.[4]

So, Locke distinguished four state functions, that of legislating, of judging, of employing forces internally in the execution of the laws and of employing those forces abroad, in defence of the community. He gave the name of legislative power to the first function, that of making the laws 'to which the other powers are, and must be subordinated.'[5] The third function he called the executive power, which involved 'the execution of the municipal laws of the society within the latter and above its parts'[6] or components. The fourth function he called the federative power, which includes 'the power of war and peace, leagues and alliances, transactions with all persons or communities outside the state'.[7]

Of all the functions he assigned to any sovereign state, the only one which he did not regard as a power was the function of judging. It has been explained that this 'was not a separate power, but a general attribution of the state'.[8]

As the novelty of Locke's thesis lies in the distinction between the faculty of legislating and that of employing forces in the execution of the laws, it was not necessary to individualize the power of judging, which was a traditional state function.

In any case, it is important to note that Locke confined himself to rationalizing and systematizing the functions of the sovereign state, but did not actually formulate a theory on the division or separation of powers. What is more, no thesis can be inferred from Locke's work to the effect that the power of the state had to be placed in different hands to preserve liberty or to guarantee individual rights, whilst allowing for the parts to coincide.[9] He did however admit that if the powers were placed in different hands, a balance could be achieved.[10]

Locke's fundamental contribution to the principle of the division of power then lay in his criterion according to which the executive and federative power must necessarily be in the same hands.[11] Moreover, he argued for the supremacy of the legislative power over the others, to the extent that both the executive and judicial functions had to be performed in execution of, and in accordance with, the laws adopted and duly published.[12] For Locke, this supremacy of the legislative power was the consequence of the 1688 Revolution where Parliament achieved its supremacy over the monarch. This is today the most characteristic feature of English public law.

This theory of the division of power has such a great influence on modern constitutionalism as a result of its conversion from the division of power to the separation of power in the revolutions in France, the United

States and in Latin America. This transformation had its fundamental formulation in Montesquieu's *De L'Esprit des lois*.

According to Montesquieu, political liberty only existed in those states in which the power of the state, together with all corresponding functions, was not in the hands of the same person or the same body of magistrates.[13] That is why he insisted that 'it is an eternal experience that any man who is given power tends to abuse it; he does so until he encounters limits ... In order to avoid the abuse of power, steps must be taken for power to limit power.'[14]

From his comparative study of the various states existing at the time (1748), Montesquieu reached the conclusion that England was the only state the direct aim of which was political liberty. He undertook to study the Constitution of England and consequently formulated his theory of the division of power into three categories:

legislative power, power to execute things which depend on international law, and power to execute things which depend on civil law. In the first case, the prince or magistrate makes laws for a period of time or for ever. In the second case, he makes peace or war, sends or receives ambassadors, establishes security, takes measures against invasion. In the third case, he punishes crimes, or settles disputes between individuals. The latter we shall call the power to judge, and the other simply the executive power of the state.[15]

Following Locke's example, Montesquieu referred to various state functions or faculties: the function of making laws, that of judging and that of executing laws. The latter encompassed what Locke called executive and federative power.

However, the novelty of Montesquieu's approach is his conclusion that to guarantee liberty, the three functions must not be in the same hands. Moreover, they were to be on an equal footing, otherwise power could not curb power. In the same chapter VI of Volume XI of *De L'Esprit des lois*, Montesquieu expressed the following opinion:

When legislative power and executive power are in the hands of the same person or the same magistrates body, there is no liberty ... Neither is there any liberty if the power to judge is separate from the legislative and executive powers ... All is lost if the same man, or the same body of princes, or people exercised these three powers: that of laws, that of executing public resolutions and that of wishes or disputes of individuals.[16]

As a result of all this, Montesquieu stated: 'those princes who wanted to become despots, always began by taking possession of all the magistracies'.[17]

Underlying this whole conception, there was also the concept of liberty seen from the same standpoint as Locke. Montesquieu even said, in terms very similar to those used by Locke:

It is true that in democracies the people seem to do what they want; but political liberty does not consist of doing what one wants. In a state, that is to say, in a society in which laws exist, liberty can only consist of being able to do what one should want to do, and not being obliged to do what one should not want to do.[18]

In contrast to what existed in the English Constitution which he was then analysing, Montesquieu's concept involved no proposal whatsoever that any particular public authority should have priority over another. It is true that by defining the legislative authority as the 'general will of the state' and the executive authority as the 'execution of that general will'[19] it could be inferred that the latter, as far as the execution itself was concerned, was to submit to the will of the former, but not, of course, in the sense of political subordination. On the contrary, he conceived the three authorities as being so equal that they could act as a mutual restraint, as the only possible form of co-operation for the maintenance of political liberty. That is why Montesquieu concluded with his proposal: 'these three powers should constitute a rest, or inaction. But since, as all things, they must necessarily move, they will be forced to move in concert.'[20]

Montesquieu's concept, like that of Locke, was devised to counter an absolute state through a scheme for the division of the sovereign's power. Since this was a legal doctrine rather than a political postulate, it does not determine who is to exercise sovereignty, but only how power should be organized to achieve certain objectives.[21]

In the political theory which led to continental reaction against the absolute state and the appearance of the *état de droit*, Rousseau's concept of law occupies a place of paramount importance in postulating the submission of the state to a law which is of its own making. That is to say, it gave rise to the principle of legality and consolidation of the *état de droit* itself. For Rousseau, the social pact or contract is the solution to the problem of finding a form of association 'which defends and protects, with the whole common force, the person and goods of each member of the association, and in which each person, united with all, nevertheless obeys only himself and remains as free as before'.[22] Thus, 'the transition is made from the natural to the civil state'.[23] But, as Rousseau himself pointed out, 'through the social pact we have given birth to the political body; we must now endow it with movement and a will, through legislation'.[24]

Thus, and this was the novelty of his proposal, it is the law, as a manifestation of the sovereign state resulting from the social pact, which sets the state in motion and provides it with the necessary will. Thus Rousseau not only built up the theory of the law as an 'act of general will' to which the conduct of the state itself and that of private individuals must be subjected, but he also established the principle of the generality of the law, which was to subsequently lead to the reaction against privileges.[25]

However, Rousseau limited state functions to two: the making of laws and their execution. To the latter, he applied the same terminology as Montesquieu, legislative power and executive power.[26] Nevertheless, it is not a question here of a doctrine of separation of powers, but, along the same lines as Locke and Montesquieu, a doctrine of the division of one single sovereign power resulting from the social pact or from the integration of the general will.[27]

Neither was Rousseau in favour of placing the two functions of power – the expression of the general will by means of laws and the execution of those laws – in the same hands. So, adopting the same approach as Montesquieu, he also recommended that they be exercised by different bodies, although, unlike Montesquieu, he insisted on the need for the subordination of the body executing the law to the body making it. This bias in the English system, pursuant to Locke's theory, was to ensure the subsequent supremacy of the legislation and the law.

With regard to the need for such laws, Rousseau agreed with Montesquieu. Rousseau in fact stated: 'Therefore, I understand a Republic to be any state which is governed by laws.'[28] Montesquieu, for his part, defined the state as 'a Society in which laws exist'.[29] This is also a declaration of the fact that the existence of laws was a fundamental requisite for the existence of the state.

## (b) The American and French Revolutions

It may be said that the writings of Locke, Montesquieu and Rousseau make up the whole theoretical and political arsenal necessary for the reaction against the absolute state and its replacement by the state according to the rule of law based on the separation of powers, as a guarantee of liberty. That reaction was to occur in continental Europe, with the French Revolution (1789), and in the United States, with Independence (1776), based on the exaltation of individualism and liberty.

In effect, all of these political theories were based on an analysis of man's natural situation and the achievement of the social pact or contract which established a sovereign as a mechanism for the protection of liberty.

This was the basis for the subsequent exaltation of individualism and the political consecration of rights, not only of the citizens of a particular state, but also those of man, with the consequent construction of political and economic liberalism.

In order to prevent the abuse of such rights, it was considered necessary for the power of the state, as a product of the social pact, to be divided and rationalized. To that end, state functions were systematized and power was divided, thereby paving the way for the adoption of a different and more radical formula: that of the 'separation of powers', as a guarantee of liberty. Thus, as Madison pointed out at the beginning of constitutionalism in the United States: 'The accumulation of all powers, legislative, executive, and judiciary in the same hands, whether of one, a few, or many, and whether hereditary, self-appointed or elective, may justly be pronounced the very definition of Tyranny.'[30]

This fear of absolute power was not merely a theoretical consideration. For example, the Constitution of Massachusetts (1780) categorically said:

In the government of this Commonwealth, the legislative department shall not exercise the executive and judicial powers, or either one of them: The executive shall never exercise the legislative and judicial powers, or either one of them: The judicial shall never exercise the legislative and executive powers, or either one of them: to the end it may be a government of laws not of men.[31]

The American revolutionary movement did not merely rely upon the separation of powers. Law itself was considered an essential element of the state and the sovereign power was considered to be updated by the production of laws. Since the legislative function occupied a superior position to that of the other executive functions, this existence of law (act of the general will) operated as a guarantee of civil and political liberty to which both the sovereign and individuals were subjected.

The principles gleaned from the examples of the American and French Revolutions show that the *état de droit* was based on the concepts of liberty, the separation of powers, supremacy of the law and the principle of legality. In this beginning of the *état de droit*, one can discover the submission of the state and its administration to legality.

Such submission, however, was not always guaranteed in European countries. At the beginning, for example, the separation of powers in France presented the non-interference of one power with another in such a fashion that the judicial power could not guarantee individuals that

Government would be submitted to legality. Proof of this was the Law of Judiciary Organization of 16–24 August 1790 which specified that:

Judiciary functions are, and shall always be separate from administrative functions. Any interference by judges in the activities of the administrative bodies, or any summons issued to the administrators by the said judges, for reasons relating to their functions, shall constitute a breach of duty.[32]

Subsequently, the Law of 16 Fructidor of the year III (1795) enacted that: 'The Courts are forbidden, under penalty of law, to take cognizance of administrative acts, whatever their nature.'[33]

The evolution of administrative jurisdiction in France constituted an extreme form of separation of powers: if the government or administrators were to be judged, a special jurisdiction, different and separate from the judicial power, had to be set up. That developed through a lengthy process which led, eventually, to the establishment of the *Conseil d'État*. Thus, any type of control over the constitutionality of the laws in continental Europe, at this time, was inconceivable. This continued to be the case up to the beginning of the present century.

In any case, throughout the last century and during the present one, the evolution of the principle of the separation of powers and the primacy of the legislator has shown a growing tendency towards the submission of the state and all its bodies to the law. This submission and control led, *inter alia*, to the birth of administrative law in Europe and in England.

## (c) The sovereignty of Parliament

In the concept of the separation of powers as a system of distributing power in such a way that power curbs power, the English system was at variance with others.

Despite Montesquieu and all the literature produced in the eighteenth century with reference to England as the living example of the separation of powers, the fact is that such separation has never existed. In fact, England has always had a *heureux mélange* – a successful mixture.[34]

Despite the mixture, there are a number of groups and institutions which bring about a balance of powers through restrictions and counter-restrictions. Yet one power has always prevailed over the others. That has been the power of Parliament or, within Parliament, the power of the government. Thus it has been said that:

the Executive has acquired an overall position of dominance, extending its authority in all three of the functional branches of Government – legislative, executive and judicial. Above all, it has acquired a practical control over the House of Commons in Parliament, from which it has virtually excluded the House of Lords as a countervailing power.[35]

The influence of the government over Parliament has been noted by almost all the constitutional lawyers of the United Kingdom[36] so that it may be concluded that 'in absence of a written constitution, there is no formal separation of power in the United Kingdom.'[37] This lack of separation is particularly noticeable between the legislative and the executive power and has arisen as a result of the practical needs of the parliamentary government which oblige Parliament to trust governmental policy and accept the cabinet's wishes as far as the legislative programme is concerned. These practical needs have also demanded that considerable power is delegated to the executive by Parliament.[38]

This principle of parliamentary sovereignty is characterized *inter alia* by the following elements: In the first place, there is an absence of any formal distinction between constitutional and ordinary laws. This implies that Parliament can institute, at any time, by the ordinary method of law making, reforms of a constitutional nature. Therefore, 'the authority of Parliament to change the law is unlimited' and 'since the Sovereignty of Parliament is recognised by law, it should be contrary to the rule of law to deny full force to enactments which change existing law'.[39]

For instance, Parliament's term of office, according to one of the conventions, is five years, but this period might be extended. Parliament can also regulate succession to the throne, exclude persons who are not members of a particular religion, limit royal prerogatives, change the state religion, in short, make any decision with no limitation whatsoever. The principle implies that any Act of Parliament can always be revised and changed by a subsequent Act, either expressly or, in the case of conflict, implicitly. Consequently, important Acts of Parliament such as the *Habeas Corpus Act* 1679, the *Bill of Rights* 1689, the *Act of Settlement* 1700, the *Statute of Westminster* 1931 and even the *European Economic Kaufman, J Act* 1972 can very well be revised by Parliament. No special majority is even needed for this.[40]

The second element that characterizes the principle of sovereignty of Parliament is the absence of any possibility of control over parliamentary activity. This implies that there is no court competent to decide upon the constitutionality of laws or Acts of Parliament. Consequently, any Act of Parliament, whatever its content, must be applied by the courts of law. This element of the principle of Parliamentary sovereignty has been recognized both by academic writers and the courts. As Dicey said at the

17

beginning of his *An Introduction to the Study of the Law of the Constitution,*

The principle of Parliamentary sovereignty means neither more nor less than this, namely, that Parliament ... has, under the English Constitution, the right to make or unmake any law whatever; and, further, that no person or body is recognised by the law of England as having a right to override or set aside the Legislation of Parliament...[41]

In the House of Lords decision of the *British Railways Board* v. *Pickin* (1974) Lord Reid stated that: 'The idea that a court is entitled to disregard a provision in an Act of Parliament on any ground must seem strange and startling to anyone with any knowledge of the history and law of our constitution.' Later he said 'no court of justice can inquire into the manner in which [an Act] was introduced into Parliament, what was done previously to its being introduced, or what passed in Parliament during the various stages of its progress through both Houses of Parliament'. Finally, he concluded that: 'the function of the Court is to construe and apply the enactments of Parliament. The Court has no concern with the manner in which Parliament or its officers carrying out its Standing Orders perform these functions.'[42]

The third point that emerges from the principle of the supremacy of Parliament is that the law created by Parliament, that is to say, the statutes and the regulations which flow from them, have primacy over common law and over any form of legal creation. In the Chancery Division decision of *Cheney* v. *Conn* (*Inspector of Taxes*) (1968) the Court stated: 'what Statute says and provides is itself the law, and the highest form of law that is known to this country. It is the law which prevails over every other form of law, and it is not for the Court to say that a parliamentary enactment, the highest law in the country, is illegal.'[43] Thus Parliament also prevails over judicial decisions themselves, to the extent that a bill could even be approved for the purpose of legalizing an illegal act, or exempting somebody from the legal consequences of a committed act. Thus it is said that 'the legal authority of Parliament is absolute, not limited'.[44]

One of the consequences of the first element of parliamentary sovereignty is that, because Parliament can change any law at any time, there are no constitutional guarantees, such as a Bill of Rights, from Parliament itself. This is undoubtedly an exception in the modern world, since most countries have a written Constitution represented by a formal document, protected, as a fundamental law, against any attempt by simple majorities to introduce reforms.[45]

Not only are these constitutional guarantees non-existent in the United Kingdom. It appears difficult to create them. Since an ordinary Act of Parliament can reform any law, then it is presently not possible for Parliament itself to declare a law or statute to be unreformable, or to be only reformable subject to certain conditions. In other words, Parliament cannot modify or destroy its own 'continuing sovereignty' for the courts will always obey its most recent commands.[46] In order to institute fundamental guarantees beyond the reach of Parliament, it is necessary to limit the power of Parliament. One such method may involve the transfer of power to the courts, by ensuring that their first loyalty is to constitutional norms separate from Parliament itself.[47] In any case, parliamentary sovereignty in the United Kingdom, as it exists today, has a profound effect on the position of judges. They are not guardians of a Constitution or of constitutional rights, with the power to declare certain legislative acts unconstitutional. Therefore, as Parliament is not limited by any text or superior fundamental rule, there is no possibility of exercising any political control over the conformity of parliamentary acts with a higher law.

### (d) The distribution of power

The idea of the state according to law, with or without Parliamentary sovereignty, is based on the concept of the limitation and distribution of power. There are three aspects to this.

In the first place, there may be a distribution of power between the state, on one hand, and individuals or citizens on the other, in the sense that a sphere of liberty is established for individuals and citizens. This implies limitations to state powers, in the sense that the faculty of the state to invade the sphere of fundamental rights is, in principle, limited.

In a certain way there is a defined sphere of prohibited political activity even in the United Kingdom, notwithstanding the existence of parliamentary supremacy, the absence of an entrenched Bill of Rights and the consequent inability of courts to review legislation. As has been pointed out:

For centuries, and certainly at the time of the 1688 Revolution, the concept of practically 'inalienable' personal liberties has been a very strong feature of the British Constitution: it is implicit in the British concept of the Rule of Law, and has led to the doctrine of natural justice in administrative law, as well as the rules for interpreting states so as not to threaten individual liberty.[48]

Unfortunately, while this enclave of personal liberties may be practically exempt from political interference, to a greater or lesser degree, there is no guarantee in the United Kingdom that Parliament must not interfere.

The second possible aspect of the distribution of power in the *état de droit* relates to its organization by means of a principle of distribution of power between constituent and constituted power. Constituent power belongs and corresponds to the people who are sovereign and is reflected in a Constitution, so that constituent acts can only be taken by the people, in accordance with the provisions of the Constitution itself. Thus the bodies of the constituted power cannot invade the activities which correspond to the constituent power established in the Constitution, and all invasions of those activities invalidate acts taken in such a way.

Finally, this principle of the distribution of power in the *état de droit* also refers to the organization of state power itself in the sphere of constituted power, by means of a system of division of power consisting of a series of attributions to the different state bodies.

This principle of organization or distribution of power has two connotations: in the first place, the classical horizontal division or separation of powers, that distinguish the various branches of public power in a nation, between the legislative, the executive (government and administration) and the judicial bodies. The aim of this division and distinction is to establish reciprocal restrictions and controls among such various state powers, established in the Constitution. In addition there is a second, vertical connotation that seeks a distribution of state power among its different territorial levels. This results in a federal or politically decentralized form of state. In these, the different territorial levels (national, federate states or regions and municipalities) are permitted to exercise part of the public power. This distribution of jurisdictions is also established by the Constitution.

These three forms of distribution and limitation of state powers often result in constitutional issues of jurisdiction which then necessarily lead to a system of judicial review to control unconstitutional invasions or interferences of powers in the sphere reserved to the other. None of these aspects of the *état de droit* based on a limitation or distribution of power is applicable to the constitutional system of the United Kingdom. As a result, no judicial review of the constitutionality of state acts is possible by the courts of that country.

# 3

## THE SUBMISSION OF THE STATE TO THE LAW

The second main feature of the concept of the *état de droit* is the submission of the state to the law. This implies that all the actions of the public bodies of a given state and its authorities and officials must be carried out subject to the law and within the limits set by the law.

This feature is perhaps one of the main characteristics of legal systems today, and can have as many interpretations as legal systems or authors. It is also referred to by various expressions: for instance, in the continental and Latin American legal systems, this feature of the submission of the state to the law is commonly identified with the 'principle of legality'; in the system of the United States, with the whole idea of constitutionalism or government under the law; and in the British constitutional system by the classical expression 'rule of law'.

Although these terms do not always have the same meaning and scope in every system, they ultimately mean that state bodies should be subject to the law. Thus, it has been said that the rule of law or government according to law, means 'that all power came from the law and that no man, be he King or Minister or private person, is above the law'.[1] However, this definition does not resolve the issue of the subjection of the sovereign or, of Parliament, in the case of the British Constitution, to the law.

### (a) The sovereign and the law

The analysis of this issue, of the submission of the state to the law, must begin with the following statement of Professor H.L.A. Hart in his book, *The Concept of Law*, when he said: 'whenever there is law, there is a sovereign incapable of legal limitation'.[2] In similar terms, C.M. McIlwain, speaking of the sovereign said: 'it is the highest body legally able to make rules for the subject, and itself free of the law'.[3]

If we therefore accept the principle that in all legal order there is a sovereign not submitted to the law or legal limitations, how can we talk about the *état de droit* or the state submitted to the law? This question,

21

leads us to the problem of identifying within the bodies and organs of the state, which one is the sovereign and therefore, not subjected to the law.

Austin claimed that, in a democracy, it is the electorate not the elected representatives who constitute or form part of the sovereign body. With regard to the United Kingdom, 'the members of the House of Commons are merely trustees for the body by which they are elected and appointed: and consequently the sovereignty always resides in the King's peers and the electoral body of the Commons.' Similarly, within the United States, sovereignty of each state of the federal union, 'resides in the states government as forming one aggregate body, meaning by a state's government not its ordinary legislature but the body of citizens which appoints its ordinary legislature'.[4]

Thus it is possible to distinguish between two powers: that of the constituent sovereign body and that of the constituted, formed by all the state organs. As indicated earlier, this is one of the main consequences of the principle of limitation of state power: the division in a given society between the constituent and the constituted power.

With regard to this distinction in a democracy, between the sovereign itself, the people and the organs of the state, the Germans have made a useful distinction between what they choose to call the sovereign and the sovereign organ (*Träger der Staatgewalt*, or *Staatorgan*).[5] The sovereign, that is to say the electoral body, has no legal limitations as a constituent power,[6] but the sovereign organs have limitations imposed on them by the constituent power in the Constitution, as well as by various other types of control such as the political one by the people who gave them power.

In this perspective, we must again consider the concept of parliamentary sovereignty. Hart points out the following alternative:

there could only be legal limits on legislative power if the legislator were under the orders of another legislator whom he habitually obeyed; and in that case he would no longer be sovereign. If he is sovereign he does not obey any other legislator and hence there can be no legal limits on his legislative power.[7]

That, therefore, is the main question. Is the legislative organ legally bound to observe constitutional restriction imposed by a constituent power, that is to say, by the people as sovereign? If it must, then according to the definitions which have been proposed, the legislative body would not then be the sovereign but only the sovereign organ. Conversely if the legislative body in a state is free of constitutional or legal limits to its power, then it must be the sovereign itself.

Almost all legal systems establish legal limitations on the exercise of legislative organ power and therefore do not identify the sovereign with that legislator or Parliament but rather with the people. This conclusion may be examined from the perspective of a system with very few limits on the power of the legislator. In spite of the existence of parliamentary sovereignty, Hart noted that 'Austin himself did not identify the sovereign with the legislature even in England ... This was his view although the Queen in Parliament is, according to normally accepted doctrine, free from legal limitations on its legislative power, and so is often cited as a paradigm of what is meant by "a sovereign legislature" in contrast with Congress or other legislatures limited by a "rigid" constitution.'[8]

The difference between the British Constitution and the other constitutional systems in the world, is the degree of delegation of sovereign power given by the people to the legislative organ, in other words, 'the manner in which the sovereign electorate chooses to exercise its sovereign power'.[9]

The distinction has been pointed out by Professor Hart in the following passages from his book:

In England ... the only direct exercise made by the electorate of their share in the sovereignty consists in their election of representatives to sit in Parliament and the delegation to them of their sovereign power. This delegation is, in a sense, absolute since, though a trust is reposed in them not to abuse the powers thus delegated to them, this trust in such cases is a matter only for moral sanctions, and the courts are not concerned with it, as they are with legal limitations on legislative power.[10]

By contrast, Hart added:

in the United States, as in every democracy where the ordinary legislative is legally limited, the electoral body has not confined its exercise of sovereign power to the election of delegates, but has subjected them to legal restrictions. Here the electorate may be considered an 'extraordinary and ulterior legislature' superior to the ordinary legislative which is legally 'bound' to observe the constitutional restrictions and, in cases of conflict, the courts will declare the acts of the ordinary legislature invalid. Here then, in the electorate, is the sovereign free from all legal limitations which the theory requires.[11]

In order to distinguish the constituted from the constituent power, it is necessary to be clear about what law is, in respect of creating limits on power. In this concept of law, all sources of the legal order have been included as well as the Constitution itself and all norms deriving from it. This is different from the concept in the expression 'rule of law', which has been taken to mean 'rule of law as enacted by Parliament',[12] with no legal limits on its activity.

Nevertheless it is noted that, in spite of everything that is said about the unlimited, absolute, omnipotent, all-powerful or unrestrained powers of the Parliament of the United Kingdom, a number of limitations do exist so as to make that power a constituted one.[13] Lolme's famous statement that 'Parliament can do everything but make a woman a man and a man a woman'[14] is no more than an exaggeration tending to mean that Parliament has no legally entrenched limits upon its actions, because of the absence of a written and rigid Constitution. But it does not mean that there could be arbitrariness in the exercise of parliamentary powers, and that in certain aspects, in political practice, there are absolutely no limits over Parliaments.

Firstly, there are some Acts of Parliament that can be considered, from the perspective of constitutional law, as 'constituent documents' limiting parliamentary action. Thus the *Act of Union* of 1707 and the *Ireland Act* of 1800 may be qualified as constituent documents even though the limitations imposed by them upon Parliament are established 'in such a way that any infringement of them is improbable'.[15] Moreover, there are those limits established by convention, or habits of thought, such as the 'doctrine of mandate' which states that a government which has lost general support in the country should not force major legislation through Parliament shortly before an election, even though such legislation may have been in its electoral programme.[16]

There are also limits imposed by political expediency which undoubtedly bind all Parliaments in such a way that they cannot reverse what a previous Parliament has done. For instance, one cannot imagine that Parliament could reverse the *Statute of Westminster* 1931, which limits the power of Parliament to legislate over a Dominion without its consent;[17] nor can one imagine that Parliament could reverse the acts granting independence to the Dominions or territories overseas and thus try to take away their independence.[18] In the same context, it would be difficult for Parliament to legislate contrary to the *European Communities Act*, 1972, which provides for primacy of community laws over domestic law, while the United Kingdom remains a member of that community.[19]

Finally, in spite of the absence of judicial review of legislation, the courts do exercise some limiting force over Parliament's constitutional power. Thus it may be said:

Judges, however, usually manage to get their own way: The House of Lords has been able to attain some of the same results which in the United States, are achieved by the first ten amendments. By a convenient fiction it assumes that Parliament always intends that its statutes will accord with natural justice; no statute will therefore be constructed to be retrospective or to deprive a person of a fair hearing or to prevent freedom of speech unless Parliament has so provided in the most specific terms.[20]

Thus, rather than judicial review the courts exert a judicial interpretative effect over Parliament's sovereignty. Accordingly, 'A statute is presumed, in the absence of clear words to the contrary, not to take away property without compensation, not to exclude the jurisdiction of the court, not to be retrospective, not to impose taxation.'[21]

It has been considered that through such presumptions, effective protection can be given to fundamental rights and liberties, so much so that it is uncertain that the enactment of a formal Bill of Rights as part of English law would achieve better protection of traditional liberties.[22]

Although these limits to Parliament's authority do exist, entrenched limits do not. Perhaps this has been as a result of the absence of real threats against the Constitution. They are not entrenched now because of the belief that unconstitutional law would not be enforced.[23]

This confidence is largely justified in the United Kingdom because of the continuity of constitutional rule in the last 300 years. In most other countries, however, this confidence does not exist. On the contrary, experience abroad has shown that it has been precisely because of the actions of Parliaments, dominated by circumstantial majorities, that the worst attacks against human rights have been committed. In these other countries the sovereign does not fear fictions or presumptions, duly applied, as a means of judicial protection of human rights. Accordingly, the majority of countries today[24] feel the trend to establish a written and rigid Constitution, with an entrenched declaration of fundamental rights and liberties, precise dispositions for the limitation and distribution of legislative, executive and judicial powers with judicial independence assured, so as to maintain these limits on power according to the Constitution. Thus, the concept of the *état de droit*.

### (b) The law and the legal order

As has been noted, in the concept of the *état de droit* the word law must be understood in the broader sense of legal order, comprising all the norms that regulate a given society according to its political constitution. It is in this broader sense that the expression 'principle of legality', the

25

continental law equivalent to the rule of law, must be understood.

Therefore, 'legality' in contemporary constitutional law is not only the submission to 'formal law' as an act passed by the legislator, but means submission to law as the legal order including the Constitution and other derivating sources of law. Furthermore, the rule of law or the principle of legality not only refers to the submission of the executive to law controlled by the courts, but also the submission of all the state organs to the laws that regulate its functioning. In this sense, the principle of legality or the rule of law applicable to Parliament or to the legislative body, in systems with a written Constitution, are the rules contained in that Constitution.

However, from the historical point of view the principle of legality in continental Europe was understood in the restricted sense. It was considered that, if the state were to be subject to the law, it must mean an act issued by the legislator.

Since the law as an act of the legislative body was considered by certain theoreticians to be 'the expression of the general will', it could be used to define the liberty of man under the law: 'The liberty of man in society is to be under no other legislative power but that established, by consent, in the commonwealth; nor under the dominion of any will or restraint or any law, but what that legislative shall enact according to the trust put in it.'[25]

Since it was in this manner that the law was conceived by French authors[26] the French Declaration of the Rights of Man and Citizen of 1789 was drafted as follows: 'The Law is the expression of the general will; all citizens have the right to participate personally, or through their representatives, in its formation.'[27] In this tradition, the law is the fundamental guarantee of liberty. The laws proposed for the limitation of power, at the time of the beginning of the *état de droit* and after the French Revolution were not perceived, as far as their contents were concerned, as statutes such as are usually approved by today's Parliaments. Instead they were perceived as laws of liberties,[28] that is to say, laws designed to enable the members of the social body to evolve freely. This different perspective existed as a result of the different perception of the state; that is that it had, as its main function, the formulation of the exercise of liberties by the citizens. That was the essence of liberalism in its political perspective, and in this regard, the 1789 Declaration of the Rights of Man and the Citizen stated:

The aim of every political association is the preservation of the natural and inalienable rights of Man; these rights are liberty, property, security and the resistance to oppression.

Liberty consists of the power to do whatever is non injurious to others; thus, the enjoyment of natural rights of every man has, for its limit, only those that assure other members of society the enjoyment of those same rights; such limits may be determined by the law.[29]

This restricted meaning of the concept of legality has been followed in contemporary times by some French administrative writers,[30] and has normally been formulated in relation to the control of the executive or administration, due to the traditional concept of the supremacy of the law and to the absence of any protection given to the people against legislative actions contrary to the Constitution.[31]

It has only been with the development of the judicial control of the constitutionality of laws in France by the Constitutional Council, and with the spreading of the American and Austrian models of judicial review, that the difference between the Constitution and the law has been accepted. With this, the expansion of the concept of legality or rule of law has been effected.

It must be noted that in all legal systems[32] there exists a distinction between those rules which form the Constitution itself, as a higher positive law, and those provisions or rules of law which may be made by an authority delegated by the Constitution. Thus, as McIlwain pointed out when referring to Bodin's thoughts on the matter:

There is and there must be, in every free state, a marked difference between those laws which a government makes and may therefore change, and the ones which make the Government itself. The Government...is 'free of the law' [said Bodin]...but by this he meant free only of the ordinary laws which the government itself has made or may make. He does not include among these laws the fundamental principle of the Constitution under which the government itself comes into being, which defines and sets bounds to the supreme organ in the government so created...The...supreme authority established and defined by a fundamental law is bound absolutely by that law, though he is free of all other laws.[33]

In this perspective, since acts of the legislative body are *per se* derivative norms of the Constitution, they are therefore subordinate to it. As a consequence, the rule of law or the principle of legality must be able to comprise the 'rule of the Constitution' or the 'principle of constitutionality'. With this expansion it is assumed that legislative acts must be issued as a direct consequence of the Constitution. Those that are not are unconstitutional; hence the judicial control of the constitutionality of laws.

When legality is seen in this wider context, so as to include not only the decrees of the legislative or executive branches, but also the Constitution itself, all state organs and bodies become subject to control by the law of the Constitution. Their activities are limited by this law so that the courts can review them to test their constitutionality.

As an integral part of this process it becomes necessary to determine which is the rule of law to which each act of the state must conform. For this purpose, the rules of law that comprise a legal system are deliberately or spontaneously organized in a hierarchical way so that there are norms of superior level that prevail over norms of inferior level.

### (c) The hierarchical or graduated legal system and the confines of the principle of legality

Kelsen's theory of a legal system as a hierarchy of norms is a useful method identifying the hierarchical relation between the rules of law composing a legal system. In this sense, each norm belonging to the system has its derivation in another norm, ending the chain of derivation in a *Grundnorm* or Constitution, which is the ultimate reason for the existence of all the norms of the whole system.

When speaking of derivation, Kelsen refers to the mode of creation of norms, in the sense that a norm is always created according to a power established by another norm.[34]

A plurality of norms or of rules of law constitute a unity, a system or an order when their validity depends on, in the final analysis, a unique rule or norm. This fundamental norm is the common source of validity of all the rules or norms that belong to the same order and form its unity. A rule of law thus belongs to a given order only when the possibility exists of making its validity depend on the fundamental norm, that is in the foundation of this order.[35]

In effect, the law of any state, at a given point in time, consists not only of the formal acts of Parliament, but also of delegated legislation, administrative acts, judicial decisions and customs, and general principles of law. All these precepts, which make up the legal order in force at a given time, not only have different origins but also different ranks, and it is not a question of considering them as coordinated rules in juxtaposition[36] but as being in a hierarchical structure with the rules distributed in various strata, more or less one above the other. Within this hierarchy there must necessarily be a formal connection between the rules, because they are linked organically despite their different origins and characteristics.

One can therefore speak of a superior rule and of an inferior one. For example, the establishment of Acts of Parliament is regulated by the Constitution; the decision as to who is to enact delegate legislation and how it is to be enacted, is regulated by certain formal laws; judicial decisions and their procedural rules are subject to primary and delegated legislation. Likewise, the validity of administrative acts is established in primary and delegate legislation and in judicial decisions.

The principle which establishes the relationship between all these legal rules of such varied origin, rank and scope and which shapes them into a system, is the existence of a common basis of validity in the form of a fundamental or superior rule. Thus, a set of rules of law constitutes a relatively independent legal system when the justification or validity of them all has its derivation in a single rule on which they are all formally based. And this single rule is referred to, in relation to all the others, as the fundamental rule or the Constitution.

This method of submitting state organs and activities to the rule of law is applicable to legal systems with written Constitutions and to those with unwritten Constitutions. In the former, the application of the theory of the graduated or hierarchical system of rules is evidently clear, precisely because a formal constitutional document established as a supreme constituent rule exists. In other legal systems, however, the process of systemization of the legal order is much more complicated and the supreme constituent rule consists of an amalgam of heterogeneous rules, established in statutes, common law[37] and conventions, all recognized by the courts as rules of law.

In either case, the formal systemization of a legal order is nevertheless indispensable to the determination of the scope of application of the law to state bodies, because situations often arise in which two contradictory provisions claim to be in force. In such cases it will be necessary to choose one over the other by determining which one ranks higher than the other. It may also be necessary to determine which state body is competent to decide this hierarchy.

Thus it is necessary to distinguish between acts whose authority stems directly from the Constitution, such as legislation from the Parliament or from any politically decentralized territory, and those whose authority stems indirectly from the Constitution.

There are, in addition, acts whose authority stems directly from the Constitution, but which do not regulate the conduct and activities of individuals. Some of these are called *interna corporis*, that is to say, acts which regulate the functioning of the Houses of Parliament. Others exist

29

because of the check and balancing system of the separation of powers. In these instances the legislative branch intervenes in executive activities in order to validate executive actions. That happens, for instance, in the appointment of some high ranking state officials in domestic administration or in the diplomatic corps; in contracting foreign loans or in the approval of various budget modifications. In many countries, the executive requires the approval, or the authorization, of the legislative branch before taking any such actions.

All these acts enjoy the same formal hierarchy as a result of their direct relation to the Constitution. Being subject to the Constitution, they participate in that same concept of legality (constitutionality) and they are therefore also subject to judicial review to enforce the constitutional rule with which they must be in accordance.

In systems with written Constitutions, it is often the case that the Constitution directly attributes powers to the head of state or to the head of government to exercise certain activities which are not subject to regulation by the ordinary legislator. These powers normally concern the government in the political sense and are referred to in continental European law as 'acts of government' or 'political acts'. This is roughly equivalent to the notion in the United States of 'political questions'. Because the validity for these powers stems directly from the Constitution, they are equal in rank to laws enacted by Parliament, and accordingly cannot be submitted to regulation by other laws. Only the Constitution determines its confines of legality.

Because of the traditional absence of judicial control of the constitutionality of state acts and because of the limited power conferred upon the administrative judicial courts or tribunals, in France and in other continental European countries, the doctrine of the *actes de gouvernement* or 'political acts' as an exception to the principle of legality was developed during this century in the sense that they were not subject to judicial control by the administrative judicial courts.

In France the decisions of the Conseil d'Etat declaring its incompetence to control such acts led to the development of that doctrine and established a distinction between administrative action, which was subject to judicial control and governmental action, which was not. This governmental action was progressively reduced to basically two fields: the acts of the head of state or of the government in relation to the legislative body, which included the power of the executive to submit bills to the legislature and the government acts concerned with international relations, such as the process of making or denouncing a treaty.[38] Although these 'acts of government' would escape judicial review of the administrative judicial court because they could not be subject to formal law and were not administrative acts, nevertheless they would be subject to judicial control of their constitutionality.

In addition to 'acts of government', a Constitution often directly attributes some legislative power to the head of state. These powers, when exercised, are called 'decree laws'. By virtue of their legislative content, these are normative acts of government which are also issued on the basis of power established directly by the Constitution or, on some occasions, delegated by Parliament in accordance with the provisions of, and as a result of their direct relation to, the Constitution. These decree-laws have the same hierarchy as other ordinary laws although, by virtue of their content, they could be replaced by ordinary formal law enacted by Parliament.

In all these cases, acts issued by constitutional bodies are acts whose authority stems directly from the Constitution and are, therefore, submitted only to the Constitution. Those state acts must be compared with those, particularly in the administrative and judicial fields, whose authority stems directly from the legislation, that it to say, of the formal laws or Acts of Parliament and of acts of government or decree laws issued by the appropriate constitutional bodies.

Thus, all administrative activities are ultimately acts done under the direct authority of legislation, and under the mediate authority of the Constitution, that is to say, whose authority stems directly from the legislation and indirectly from the Constitution.

Consequently, the extent of the administration's submission to legality in the *état de droit* is greater than that of the submission which supreme state bodies incur. Legislative and executive branches are controlled only by the Constitution whereas administrative bodies and authorities are involved in a much more extensive area of legality, since they must be submitted not only to the Constitution but to all the state acts whose authority stems directly from it, i.e., legislation.

This approach to the graduated system of legal order or the analysis of legal systems has enormous implications in the area of judicial control of the activities and actions of the state.

There would be no use formulating the principle of legality in the *état de droit*, in the sense of submission of the state to the rule of law, if some mechanism were not set up whereby individuals could control the effective submission of state bodies to the law, by court action.

In those legal systems in which a written Constitution exists, the

31

maximum demonstration of the concept of legality is reflected in the establishment of two major systems of judicial control over the exercise of power: the control of constitutionality and the control of legality in the strictest sense of the term.

State acts whose authority stems directly from the Constitution must be subject to some system of judicial control of constitutionality. It is to this end, for example, that constitutional tribunals have been set up in the continental European states. As constitutional bodies, these tribunals have the basic aim of controlling the constitutionality of these state acts.

The first Constitutional Tribunals set up were those in which the organization of the constitutional system was directly influenced by Kelsen's theory of a legal system as a hierarchy of norms. That was the situation in Austria and Czechoslovakia in 1920. It was not until the 1940s that other Constitutional Tribunals were established in continental European countries.

In those countries which failed to establish Constitutional Tribunals, the concept of legality could not stretch to include the concept of constitutionality. This caused distortions in the *état de droit* through the concept of 'acts of government' in French law, or 'political acts', in Italian or Spanish law previously referred to. These were not submitted to the control of legality by the administrative judicial courts because they were considered to have been formulated initially for political reasons, or later, when that argument failed to remain convincing, because it was considered that they referred to issues stipulated directly in the Constitutions, with reference to the relations between the different state powers or constitutional bodies, or to other states in the international order.

In fact, such acts were actually exempt from administrative judicial control because they were not really administrative acts. In effect, they were acts of government whose authority stems directly from the Constitution, and the only control to which they could be submitted was the control of constitutionality. The subsequent establishment of control over the constitutionality of legislative and executive acts, in Spain and Italy, resulted in the reduction or disappearance of the doctrine of the judicial immunity of political acts. They now come under the control of the Constitutional Tribunals.

In France, since there is yet no genuine control of the constitutionality of these acts, the doctrine of the exemption of 'acts of government' from judicial control still exists.

In the legal system of the United Kingdom, in the absence of a written Constitution establishing entrenched rights and constitutional guarantees, there can be no judicial control over the constitutionality of certain acts. Instead, the unwritten Constitution of the United Kingdom recognizes parliamentary sovereignty, which itself implies that Parliament is not submitted to any superior rule but produces these superior rules itself. Therefore, an Act of Parliament is not submitted to any superior rule, its constitutionality could not be controlled.

Nevertheless, it is possible to establish a system of a graduated or hierarchical legal order based, naturally, on the concept of the superiority of Acts of Parliament.

In any case, apart from acts whose authority stems from the Constitution, it is evident that the principle of legality plays a more important role with regard to state acts whose authority stems indirectly from the Constitution. Here the concept of legality has developed in the fullest sense of the term, particularly in connection with the administration, both in the continental European and in the British legal systems. This in itself had given rise to the judicial control of the legality of administrative acts or actions, and therefore to administrative law.

The broader concept of legality implies not only that the executive or administrative power is subject to the rule of law, but that the legislative power is also subject to the rule of law. Thus the individual perspective of the rule of law varies according to the level of law, those whose authority stems from the Constitution, or from the legislation. Thus, for the legislator and for certain acts of the executive, legality means constitutionality or submission to the Constitution; for administrators, legality means compliance with enacted laws.

### (d) The principle of legality and the executive

As far as executive and judicial powers are concerned, the concept of legality or the rule of law has a wider sense than merely that of legislative enactments. Thus it includes constitutional rules as well as those acts of the head of state issued within its constitutional powers. In fact, it includes all the other sources of legal rules that bind administrative action as well as general principles of law or principles of natural justice that are to be observed by public administration.

In the evolution of the contemporary state, the submission of the executive branch to the law began with the submission of its administrative actions to the law. Law in this sense was conceived as formal law, that is to say, Acts issued by Parliament. Thus the administration had always to act on the basis of a pre-existent rule of law.

In continental legal systems, however, this principle of legality has been expanded to the extent that the term legality has become synonymous with legal order, in the sense that in a graduated legal system, the administration must submit to all the superior rules governing its activities. In this context, therefore, law is not just law in the formal sense but it also includes international treaties signed by the respective states, delegated legislation, decree laws and general principles of law.

Naturally, this principle of legality as applied to the administration has been implemented by the establishment of a system of control of the administration through the courts, either the ordinary courts or special administrative judicial courts, and by the establishment of the principle of the responsibility of the state, particularly, for damage caused to individuals by state actions.

In this sense, in the *état de droit* the activities of the administration are subject to complete judicial supervision through the judicial mechanisms provided for in ordinary law, or established in a particular administrative law system, to control the administration itself.

Occasionally, the theory of discretionary powers opened a void in the principle of legality. Thus the administration was given a certain amount of freedom to take the most convenient action or decision according to its own interpretation. But little by little, judicial control of these discretionary acts progressed because the courts could not let such actions become into arbitrary. As a result, such acts became subject to a judicial control of legality. In continental European administrative law, these controls were derived from the principles of proportionality, rationality, non-discrimination, equity and justice.

It has also been accepted that the use of discretionary power by the administration cannot lead to the violation of the general principles of administrative procedure, in particular, those connected with the right to a fair due process of law, granting the general right of citizens to look for their own defence. A demonstration of this is the right to a hearing before an administrative action could be taken, so that the individual who may be affected by that decision could have the opportunity to express his position regarding the administrative action and argue his rights.

Although many of these principles which lead to the limit of discretionary power originated in case law, in various countries they have been codified in legislation relating to administrative procedures. Venezuela can serve as an example of this process. Its Administrative Procedures Act of 1981[39] states in Article 12:

'When a norm of a Statute or of a general regulation issued by the

Executive, leaves an administrative measure or decision to be taken by the competent authority on his own understanding, such a measure or decision must maintain due proportionality and adequacy with the facts and aims established in the norm, and follow all the procedural rules and formalities needed for its validity and effectiveness.' That is to say, when an administrative authority has been given the authority by a legislative or executive norm, the authority to take any measure or decision based on its own understanding of the circumstances and timing of the given action, it must, first, respect due proportionality between the facts that motivated the administrative actions and the consequences established in the law.

In that respect, if the norm authorizes the administrative organ, for example, to apply a fine or penalty measured against two extremes, in accordance with its appreciation of the gravity of the offence, the action, that is to say, the fine or penalty imposed, must have some proportion with the actual facts which occurred and which cause the administrative action, deriving from rationality, justice and equity.

This principle of proportionality leads to another – the principle of equality and non-discrimination. Thus, in relation to a given fact, if a measure or decision has been taken against an individual, the same measure or decision must be taken against other individuals if the facts coincide. This also implies that impartiality, as a general principle of administrative action, is also a limit on discretionary power.

But this article of the Venezuelan Administrative Procedures Act also establishes the need for an administrative authority to try to attain, when taking a measure or a decision, the aims or goals which are established in the law which granted him power to act. Any deviation in obtaining or pursuing those aims can lead to judicial control of the administrative action by means of illegality, through a procedure similar to the *détournement de pouvoir* in French administrative law.

Moreover, that same article of the Venezuelan Administrative Procedures Act established the due fitness of the actual facts that motivated an administrative action with the ones established in the particular norm. That means that public authority must first determine the facts that had occurred; second, it must prove them, through the usual or technical means; third, it must qualify them appropriately, and finally, the facts must coincide with the ones established in the law authorizing the administrative action. All these steps must be taken in accordance with the principles of equality, impartiality and justice, so that any violation thereof leads to judicial control through a declaration of illegality.

Finally, the article states that in the use of discretionary powers, the

35

administrative organ must always respect the procedural steps normally required for the validity and effectiveness of the administrative action. These procedural rules must include the right to defend oneself. This right of every citizen to look for his own defence leads, in the Administrative Procedures Act of Venezuela, to the establishment of other derivative rights of the individual *vis à vis* the public administration: the right always to be heard prior to a decision which affects rights and interests; the right to participate in those procedures; the right to be formally and personally notified of the decision; the right to have access to all official documents filed in the dossier concerned and the right to copy those documents; the right to present evidence in defence; and the right to be notified of the means of appeal or other actions that can be used for defence.[40]

As can be seen from this example, the control of administrative action through the concept of legality can have many options available to it. Whether these controls occur through legislation, as in the Venezuelan example, or through the case law method particularly, relying upon principles of natural justice,[41] the object is the control of administrative action through legal means and the exclusion of the discretionary power as an exemption to the rule of law. A similar process has occurred with regard to government or political acts.

Although certain acts of the executive, such as political acts, were traditionally seen in continental Europe as being exempt from submission to legality, the *état de droit* has made an effort to gradually reduce the number of such political acts exempt from control. Moreover, with the establishment of Constitutional Tribunals, it has been possible in some countries to control the constitutionality of such acts of government, as acts whose authority stems directly from the Constitution.

Because the state act depends upon a Constitution and the legal codes for its validity, all the activities of the executive must be submitted to the concept of legality and to judicial review.

### (e) The rule of law and Dicey's concepts

In the legal system of the United Kingdom, the term 'rule of law' is roughly equivalent to what the continental European legal systems call the concept of legality or the *état de droit*, that is to say, it is the laws which govern and not men.

But there is perhaps a radical historical difference between the two systems; whereas the *état de droit* came into being on the continent as a rational system substituting the *Ancien Régime*, the rule of law is directly linked to the medieval doctrine of the 'Reign of Law' in the sense that law, whether it be attributed to supernatural or human sources, ought to rule the world.[42] Thus an absolute monarchical system has never existed to the same extent in the United Kingdom as on the continent.

Therefore, Dicey did not invent the notion of the rule of law[43] although he was the first writer to systematize and analyse the principle. Thus it is impossible to refer to the rule of law in the United Kingdom, without referring in one way or another to Dicey's approach.[44] According to Dicey's classical definition, the rule of law means three things: the absolute predominance of the law; equality before the law; and the concept according to which the Constitution is the result of the recognition of individual rights by judges. With regard to the first meaning, Dicey stated that by rule of law,

We mean ... that no man is punishable or can be lawfully made to suffer in body or goods except for a distinct breach of law established in the ordinary legal manner before the ordinary courts of the land. In this sense the rule of law is contrasted with every system of government based on the exercise by persons in authority of wide, arbitrary or discretionary powers of constraint.[45]

As Dicey himself stated, in this sense, the rule of law means:

the absolute supremacy or predominance of regular law as opposed to the influence of the arbitrary power and excludes the existence of arbitrariness of prerogative, or even wide discretionary authority on the part of the government. Englishmen are ruled by the law, and by the law alone; a man may with us be punished for a breach of law, but he can be punished for nothing else.[46]

In relation to this first meaning of the rule of law, power granted by the law to the government is not equivalent to arbitrariness, for the government itself has limits in its exercise.

Yet while it is true that the government lacks arbitrary power, the same may not be said about the British Parliament, since its powers are not limited by a written Constitution. Consequently, the British Parliament, by virtue of its sovereignty, possesses in principle unlimited powers, not only to establish general laws, but also particular laws with any content.

Arbitrary law-making is not, therefore, constitutionally excluded in the United Kingdom, although it must take the form of an Act of Parliament or be authorized by such an act. But bearing in mind the government's factual supremacy over Parliament, which exists because of the party system, the government may request ratification from Parliament even after arbitrary or illegal measures have been taken. Thus, for example, it has been said that Parliament ratified and legalized in 1931 a series of illegal acts issued by the Cabinet with reference to the abolition of the gold standard. In this case, the arbitrary or uncontrolled power of Parliament served to sanction illegal acts.[47]

According to Dicey, the rule of law also means legal equality. In this sense, Dicey wrote:

We mean in the second place, when we speak of the rule of law as a characteristic of our country, not only that with us no man is above the law, but (what is a different thing), that here every man, whatever be his rank or condition, is subject to the ordinary law of the realm and amenable to the jurisdiction of the ordinary tribunals.[48]

In explaining this second meaning, he went further and applied the concept to government officials. He said:

It means, again, equality before the law, or the equal subjection of all classes to the ordinary law of the land administered by the ordinary law courts. The rule of law in this sense excludes the idea of any exemption of officials or other from the duty of obedience to the law which governs other citizens or from the jurisdiction of the ordinary tribunals.[49]

Since this aspect of Dicey's concept of the rule of law ensures that all individuals, including public officials, are governed by the ordinary law in ordinary courts, it naturally excludes any idea of special administrative courts in the French manner.

As a consequence of this aspect of the rule of law, Dicey formulated his mistaken approach to administrative law which concludes that 'there can be with us nothing really corresponding to the administrative law, *droit administratif* or the administrative tribunals (*tribunaux administratives*) of France.'[50]

Dicey, in reality, denounced what he understood French administrative law to be. He said that the *droit administratif* rested at bottom on various 'leading ideas alien to the conceptions of modern Englishmen', within which he referred to the idea:

that in France the government and every servant of the government, possesses as representative of the nation, a whole body of special rights, privileges, or prerogatives as against private citizens, and that the extent of these rights, privileges or prerogatives is to be determined on principles different from the considerations which fix the legal rights and duties of one citizen towards another.[51]

This body of privileges and prerogatives referred to by Dicey was embodied in one main aspect of the French system: the existence of special administrative courts to judge public bodies and officials ranked in a separate system of judicature different from the judicial power, having at its apex not the *Cour de Cassation* but the *Conseil d'Etat*.

It has long been realized in Great Britain that Dicey's picture of administrative law was wrong,[52] and that legal equality does not mean that the state bodies would be submitted to the same laws applicable to ordinary citizens. As Professor J.D.B. Mitchell stated:

While the subjection of officials to law is desirable, it does not follow that this should in all cases, or generally, be a subjection to the law which is applicable to the ordinary citizen [because] ... it is clear that the powers of government cannot be those of an ordinary citizen...and that as far as rights are concerned public bodies and public officials cannot be governed by the ordinary law.[53]

Therefore, if it is desirable in principle that the executive be subject to the same law as that governing the citizen, this does not exclude the possible need for the government, in view of its very nature, to have special prerogatives and powers. What the principle of the rule of law actually requires, is that the government be granted no unnecessary privileges or exemptions in relation to ordinary laws. In this respect, for example, the fact that the Crown could not be taken to court on the ground of responsibility constituted an unnecessary privilege and was eliminated in 1947 by the Crown Proceeding Act.[54]

In any event the second aspect of the rule of law as developed by Dicey means that government bodies should be subject to the law so that all government actions must be carried out in accordance with the law although Parliament, through its supremacy, can make any law whatsoever. Thus, all administrative or governmental authorities can only act by means of an authorization granted in a law which in general, must be understood to be an Act of Parliament.

But the principle of the rule of law does not consist solely of submission to formal law. It also implies that administrative authority must submit to those principles and rules which limit any discretionary power granted to the said authority by an Act of Parliament. Because of this aspect of the rule of law, it has been said that the concept was developed in relation to the administration, on the basis of judicial limitations upon the powers which may have been granted to the administrative authorities by Acts of Parliament.[55] The object of all this is to prevent and avoid abuse in the exercise of discretionary powers.

In any event, in the United Kingdom, the concept of the rule of law implies that claims brought by individuals against administrative and government acts and officials must be judged by the judicial authority, that is to say, by judges completely independent of the executive bodies. Logically, this requirement of judicial independence does not necessarily require that those judicial bodies which control administrative actions be separate from the ordinary judicial bodies. What the rule of law demands instead is that control be exercised by judicial bodies.

In many continental systems, as for example in the French system, disputes relating to the control of the legality of administrative action are brought before administrative courts organized separately from the judicial hierarchy, yet they are independent of the government. In many of the common law systems, such as in the United States and the United Kingdom, administrative matters are brought before ordinary courts and independent judges, maintaining one of the most important elements of the concept of the rule of law.

The third aspect of the rule of law, according to Dicey, was that the Constitution was the result of the recognition of individual rights by judges although these rights were not included in a written Constitution. Dicey explained this third meaning of the rule of law as follows:

We may say that the constitution is pervaded by the rule of law on the grounds that the general principles of the constitution [as for example the right to personal liberty, or the right of public meeting] are with us the result of judicial decisions determining the rights of private persons in particular cases brought before the courts; whereas under many foreign constitutions the security [such as it is] given to the rights of individuals results, or appears to result, from the general principles of the constitution.[56]

In other words, he described this third meaning of his conception of the rule of law by saying that this expression: 'may be used as a formula for expressing the fact that with us the law of the constitution, the rules which in foreign countries naturally form part of a constitutional code, are not the source but the consequence of the rights of individuals, as defined and enforced by the courts.'[57]

Naturally this common law protection can only extend to certain personal liberties such as free speech, but cannot 'assure the citizen's economic or social well being'[58] such as the protection of physical well-being, having a proper home, or education or the provision of social security or a proper environment; these require complex legislation.[59]

Thus, as a result, the ability of the common law to deal with economic or social needs, and with that law's creation in the field of personal liberty being subject to the supremacy of Parliament, the faith shown by Dicey in the common law as the primary legal means for the protection of the citizen's liberties against the state has been superseded. Instead the experience of many Western countries has shown that entrenched declarations of human rights which impose legal limits on the legislatures have proved to be of greater value.

Since Dicey's description, the concept of the rule of law has received a much closer analysis. Professor H.W.R. Wade identified five different although related aspects of the rule of law. First, it means that all governmental action must be taken according to the law, in the sense that all administrative acts that infringe individual rights must be authorized by law. Second, that government should be conducted within a framework of recognized rules and principles which restrict discretionary power, in the sense that an essential part of the rule of law is that of a system of rules for preventing the abuse of such discretionary power. Third, that disputes as to the legality of acts of government are to be decided upon by courts which are wholly independent of the executive, which in the United Kingdom means the ordinary courts of law. Fourth, that the law should be even-handed between government and citizen, in the sense that even though it cannot be the same for both, government should not enjoy unnecessary privileges or exemptions from ordinary law. And fifth, outside the sphere of public administration, the rule of law means that no one should be punished except for legally defined crimes, a principle that applies, moreover, to administrative action in the sphere of administrative sanctions.[60]

In another more descriptive perspective, Joseph Raz enumerates a few principles as a complement to the view of Professor Wade. Those principles are as follows: all laws should be prospective, open and clear; laws should be relatively stable; the making of particular laws should be guided by open, stable, clear and general rules; the independence of the judiciary must be guaranteed; the principles of natural justice must be observed; the courts should have review powers over the implementation of those principles; the courts should be easily accessible; and the discretion of the crime prevention agencies should not be allowed to hinder the law.[61]

It is in this manner that the rule of law, as a general concept, can be described. This concept is applicable, within the British constitutional system, as it relates to the activities of executive administrative action. Parliament, because of its sovereignty, is not included in the principle.

This sovereignty continues to exist because there is no written Constitution or entrenched law to which it must submit.

In continental Europe and in the United States, the rule of law applies to the legislative branch in the sense that Congresses, General Assemblies or Parliaments must submit to and are limited by a written and rigid higher law.

# 4

## THE DECLARATION OF
## FUNDAMENTAL RIGHTS AND LIBERTIES

The third characteristic of the *état de droit* is the establishment of a set of fundamental rights and liberties. These are normally enumerated in a formal declaration of constitutional rank or in a written constitution; in an entrenched way and with the necessary guarantees and legal security to prevent their violation by the state itself. This process of constitutional entrenchment distributes power between the state and its citizens in such a manner that the state cannot interfere with that area that has been reserved for the individual.

This constitutional establishment of fundamental rights appeared as a central element of liberalism and, as part of the *état de droit*, is designed to ensure the protection, guarantee and fulfilment of human rights and fundamental liberties.

### (a) Theoretical background and historical antecedents

This conception of the entrenchment of fundamental rights and liberties lies beneath the whole construction of the *état de droit* and has done so from its philosophical beginnings. This beginning was established with Locke's *Two Treatises of Government* (1690). According to Locke, the establishment of a political or civil society implied an agreement between men, 'to join and unite into a community for their comfortable, safe and peaceful living one among the other, in a secure enjoyment of their properties and a greater security against any that are not of it'.[1] Accordingly, the power granted to the Commonwealth, and in particular to the legislative branch

is not, nor can possibly be, absolutely arbitrary over the lives and fortunes of the people, for it being but the joint power of every member of the society given up to that person or assembly which is legislator. It can be no more than those persons in a state of nature before they entered into society and gave up the community; for nobody can transfer to another more power than he has in himself, and nobody has an absolute arbitrary power

43

over himself, or over any other, to destroy his own life, or take away the life or property of another. A man, as has been proved, cannot subject himself to the arbitrary power of another and having in the state of nature no arbitrary power over the life, liberty or possession of another, but only so much as the law of nature gave him for the preservation of himself and the rest of mankind, this is all he does or can give up to the commonwealth, and by it to the legislative power, so that the legislative can have no more than this. Their power, in the utmost bounds, is limited to the public good of the society. It is a power that has no other end but preservation, and therefore can never have a right to destroy, enslave, or designedly to impoverish the subject.[2]

On this basis, Locke defined the end of government as 'the good of mankind', and stated that 'all the power government has is only for the good of the society'. Opposed to civil society was the absolute arbitrary power or government without settled standing laws. Those,

can neither of them consist with the end of society and government which men would not quit the freedom of the state of nature and tie themselves up under, were it not to preserve their lives, liberties, and fortune, and by stated rules of right and property to secure their peace and quiet. It cannot be supposed that they should intend, had they a power so to do, to give to anyone, or more, an absolute arbitrary power over their persons and estates, and put a force into the magistrate's hand to execute his unlimited will arbitrarily upon them. This were to put themselves into a worse condition than the state of nature, wherein they had a liberty to defend their right against the injuries of others, and were upon equal terms of force to maintain it, whether invaded by a single man or many in combination.[3]

Locke was therefore able to conclude that fundamental rights, or property as he termed them, were beyond the power of government. Thus 'the supreme power cannot take from any man part of his property without his own consent; for the preservation of property being the end of government and that for which men enter society, it necessarily supposes and requires, that the people should have property'.[4]

The concept that the state was based on the idea of the existence of man's inalienable liberties was also propounded by two other theoreticians. Rousseau referred to the nature of the rights of citizens by saying:

To renounce one's liberty is to renounce one's equality as a man, the rights and also the duties of humanity...such a renunciation is incompatible with man's nature, for to take away all freedom from his will is to take away all morality from his actions. In short, a convention which stipulates absolute authority on the one side and unlimited obedience on the other is vain and contradictory.[5]

Montesquieu, for his part, argued that 'political liberty' was to be found only in 'moderate governments', that is to say, those where 'there is no abuse of power'.[6] Those governments could only exist in systems, like the British, where power checked power. Thus Montesquieu's theory relied upon the distribution of power as a prerequisite for political liberty.

Britain had had a long tradition of fundamental rights, even though the idea of such rights has been said to be 'strictly an [English] commodity for export, particularly to France, and to the American colonies'.[7] The Magna Carta of 1215, is often referred to as the first declaration of fundamental rights. This Charter was the result of the struggle between the centripetal and centrifugal feudal forces, that is to say, on the one hand, the king's forces, and the established central institution which administered a common law and, on the other hand, the forces of the barons, the landowners, the ecclesiastics and traders,[8] all of whom sought disintegration as a means to independence and power.

The result of that struggle, the Great Charter, was a code passed by the whole body of barons and bishops and thrust upon a reluctant king.[9] Because it attempted to establish one standard for reforming laws, it opened up a new chapter in English history and has thus been seen as the origin and source of English constitutional law.[10]

As one of many formal examples of stipulations between the king and the feudal knights, the Great Charter was a *stabilimentum* or an enactment formulated by the king, church, barons and merchants as partners in the legislative powers of the nascent state. Thus, the Charter set forth a series of rights of a heterogeneous nature, all relating to the different classes participating in its enactment. Its clauses were classified into five groups; those granting the liberty of the church; those dealing with feudal grievances; those relating to trade; those relating to central government; and those which placed limitation upon arbitrary power.[11]

However, the Great Charter contained nothing resembling a general declaration of fundamental rights of the English people. The freemen, whose rights the document refers to, were just a fraction of the English people, and although it is true that some clauses could be interpreted so as to include the villain 'it is fairly clear that they were thus protected, not because it was intended to confer any rights upon them, but because they were the property of their lords and excessive amercements would diminish their value'.[12] As the Charter was therefore primarily concerned with *liberi homines,* it must be seen only as an agreement between a feudal aristocracy and its king.

Yet this historical fact does not detract from its crucial symbolic importance in British constitutional history, which began to take effect after the middle ages and before the sixteenth century when the idea of duty gave way to the idea of rights.[13] This change itself was due to theoreticians such as Locke and Rousseau.

The first formal expression of this new concept, based upon the symbol of the Great Charter, was the writ of *habeas corpus*. As Sir William Holdsworth pointed out:

> Whether or not the famous clause of Magna Carta, which enacted that 'no free man shall be taken or imprisoned or disseised or exiled or in any way destroyed except by the lawful judgment of his peers or by the law of the land', was intended to safeguard the principle that no man should be imprisoned without due process of law, it soon came to be interpreted as safeguarding it. Because it was interpreted in this way, it has exercised a vast influence, both upon the manner in which the judges have developed the writs which could be used to safeguard this liberty, and upon the manner in which the Legislature has assisted that development.[14]

This original judicial interpretation of the Magna Carta became, in 1679, an Act of Parliament. This was followed, a few years later in 1689, by the first Act which referred to fundamental liberties in a wider sense, as 'rights of the nation'.[15] This Bill of Rights (1689) was enacted at the end of the English Revolution of 1688 and marked the ultimate triumph of Parliament in its struggle against the Crown. In so doing, however, the Bill resolved long-standing disputes in ways favourable to Parliament and the individual, and according to the libertarian political principles that the revolution embodied. Thus it has been said that the Bill of Rights

> dealt with royal prerogatives that lie at the very heart of sovereignty; royal power respecting law, military authority and taxation. They sought also to strengthen the role of Parliament, by claiming the rights of free election, free speech, free debate, free proceedings and frequent meetings. And they guaranteed rights to the individual to petition the King without fear of reprisal, to bear arms [under certain restrictions]; and to be protected against certain judicial procedures [excessive bail, excessive fines, cruel and unusual punishments, and the granting and promising of fines and forfeitures before conviction].[16]

The importance of the Bill of Rights (1689) therefore lies in two principal aspects; first because it paved the way for the transition from the ancient system of class rights towards modern individual rights, in the sense that the Bill of Rights declared individual rights not of some privileged classes but of English people as a whole; and second, because of its influence on other declarations of fundamental rights, those of the English colonies of North America.

## (b) The American and French Declarations and their influence

The Declaration of Rights of the American colonies differed from their English precedents, partly because they did not refer to rights based on the common law and tradition, but rather to the rights derived from human nature and reason. Thus the rights 'do pertain to ... [the people] and their posterity, as the basis and foundation of government'.[17] With this affirmation, and the ensuing content, it is clear that Locke's theories of the reasons for political associations had a direct influence. The first three sections were declared as follows:

Section 1: That all men are by nature equally free and independent and have certain inherent rights, of which, when they enter into a state of society, they cannot by any compact, deprive or divest their posterity; namely, the enjoyment of life and liberty, with the means of acquiring and possessing property and pursuing and obtaining happiness and safety.

Section 2: That all power is vested in, and consequently derived from the people; that magistrates are their trustees and servants and at all times amenable to them.

Section 3: That government is, or ought to be, instituted for the common benefit, protection and security of the people, nation, or community; of all the various modes and forms of government, that is best which is capable of producing the greatest degree of happiness and safety, and is most effectually secured against the danger of maladministration; and that, when any government shall be found inadequate or contrary to these purposes, a majority of the community hath an indubitable, inalienable, and indefensible right to reform, alter, or abolish it, in such manner as shall be judged most conducive to the public weal.[18]

In addition, Section 4 established the prohibition of privileges and Section 5 prescribed the separation of powers and the temporal condition of public offices.

With these sections in the Declaration, the English colonies in North America accepted the theory of the social contract or pact, based on the existence of inherent and inalienable rights of man; the democratic basis of government with democratic representation through free elections; and the right of resistance.

These same fundamental liberal principles can also be found in the Declaration of Independence of the United States of America, approved less than one month later. That declaration stated:

We hold these truths to be self-evident that all men are created equal; that they are endowed by their Creator with certain unalienable rights; that among these are life, liberty and the pursuit of happiness; that, to secure these rights, government is instituted among men, deriving their just powers from the consent of the governed; that, whenever any form of government becomes destructive of these ends, it is the right of the people to alter or to abolish it and to institute new government, laying its foundation on such principles, and organizing its powers in such form, as to them shall seem most likely to effect their safety and happiness.[19]

Although these declarations marked the beginning of the democratic and liberal era of the modern state, the 1787 Constitution of the United States did not contain a declaration of fundamental rights. This deficiency was resolved two years later when ten amendments to the Constitution were drafted by the first Congress. They were approved on 25 September 1789, and adopted 15 December 1791.

Earlier, on 27 August 1789 the representatives of the French people, organized in the National Assembly, approved a Declaration of the Rights of Man and the Citizen.[20] The mutual influences between the two continents at the time are well known; the French philosophers, including Montesquieu, and Rousseau were studied in North America; French participation in the War of Independence was important, Lafayette was a member of the drafting committee of the Constituent Assembly which produced the French Declaration and submitted his own draft based on the Declaration of Independence and the Virginia Bill of Rights; the rapporteur of the Constitutional Commission proposed 'transplanting to France the noble idea conceived in North America'; and Jefferson himself was present in Paris in 1789, having succeeded Benjamin Franklin as American Minister to France.[21] Moreover, the main objectives of both declarations were the same: to protect the citizen against arbitrary power and to establish the rule of law.

The drafters of the French Declaration took from Rousseau the concept of the role of society as being related to the natural liberty of man, and the idea that the law was the expression of the general will which could therefore not be used as an instrument for oppression. They also took, from Montesquieu, the distrust of power and therefore the principle of the separation of powers.[22] The Declaration was designed as an attempt to remind government of the 'natural inalienable and sacred rights of man'.[23] The first articles of the Declaration were a compilation of liberal principles based on the ideas of Locke, Montesquieu and Rousseau and formalized in the American Revolution. They were:

48

1 Men are born and remain free and equal in rights; social distinctions may be based only upon general usefulness.

2 The aim of every political association is the preservation of the natural and inalienable rights of man; these rights are liberty, property, security and resistance to oppression.

3 The source of all sovereignty resides essentially in the nation; no group, no individual may exercise authority not emanating expressly therefrom.

4 Liberty consists of the power to do whatever is not injurious to others; thus the enjoyment of the natural rights of every man has as its limits only those that assure to the members of society the enjoyment of those same rights; such limits may be determined only by law.

5 The law has the right to forbid only actions which are injurious to society. Whatever is not forbidden by law may not be prevented and no one may be constrained to do what it does not prescribe.

6 Law is the expression of the general Will; all citizens have the right to concur personally, or through their representatives in its formation; it must be the same for all, whether it protects or punishes...

7 Every society in which the guarantee of rights is not assured or the separation of powers not determined, has no constitution at all.[24]

The remainder of the Declaration was concerned with individual rights such as the principle of *nullum crimen nulla poena sine legge*, the presumption of innocence until a declaration of guilt; the right of free expression and to free communication of ideas and opinions; and the right to property. In 1791 the Declaration of the Rights of Man and of the Citizens was incorporated into the French Constitution. With the United States and French Constitutions establishing a new form of limitation of power, it is surprising that other European countries were not the next to follow. Instead, the third formal declaration of rights was the Declaration of Rights of the People adopted by the Supreme Congress of Venezuela in 1811, four days before the formal Independence Act of July 1811.[25] That Declaration followed the French one but was much more detailed in its enumeration of rights in that it included new rights such as the right to industrial and commercial freedom and the freedom to work; the right to consider one's home as inviolable, and the right to petition state authority without limitation. The Declaration was later incorporated as the final chapter of the Venezuelan Constitution of 21 December 1811.[26]

The United States, Latin American and French Declarations of Rights were different in their content and meaning. Because the French Declaration was given in circumstances where the French state was to continue, although in an altered condition, the concept of the citizen was taken for granted. As stated in its introduction, the purpose of the Declaration was to solemnly remind all members of the community of their rights and duties. Hence the concept of individual liberty appeared only as an important modification within the context of a political unity already in existence. In the Venezuelan and United States' Declarations, the enforcement of rights was an important factor in the independence process in that these new states were built upon a concept of the sovereignty of the people with all its democratic content.

After these initial steps during the first decades of the last century, declarations of fundamental rights and liberties became more common throughout the world, so that it is difficult to find written Constitutions without such declarations in the present century.

As these written Constitutions are usually rigid, the declarations of fundamental rights become entrenched declarations in the sense that the ordinary legislator cannot eliminate or modify their contents. This establishment of an entrenched declaration of fundamental rights and freedoms implies that the first and most important guarantee of those rights is the inability of any branch of government to amend those rights, this then, must take place through special constitutional procedures for amendment; and in all cases in which the Constitution allows possible further regulations and limits to the enjoyment of right, those regulations and limits can only be established through formal laws or Acts of Parliament. Therefore the executive itself cannot set any limit whatsoever on constitutional rights.

In this concept of the *état de droit*, in which the Constitution has supremacy over legislative, executive and administrative actions, judicial independence becomes fundamental as it is the only instrument capable of guaranteeing that fundamental laws will not be violated. Hence the definition of the *état de droit* as one in which judicial control exists is also referred to as a 'state of justice'.

### (c) The situation of fundamental rights in the British constitutional system

England has rightly been called the land of liberalism: Locke was English; Montesquieu's system was based on his interpretation of the English Constitution; and from the point of view of positive law, the declarations of rights have their antecedents in English constitutional history. Because of those antecedents, many liberal democratic constitutions contain a declaration of rights. However, in the United Kingdom, there is no written constitution and, apart from references to historical statutes, 'there are no fundamental rights'; and 'there is no special protection' for 'fundamental rights'.[27]

Instead, the rights of the British people are based on two assumptions: in the first place, that citizens can do or say anything, provided it is not an infringement of a law or of other citizens' rights; and in the second place, that the authorities can only do what is permitted by statutory or common law.[28] Thus 'the approach of the law in Britain to the citizen's liberty has often been to treat it as a residual concept: the citizen may go where he pleases, and do or say what he pleases provided he does not commit a criminal offence or infringe the rights of others'.[29] As a consequence, rights are expressed in a negative manner, in terms of liberties, rather than in a positive manner. Accordingly, 'anything is lawful which is not unlawful', in other words, 'it is lawful to do anything which is not unlawful or which cannot be prohibited by public authorities'.[30]

It was precisely this negative approach to fundamental rights in England that caused Dicey to point out the contrast between the continental and the English Constitutions, saying that on the continent, 'individual rights result, or appear to result from the general principles of the Constitution', whereas in England, 'the general principles of the Constitution [as for example the right to personal liberty, or the right of public meeting] are ... the result of judicial decisions determining the rights of private persons in particular cases brought before the courts'. Consequently, Dicey concluded that 'the rules which in foreign countries naturally form part of a constitutional code, are not the source but the consequence of the rights of individuals, as defined and enforced by the courts'.[31]

This situation has changed from the time of Dicey's first edition of *An Introduction to the Study of the Law of the Constitution* in 1885. As makers of law, the courts have declined in importance. In part this is the obvious result of the development of Parliament, in part it is the result of 'changes in ideas about the functions of a state... the development of the welfare state has meant that rights with which individuals are increasingly concerned, protections or hedges against poverty, ill-health, and the like, cannot be the creation of judge-made law as could be the rights of speech, etc., with which Dicey was concerned. These newer rights can only be the result of complex legislation.'[32]

Despite the British tradition of civil rights being protected through the democratic institution of Parliament, discussions have been held during the last two decades on the need and possibility of the enactment of an entrenched Bill of Rights. The principal argument in favour of a Bill of Rights, the restraint of excess power or abuse of power by public authorities, has been summarized by P.S. Atiyah as follows:

that there ought to be, and are, certain basic human rights which ought not to be at the mercy of government and legislature; that governments and legislatures derive their power from the people, and that the people cannot be assumed to have granted away unlimited and despotic powers just because they have elected a Parliament [by a process set by Parliament itself]; that a majority of the people is no doubt entitled to elect a majority government and parliament to represent their views, but this does not give, and ought not to give, that government and parliament unlimited power to oppress the minority or minorities; and that at the very least, the basic structure of the democratic process – which alone gives legitimacy to the power of governments and parliaments – ought to be entrenched so as to be unalterable by Parliament.[33]

Obviously, arguments in favour of the entrenchment of a Bill of Rights in Britain must take into account that it would limit the powers of the ordinary legislator to modify it, which is contrary to the concept of sovereignty of Parliament in the British Constitution. Such a Bill of Rights would mean that judges would become the ultimate arbiters of the powers of Parliament. In order to ensure the effective operation of such a Bill, judges would have to be persuaded to alter their traditional methods of interpretation. 'For traditional and crabbed methods of interpretation could often lead to the invalidation of legislation which is absolutely necessary to keep pace with changing values or conditions; huge tensions would then build up in the legal and political system, and general discredit could be thrown on the law.'[34]

The main arguments against the enactment of a Bill of Rights have been exposed, clearly summarized and criticized by Michel Zander in his pamphlet entitled *A Bill of Rights*.[35] In the first place, it has been said that a Bill of Rights, is an 'un-British way of doing things'. Yet to say that a Bill of Rights is 'un-British' responds M. Zander, 'is to show an ignorance of history.'[36] In fact, it was in the United Kingdom that the concept of a Bill of Rights was first conceived.

The second argument against the enactment of a Bill of Rights, or against incorporating the European Convention of Human Rights into domestic law, is that it is not needed because human rights are adequately protected in Britain.[37] 'At the time of ratification [of the European Convention], the government of the day assumed that domestic law was in full conformity with the Convention's provisions, and successive governments have, since that time, expressed the opinion that the rights and freedoms enumerated are in all cases already secured in domestic law.'[38] In response to this argument, bearing in mind that in Britain a system of remedies rather than of rights exists, Professor Zander says that 'the existing ways of getting remedies all leave much to be desired',[39] and, as has been pointed out, 'no other country which belongs to the convention system has been faced with so many cases' of importance, adding 'it is not the sheer volume of cases which is so telling, but the proportion of cases declared admissible by the commission and of cases decided against the United Kingdom'.[40]

The third argument against the enactment of a Bill of Rights is based on the principle of the sovereignty of Parliament. Since a Bill of Rights needs to be entrenched, Parliament's freedom to legislate in the future would necessarily have to be restricted. This may not be possible. As Professor H.W.R. Wade has said: 'the one inherent limit on [Parliamentary] omnipotence, which is the consequence of that omnipotence itself, is that the Parliament of today cannot fetter the Parliament of tomorrow with any sort of permanent restraint, so that entrenched provisions are impossible.'[41]

The final argument against the enactment of an entrenched Bill of Rights in the United Kingdom is that it could imply the powers of courts to review the conformity of Acts of Parliament with that Bill. This would not be acceptable in the British constitutional system unless greater modification of the Constitution itself took place.[42]

All these arguments could be overcome if the United Kingdom granted domestic status to the European Convention on Human Rights. This would allow the courts to apply and interpret the Convention and to secure speedy and effective domestic remedies for British citizens against the violation of their fundamental human rights.[43] This is probably the best solution to the problem of Parliamentary sovereignty,[44] although its adoption would involve a number of questions regarding relations between international law and English law and the interpretation of the Convention in English law.[45]

# Part II

# THE PROCESS OF CONSTITUTIONALIZATION OF THE *ÉTAT DE DROIT*

# 5

## THE WRITTEN CONSTITUTIONAL PROCESS

The consolidation and further development of the *état de droit* from the beginning of the last century is closely related to the process of constitutionalization of the state. This process was characterized by the establishment of a system of higher norms containing, in a global way, the basic rules related to the fundamental functions of the state and to the fundamental rights and liberties of the citizens.

This constitutionalization of the state started with the introduction of written Constitutions which were conceived as formal documents containing the will of the people considered as sovereign in regard to the political organization of a nation. As a consequence of this process, sovereignty was depersonalized and the constituent organs of the state, including kings and Parliament, were converted into constituted organs of the state with constituent sovereignty attributed to the people.

During the last two centuries, after the approval of the 1787 Constitution of the United States of America, the practice of written Constitutions has become widespread so that they are now in existence in almost every country in the world.

Yet the fact that in the United Kingdom, Israel or New Zealand there is no written Constitution, does not mean that there is no Constitution at all. On the contrary, in these countries a collection of rules exists, partially written, partially unwritten, which establish, regulate and govern their government.[1] Thus the constitutionalization of the state has also taken place in legal systems with no written Constitutions.

In any case, this process of constitutionalization of the *état de droit*, reflected in a written Constitution, has produced a system of guarantees of individual liberties, which are specified in the recognition of fundamental rights; the establishment of the division of powers; provision for the people's participation in legislative power by means of popular representation; submission of the state to the rule of law and, most importantly, a system which responds to a political decision of society adopted by the people as a constituent power through a particular constituted Assembly.

Although the United States' Constitution of 1787 was the first of the modern Constitutions, the idea of a higher and fundamental law established as a social contract had English origins and antecedents. One can go back perhaps as far as the medieval doctrine of the supremacy of law, as interpreted by Coke and Bracton.

## (a) Historical origins

The remote antecedents of written Constitutions can be found in the medieval formal pacts made between a prince and his vassals, or a prince and popular representation, which was subsequently taken as the expression of the will of the people.

Certainly, in the Middle Ages, these charters were established between the princes and their barons. However, these documents were not Constitutions in the modern sense of the word. They have been termed laws, because they were issued by the king and took the form of royal concessions and, as such, they have even been described as public law contracts. Yet because they have been present throughout British history, acting either as a factor of real integration, or as the ideological content of competition between parties, or as a symbol of the parliamentary party, they symbolized the spirit of the Constitution in its entirety.

The greatest of the Charters, the Magna Carta of 1215, was the result of a resistance movement by the privileged barons against crown policy during the reign of King John (1199–1216).[2] It was just one of the many feudal charters established between the prince and his barons, guaranteeing them privileges in exchange for certain commitments on their part.

The Magna Carta was a *stabilimentum*, that is to say, an agreement or stipulation lacking any precise sense of political law. The fact that it was in writing is no argument in favour of its characterization as a Constitution, and its name, Magna Carta, was merely a popular description to distinguish it from the *Carta Foresta* or Charter of the Forest of 1217 relating to hunting rights.[3]

The original name of the Magna Carta was *Cartam Libertatis* or *Carta Baronum*, and it was only centuries later, with Parliament's revolution against the absolutism of the Stuarts, that the modern sense was attributed to it. While the magnified sense may be sufficient to credit it with the origin of a modern Constitution, it would be a historical error to see anything in it analogous to a modern liberal or democratic Constitution.[4]

Nevertheless, in medieval times, it was considered to be an unalterable, fundamental and perpetual[5] part of the enacted law, and was confirmed by different kings on more than thirty different occasions.[6]

Within the same British context, the first real example of a modern written Constitution is the *Instrument of Government* (1653). This document occurred as a result of the only real break in the political continuity of English constitutional history.[7]

The Civil War of 1642, which divided Great Britain into Parliamentarians and Royalists, can be thought of as the final step in the long struggle between Parliament and king. Charles I was tried and executed in January 1649, and soon afterwards the monarchy and the House of Lords were abolished and England was named a Commonwealth or Free State, under the control of the army and of Oliver Cromwell.[8] Parliament carried out the wishes of the army, except when setting a limit on its own powers and its own existence. After long and futile negotiations, Cromwell finally dissolved Parliament by force in 1653. In its stead he invited a number of proven Puritans to form an Assembly of Saints. They shortly afterwards resigned their powers, and gave back their authority to Cromwell. The Council of army officers then produced a written Constitution for the government, known as the *Instrument of Government* (1653).[9] This document shows all the characteristics of a Constitution as it is understood today.

The *Instrument of Government* made Oliver Cromwell Lord Protector of the Commonwealth of England, Scotland and Ireland and conferred executive powers upon the Protector assisted by a Council of State.[10] But when Parliament met, not all its members accepted the fundamentals of the Protectorate Government and they refused to accept the Constitution under which it was assembled. Eventually it was dissolved, because it attempted to deprive Cromwell of sole control over the army, and Cromwell again found himself obliged to rule by means of the army.[11] This happened again and again until Cromwell's death in 1658.

Thereafter, King Charles II was restored to his throne by a new Parliament under the terms of the *Declaration of Breda* (1660), which contained four principles or conditions: a general amnesty, liberty of conscience, security of property and payments of arrears to the army.[12] This Declaration was not a Constitution, in the sense of the *Instrument of Government*, because the Restoration meant a return to the old form of government and no Constitution was needed to that end.[13] In this sense, the *Instrument of Government* which made Cromwell Lord Protector and established a new legislature, was the first and only example of a written

Constitution in England. However, it only remained in force for a few years and did not even survive Cromwell himself.

Nevertheless, this Constitution anticipated many of the constitutional developments of the nineteenth and twentieth centuries. As Sir William Holdsworth pointed out this *Instrument of Government* and its immediate modifications:

were the first attempt that Englishmen had made to construct a written constitution, and therefore they raised for the first time all the problems connected with its construction. Thus we get the idea of a separation of powers as a safeguard against the tyranny both of a single person and a representative assembly; the idea of stating certain fundamental rights of the subject; and the idea of rendering these rights permanent, by denying validity to any legislation which attempted to affect them.[14]

## (b) The American Constitution 1787

The movement towards independence from England began in the United States long before independence was finally declared in 1776. An independent spirit had developed through the Colonial Assemblies, which had grown in power and influence during the first half of the eighteenth century, as they resolved many of the colonists' problems at local level.[15]

Thus the process of the separation of thirteen English colonies in America from Great Britain took place on the basis of two fundamental elements: the process towards independence of each one of the colonies through their own representative governments and progress towards the unity of the colonies through the continental congresses. Consequently, it was perceived that 'the Revolution and the Union developed gradually from 1770 to 1776'.[16]

During that period, the colonies established a number of intercolonial agreements designed to resist the tax claims of England. In this context the New York Congress of 1765 met to demonstrate the colonies' rejection of the *Stamp Act* passed by the English Parliament on 22 March 1765. This Act placed stamp duties on all legal documents, newspapers, pamphlets, college degrees, almanacs, liquor licences and playing cards, and aroused widespread hostility in the colonies.[17]

Although the due subordination of this Congress to the Parliament of Great Britain was declared, its representative character was questioned on the grounds that the taxes established in the Stamp Act had not been approved by the Colonial Assemblies. England later annulled the Stamp Act but imposed a series of customs duties on colonial products.

By 1774, it had become clear that the problems of individual colonies were common to them all. Consequently, Virginia proposed that an annual Congress be held to discuss the joint interests of America. In 1774 the first continental Congress met in Philadelphia with representatives from all the colonies except Georgia. The colonies discussed whether they should concede authority to Parliament and whether the basis of such submission would be the law of nature, the British Constitution or the colonial Charters.[18] It was decided that the law of nature should be recognized as one of the foundations of the rights of the colonies. Thus the Congress declared, as a right of the inhabitants of the English colonies in North America:

That the foundation of English Liberty, and of all free government, is a right in the people to participate in their legislative council; and as the English colonists are not represented, and from their local and other circumstances, cannot properly be represented in the British Parliament, they are entitled to a free and exclusive power of legislation in their several provincial legislatures, where their rights of representation can alone be preserved in all cases of taxation and internal polity, subject only to the negative of their sovereign, in such manner as has been heretofore used and accustomed ...[19]

Thus loyalty to the king was maintained although Parliament was denied competence to impose taxes on the colonies.

As a result of this Congress, economic war was declared with Britain by the suspension of imports and exports. The economic war rapidly became a military one and Congress met again in Philadelphia and adopted the 'Declaration of the Causes and Necessity of taking up Arms' (1775), as a reaction against the enormous and unlimited power of the Parliament of Great Britain. The sovereignty of the English Parliament was not long to be found in these united colonies. One year later, the Second Continental Congress, in its session of 2 July 1776, adopted a proposition whereby the colonies declared themselves free and independent:

That these United Colonies are, and of right, ought to be, Free and Independent States; that they are absolved from all allegiance to the British Crown, and that all political connexion between them, and the State of Great Britain, is, and ought to be, totally dissolved.[20]

The Congress agreed to draw up a declaration proclaiming to the world the reasons for its separation from Great Britain, and on 4 July, the Declaration of Independence was adopted, in formal ratification of the act already executed. There was no longer recourse to common law, nor to the rights of Englishmen, but exclusively to the laws of nature and to God. There was no longer recourse to historic documents, but to self-evident truths namely:

that all men are created equal; that they are endowed, by the Creator, with certain unalienable rights that among these are life, liberty, and the pursuit of happiness. That to secure these rights, Governments are instituted among men, deriving their just powers from the consent of the governed that whenever any form of government becomes destructive of these ends, it is the right of the people to alter or to abolish it, and to institute a new government, laying its foundation on such principles and organizing the powers in such form, as to them shall most likely effect their safety and happiness.[21]

Consequently, anything which was not rationally adapted to the objectives established was unjustified and illegitimate; the state was also organized so as to achieve these objectives.

Apart from the importance of this document for the United States, it is also of universal significance: its basic premise, as a syllogism, is constituted by all those acts of the Crown which, according to Locke, define tyranny, and the conclusion of the syllogism is obvious: by violating the pact uniting him to his American subjects, the King had lost all claim to their loyalty, so that the colonies became independent states.

Once the colonies had acquired their independence, they had to regulate their own political organization. After the king's proclamation of rebellion (1775) before the Declaration of Independence, Congress urged all colonies to form separate governments for the exercise of all authority. Thus was created the Bill of Rights and the Constitution or Form of Government of Virginia (1776).

The idea of a confederation or union of colonies was also formulated at this time as an attempt to satisfy the need for a stronger political, economic and military union. Hence, by adopting the *Articles of Confederation* (1777),[22] Congress established a confederate union between the states. The aim of the union was the 'common defence, the security of their Liberties and their mutual and general welfare'[23] while each state retained 'its sovereignty freedom and independence'[24] and any power, jurisdiction and right not expressly delegated to the United States in Congress.

However, this first confederation was weak. It lacked direct taxation power, it depended economically on the contributions of the states and it had no executive body and only an embryonic form of judicial organization. After their victorious completion of the revolutionary war, a

Federal Convention was called to meet 'for the sole and express purpose of revising the articles of Confederation'.[25] This led to the adoption by Congress of the Constitution of the United States.

This Constitution was the result of a series of general compromises[26] between the political and social components of the independent colonies, of which the following are the most outstanding. One of the most important involved the distribution of governmental powers so as to provide the Union with the necessary competences for its existence, on the one hand, while on the other to maintain the autonomy of the Federate States. From this compromise emerged the form of the federal state.[27]

The second great compromise was required as a result of a long brewing confrontation between large and small states of the Union regarding representation. The larger states preferred a Congress in which the states would be represented in proportion to their population while the smaller preferred a confederal type of representation. The result was a bicameral system in which the House of Representatives was to be made up of a number of Deputies proportional to the population of each state, whereas the Senate would comprise two representatives per state, regardless of its size.[28]

The third situation which required a compromise occurred as a result of the slavery issue. Pro-slavery states wished to have the advantages of population, which the slaves brought, in regard to the appointment of representatives and for tax purposes but did not wish to provide them with the rights of a citizen of the state. Accordingly, it was agreed that the slave population was to be estimated at three fifths of the white population.

The great slavery issue also produced a fourth issue concerning the import of slaves or the abolition of slavery. As a compromise, it was agreed to insert a clause into the Constitution preventing Congress from taking any decision prohibiting slave importation for twenty years.[29]

The fifth compromise arose out of a conflict between democracy and the interests of the ruling classes. As a consequence of that conflict, limited voting rights were established, based on private property. Thus, while representatives to the House of Representatives could be elected directly, election of the members of the Senate could only be by indirect election.

Finally, there was a separation of powers at the federal level creating a system of checks and balances. In addition to the legislative body, therefore, a strong presidency was established, to be occupied by a president elected for four years by means of a system of indirect suffrage, and a Supreme Court was created made up of judges elected for life. This court was given the power to declare the unconstitutionality of acts issuing from the other powers against the Constitution.

In spite of the colonial antecedents and of the proposals made in the Convention, and except for the right of representative government, the Constitution did not contain a Bill of Rights. This deficiency was only made good later with the adoption of the first ten amendments to the Constitution of 15 December 1791.[30]

## (c) The French Constitution 1791

Thirteen years after the Declaration of Independence of the United States, the French Revolution (1789) developed into a social revolution aimed at liquidating the *Ancien Régime* represented by an absolute and personal monarchy.[31] The problem was not how to find a common denominator between thirteen independent states and create a new state from the remains, but rather to transform an over-centralized state constructed around the old French monarchy into a new form of state in which the people were to participate. A revolution was needed and its first result was the weakening of the monarchy itself.

After the 14 July 1789, two main decisions were taken by the French National Assembly: the abolition of seignorial rights on 4 August and the Declaration of the Rights of Man and of the Citizen on 26 August. Two years later the first French Constitution of 3 September 1791 was adopted. Although it was still a monarchical Constitution, it conceived the king as a delegate of the nation and subject to the sovereignty of the law. From that time onwards, the state was no longer the king as absolute monarch, but the organized people in a nation subject to its Constitution.

The Constitution of 1791 adopted a structure which was later followed by a number of Constitutions including some of the state Constitutions in the United States. This structure established a clear distinction between a dogmatic part, containing individual rights and the limits and obligations of state power, and an organic part, establishing the structure, attributions and relations between the various state bodies.[32]

Firstly, the Constitution began with the *Declaration of the Rights of Man and of the Citizen*, previously adopted by the Assembly. This text had been inspired by the Declarations of the American states recently emancipated from England, particularly the Virginian Bill of Rights (1776), and to a large extent, by the rationalist French works of Rousseau and Montesquieu.[33]

Its content constituted a formal adhesion to the principles of natural law and to the natural rights with which man is born. This ensured that the Declaration had a universal character. It was not a declaration of the rights only of the French, but the acknowledgement by the revolutionaries of the existence of the fundamental rights of man, for all time and for all states. Thus De Tocqueville later compared the political revolution of 1789 with a religious revolution, by noting that in the fashion of great religions the political revolution established general rules and adopted a message that spread abroad. This important aspect of the Declaration is related to the fact that the rights declared were natural rights.[34]

Secondly, under Rousseau's influence, the Declaration was based on man's natural bounty and implicitly rejected the idea of original sin. As it stated, 'ignorance, forgetfulness and contempt of the rights of man are the sole causes of public misfortunes and of the corruption of governments'.

Thirdly and fundamentally, the powers of the state were limited inasmuch as it had to act within the limits imposed on it by the rights declared in the Constitution.

Moreover, both the Declaration of Rights and the Constitution were based on the affirmation of national sovereignty. Although this idea of the nation emerged for the purpose of depriving the king of his sovereignty, as sovereignty existed only in the person who exercised it, another concept of the nation had to emerge to replace the deposed king. The concept of the nation which emerged was a personification of the people.[35]

But the nation in revolutionary theory was identified with what Sieyès called the Third Estate. The Third Estate in the revolutionary Estates, compared to the other two estates (the nobility and the clergy), generally was the lower estate or the nation as a whole. *Qu'est-ce que le tiers état?* was the question posed by Sieyès in his book, and the answer he gave was 'all the nation'.[36] The privileged strata was excluded from the concept of the nation, confined then to the bourgeoisie.

The bourgeoisie, as stated by Sieyès, sought the 'modest intention of having in the Estates General or Assembly an influence equal to that of the privileged',[37] but the real situation led the bourgeoisie to obtain power, particularly because of their economic power and the reaction against privileges, through the French Revolution, with popular support.[38] The French Revolution therefore has been considered a revolution of the bourgeoisie, for the bourgeoisie and by the bourgeoisie,[39] and was basically an instrument against privileges and discrimination and to seek equality of all men in the enjoyment of their rights. Thus the Declaration of Rights of Man and of the Citizen was qualified as being 'the ideological expression of the triumph of the bourgeoisie'.[40]

As the Declaration of Rights expressly established, sovereignty was in the nation. 'The source of all sovereignty is essentially in the nation; no body, no individual, can exercise authority that does not proceed from it in plain terms.'[41] Thus since the nation exercised its power through representatives, the French Constitution was also a representative Constitution although a large number of citizens were excluded from electoral activity.[42] Moreover, the French Constitution established another principle of modern public law, which was particularly developed in France and which is summarized in the following statements: 'There is no authority in France superior to that of the law'[43] and the law was considered to be the 'expression of the general will'.

This is an affirmation of the *état de droit* and of the idea that it is not men who command, but laws. Hence the state bodies could demand obedience only insofar as they are an expression of the law, to the extent, said the Constitution, that the king himself 'only reigns by law, and it is only in the name of the law that he can demand obedience'.[44]

The first Constitution of France of 1791, in spite of the revolution, continued to establish a monarchical government: the exercise of the executive power and a share, though very limited, of the legislative power was conferred upon the king. But he was nothing more than the chief public functionary; he was considered a delegate of the nation, subject to the sovereignty of the law. Consequently, the monarchy became a state body for the first time, and the ancient institution of divine right became a body of positive law. The king became king of the French people instead of king of France.[45]

Moreover, the Constitution also established a system with a strict separation of powers. This was in accordance with what was stated in the Declaration of the Rights of Man and the Citizen, in the sense that 'any society in which the separation of powers is not determined has no constitution at all'.[46]

In the French system of separation of powers, a clear predominance of the legislative power was shown. Thus the king neither convened, nor suspended, nor dissolved the Assembly; he had the power of veto, but only for suspension, and could not take any initiative, although he could invite the legislative body to take something into account. The Assembly, for its part, had no control over the executive, since the king's person was sacred and inviolable. Ministers were only subject to penal responsibility. However, the Assembly had important executive attributions such as the appointment of principal officials, the surveillance of departmental administration, the declaration of war and the ratification of treaties.[47]

The significance of the French Revolution lies in the fact that it led to the establishment of an *état de droit*, in the sense that it produced a Constitution which limited and controlled the exercise of state power, thereby endowing the modern state with a new political character. In this system, the nation, as subject of the constituent power, confronted the absolute monarch, eliminated his absolutism and completely took his place. This led to an increase in the power of the state itself and to the concept of the Constitution of the nation, as a fundamental law which could not be modified by ordinary legislation.

Because the Declaration of Independence of 1776 and the American Constitution of 1787 were also the result of decisions adopted by the people of the United States, the American model exerted considerable influence in this respect.

### (d) The inspiration of France and America and Latin American constitutionalism

The constitutionalization of the *état de droit* under the American and French Constitutions was duplicated all over the world and particularly in Latin America and Europe during the nineteenth century.

In Europe, the French Constitution of 1795 inspired the Spanish Constitution of Cadiz 1812 and the Norwegian Constitution 1814,[48] but in the Latin American countries, being colonies of Spain and Portugal, the influence of the American and French Revolutions and constitutionalism was immediate and definitive. Venezuela was the first Latin American country to gain independence from Spain, the third country in the world in which a Declaration of Rights of the People was approved by an elected Congress, and had the first independent Latin American Constitution to be adopted.

One of the first French inspired reactions against the Spanish monarchy was the San Blas conspiracy in Madrid, intended to take place on 3 February 1796. It ended before it began; the conspirators were detained the day before, tried and a few of them deported to the colonies for life imprisonment. The principal conspirators, including Juan Bautista Picornell, were sent to Venezuela where they managed to get in touch with local conspirators, and in 1797 they developed what has been called the conspiracy of Gual y España, named after the two main participants: Manuel Gual and José María España.

The conspiracy failed but it remained as a symbol of liberation in Latin America. Moreover, it produced an important inspirational document for the constitutionalization of Latin America. This was a booklet entitled *Rights of Man and Citizens with an 'address to the Americans'* (1797). In fact this was a translation of the French Declaration of the Rights of Man and the Citizen contained in the 1795 French Constitution.[49] Yet this document inspired the Declaration of Rights of the People, approved by the first Venezuelan Congress (1811). Four days later, on 5 July 1811, inspired by the American Declaration of Independence, the Venezuelan Declaration of Independence was proclaimed.

Subsequently, on 21 December 1811, the Federal Constitution of the States of Venezuela was adopted. This document evidences the general trends of the constitutionalization process of the *état de droit* existing at the time[50] as well as the fundamental ideas of Hobbes, Bodin, Locke, Montesquieu and Rousseau. In structure, the Constitution resembled the formal shape of the French Constitution. It contained 228 Articles and had both a dogmatic part, containing a declaration of The Rights of Man, and an organic part, establishing the fundamental framework of the state and its organs.

The foundation of the Constitution followed the American and French concept of national sovereignty and representation in that it was adopted by the 'people of the States of Venezuela, using our sovereignty'. Article 144 of the Constitution, in this respect established:

The sovereignty of a country or supreme power to govern or direct community interests equitably, essentially and originally lays in the general mass of its inhabitants, and is exercised by means of agents or representatives appointed and established in accordance with the Constitution.

Thus, continued Article 145 and 146:

No individual, no family or portion or group of citizens, no particular corporation, no village, city or county can confer upon itself national sovereignty, which is inalienable and indivisible, in essence and origin. Neither may any individual exercise governmental public functions unless it has been obtained by the Constitution.

Magistrates and officials of Government, invested with any kind of authority whether in the Legislative, Executive or judicial Departments, consequently are simple agents and representatives of the people in their functions and are always responsible to the inhabitants for their public conduct through legal and constitutional means.

The Constitution was conceived as a manifestation of the social contract according to Locke's and Rousseau's concepts, with a duty to protect the rights of the people once they had renounced their natural condition of man. In this sense, Articles 141 and 142 stated:

Once men have set themselves up in a Society, they renounce that unlimited and licentious liberty – in which their passions easily led them to indulge, passions characteristic only of the wild state. The establishment of a society presupposes the renouncement of those ill-fated rights, the acquisition of other sweeter and more pacific rights and subjection to certain mutual duties.

The social pact assures each individual the enjoyment and possession of his goods, without prejudice to the right of others to have theirs.

Articles 151 and 152 also stated:

The aim of society is the common happiness, and governments have been instituted to make man secure, protecting his physical and mental faculties, improving the sphere of his enjoyment and to produce the honest and equitable exercise of his rights. These rights are liberty, equality, property and security.

The supremacy of law was formally declared in accordance with Rousseau's concept as the expression of the general will, and secured by sanctioning illegal acts as tyrannical. In this respect, Articles 149 and 150 stated:

The law is the free expression of the general will or of the majority of the citizens, indicated by the body of its representatives legally constituted. The law is founded on justice and on the common needs and must protect public and individual liberty against any oppression or violence.

Those acts committed against any person which do not fall within the cases and forms determined by the law, are iniquitous, and when they involve the usurpation of constitutional authority or the liberty of the people, they shall be considered to be tyrannical.

The Constitution adopted the principle of separation of powers in accordance with Montesquieu's thoughts. In the Preamble to the Constitution, when establishing the basis of the federal pact, it was stated:

The various functions of the authority entrusted to the Confederation shall never be performed together. The Sovereign Power must be divided into Legislative, Executive and Judicial power, and entrusted to different bodies, independent both reciprocally and in their respective faculties.

Furthermore, Article 189 stressed that:

The three essential government departments, namely the Legislature, the Executive and the Judiciary must be as separate and mutually independent as is required by the nature of a free government or as is in keeping with the links which bind together the system of the Constitution in indissoluble friendship and unity.

Finally, the Venezuelan Constitution of 1811 adopted the federal form of state, following the American model, as a means to unite several former highly decentralized colonial provinces. As in the federal scheme adopted by the United States, the provinces kept their 'sovereignty, liberty and independence' in all matters not assigned by the Federal Pact to the general authority of the Confederation. This weakened the uniting factor of the Federal government and undoubtedly assisted in provoking the crisis of the First Republic and the beginning of a ten year war of independence.

The federal form of the state was severely criticized by Simón Bolívar who attributed the absence of political stability and continuity to the weakened and powerless Republic that resulted. In 1815 he said:

In the same way that Venezuela has been the American Republic that has made most progress in its political institutions, it has also been the clearest example of the inefficiency of the federal-democratic form for our nascent states.[51]

Four years later, in 1819, on the same matter, he insisted;

The more I admire the excellencies of the Federal Constitution of Venezuela, the more I am persuaded of the impossibility of its application to our State and from my point of view it is a prodigy that its model in the North part of America be still in force, so prosperily...[52]

Bolívar looked upon the federal Constitution of the United States as the most perfect of the time, but blamed the 1811 Venezuelan legislators for being:

seduced by the dazzling shine of happiness of the American people, thinking that the blessings they enjoy are the exclusive result of its form of government and not of the character and customs of its citizens. And in effect, the example of the United States because of its prosperity, was too flattering so as not to be followed.[53]

He concluded his argument against the federal form of state by stressing that at the beginning of the Republic, Venezuelans were not yet prepared for a highly decentralized form of vertical division of power or for adopting weak central government. He concluded, in relation to the copying of the North American federal system, 'I think that it would be better for [Latin] America to adopt the Koran, than the [form of] government of the United States even if it is the best in the world.'[54] Yet in spite of Bolívar's recommendations, federalism spread throughout Latin America.

# 6

## GENERAL TRENDS
## OF CONTEMPORARY CONSTITUTIONALISM

One can say that certain fundamental principles and institutions of modern constitutional law had their factual origin in the American Revolution. This event and the whole process of independence and constitutionalism in the United States radically transformed the constitutional trends of the time and established the basis of contemporary constitutional law.

An exceptional witness to those processes was Alexis de Tocqueville, perhaps the first modern constitutional thinker whose studies regarding the American and French Revolutions and their constitutional consequences were highly regarded by his contemporaries in France and other European countries. His books are still essential works for understanding the fundamental changes and trends that took place after the American and French Revolutions, as well as the causes of those processes.

De Tocqueville stressed certain points where the constitutional situation of the states of the United States, and particularly those of New England, departed from the constitutional situation of their European sources. He stated:

All the general principles on which modern constitutions rest, principles which most Europeans in the seventeenth century scarcely understood and whose dominance in Great Britain was then far from complete, are recognised and given authority by the laws of New England; the participation of the people in public affairs, the free voting of taxes, the responsibility of government officials, individual freedom, and trial by jury – all these things were established without question and with practical effect.[1]

These general principles, on which modern Constitutions subsequent to American independence rest, are the following:

(a) The notion of Constitution itself, as a written document, of permanent value, containing a fundamental or higher law and which forms the basis of the constitutionalization process.

(b) The notion of democracy and the democratic regime or state with the concept of sovereignty belonging to the people rather than to state organs.

71

(c) Political centralization or decentralization as a basic method for state organization.

(d) The principle of separation of powers and its effect on the formation of different forms of government, particularly presidential or parliamentary governments.

(e) The role of the Judicial power, the Supreme Court of Justice and judicial control of the constitutionality of legislation, and

(f) The establishing of an entrenched declaration of fundamental rights and liberties.

Although de Tocqueville was 'very far from believing that they [the Americans] have found the only form possible for democratic government'[2] and he did 'not think that American Institutions are the only ones, or the best, that a democratic nation might adopt',[3] he nevertheless made a precise examination of the American system in light of the six principles of constitutional law just enumerated.

## (a)  Constitutionalism

The first of the principles of contemporary constitutional law is constitutionalism, that is to say, the trust which men place in the power of words formally written down in a Constitution to keep a government in order.[4]

This practice of written Constitutions was initiated in the thirteen English colonies in America when they became independent states in 1776. These early documents referred to the political organization of society, established the powers of the different state bodies and were generally preceded by a list of rights inherent in man. Thus was born the general division of the contents of modern Constitutions into an organic and a dogmatic part, the former comprising the concept of separation of power and supremacy of the law, and the latter the declaration of fundamental rights.

The basic element in the process of constitutionalization or of constitutionalism, is the concept that the Constitution is a supreme and fundamental law, placed above all state powers and individuals. In this respect, De Tocqueville compared the Constitutions of France, England and the United States as follows:

In France, the Constitution is, or is supposed to be, immutable. No authority can change anything in it; that is the accepted theory.
In England, Parliament has the right to modify the Constitution. In

England, therefore, the Constitution can change constantly, or rather it does not exist at all. Parliament being the legislative body, is also the constituent one.

American political theories are simpler and more rational.

The American Constitution is not immutable, as in France; it cannot be changed by the ordinary authority of society as in England. It is a thing apart; it represents the will of the whole people and binds the legislators as well as plain citizens but it can be changed by the will of the people, in accordance with established forms....[5]

and he concluded:

In America, the Constitution rules both legislators and simple citizens. It is therefore the primary law and cannot be modified by a law. Hence it is right that the courts should obey the Constitution rather than all the laws.[6]

From this concept of the supremacy of written, rigid constitutions, Chief Justice Marshall in the case of *Marbury* v. *Madison* (1803) was able to reason that:

It is a proposition too plain to be contested, that the Constitution controls any legislative act repugnant to it; or, that the legislature may alter the constitution by an ordinary act.

Between these alternatives there is no middle ground. The constitution is either a superior paramount law, unchangeable by ordinary means, or it is on a level with ordinary legislative acts, and, like other acts, is alterable when the legislature shall please to alter it.[7]

Marshall then concluded with his formidable proposition related to written constitutions :

Certainly all those who have framed written constitutions contemplate them as forming the fundamental and paramount law of the nation, and consequently, the theory of every such government must be, that an act of the legislature, repugnant to the constitution, is void.

This theory is essentially attached to written constitutions, and is, consequently, to be considered by this court as one of the fundamental principles of our society.[8]

### (b) Democracy and the people's sovereignty

The second principle influenced by constitutionalism in the United States is that of democracy based on the concept of people's sovereignty. With the American Revolution, the traditional monarchical legitimacy of government was substituted for that of the people.

This was the fundamental concept of De Tocqueville's work, *Democracy in America*, in which he said that 'Any discussion of the political laws of the United States must always begin with the dogma of the sovereignty of the people,'[9] a principle that De Tocqueville considered to be 'over the whole political system of the Anglo-Americans'.[10] He added that 'If there is one country in the world where one can hope to appreciate the true value of the dogma of the sovereignty of the people, study its application to the business of society, and judge both its dangers and its advantages: that country is America.'[11]

Of course, democracy developed in America long before independence and De Tocqueville located its exercise 'in the provincial assemblies, especially that of the township' where it 'spread secretly'[12] during colonial rule. But once the American Revolution broke out 'The dogma of the sovereignty of the people came out from the township and took possession of the government; every class enlisted in its cause; the war was fought and victory obtained in its name; it became the law of laws.'[13]

In accordance with this dogma of the sovereignty of the people, when it prevails in a nation 'each individual forms an equal part of that sovereignty and shares equally the government of the state'.[14] Thus his assertion that 'America is the land of democracy.'[15] In answer to his own question as to 'Why it can strictly be said that the people govern in the United States,' De Tocqueville replied:

In America the people appoint both those who make the laws and those who execute them; the people form the jury which punishes breaches of the law. The institutions are democratic not only in principle but also in all their developments; thus the people *directly* nominate their representatives and generally choose them annually so as to hold them more completely dependent. So direction really comes from the people, and though the form of governments is representative, it is clear that the opinions, prejudices, interests, and even passions of the people can find no lasting obstacles preventing them from being manifest in the daily conduct of society.[16]

De Tocqueville attributed three main causes which tended to maintain a 'Democratic Republic in the United States'.[17]

The first is the federal form adopted by the Americans, which allows the Union to enjoy the power of a greater republic and the security of a small one.

The second are communal institutions which moderate the despotism of the majority and give the people both a taste for freedom and the skill to be free. The third is the way judicial power is organized. I have shown how the courts correct the aberrations of democracy and how, though they can never stop the movements of the majority, they do succeed in checking and directing them.[18]

### (c) The vertical distribution of state powers: federal state, decentralization and local government

Because political decentralization, or the vertical distribution of state powers among different political territorial units, appeared to be vital to democracy in the United States, De Tocqueville observed that 'nothing strikes a European traveller in the United States more than the absence of what we call government or administration ... Functions [are] multiplied ... [and] by sharing authority in this way its power becomes, it is true, both less irresistible and less dangerous, but it is far from being destroyed...'[19] He concluded his observation by noting that 'There is nothing centralized or hierarchic, in the constitution of American administrative power, and that is the reason why one is not at all conscious of it. The authority exists but one does not know where to find its representative.'[20]

De Tocqueville noted that this vertical distribution of powers had not occurred in the same manner as in its European counterpart. It was one of the incidents of history that, in Europe, political existence began with the ruling classes and eventually worked its way down while in the United States, political activity began in the community which gradually formed into a nation.[21] Yet in becoming a nation, the United States maintained their local communities, the source of their democracy, and necessarily became a democratic nation. Within this process, the importance of the local communities cannot be dismissed. The strength of free peoples 'resides in the local community. Local institutions are to liberty what primary schools are to society; they put it within the people's reach; they teach people to appreciate its peaceful enjoyment and accustom them to make use of it.'[22] 'In the townships ... the people are the source of power, but nowhere else do they exercise their power so directly';[23] thus local institutions 'exercise immense influence over the whole of society',[24] so much so that it can be said that 'political life was born in the very heart of the townships'.[25]

De Tocqueville regarded the federal system of government, which was the structure of the decentralized form of democracy, as a new discovery. 'This constitution, which at first sight one is tempted to confuse with previous federal constitutions, in fact rests on an entirely new theory, a theory that should be hailed as one of the great discoveries of political science in our age.'[26]

Although previous federal states had existed, the federal system of the United States was unique. It did not respond to a previous scheme, but to practical need: its purpose was to seek a formula that made the existence of independent states compatible with a central power that had sufficient attributions to act as a separate unit. Unlike the European confederations that existed prior to 1776, the central power in the Constitution of the United States acted 'without intermediary on the governed, administering and judging them itself, as do national governments'. In this regard, De Tocqueville commented: 'Clearly here we have not a federal government but an incomplete national government. Hence a form of government has been found which is neither precisely national nor federal; but things have halted there, and the new word to express this new thing does not yet exist.'[27]

This 'new thing' is precisely what in constitutional law is known as a federal state, and although De Tocqueville admired its novelty, he also pointed out its defects, and clearly observed that it was not a product for export. He said that 'The Constitution of the United States is like one of those beautiful creations of human diligence which give their inventors glory and riches but remains sterile in other hands.'[28]

In contrast to the centralized states of Europe, with their national concentrations of political power, De Tocqueville pointed out that the 'most fatal of all the defects which I regard as inherent in the federal system as such is the comparative weakness of the government of the Union', adding that 'a divided sovereignty must always be weaker than a complete one'.[29] Yet he also praised the beneficial effects of political decentralization and local government by stating that 'The partisans of centralization in Europe maintain that the government administers localities better than they can themselves; that may be true when the central government is enlightened and the local authorities are not, when it is active and they lethargic, when it is accustomed to command and they to obey.' But when people are enlightened, awake to their own interests, and used to thinking for themselves, as he had seen in America, he said that he was 'persuaded that in that case the collective force of the citizens will always be better able to achieve social prosperity than the authority of the government'.[30] As a result, he was able to conclude that 'the political advantages derived by the Americans from a system of decentralization would make me prefer that to the opposite system'.[31]

## (d) Separation of powers
## and the presidential system of government

In the Constitution of the United States of 1787, and previously in the various Constitutions of the former colonies, the principle of separation of powers first became a juridical fact. For instance, Article 3 of the Constitution of Virginia of 1776 stated: 'The Legislative, Executive and Judiciary departments, shall be separate and distinct, so that neither exercise the powers properly belonging to the other; nor shall any person exercise the powers of more than one of them at the same time...'

The Constitution of the United States contained no such norm although its organization was based upon a separation of powers. Nevertheless, this separation allowed various interferences between the powers, as a system of checks and balances. Thus the powers of the executive were regulated in a new way, giving rise to presidentialism as opposed to parliamentarism, and to judicial duties and obligations never previously known in constitutional practice.

Thus, in referring to the executive power, De Tocqueville noted that in the United States, 'maintenance of the republican form of government required that the representative of executive power should be subject to the national will'; thus, 'the president is an elective magistrate . . the one and only representative of the executive power of the Nation'. But, he noted, 'in exercising that power he is not completely independent'.[32]

One of the particular consequences of this separation of powers is that the executive is not dependent on Parliament. That is why when comparing the European parliamentary system with the presidential system of the United States, De Tocqueville observed that a constitutional king 'cannot govern when opinion in the legislative chambers is not in accord with his'.[33] However, in the presidential system the sincere aid of Congress to the President 'is no doubt useful, but it is not necessary in order that the government should function'.[34]

## (e) The role of the judiciary

Among the constitutional institutions which originated in the United States, the one that is the most original is the role assigned to the judicial power in the separation of powers system. De Tocqueville observed that 'Confederations have existed in other countries beside America, and there are republics elsewhere than on the shores of the New World; the representative system of government has been adopted in several European States; but so far, I do not think any other nation in the world has organized judicial power in the same way as the Americans.'[35]

Three aspects of the organization and functioning of judicial power can be considered as a fundamental American contribution to constitutional law: the political role of judges; the institution of a Supreme Court; and judicial review of legislation. All three aspects were noticed by De Tocqueville.

The first aspect which De Tocqueville observed in the American judicial system was the 'immense political power'[36] attributed to judges. This he considered the most important political power in the United States.[37] The reason for this immense power 'lies in this one fact: The Americans have given their judges the right to base their decisions on the Constitution rather than on the laws. In other words, they allow them not to apply laws which they consider unconstitutional.'[38] Therefore, 'there is hardly a political question in the United States which does not sooner or later turn into a judicial one'.[39] Consequently, Supreme Court decisions have resulted in fundamental changes in the political and social life of the United States.

The second aspect of the American judiciary was the high standing of the Supreme Court among the great authorities in the state. De Tocqueville observed that 'The Supreme Court has been given higher standing than any known tribunal, both by the nature of its rights and by the categories subject to its jurisdiction... A mightier judicial authority has never been constituted in any land.'[40] De Tocqueville justified these powers of the Supreme Court by concluding that:

without [the judges of the Supreme Court] ... the Constitution would be a dead letter; it is to them that the executive appeals to resist the encroachments of the legislative body, the legislature to defend itself against the assaults of the executive, the union to make the states obey it, the states to rebuff the exaggerated pretensions of the Union, public interest against private interest, the spirit of conservation against democratic instability.[41]

In relation to the supremacy of the constitution, De Tocqueville observed that it 'touches the very essence of judicial power; it is in a way the natural right of a judge to choose among legal provisions that which binds him most strictly'.[42] This led to the control of the constitutionality of law, a creation of American constitutionalism, referred to by De Tocqueville with these simple and logical words: 'if anyone invokes in an American court a law which the judge considers contrary to the

Constitution, he can refuse to apply it. That is the only power peculiar to an American judge, but great political influence derives from it.'[43]

## (f) The entrenched declaration of fundamental rights and liberties

The sixth major contribution of North American constitutionalism to modern constitutional law, has been the practice of establishing formal and entrenched declarations of fundamental rights and liberties.

However, De Tocqueville did not devote particular comments in his book to the declaration of rights, undoubtedly, because by the time he visited America, the adoption of the French Declaration of 1789 had already destroyed the uniqueness of the Bill of Rights. Nevertheless he referred to specific rights particularly important in the United States, like equality, freedom of the press and political association.[44] Yet these comments were not always made with complete acceptance. For instance, referring to freedom of the press he said: 'I admit that I do not feel toward freedom of the press that complete and instantaneous love which one accords to things by their nature supremely good. I love it more from considering the evils it prevents than on account of the good it does.'[45]

# 7

## THE *ÉTAT DE DROIT* AND JUDICIAL REVIEW

The *état de droit* can be characterized by three main trends. The first is as a state in which powers are limited through a system of distribution and separation of powers. This limitation of powers shows itself in three sorts of state power distribution: in the first place, by a distinction between the powers of the state itself and an area of liberties, freedoms and rights of citizens which is beyond the sphere of state action. In the second place, by a distinction in the state between constituent power, attributed to the people as sovereign electorate and the constituted powers, represented by the organs of the state. In the third place by a separation of powers within the constituted organs both vertically and horizontally. The vertical separation leads to a system of political decentralization throughout state organs at various territorial levels, while the horizontal separation of powers leads to the classical division between the legislative, executive and judicial organs.

The second main feature of the *état de droit* is that the state is submitted to the rule of law so that all state organs are submitted to limits imposed by the law. The only body not submitted to legal limitations is the sovereign, identified in most states with the electoral body. In relation to the state organs, however, the rule of law necessarily implies their submission to the law, although this concept of legality may vary in relation to the level that the state organs occupy in the graduated or hierarchical system of rules of law.

Finally, there is an establishment of an entrenched Bill of Rights, as a guarantee to individuals against the state organs.

In order to be protected from changes introduced by the ordinary legislator, these three characteristics of the *état de droit* must be constitutionalized, that is, they must be embodied in a rigid Constitution which is not amendable by ordinary legislative process. This usually means that these characteristics must be embodied in a written Constitution. This process of constitutionalism necessarily requires some means of protection in order to guarantee the existence of the limits imposed on the state organs and on the enjoyment of individual rights. In this respect the argument of Justice Marshall in the case of *Marbury* v. *Madison* decided by the United States Supreme Court was precise:

To what purpose are powers limited, and to what purpose is that limitation committed to writing, if these limits may, at any time, be passed by those intended to be restrained? The distinction between a government with limited and unlimited powers is abolished, if those limits do not confine the persons upon whom they are imposed, and if acts prohibited and acts allowed are of equal obligation.[1]

Therefore, the *état de droit* with all its characteristics only exists if means of protecting the Constitution and therefore of legality are established. This means that the judicial branch of the state must be in charge of the effective protection of the Constitution.[2]

Consequently, it can be said that the basic element of the *état de droit* is the existence of a system of judicial review, aimed at controlling that submission to the rule of law of all legislative, administrative and even judicial acts. The two fundamental objectives of this system of judicial review are obviously: one, to ensure that all those acts of the state are adopted or issued in accordance with the law of the said state; two, to ensure that state acts respect the fundamental rights and liberties of citizens.

### (a) The judicial control of the conformity of state acts with the rule of law

Within the context of the courts' attempt to ensure the effective submission of state acts to the rule of law or to the principle of legality, it must be noted that the spheres or confines of legality are certainly not the same for all state acts. Its meaning or the confines of legality for each of these acts depends upon the rank the specific act holds in the legal order.

It must be noted that there are three different categories of state acts. Firstly, there is the Constitution; this is the supreme law of the land. From this it can be said that there are acts whose authority stems directly from the Constitution and acts whose authority stems indirectly from the Constitution. This distinction between state acts, leads to a distinction between the various systems of judicial review or control that are laid down.

In relation to those acts whose authority stems directly from the Constitution, the system of judicial review has and can only have the purpose of ensuring that they are issued or adopted in accordance with the constitution itself. In this case, as Hans Kelsen pointed out in 1928, the 'guarantee of the Constitution means guarantees of the regularity of the Constitution's immediate subordinated rules, that is to say, essentially, guarantee of the constitutionality of laws'.[3] Therefore with respect to those acts of the state, legality is equivalent to constitutionality, and judicial review or control of legality means judicial control or review of the constitutionality of such acts.

Of course, this distinction between acts whose authority is directly and indirectly reliant upon the Constitution and consequently the distinction between judicial control of constitutionality and the judicial control of legality, only exists in the strictest sense of the term in those legal systems possessing a written Constitution as a fundamental law. In systems without a written Constitution, where Acts of Parliament are the supreme law, the distinction cannot be made and a system of judicial review of constitutionality cannot exist.

The same happens when, although this fundamental law exists, the courts do not have the power to control the constitutionality of legislative acts. As Professor J. D. B. Mitchell pointed out:

The mere fact of there being a written Constitution does not by itself necessarily mean that courts play any greater role in protecting individual rights or policing the Constitution.

Where there is such a Constitution but courts do not possess the power to declare legislation unconstitutional, the only means by which the courts can protect the basic principles of that constitution from encroachment of erosions is by the restrictive interpretation of legislation. In such circumstances the position of the courts and the protection for fundamental constitutional principles do not differ materially from those which exist when there is no written Constitution.[4]

Therefore, the real difference between a legal system with a written Constitution and one without a written Constitution really lies in the powers granted to the courts to control the constitutionality of state acts. This was also mentioned by Professor Mitchell in relation to the British constitutional system: 'the real contrast with our own system is afforded by a system under which there is not only a written constitution but also a recognised power in the courts to declare legislation invalid as being unconstitutional.'[5] In any case, the control of the constitutionality of formal laws, or of any other state act whose authority stems directly from the Constitution, is only possible in those constitutional systems possessing a written, rigid Constitution, that is, unable to be changed through the process of ordinary legislation.

The rules established in this type of Constitution are, of course, applied directly, and the Constitution itself occupies a pre-eminent rank in the hierarchy of the legal order. In this respect, it is precisely in the countries where the courts have been granted the power to control the constitutionality of the laws that the juridical normative nature of the Constitutions, that is to say, their obligatory nature, is clearest. Likewise, it is in those countries that the principle of the hierarchical pre-eminence of the Constitution in relation to the ordinary laws has its origin.

Within those legal systems with written Constitutions, judicial review has been developed particularly in relation to legislative acts. Hence, one usually speaks of judicial control of the constitutionality of legislation or simply of 'judicial review of the constitutionality of legislation'.[6]

Thus, although Parliament, Congress or the National Assembly legislates as a representative of the sovereign people, it must do so subject to constitutional rules which are the fundamental expression of these same sovereign people. Consequently, the act of a legislator is always submitted to the Constitution, and when it exceeds those limits, that act is unconstitutional and therefore either invalid or liable to be invalidated. As stated in *Marbury* v. *Madison*:

Certainly all those who have framed written Constitutions contemplated them as forming the fundamental and paramount law of the nation, and consequently, the theory of every such government must be, that an act of the legislature, repugnant to the Constitution, is void.[7]

Judicial control or review of constitutionality therefore affords the courts the possibility of determining the constitutionality of the laws and, in that process, always to give preference to what is stated in the Constitution. However, judicial control of constitutionality is not restricted to formal law. Thus, matters such as the enactment of internal regulations for the functioning of legislative bodies or of parliamentary acts with the specific effect of authorizing or approving some executive acts, so long as they are contained in and controlled by the Constitution, they are subject to judicial control. In fact, all acts of state bodies and organs whose authority stems directly from the Constitution are also subject to such control. These other acts would include acts of government issued by the head of state or of the government.

There is another aspect of judicial review where the courts combine rules to ensure submission both to the fundamental law of the Constitution as well as to those valid laws which stem directly or indirectly from the Constitution. In this sense, therefore, legality means submission to the legal order considered as a whole. The acts being subjected to such control are administrative actions and other judicial decisions themselves. So important has this aspect of judicial review been, that it can be said that judicial review of administrative action has given rise to the development of administrative law itself, not only in continental European countries but also in common law countries.

Although judicial review of administrative actions in these countries is based upon the same inherent duty of the courts to ensure that each legal action conforms to a superior law, there is a substantial difference with regard to its organization. Judicial review in the Latin and German tradition is the power of special courts to decide on the legality of administrative action. This led to the development of the *contentieux administratif* recourses in continental Europe, which are to be decided by special judicial administrative courts. In some cases, these special courts were established completely separately from the ordinary courts, as is the case in France with the *juridiction contentieux administratif*; in other cases, the special administrative courts are established within the ordinary judicial order, in the same manner as there are special courts in labour law, civil law or commercial law. In all these cases, both remedies for judicial review and the courts which are to exercise the review power are special.

In contrast to this situation, the common law tradition on judicial review generally implies that the ordinary courts of justice are the ones that exercise the power of judicial review of administrative action through the ordinary common law remedies, although in more recent times special legislative remedies have been developed

With the legislative and executive branches subject to the rule of law, it can be seen that the formation of the *état de droit* is not complete until the judicial branch is brought under the control of legality as well. This is normally implemented through two mechanisms. On the one hand, the ordinary appeal system allows for control of the decisions of the inferior courts by the superior courts, within the hierarchy of the judicial system; and on the other, this control may be obtained through extraordinary remedies as, for example, with the *recours de cassation* developed in the systems influenced by continental European procedural law. Through these methods, superior courts have the power to verify the legality of decisions taken by inferior courts.

## (b) Judicial guarantees of fundamental rights and liberties

There is another system of control of state actions aimed specially at the protection of fundamental rights and liberties which have been established in a Constitution as a guarantee for the effective fulfilment of such rights and liberties. This judicial protection of fundamental rights is in fact a protection of the Constitution itself as all violations or infringements upon such rights and liberties are necessarily violations of the Constitution.

The *état de droit* has developed mechanisms to assure the protection of these fundamental rights and liberties and to avoid their violation mainly by public bodies, either by ordinary actions brought before the ordinary courts or by special actions of protection brought before either ordinary courts or before a special constitutional court.

# Part III

# THE FOUNDATION OF JUDICIAL REVIEW OF THE CONSTITUTIONALITY OF LEGISLATION

# 8

## THE LIMITED STATE ORGANS AND JUDICIAL REVIEW

With the courts controlling the conformity of state acts with the Constitution, judicial review becomes the ultimate consequence of the consolidation of the *état de droit* where the state organs are not sovereign but subject to limits imposed by a superior law or Constitution. This argument was made a few decades ago by Professor Paul Duez in an article published in the *Mélanges Hauriou* when he wrote:

Modern Public Law establishes as an axiom that Governments are not sovereign and that in particular, the Parliament is limited in its legislative action by superior legal rules, that it could not infringe; Acts of Parliament are submitted to the law, and no Act of Parliament can be contrary to the law.[1]

In the process of formulating the principle of the limitation of all state organs by a Constitution as a superior rule, Professor Duez added: 'But it is not sufficient to proclaim such a principle: it must be organized, and practical and effective measures must be adopted to ensure it.'[2] He subsequently referred to the French system of judicial control, related to Public Administration and to administrative action, through the *recours pour excès de pouvoir*; but nevertheless said 'The spirit of legality requires that a similar control be established in relation to legislative action'[3] and concluded by saying that 'there is not a real organized democracy, and an *état de droit*, except only where this control of legality of laws [Acts of Parliament] exists and functions.'[4]

Professor Duez's statement establishes the corollary of judicial review, which is that all state organs, particularly the legislator, are submitted to limits established in superior rules embodied in a Constitution. No organ of the state can then be considered sovereign. Therefore, in order to ensure that a sovereign or unlimited organ does not exist, administrative, judicial and legislative acts must always be submitted to the law. Only in countries where this control exists, are there truly organized democracies and the *état de droit*.

This judicial review of constitutionality is normally possible only in those legal systems which have established rigid or entrenched fundamental values of the society, which normally occurs in legal systems with a written Constitution. This ensures that the fundamental values cannot be modified by ordinary legislation. Ideally, this Constitution would also provide a guarantee to prevent or sanction such violations.[5] Thus, the judicial review of constitutionality becomes the power of the judiciary to control the submission of state organs to the superior rule of the country.

### (a) The relationship of state acts to the Constitution and their control

Since not all state acts have the same level of authority under the Constitution, a hierarchy of rules exists in all legal systems with written and rigid Constitutions. There are acts which are done under the direct and immediate authority of the Constitution and which are therefore subject to this superior rule alone; there are also state acts which are indirectly done under the authority of the Constitution. The latter, usually judicial and administrative acts, are usually done under the direct authority of the former and the former are the formal laws and other Acts of Parliament and acts of government issued in accordance with their constitutionally attributed powers.

With regard to this hierarchy in an *état de droit*, control exists in three ways. First, judicial review ensures that state acts, which are done under the direct authority of the Constitution, are in conformity with it; second, judicial control ensures that administrative action conforms to the Constitution and to laws which stem directly from the Constitution; and finally, the judicial control of the courts is established by systems of appeal or cassation in order to ensure that the courts conform to the Constitution and to laws which stem from the Constitution. Moreover, as the *état de droit* implies that fundamental rights and liberties ought to be established in the Constitution, judicial mechanisms of control must also be provided to protect and guarantee such rights against any act by the state which may violate them.

Within the context of the first type of judicial review, there are a number of different types of acts which are done under the direct authority of the Constitution and which are controlled by it. The most common are the formal laws or Acts of Parliament.[6] However, Parliament also creates acts which are not formal laws but which are nevertheless done under the direct authority of the Constitution. These include internal parliamentary rules of procedure and even rules regarding the relations between a

Congress or Assembly and the other constitutional organs of the state.[7] Moreover, there are a variety of acts which have the same force as the formal laws. These are executive acts with legislative content (decree-laws) and are also liable to judicial review.[8]

Governments also have the powers to produce certain acts without any legislative interference, such as when declaring a state of siege or the restriction of constitutional guarantees, when directing international relations or when vetoing an Act of Parliament. All these acts, shaped by the continental European doctrine of administrative law, as acts of government, are also subject to judicial review of constitutionality. It is true that in the traditional criteria of administrative law, such acts of government were developed to exclude them from judicial administrative control either because of their political content or motives or because they were issued by the government in its relations with other constitutional bodies.[9] These acts too, being subject to the Constitution, are liable to judicial review.[10]

Finally, international treaties and agreements are also subject to judicial review of constitutionality in the *état de droit* [11] whether this be directly, or by review of the Acts of the Parliament or government which introduce them into domestic law.

## (b) The variety of judicial review

It is evident, however, that in comparative law no single system for judicial review of constitutionality exists. Instead there is a varied range of systems. Different criteria can be adopted for classifying the various systems of judicial review of the constitutionality of state acts.[12] One type refers to the state organ which carries out this constitutional function. One system permits judicial review of constitutionality to be exercised by all the courts of a given country while others permit review only by the Supreme Court or by a court specially created for that purpose.

In the former, the system was first adopted in the United States as a result of the 1803 case of *Marbury* v. *Madison* and has since been identified as the American system. This system has also been qualified as a diffuse system[13] because all the courts in the country, from the lowest level to the highest, are permitted the power of judicial review. This system is followed in many countries, with or without a common law tradition, such as Argentina, Mexico, Greece, Australia, India, Japan, Sweden, Norway and Denmark.

By contrast, there is the concentrated system in which the power of judicial review is assigned to a single organ of the state. This may be either a supreme court or a special court created for that particular purpose. This system is also called the Austrian system because it was first established in Austria in 1920. It is also referred to as the European model because it is now followed in other European countries, for instance, in Germany, Italy, and Spain. Other countries have adopted a mixture of the diffuse and concentrated systems. Such is the case, for example, in Colombia and Venezuela.

Moreover, distinctions, other than the type of organ which carries out the judicial review function, can be observed. One such distinction may be the moment at which control of the constitutionality of laws is performed. This may be prior to the formal enactment of the particular law, as in France, or after the law has come into effect, as in Germany and Italy. Other countries have established both possibilities as e.g., Spain, Portugal and Venezuela.

Methods of judicial review in the concentrated systems can also be distinguished according to whether the constitutional issue can only arise as incidental to another litigious issue or whether it can be the subject of an independent action. In the first place, the constitutional question is not usually considered justiciable unless it is closely and directly related to an otherwise justiciable process. In such a case, the Supreme Court or constitutional tribunal can only decide the constitutional issue when it is required to do so by the ordinary court that has to decide the case. In this circumstance, it is the function of the ordinary courts to place the constitutional issue before the constitutional court. This incidental nature of judicial review is essential to the diffuse systems. When the control granted to the constitutional court can be exercised through a direct action, the constitutionality of a particular law will be the only issue.

Most countries with a concentrated system of judicial review limit the bringing of direct actions of constitutionality to other organs of the state, such as the head of government or a number of representatives in Parliament. Yet other systems of concentrated judicial review grant the action of constitutionality to individuals, sometimes ensuring that the questioned law affects a fundamental right of the individual, or permit popular actions whereby any citizen can request the constitutional court or the Supreme Court to decide upon the constitutionality of a given law.

Finally, we can classify the various systems according to the legal effects given to the particular judicial decision of review. There are decisions with *in casu et inter partes* effects and decisions with *erga omnes* effects; that is when the judicial decision has effects only within the parties in a concrete process or when it has general effects applicable to all the members of the society. Generally, decisions under a diffuse system will affect only the parties to the action, whereas under concentrated systems the decisions will usually affect everyone.

Constitutional systems also vary according to the time when the decision will have effect. In diffuse systems, the court decision which declares a law unconstitutional is generally considered to be retroactive, that is that it has *ex tunc, pro praeterito* consequences in the sense that the law is considered never to have existed and never to have been a valid law.

By contrast, in the concentrated systems a law declared unconstitutional is considered to be annullable. In this case, the decision has *ex nunc, pro futuro* consequences, that is to say, the law declared unconstitutional is considered as having produced its effect until its annullation by the court.

Nevertheless, the basic distinction between *inter partes* and *erga omnes* effects is not entirely correlative to the diffuse and concentrated systems. Although it is true that in the diffuse systems the decision will have *inter partes* effects only, when a decision is adopted by a Supreme Court, the practical situation will be that all lower courts of the country will be bound. On the other hand, when a judicial decision is adopted on an incidental issue of constitutionality in a concentrated system, certain constitutional systems have maintained that the effects of that decision must be restricted between the parties and to the particular process in which the constitutionality question was raised.

In relation to the declarative or determinative effects of the decision, or its retroactive or prospective effects, the absolute parallel with the diffuse and concentrated systems has also disappeared. Practical exceptions have been made in civil cases, in diffuse systems, to allow for the invalidity of the law not to be retroactive. In the same manner, the concentrated systems have permitted certain exceptions in criminal cases to allow for the invalidity of the law to be retroactive and to benefit an accused.

## (c) The controlled and limited legislator

Judicial review is the 'culmination of the building of the *état de droit* '[14] and the direct consequence of the adoption of a Constitution as a higher law. In this sense, judicial review as the power of the courts to control the constitutionality of legislation is, without doubt, the ultimate triumph of the individual against the absolute power of state organs, and particularly against the supremacy and sovereignty of parliaments.

Even in its origin, in the same manner as United States

constitutionalism emerged as a reaction against the sovereignty of the English Parliament, judicial review in its original American conception was a reaction against the legislative body and its powers.[15] The Congress, like all state organs, was to be submitted to the Constitution and therefore, all the laws of Congress sanctioned in violation of the Constitution, were to be considered null and void. Otherwise the Constitution 'would amount to nothing'.[16] These sentiments were echoed in the 2nd Colloquium held in Aix-en-Provence in 1981 on the subject *Cours Constitutionnelles Européennes et Droits Fondamentaux* :

the logic of the *Rechtstaat* places the Constitution at the summit of the pyramid of norms, from which all other norms draw their validity. But we must recognize that over a long century this logic was stopped ... because of the myth of the supremacy of the law, and therefore, to attain the last stage of the building of the *état de droit*, the one in which the legislator itself is subject to a superior norm, [the concept of the law] ought then to be transformed.[17]

The role of courts within this constitutional process is logically established as the result of its independent position. 'Constitutionalism, in its most advanced state, has needed a State organ or a group of State organs, sufficiently independent of political powers – the legislative and the executive – in order to protect a superior and relatively permanent rule of law, against the inherent temptations of power.'[18]

As independent bodies, the courts are the most likely to objectively evaluate the rules of the Constitution against those promulgated by the legislative, executive and even the judicial branches. Moreover, the courts are considered to be the politically less dangerous or the weakest of the three state powers and therefore the least likely to dominate the other two branches as a consequence of their role.

# 9

## THE CONSTITUTION AND ITS SUPREMACY

As indicated, the fundamental rule in the *état de droit* is the primacy of the rule of law in the sense that all state organs are subject to the rule of law. This fundamental rule of the *état de droit* has manifested itself in two distinct ways: first, in the primacy of the Constitution over all state acts, particularly those whose authority stems directly from the Constitution; and secondly, in the primacy of laws enacted by Parliament so that all other state acts are regulated by and must submit to their dictates.

When it is said, however, that the first consequence of the constitutionalization process in the *état de droit* is the primacy of the Constitution, this does not mean that the only constitutional norms that have primacy are the sole formal written articles of the Constitution. The concept of the Constitution contains all values that are considered to be fundamental to a particular legal society, as well as those values which can be inferred from these norms.[1] The role of the judiciary in this respect has been and is essential.

### (a) The Constitution as a higher and effective law

The whole possibility of judicial review of constitutionality is seen not only as the ultimate result of the consolidation of the *état de droit*, but as an integral part of the concept of the Constitution as a higher and fundamental positive law. That is to say, the Constitution conceived 'not as a mere guideline of a political, moral, or philosophical nature, but as a real law, itself a positive and binding law, although of a superior, more permanent nature than ordinary positive legislation'.[2]

One of the fundamental trends in modern constitutionalism, therefore, is the concept of the Constitution as a normative reality and not as an occasional political compromise of political groups, changeable at any moment when the equilibrium between them modifies itself. In this sense, Constitutions become effective juridical norms which overrule the whole political process, the social and economic life of the country, and which give validity to the whole legal order.[3] In this sense if a Constitution is to be seen as a real and effective norm, it must contain rules applicable directly to state organs and to individuals.

In relation to the state, Constitutions today have the same fundamental character that they originally had in the United States and that were changed later in Europe during the course of the last century. The Constitution was originally a fundamental law limiting state organs, and declaring the fundamental rights of individuals, as a political consensus given by the people themselves and therefore directly applicable by the courts. The adoption of this concept in continental Europe, as a result of the French Revolution, was later modified by the monarchical principle that turned the concept of the Constitution into a formal and abstract code of the political system, given by the monarch and not to be applied by the courts. The Constitution, in this context, had no norm directly applicable to individuals who were only ruled by the formal laws, and although it contained an organic part, the absence of means of judicial review brought about the loss of its normative character.

Nevertheless, in the European continental legal systems the concept of the Constitution has changed and is again closer to its original conception as a higher law with norms applicable to state organs and to individuals, judged by the courts. In this later sense one can consider a statement from the United States Supreme Court in *Trop* v. *Dulles* (1958):

The provisions of the Constitution are not time-worn adages or hollow shibboleths. They are vital, living principles that authorise and limit governmental powers in our nation. They are rules of government. When the constitutionality of an Act of Congress is challenged in this Court, we must apply those rules. If we do not, the words of the Constitution become little more than good advice.[4]

In contemporary legal systems, therefore, Constitutions are not those simple pieces of 'good advice' or time-worn adages; their contents are of a normative character which rule both governments and individuals. This is true even in France, where in the traditional constitutional system after the 1875 Constitutional Laws, due to the exclusion of the declaration of rights from the text of the Constitution,[5] its provisions were considered not to be directly applicable to individuals. Yet after recent decisions of the Constitutional Council adopted in the seventies, the *bloc de la constitutionalité* [6] has been enlarged to include the Declaration of the Rights of Man and Citizens of 1789, the Preambles of the 1946 and 1958 Constitutions, and the fundamental principles recognized by the laws of the Republic.[7]

This normative character of the Constitution, relating to state organs and to individuals, and its enforcement by the courts, has also brought about a change in the 'programmatic norms' of the Constitution, norms which have been considered to be directly applicable only to the legislator.[8]

In effect, it is common to find in modern Constitutions, even in the context of social and economic rights, norms that are formulated as a political guideline for the legislator. This has led to the consideration that those constitutional norms were not directly applicable to individuals until the legislative itself had adopted formal laws in accordance with the programme established in the Constitution. Therefore, only the laws issued for its legal development were to be applied by the courts.

However, the normative character of the Constitution, as a fundamental trend of contemporary constitutionalism, tends to overcome this programmatic character attributed to certain constitutional norms and seeks its enforcement by the courts as norms directly applicable to individuals. Therefore those pragmatic norms or provisions of state aims, must also be enforceable by the courts as principles that must orientate the actions of the state.

In contemporary constitutional law and in relation to judicial review, however, this judicial control of the Constitution is essentially possible when a Constitution exists as a real norm enforceable by the courts, but moreover when it has supremacy over the whole legal order. This supremacy of the Constitution over the other rules of law, and particularly over Acts of Parliament, implies that the Constitution is the supreme norm which establishes the supreme values of a legal order. This position of supremacy can be taken as the parameter for the validity of the remaining legal rules of such a system.

### (b) The English background to the concept of constitutional supremacy and American constitutionalism

The concept of the Constitution as a higher law is one of the United States' great contributions to the universal history of law. This concept incorporates the tradition of natural law in the version of Locke and Coke,[9] as the 'law of laws', the 'immutable law', that is to say, *lex legum, lex aeterna* and *lex immutabile*. Yet it incorporates this concept in the concrete form of the pacts and charters of the colonies which formed the United States.

In the English legal system, prior to the seventeenth century, statute law was considered merely as exceptionally created norms in relation to the previously established common law.[10] In fact, Coke was of the opinion that the common law was superior to the authority of Parliament.[11] This reasoning culminated in *Bonham's* case (1610) in which he stated:

> it appears in our books, that in many cases, the common law will control acts of Parliament, and sometimes adjudge them to be utterly void: for when an act of Parliament is against common right and reason, or repugnant, or impossible to be performed, the common law will control it and adjudge such act to be void.[12]

Reference may also be made to the decision of *Day* v. *Savadge* (1614) where Chief Justice Hobart, even though without direct reference to *Bonham's* case, stated:

> Even an Act of Parliament, made against Natural Equity, as to make a Man Judge in his own cause, is void in itself; for *jura naturae sunt immutabilia* and they are *leges legum*.[13]

These norms which Coke referred to were something fundamental, something permanent, in short, a higher law, binding on Parliament and on ordinary courts. One of these fundamental laws, according to Coke, was the Magna Carta which he said was called 'Magna Carta, not for the length or largeness of it ... but ... in respect of the great weightiness and weighty greatness of the matter contained in it; in a few words, being the fountain of all the fundamental laws of the realm'.[14] The Magna Carta was therefore considered a fundamental law and it is in this sense that it must be considered as the remote antecedent of modern Constitutions.

With the 1688-9 Revolution, the principle of the supremacy of Parliament was firmly entrenched in English law. Yet even then, twelve years after the Revolution, Chief Justice Holt commented on *Dr Bonham's* Case in *City of London* v. *Wood* (1701) stating:

> And what my Lord Coke says in Dr. Bonham's case is far from any extravagancy, for it is a very reasonable and true saying, that if an Act of Parliament should ordain that the same person should be party and judge, or which is the same thing, judge in his own cause, it would be a void Act of Parliament; for it is impossible that one should be judge and party, for the judge is to determine between party and party.[15]

Nevertheless, Holt accepted the principle that the basic rule was that 'an Act of Parliament can do no wrong' although if it was against the principles of natural law, it would 'look pretty odd'.[16]

Paradoxically, the development of Parliamentary supremacy in England had a direct effect on the development of judicial review in the United States.[17]

Though the Glorious Revolution of 1688 marked the triumph of legislative supremacy in England, the American colonies had nonetheless inherited both Coke's ideas regarding the subordination of Crown and Parliament to higher law and a judiciary accustomed to interpreting and at times ignoring legislative acts violating higher principles ... Paradoxically the Glorious Revolution not only did not hinder, but rather it spurred the development of the new doctrine of judicial review.[18]

Thus, with regard to the subordination of the law maker to a higher law, the colonists in the United States linked up directly with the tradition of Coke. That is why in a few States after 1776, particularly in Pennsylvania and Vermont, the idea that state laws could not be repugnant to their basic laws was emphasized; and the courts of New Jersey started to put the idea of judicial review into practice in 1780.[19]

During the Constitutional Convention of 1787 the problem of judicial review was considered only incidentally, and the discussions on the matter were related more to the supremacy of the Constitution over legislation from the states. Thus the principle that the Constitution should be applied by judges notwithstanding any disposition to the contrary in the Constitutions or laws of the member states is expressly incorporated in the 1787 Constitution. It is known as the supremacy clause.[20]

The supremacy clause, the constitutional limitations imposed on Congress by the Constitution and the authority given to the Supreme Court to 'extend to all causes, in Law and Equity, arising under this Constitution' together with the higher law background of the constitutional system led to the formal adoption of the doctrine of constitutional supremacy and consequently to the existence of judicial review.

The supremacy of the Constitution, considered as a higher and fundamental law, was first developed in 1788 by Alexander Hamilton in *The Federalist* when, referring to the role of the courts as interpreters of the law, he stated:

A Constitution is, in fact, and must be regarded by the judges, as a fundamental law. It, therefore, belongs to them to ascertain its meaning, as well as the meaning of any particular act proceeding from the legislative body. If there should happen to be an irreconcilable variance between the two, that which has the superior obligation and validity ought, of course, to be preferred; or, in other words, the Constitution ought to be preferred to the Statute, the intention of the people to the intention of their agents.

In response to the assertion that 'the rights of the courts to pronounce legislative acts void, because contrary to the Constitution' would 'imply a superiority of the judiciary to the legislative powers', he replied:

Nor does this conclusion – that the Courts must prefer the Constitution over statutes - by any means suppose a superiority of the judicial to the legislative body. It only supposes that the power of the people is superior to both; and that where the will of the legislature, declared in its statutes stands in opposition to that of the people declared in the Constitution, the judges ought to be governed by the latter rather than the former. They ought to regulate their decisions by the fundamental laws, rather than by those which are not fundamental.

Then he concluded that:

No legislative act, therefore, contrary to the Constitution, can be valid. To deny this, would be to affirm, that the deputy is greater than his principal; that the servant is above his master; that the representatives of the people are superior to the people themselves; that men acting by virtue of powers, may do not only what their powers do not authorize, but what they forbid.

Thus Hamilton not only developed the doctrine of the supremacy of the Constitution, but equally important the doctrine of 'the judges as guardians of the Constitution'. He wrote:

limitations of this kind can be preserved in practice no other way than through the medium of courts of justice, whose duty it must be, to declare all acts contrary to the manifest tenor of the Constitution, void. Without this, all the reservations of particular rights or privileges would amount to nothing.[21]

The possibility of invalidating statutes 'repugnant to the Constitution, Treaties or Laws of the United States' by the courts, was contemplated by the First Congress, in the first *Judiciary Act* of 1789, and led the Federal Circuit Court in *Vanhorne's Lessee* v. *Dorrance* (1795) and in *Cooper* v. *Telfair* (1800) to declare state laws void on the grounds that they were repugnant to the state and the federal Constitutions.[22] In *Vanhorne's Lessee* v. *Dorrance* Justice William Paterson compared the system of England and the United States in his charge to the jury by stating:

Some of the judges in England, have had the boldness to assert, that an act of Parliament made against natural equity, is void; but this opinion contravenes the general position that the validity of an act of Parliament cannot be drawn into question by the judicial department; it cannot be disputed, and must be obeyed. The power of Parliament is absolute and transcendant; it is omnipotent in the scale of political existence. Besides, in England there is no written Constitution, no fundamental law, nothing visible, nothing real, nothing certain, by which a Statute can be tested. In America, the case is widely different: every state in the Union has its Constitution reduced to written exactitude and precision.

And he asked:

What is a constitution? It is the form of government, delineated by the mighty hand of the people, in which certain first principles of fundamental laws are established. The Constitution is certain and fixed; it contains the permanent will of the people, and is the supreme law of the land; it is paramount to the power of the legislation, and can be revoked or altered only by the authority that made it.

Along the same line of thought, he established the relationship of the legislatures to the Constitution by reasoning:

What are legislatures? Creatures of the Constitution; they owe their existence to the Constitution; they derive their powers from the Constitution; it is their commission; and, therefore, all their acts must be conformable to it, or else they will be void. The Constitution is the work or will of the people themselves, in their original, sovereign, and unlimited capacity. Law is the work or will of the legislature in their derivative and subordinate capacity. The one is the work of the Creator, and the other of the creature. The Constitution fixes limits to the exercise of legislative authority and prescribes the orbit within which it must move.

Justice Paterson concluded his statement by saying to the jury:

In short, gentlemen, the Constitution is the sum of the political system, around which all legislature, executive and judicial bodies must revolve. Whatever may be the case in other countries, yet in this, there can be no doubt, that every act of the legislature, repugnant to the Constitution, is absolutely void...[23]

However, the intentions of the framers of the Constitution and two trial court decisions were not sufficient to firmly establish judicial constitutional review in the United States. Thus it was not until the decision of *Marbury* v. *Madison* (1803)[24] that the principles of Constitutional supremacy and judicial review were clearly established. In that decision, Chief Justice Marshall was to determine whether the Supreme Court could exercise the authority given to it by the Judiciary Act 1789, in accordance with the Constitution, to issue writs of *mandamus* to public officers. In concluding that it 'appears not to be warranted by the Constitution', he decided to 'inquire whether a jurisdiction so conferred can be exercised'. To this end he developed the doctrine of the supremacy of the Constitution based on the question 'whether an act repugnant to the Constitution can or can not become the law of the land'.

To answer this question, he first established the principle of the supremacy of the Constitution. He started his reasoning by accepting the idea of an 'original right' of the people to establish the principles regulating 'their future government', as 'the basis on which the whole American fabric had been erected'. This original right to adopt those 'fundamental' and 'permanent' principles, he considered, was a very great exertion, so was not to be 'frequently repeated'.

This 'original and supreme will', he said, 'organises the government ... assigns to different departments their respective powers ... [and] establishes certain limits not to be transcended by those departments'. He considered that the government of the United States was of that kind, in which 'the powers of the legislature are defined and limited', and it was precisely for the purpose 'that those limits may not be mistaken, or forgotten', that a written Constitution containing those fundamental and permanent principles was adopted. He then asked:

To what purpose are powers limited, and to what purpose is that limitation committed to writing, if these limits may, at any time, be passed by those intended to be restrained? The distinction between a government with limited and unlimited powers is abolished if those limits do not confine the person on whom they are imposed, and if acts prohibited and acts allowed are of equal obligation.

The only alternative conclusions were that 'the Constitution controls any legislative act repugnant to it'; or, that the legislative may alter the Constitution by an ordinary act. In relation to these alternatives he stated:

Between these alternatives there is no middle ground. The Constitution is either a superior paramount law, unchangeable by ordinary means, or it is on a level with ordinary legislative acts, and, like other acts, is alterable when the legislature shall please to alter it.

If the former part of the alternative be true, then a legislative act contrary to the Constitution is not law; if the latter part be true then written Constitutions are absurd attempts on the part of the people to limit a power in its own nature illimitable.

Marshall's conclusion was that the Constitution was the 'fundamental and paramount law of the nation', a principle that he considered 'as one of the fundamental principles of our society'. The necessary consequence of this was that 'an act of the legislature repugnant to the Constitution, is void'. He consequently reasoned that it is 'the very essence of judicial duty' to determine the rules that govern the case when a law is in opposition to the Constitution. In such cases, he concluded, 'the Constitution is superior to any ordinary act of the legislature, the Constitution and not such ordinary acts, must govern the case to which they both apply'. The contrary would mean to give 'to the legislature a practical and real omnipotence ... would be the same as prescribing limits and declaring that those limits may be passed at pleasure'. This would 'subvert the very foundation of all written constitutions'.

As a result of this decision, and through logical reasoning, the principle of the supremacy of the Constitution and of judicial review of legislation became entrenched in the legal system of the United States. Many other Constitutions establish the same principle in express declarations within the Constitution itself. Such was the case in the 1920 Czechoslovakian Constitution which stated in Article 1, 1:

All the laws contrary to the Constitutional Charter, to its parts and also to the Laws that modify or complement it, are invalid.

This sort of express declaration was considered by Hans Kelsen as one of the 'objective guarantees' of the Constitution[25] and can be considered a common trend in contemporary constitutionalism, particularly, in the Constitutions of Latin America[26] and Africa.[27] In the latter, as B.O. Nwabuese said, 'when a court declares a statute invalid for unconstitutionality it is merely acting as a mouthpiece, an instrumentality, of the Constitution'.[28]

Whether implied or express, constitutional supremacy did not occur in Europe until the twentieth century. This reception in Europe took place only after the First World War,[29] mainly through the constitutional system designed by Hans Kelsen for his own country, Austria, and in Czechoslovakia. Years later, after the Second World War, the Austrian system of constitutional supremacy and judicial review was adopted in Germany and Italy and later, through their influence, in other European constitutional systems.

### (c) Supremacy and rigidity of the Constitution

The supremacy of a Constitution is closely related to its rigid character, which means that the norms of the Constitution are immune to the powers of the ordinary legislator. This characteristic of the Constitution is the general trend in constitutional law all over the world, with the exception of systems like those of the United Kingdom, New Zealand and Israel, which have unwritten and therefore flexible Constitutions.[30]

In principle, judicial review is essentially related to rigid Constitutions,[31] although not all countries with rigid Constitutions have a system of judicial review and although some systems with flexible Constitutions have certain kinds of judicial review. Nevertheless, the judicial control of the constitutionality of legislation finds its complete sense and meaning in constitutional systems with written and rigid Constitutions in which amendments and reforms can only take place through special procedures and not through ordinary legislative processes.

In rigid constitutional systems the principle of *lex superior derogat legi inferiori* is the one to be applied when judging the constitutionality of laws; whereas in flexible constitutional systems, in which the Constitution does not have the character of supreme law, the conflict between legal norms is not that expressed by Chief Justice Marshall in *Marbury* v. *Madison*, but between norms of equal rank. Therefore, in such cases, the traditional principles of interpretation: *lex posterior derogat legi priori* and *lex specialis derogat legi generali* [32] are normally applicable.

Although flexible Constitutions can be reformed or amended by ordinary legislation, some distinction can nevertheless be established between constitutional norms and ordinary legislative norms. This distinction exists in the content of the respective norms.[33] Thus, although legislation under flexible Constitutions cannot result in judicial review in the formal sense, it is possible that legislation itself can result in its own system of judicial review regarding the content of such norms.[34] Also, legislation can establish its own formal barriers to subsequent legislation which may attempt to amend it. Thus some basic legislative values may be 'constitutionalized'. In this respect, note must be made to the flexible Constitution of the State of Israel.

In the 1948 *Declaration of the Establishment of the State of Israel* adopted on the eve of the termination of the British Mandate for Palestine, some fundamental principles were proclaimed by the People's Council, among which it was stated that a Constitution was 'to be drawn up by the Constituent Assembly not later than the 1st of October, 1945'.[35] The Constitution was never drafted and instead the Knesset passed the *Harari Resolution*, in which 'the Constitutional Legislative and Judicial Committee' was charged 'with the duty to prepare a draft Constitution for the State', following these guidelines:

The Constitution shall be composed of individual chapters in such a manner that each of them shall constitute a basic law in itself. The chapters shall be brought before the Knesset to the extent to which the Committee will terminate its work and all chapters together will form the State Constitution.[36]

It has been considered that with this resolution, the constituent powers inherent in the First Knesset have passed on to all successive Knessets. Thus with its continuing constituent authority, the Knesset has approved various basic laws related to the Knesset itself, to Israeli lands, to the president of the state, to the government, to the state economy, to the army, and to Jerusalem capital of Israel.[37] Some of these basic laws have been passed in such a way that their repeal or amendment can only be adopted by 'a majority of the members of the Knesset'. Among these basic laws is the Basic Law: The Knesset passed in 1958, in which the Knesset limited its own parliamentary supremacy.

In 1969 the problem of the reviewability of ordinary legislation which is inconsistent with the basic laws was placed before the Supreme Court in *Bergman* v. *Minister of Finance*.[38] The facts were the following: the Knesset passed a law providing for the financing of the political parties' election costs out of public funds. The funds were to be distributed in proportion to the party's representation in the outgoing Knesset and not in strictly equal terms. Dr Bergman, a Tel-Aviv lawyer, challenged this statute as being inconsistent with the Basic Law: The Knesset, which provided, not for proportional participation in the election but, 'for general, national ... equal ... elections'. He argued that the law could not be an amendment of the Basic Law because it was passed by less than the required absolute majority of the total membership of the Knesset. Although the Supreme Court did not expressly decide upon the constitutional questions, by stating that it was 'far from purporting to affect whosoever the sovereignty of the Knesset as the legislative authority', in fact it opened the way to judicial review of legislation inconsistent with the basic laws.[39] The decision offered the Knesset two possible courses of action: it could either re-enact the *Financing Law*, tainted with inequality as it was, by the absolute majority needed under the Basic Law: the Knesset; or it could rectify the legislative scheme of financing so as to remove therefore the unacceptable element of inequality.

Reacting to the *Bergman* case, the Knesset took two steps to rectify its mistakes: first, it adopted an amendment to the *Financing Law* which cured its original defect of inequality; second, the Knesset passed, by an absolute majority, the *Elections Law*, 1969, which provided that: 'For the purpose of removing doubt it is hereby laid down that the provisions contained in the *Knesset Election Law* are from the date of their coming into effect valid for every legal proceeding and for every matter and purpose.'[40]

Of course the Supreme Court did not invalidate the challenge law, but did not hesitate to investigate its validity by looking at the legislative journals to see if the *Financial Law* had or had not been passed by an absolute majority. Furthermore, by not declaring the defective *Financing Law* unconstitutional but by ordering the Minister of Finance not to give effect to it, the court recognised both the sovereignty of the Knesset as well as the constituent power of the Knesset to bind itself and its successors through an entrenched clause of its Basic Law. Finally, although it attempted to not establish a precedent, in fact it revolutionized the Israeli legal system 'by introducing *de facto* judicial supervision of the constitutionality of primary legislation'.[41]

Therefore, while Israel does not have a written, rigid Constitution, a differentiation between higher law (Basic Laws) and ordinary law (regular Knesset legislation) can be distinguished and a system of judicial review can be established. Notwithstanding this exception, judicial review of legislation is normally found in legal systems with written and rigid Constitutions.

### (d) Supremacy and the unwritten constitutional principles

There is a question as to whether judicial control of the constitutionality of legislation must only be exercised in relation to norms contained in written articles of a Constitution, or whether it can be exercised in relation to non-written norms as a result of deduction from the Constitution and its spirit.[42] The problem has been widely discussed in the United States, particularly over the protection of fundamental rights, and has produced two antagonistic alternatives concerning the role of judges in judicial review: the interpretative and the non-interpretative role.[43]

According to the interpretative model, constitutional judges are limited to the application of the concrete norms established in the written Constitution itself or clearly implicit therein. This was the model originally followed by Hamilton and Chief Justice Marshall and in accordance with which legislation can only be invalidated by a deduction from a fundamental premise clearly found in the Constitution.

At the other extreme, the non-interpretative model wants judges to go beyond the literal references of the Constitution and to execute the norms that are not to be found within the boundaries of that written document, but which form the permanent and fundamental values of a given society and its political system. The purest form of the non-interpretative model, recognises that the general principles of republican government and natural justice of human rights establish limitations on legislative authority. The actual words of the written text of the Constitution or even its existence are not vital to the existence of constitutional limitations.[44] This non-interpretative model was followed by the Warren Court in its decisions concerning issues of discrimination and the protection of minorities.[45]

The question regarding the choice between the interpretative model and the non-interpretative model, has been and will continue to be one of the most important issues of the role of constitutional justice and of judicial review of legislation. The adoption of one model or the other depends on the content of the Constitution, the way the articles of the constitutional text were written, and the time period in which they were written. The fact is that when a Constitution is two centuries old, like that of the United States, it is impossible to know the known intentions of the framers who lived in a patriarchal society which vanished long ago, particularly in relation to the open-ended or open clauses of the Constitution.[46] Yet it is the role of the courts to determine the content of these clauses.

Of course, the situation is different in constitutional systems with modern and detailed constitutional codes. Here the non-interpretative model is difficult to develop, depending of course on the juridical tradition of the particular country. For instance, the Swiss Federal Tribunal has largely developed the non-interpretative model for the protection of fundamental rights. Important fundamental rights like personal liberty, freedom of opinion, the right to a previous hearing are not in the text of the Federal Constitution, but are recognized by the Federal Tribunal as non-written constitutional rights. In this respect, it has been said that the Tribunal does not interpret the Constitution but rather perfects it. This is because the members of the Tribunal consider that it is their duty as constitutional judges to do so. They justify this attitude by considering that the court's function is to guarantee the foundations of the democratic society and to ensure that the federal states are submitted to the law.[47]

The Austrian Constitutional Court, however, follows the interpretative method and considers itself bound to the constitutional text even though it has to be interpreted. Nevertheless, this interpretation is considered as being of great importance in Austria because the important constitutional norms relating to fundamental rights were written in the last century and have a formalistic and lapidarian style. Yet even in these cases, the positivist orientation of the Constitutional Court is determinant and shows itself in a careful application of interpretative methods. Thus, when the Constitutional Courts consider that the absence of a constitutional norm in a particular context is wrong, its role is to ask the constitutional legislator to fill the gap, considering itself incompetent to do so.[48]

In the sphere of the protection of fundamental rights, the role of the French Constitutional Council during the last decade, as an example of the non-interpretative model, must be stressed. It is considered that the constitutional judges in France have reached the purest form of the non-interpretative judicial control model when they control the conformity of executive legislation to general principles or undefined and non-written republican traditions, which the judges found and defined as having a superior law rank.[49]

In 1958, when the Constitution was drafted, the Consultative Constitutional Committee considered the Preamble to the Constitution to be excluded from the substance of the Constitution, and therefore beyond the reach of the Constitutional Council. The Preamble reads: 'The French people, solemnly proclaim their subjection to the rights of Man and to the national sovereignty principles as have been defined by the Declaration of 1789, confirmed and completed by the Preamble to the Constitution of 1946.'

This Preamble to the Constitution was considered by the Constitutional Council, up to the 1970s, as only a principle for the orientation of constitutional interpretation.[50] Yet in 1971, when a proposed law established a procedure for preliminary judicial controls for the acquisition of legal capacity by associations, the Council concluded that this law was contrary to the Constitution.[51] Their reasoning was as follows: The 1958 Constitution, through the Preamble of the 1946 Constitution, referred to the 'fundamental principles recognized by the laws of the Republic'. Among these principles, liberty of association must be listed. In accordance with this principle, associations were to be constituted freely and could publicly develop their activities; their validity was not to be submitted to a previous intervention by either administrative or judicial authorities. Thus, the Constitutional Council decided that the limits imposed on associations by the proposed bill established a prior judicial control and were unconstitutional.[52] The significance of this decision has been summarized as follows:

It made an unambiguous breach with the constitutional tradition of the supremacy of *loi*. It declared beyond any question that even within the area set aside for legislation by article 34 of the Constitution there were fundamental principles which Parliament could not alter or contravene. And above all, it declared that those fundamental principles were to be found not only in the Constitution proper but also in its Preamble and via that Preamble, in the Preamble of 1946 [and presumably also in the Declaration of 1789].[53]

In this instance, at least, the Constitutional Council relied upon a written statement in a statute. Yet in other cases,[54] as has happened with the right to self defence, the Constitutional Council has deduced a result based on 'the fundamental principles recognized by the laws of the

Republic'. Before 1981,[55] the right to one's own defence was considered by the *Conseil d'etat* simply as a general principle of law.[56] After the January 1981 decision, the Constitutional Council recognized it as part of the 'principles and rules of Constitutional value'. This was an expression used by the Constitutional Council, 'to designate in a generic manner all the norms that, without being contained in the text of the Constitution itself, have constitutional rank'.[57]

Therefore, in France since the 1970s, the notion of constitutional norms that could serve as reference norms to control the constitutionality of legislation is progressively understood in a wider sense. Particularly, it now comprises dispositions or principles outside the constitutional text including the Declaration of 1789, the Preambles to the 1946 and 1958 Constitutions, the fundamental principles recognized by the laws of the Republic, and the general principles of constitutional value.[58] All these sources of the principle of constitutionality enjoy the same supremacy as the written articles of the Constitution.

## (e) The adaptation of the Constitution and its interpretation

The normal and customary type of judicial control of constitutionality that has been developed in constitutional systems where the principle of the supremacy of the Constitution has been established, is based on the existence of written rules in the Constitution. In this instance, the basic problem regarding judicial review of constitutionality on the interpretative model is with regard to the degree of clarity of the particular constitutional text.

The situation varies depending to the modernity or antiquity of the Constitution, on whether there are numerous or few provisions and whether the articles are precise or vague. In modern Constitutions, fundamental rights are written down in a synthetic, vague and elusive way, and their norms are generally expressed in ambiguous terms, full of worthy characteristics like liberty, democracy, justice, dignity, equality, social function, and public interests.[59] These vagaries require an active role by judges, when interpreting the 'precious ambiguities'[60] in which Constitutions are written down.

In the continental European legal systems, these vague phrases are called the 'undetermined legal concept' or 'imprecise juridical notions'.[61] Since they always express certain concepts or values related to the general foundations of the given society and its political system, it is in relation to these that the constitutional judge must play his creative role determining the exact meaning of the concept. The constitutional judge must fill in these concepts, pinpoint and determine their boundaries through an interpretative process, bearing in mind the superior values followed by the Constitution and generally established in the preamble or in its first articles.

The position of the judge facing the Constitution, therefore, is not fundamentally different from the position he normally has in other types of laws which must be interpreted. If it is true that the judges must not substitute for the legislator in deducing concepts which could be against what is written in the law, neither must they interpret the Constitution in a way so as to arrive at concepts that could be contrary to the constitutional text and its fundamental values.[62] The constitutional judge, however, always has an additional duty compared to the ordinary judge: he must defend the Constitution and the values that are at its foundation. That is why the constitutional judge in his interpretative process must adapt the Constitution to the current values of society, and of the political system, in order precisely, 'to keep the Constitution alive'.[63]

The role of the constitutional judge in this process of adaptation of the Constitution is crucial, as the United States Supreme Court has demonstrated. In this respect it suffices to recall the important decisions of the Supreme Court in the matter of discrimination in the educational system.

When referring to the Fourteenth Amendment, Chief Justice Warren said in *Brown* v. *Board of Education of Topeka* (1954) that:

In approaching this problem we cannot turn the clock back to 1868 when the Amendment was adopted, or even to 1896 when *Plessy* v. *Ferguson* was written. We must consider public education in the light of its full development and its present place in American life throughout the Nation. Only in this way can it be determined if segregation in public schools deprives these plaintiffs of the equal protection of the laws.

This assertion led Chief Justice Warren to conclude,

that in the field of public education the doctrine of 'separate but equal' has no place. Separate educational facilities are inherently unequal. Therefore, we hold that the plaintiffs, and others similarly situated from whom the actions have been brought are by reason of the segregation complained of, deprived of the equal protection of the laws guaranteed by the Fourteenth Amendment.[64]

In the same sense, this adaptation of the Constitution has recently been demonstrated in France by the Constitutional Council's decision in the *Nationalization* case (1982). In this case an article concerning the right of property in the Declaration of the Rights of Man and Citizen of 1789 was applied so as to give present day constitutional validity to the right of property itself. Previous to this decision[65] it was thought that the article was obsolete and that it could not be given any interpretation other than that which applied in 1789.[66] The Constitutional Council stated:

Taking into account that if it is true that after 1789 and up to the present, the aims and conditions of the exercise of the right to property have undergone an evolution characterized both, by a notable extension of its application to new individual fields and by limits imposed by general interests, the principles themselves expressed in the Declaration of Rights of Man have complete constitutional value, particularly regarding the fundamental character of the right to property, the conservation of which constitutes one of the aims of political society, and located on the same rank as liberty, security and resistance to oppression, and also regarding the guarantees given to the holders of that right and the prerogatives of public power.[67]

Thus by giving the 1789 Declaration a constitutional rank and value, the Constitutional Council adapted the sacred right to property established two hundred years ago, to the limitable right of our times.

# 10

## THE JUDICIAL GUARANTEE OF THE CONSTITUTION

In systems with written Constitutions, one of the basic elements of the state submitted to law is the principle of the supremacy of the Constitution over all other norms in the legal order and over all state acts. This supremacy implies not only submission to the procedural and organic rules established in the Constitution, but also the respect of the fundamental rights of individuals contained therein.

The Constitution is therefore seen as an organic and procedural as well as a substantive rule. A statute could be unconstitutional, therefore, not only because of procedural irregularities, but also when its contents are contrary to the principles established in the Constitution regarding the rights of individuals.[1] Thus constitutional supremacy would mean nothing if there were no particular means of protection of the Constitution.

### (a) Judicial review and the end of parliamentary absolutism

Two types of guarantees of the supremacy of the Constitution can be distinguished: the political and the judicial. In general, the political guarantee of the Constitution is exercised by the supreme representative political organ of the state, and is commonly adopted in legal systems where an extreme interpretation of the principle of the separation of powers or of the unity of state powers prevails. The political guarantee of the Constitution was the method adopted in France prior to the establishment of the Constitutional Council under the 1958 Constitution and it is the solution in almost all socialist countries where the supreme representative political organ is the only one which can control the constitutionality of legislation. Obviously, this system identifies the controlled organs with the organs of control,[2] and has been criticized in the socialist world as being an inconvenient system for the protection of the Constitution, or at least a system with an 'insufficient suitability'.[3]

The argument in favour of this kind of means for the protection of the Constitution is based on the principle of the unity of state power and on the rejection of the principle of separation of powers as a result of the supreme power of the representative political organ of the state. The logical consequence of this supremacy is that it excludes the possibility of giving power to control the constitutionality of laws to any other organ, and to consider illegitimate any control that could be exercised by any other organ of the state different to the representative supreme one. Nevertheless, three of the socialist countries (Yugoslavia, Czechoslovakia and Poland), have established a system of judicial review, assigning the power of control of the constitutionality of legislation to a special Constitutional Court.[4]

Likewise, in systems with an extreme interpretation of the separation of powers, no system of judicial control of the constitutionality of legislation can be accepted. In Europe, the monarchical regime and the principle of representation developed through the elected legislator led to the adoption of the principle of the supremacy of Parliament over other state powers. The consequence of this was the primacy of laws or acts of Parliament over other legal rules.

During the last century it was inconceivable that there could be any deviation from the principle of the supremacy of the law as the expression of the general will. The enemy of the Constitution was really the executive – the monarch – who was tempted to put his individual will before that of the people as expressed in Parliament. Thus, the possibility that Parliament could be in error or act mistakenly was not conceivable. The judiciary power was simply seen as an executive instrument of the laws passed by the assembly, with no liberty to interpret the laws. In France this created the *référé législatif* according to which judges were obliged to consult the National Assembly when they had doubts about the interpretation of a statute.[5]

This limitation was based on the purest tradition of the thoughts of Montesquieu, who considered the national judges, 'as no more than the mouth that pronounces the words of the law, mere passive beings, incapable of moderating either its force or rigor';[6] and was expressly established in the Statute of 16–24 August 1790 which referred to the judiciary organization. Article 10 of this law regulated the separation between legislative and judicial power, by saying that 'the courts could not take part directly or indirectly in the exercise of legislative power, neither prevent nor suspend the execution of acts of the legislative body ...', adding in Article 12 that the courts 'could not make regulations, but they must always address themselves to the legislative body when they think it necessary to interpret a Statute or to make a new one'.[7] The *référé législatif* then was the instrument of the legislative body for interpreting the laws.

The judges, in accordance with this principle must apply laws and of course, interpret them, but they are not to control them because acts of the legislative body are the expression of the sovereign will of the people.

In this traditional framework of the separation of powers, a system of judicial review of the constitutionality of laws was considered a violation of the principle of parliamentary sovereignty, based on the pre-eminence of the legislative power over other state powers. Parliament was constituted by the representatives of the people who, as such, in the representative democratic state represented the sovereign. Any intervention by a constitutional body to limit the autonomy of the supreme representative organ of the state was considered inadmissible, and therefore, legislation could only be controlled by that supreme representative organ.

It is clear that this principle of popular sovereignty expressed in modern Constitutions is a political principle which refers to the constituent power of the state represented in all the constituted bodies of the state. Since all the bodies of the state are the product of the sovereign and are its representatives, there can be no discussion about the relative sovereignty of the various constituted state bodies. Thus, it makes no sense to rely upon a concept of the sovereignty of Parliament and thereby to reject a mechanism which guarantees the preservation and enforcement of the Constitution.

To reinforce the argument in another way, it should not be forgotten that in presidential and parliamentary democratic systems, the president of a republic or the head of a government are designated by popular election and are as much a product of the sovereignty of the people as Parliament. From the moment the Constitution attributes sovereignty to the people, it is clear that this quality cannot be exercised in one body of the state to the exclusion of others. Therefore all the powers of state and all the bodies which carry them out, find their legitimacy in the people. Thus, no constitutional body is or can be really sovereign[8] and all of them must be submitted to the Constitution.

A review of these constitutional concepts appeared in Europe after the crisis brought about by the First World War and by the tragedies which political irrationality caused throughout Europe. This led both to the transformation of the Constitution into a normative code which could be directly applicable and enforceable, and to the establishment of a constitutional body for constitutional adjudication which would ensure the supremacy of the Constitution over the executive and legislative powers of the state. Consequently, the sovereignty of Parliament ceased and judicial review of constitutionality was to become the instrument governing the subjection of Parliament to the Constitution.[9] 'It was realized that there was too much illusion in the Liberal democratic theory' in the sense that the reality had moved far from the myth of the supremacy of the peoples' will so that 'Parliaments and their legislation, too, ... [became] ... instruments of despotic regimes; and that majorities ... themselves [became] brutally oppressive'.[10]

In this way an awareness grew that it was necessary to protect liberties not only from the executive, but also from the legislative branch of government. As has been remarked,

the old idea that marked the liberal 19th century, that of the protection of liberty *by the law*, tended to be substituted by the experimental idea of the need of protection of liberties *against the law*. This evolution made the extraordinary phenomenon of the acceptance of a superior authority to the Legislator itself, of an authority in charge to impose upon the Legislator the respect of the Constitution possible.[11]

Thus, European continental countries adopted the review of the constitutionality of laws following a different path from that of the system in the United States. The European phenomenon occurred less in response to a problem of legal logic than to political logic. It was the fear of oppression by a parliamentary majority, which was decisive in the change in the position of the continental European countries regarding their review of the constitutionality of laws.[12]

This political logic of judicial review can be found in the fact that the myth of representativeness of the general will as expressed by those elected, has broken down in many countries, particularly because the legislative body is frequently made up of men chosen by the political parties, and who represent these parties rather than the general will. This lesson was firmly established by the Second World War so that, subsequent to it, the European continental countries discovered the true fundamental nature of the Constitution as a higher and supreme law, applicable to all state organs and enforceable by the courts.[13] What had changed was 'the serious attempt to conceive the Constitution not as a mere guideline of a political, moral, or philosophical nature, but as a real law, *itself a positive and binding law* although of a superior, more permanent nature than ordinary positive legislation'.[14] Therefore, the supremacy of the Constitution over Parliament marked the end of parliamentary absolutism,[15] transformed the old concept of parliamentary sovereignty and led the way to constitutional review in France through the Constitutional Council.

Another factor which contributed to the appearance of mechanisms for judicial review of the constitutionality of laws was the transformation of the notion of the law. In the nineteenth century, statutes were seen as the expression of the general will. With the evolution of parliamentary systems, they came to be seen as acts adopted by both the parliamentary majority and the government through the political parties. In this form, the statutes were not necessarily the expression of the general will, approved by a solid and mythical majority, but they were 'no more than the expression of the governmental will approved by a solidarian majority'.[16] Moreover, with the evolution of the tasks of the state, the law tended to become a more technical product whose content was frequently withdrawn from the effective control of Parliament into the hands of the technocrats within the administration.

## (b) Judicial review and its legitimacy

Once the judicial power, considered the least dangerous of all state powers,[17] has been given power to defend the Constitution and to control the constitutionality of legislation, the issue arises as to the legitimacy of power given to state organs that are not responsible to the people, to control the acts of those who are politically responsible.[18]

This discussion has been developed either to justify the absence of judicial review, in systems in which the sovereignty of Parliament prevails, or to criticize judicial review, when judges have been active in the adaptation of the Constitution and in creating non-written constitutional rules or in attributing constitutional character to certain rules. In this context, judicial review has been considered illegitimate because it is believed that non-elected bodies must not control elected bodies of the state, and that non-elected state bodies must not determine which norm of the state is law, that is to say, which is constitutional or unconstitutional.

This problem is not resolvable, particularly because it is orientated as if there were a problem of abstract legitimacy of judicial review that could be resolved in an abstract way, identifying democracy with sole representativeness. The problems of judicial review, or of the powers assigned to judges to control the constitutionality of legislation, cannot be explained or criticized on the grounds of legitimacy or illegitimacy considering the democratic principle as sole representativeness. Democracy does not exhaust itself in representativeness, because it is a way of living in which individual liberty and fundamental human rights are to be respected to a point where we can say that no effective judicial review of constitutionality is possible in undemocratic regimes.[19]

Therefore in a representative and democratic regime, the power attributed to judges to control the deviations of the legislative body and the infringements by the representative body of fundamental rights is absolutely democratic and legitimate.[20] In fact, rather than being less than a pure democratic state, it is more. As Jean Rivero stated: 'I think that the [judicial constitutional] control marks progress, in the sense that democracy is not only a way of attribution of power, but also a way of exercising it. And I think that all that reinforces the fundamental liberties of citizens goes along with the democratic sense.'[21] Along this same line of thought, it has been noted that if the Constitution establishes fundamental norms,

it is obvious that an occasional parliamentary majority who ignore or infringe them, is very far from being legitimate to do so based on the majoritarian argument, and is rather revealing its abuse of power and its possible attempts at exclusion of minorities. The protective function of the Constitutional Tribunal confronting that abuse, annulling the legislative acts which make an attempt on the liberty of a few or all citizens, is the only effective instrument against infringement; there is no other possible alternative if one prefers to have an effective guarantee of liberty, that could make it more than simply rhetoric in a constitutional document.[22]

This was also the main argument put forward by Hans Kelsen when arguing against the majoritarian argument. He said

If one sees the essence of democracy, not in the all powerful majority, but in the constant compromises between the groups represented in Parliament by the majority and the minority, and consequently in the social peace, constitutional justice appears as a means particularly proper for the achievement of this idea. The simple threat of an action to be brought before the Constitutional Court can be an adequate instrument in the hands of the minorities for preventing unconstitutional violations of juridically protected interests by the majority, and consequently being able to oppose the majority dictatorship, which is not less dangerous to social peace than the minority one.[23]

But democratic legitimacy of judicial review, however, does not arise only through judicial protection of fundamental rights, but also through the protection of the organic part of the Constitution which controls the systems of distribution of powers adopted in the Constitution. In this respect, we must point out that the problem of legitimacy has never been posed regarding the vertical distribution of state powers in the politically decentralized or federal systems; on the contrary judicial review is essentially and closely related with federalism.[24] Consequently, among the most important political principles which have led to the establishment of judicial review of legislation and upheld its justification in contemporary constitutional law is the federal form of the state.

It is thus not by chance that those countries with the federal form of state and with politically decentralized state organization were among the first to establish judicial review of the constitutionality of legislation. This happened in the United States of America and in all the federal states of Latin America in the last century. It also happened in the Federal Republic of Germany, in the decentralized forms of the Italian Regional State and in the Spanish Autonomous Communities State.

In all these cases, it is evident that the need for judicial review or the establishment of a Constitutional Court is justified by the demand for a constitutional body which could settle conflicts of powers between the national and regional bodies. One of the fundamental tasks of the Constitutional Courts in Austria, Germany, Italy and Spain, for example, is precisely the resolution of conflicts between the levels of the national state and the local states or regions. Similarly, conflicts may arise between the regions themselves, or between them and the national level. Thus it is political decentralization that has encouraged the appearance and consolidation of Constitutional Tribunals responsible for the function of constitutional review to guarantee the constitutional balance of the central state and the territorial bodies. Accordingly, in federal or in politically decentralized states, there are no doubts about the legitimacy of judicial review of constitutionality and no debate has arisen on the matter except to justify its existence and necessity.[25]

The same can not be said about the horizontal distribution or separation of powers. Although it also imposes limitations on the legislative power, judicial review with regard to this aspect of the Constitution has promoted discussions over its legitimacy. Concern has been primarily with the notion of supremacy of Parliament over the other state bodies. The principle argument in favour of judicial review in this area is that an independent mechanism to guarantee the organic part of the Constitution is required. This system of control is essential to the distribution of power particularly between the legislative and the executive power. Between them it is necessary to establish a third counter-weight system so as to maintain the equilibrium that the Constitution lays down.

However, the traditions of parliamentary supremacy, on the one hand, and of separation of powers on the other, have been so powerful in Europe that they have prevented ordinary judicial bodies from any possibility of judging the constitutionality of legislation even though judicial review of legislation has been developed but assigned to new constitutional organs. It has been this confrontation, between the need for constitutional judicial review as a guarantee or means of protection of the Constitution and the principle of separation of powers, which has led in continental Europe to the creation of special constitutional bodies with the particular and special jurisdictional task of controlling the constitutionality of legislation. Therefore the solution to this confrontation has been resolved by creating new constitutional bodies above the traditional horizontal separation of powers – equally above the legislator, the executive and the courts – to ensure the supremacy of the Constitution with respect to them all.

This Austrian or European model of judicial review [26] is characterized by the fact that constitutional justice has been attributed to a constitutional body organized outside the ordinary courts, and thus not integrated within the general structure of the judiciary. The members of the constitutional tribunal, court or council do not become so by way of a judicial career, but rather are appointed, usually by political bodies such as Parliament or the executive. This system has given rise to a special constitutional organ which, despite its not being integrated within the judiciary, resolves legal controversies according to the law and thus pursues a proper jurisdictional activity.

These constitutional bodies have been considered the 'supreme interpreters of the Constitution' as the Spanish *Constitutional Tribunal Organic Law* qualifies it,[27] or as the 'custodian of the Constitution'.[28] Professor Eduardo García de Enterría has referred to the Spanish Constitutional Tribunal as a 'commissioner of the constituent power to sustain the Constitution and to maintain all the constitutional organs in their strict quality of constituted powers',[29] and the former President of the same Spanish Constitutional Tribunal has considered it 'as a constitutional organ, established and structured directly in the Constitution', and that 'as regulator of the constitutionality, of the State action, it is the one called upon to give full existence to the *Estado de Derecho* and to ensure the validity of the distribution of powers established in the Constitution, both essential components in our times of the true Constitutional State'.[30]

In this sense, and established as constitutional organs separate from the traditional legislative, executive and judicial organs, the European Constitutional Courts are conceived of as being the supreme guarantor of the distribution of power in the various senses in which it has been referred to herein.[31] This is particularly so in the first place, as regards the distribution of the sphere of state power and the sphere of society; that is to say, between the powers of the state and the rights and liberties of individuals and groups. This principle of distribution of powers, expressly established in Constitutions when they guarantee the rights and liberties of citizens must, moreover, be jurisdictionally guaranteed. This power of guaranteeing fundamental rights is frequently a power given to ordinary tribunals as well as to Constitutional Courts, by means of writs of protection (*amparo*). In such cases the courts are the guardians of the limits on the power of the state imposed by the Constitution in relation to the respect for fundamental individual rights and liberties.

Moreover, this is true with regard, in the second place, to the distinction between the constituent power and the constituted power. The effectiveness of this division is not limited only to the moment when the Constitution is adopted, but should be demonstrated throughout its validity as a result of its very existence. The function of constitutional justice is precisely that of guaranteeing that the constituted powers act within limits established by the constituent power as set down in the Constitution. It is thus the aim of the Constitutional Court to be the custodian of the primacy of the constituent power over the constituted power. Thus, even in cases of preventive review of constitutionality, when a collision arises between a norm and the Constitution, either the norm is not to be sanctioned or a constitutional reform must take place.

Similarly, it is also true with regard to the horizontal division of powers, that is a distribution among constitutional bodies of the same constitutional rank. This division is also guaranteed by the Constitutional Courts, both at the level of the central powers of the state and at other territorial levels. In this respect, at the level of the constitutional bodies of the state it is the Constitutional Court which is called upon to resolve conflicts of powers between, for example, the government and Congress, or between the Chamber of Deputies and the Senate, or between other bodies of constitutional rank. In the horizontal distribution of power at lower territorial levels the Constitutional Tribunal must also resolve conflicts which arise between the authorities at those levels.

The fourth aspect of the division of power is the vertical division. This consists of the distribution of powers among the various political decentralized levels of the state: the powers of the national state; those at intermediate level, whether these be federal member states or autonomous regions or communities of the regional states; and thirdly, those at the municipal or local level. In these cases, the state structured by a system of vertical distribution of powers must ensure that the various legislative provisions at the different levels do not invade the sphere of power of other levels. For example, there should be no invasion of the powers of the communities or regions by the national level, or of those of the other member states of a federation, and *vice-versa*. The same holds good for the municipal level: the Constitutional Court is the body which must ensure that the municipal powers, which are normally guaranteed in Constitutions or by acts issued at national or intermediate levels, are not to be invaded.

Thus the fundamental reason for justifying the establishment of Constitutional Courts in continental Europe relates to the solution of conflicts between state bodies. It is the only body which is in a position to prevent the invasion of powers by other constitutional bodies and to objectively maintain the balance which the Constitution has established in the separation of powers. In this way, the sharing of power among the national organs of the state and the vertical system of the distribution of powers all demand that there be a body to maintain a balance. This should either be a Constitutional Court or the Supreme Court of a given country acting as a constitutional judicial organ. That is why, even though Constitutional Courts are independent and separate from the traditional legislative, executive and judicial organs of the state, and particularly, not within the organization of the judiciary, they always decide upon constitutional conflict by means of a jurisdictional action.

It must be stressed that, in order to refute the objection to constitutional justice based on the principle of separation of power, Hans Kelsen argued that the Constitutional Tribunal did not exercise jurisdictional activity but a negative legislative activity when annulling an Act of Parliament. He said that 'To annul a Statute is to establish a general norm, because the annulment of a Statute has the same general character of its adoption, being, we can say, the same adoption but with a negative sign, and consequently in itself, a legislative function.'[32] But in reality, the Constitutional Court, when annulling a statute, does not repeal it and any annulment it can pronounce is not based on discretionary powers but on legal criteria, applying a superior rule, the Constitution. Thus in no way does it exercise a legislative function.[33] Its function is jurisdictional as is that assigned to the ordinary court,[34] but characterized as being a guarantee of the Constitution. And, if it is true that constitutional judges in many cases decide political issues when considering the constitutionality of legislative acts, they do so by legal methods and criteria, in a process initiated by a party with the required standing. Even in cases in which constitutional justice allows the possibility of exercising a popular action[35] to obtain a decision upon the unconstitutionality of a law by the

Supreme Court, the judicial activity is developed by a process in which the Supreme Court decides a judicial controversy, even though there are no proper parties in the traditional procedural law sense.

Nevertheless, a court must only act on the formal instance of, or at the request of, a person whose rights or interests are infringed by the particular law, and cannot decide on its own initiative. Therefore, the role of a constitutional judge can in no way be considered a legislative function, but rather jurisdictional.

In any event, judicial review of constitutionality both on the American and European models, is conceived as being a constitutional guarantee of the distribution and limitation of state powers established in the Constitution, exercised by independent bodies. Furthermore, constitutional judges are also the guarantee of the functioning of the particular system of government resulting from the way state powers are distributed, and of democracy itself. Its legitimacy lies there.

In effect, judicial review can be considered as one of the tools for ensuring the solution of political and social conflict, and therefore, for contributing to the peaceful development of democratic political activity.[36] This has proven to be particularly useful in resolving political conflicts between government and minorities which the electorate cannot assist in resolving. As Professor L. Favoreu has pointed out,

when the majority and the opposition conflict on important issues without having recourse to an electoral decision, it is evident that recourse to a constitutional judge to decide upon the law adopted by the majority, has the virtue of calming the debate and transforming it more serenely. In many cases, when the decision of the constitutional judge has been adopted, the controversy is extinguished.[37]

As an illustration of this aspect of the legitimacy of judicial review, one can consider the political conflict which arose in Europe from the sanctioning of laws referring to abortion. The controversy raged in every country, in Parliament and in public, but once decisions were taken on the issue by the constitutional judge, the conflict died down.[38] The same happened in France over the most important aspects of the socialist government's programme executed in the early eighties, particularly in relation to nationalization and to decentralization processes.[39] The same happened, for example, in Spain, with regard to the Law for the Harmonization of the Autonomous Communities. Once the Constitutional Tribunal had resolved the conflict over the powers of the state and the Autonomous Communities, the debate declined in its intensity.[40]

Judicial review, however, has also been a guarantee of the Constitution when working as an instrument for the maintenance of political stability and continuity in democratic societies. This is particularly so in parliamentary systems of government. There is a certain 'institutional logic' in the political functioning of parliamentary systems of government, to encourage the development of mechanisms of judicial review of constitutionality as a reaction against the great power of the government block.[41] In this instance, judicial review lessens the power of a strong government and lessens the effects of political changes resulting from the alternation in power, particularly when a change in the majority in Parliament and in the government happens after a few years of leadership of one political force or party. In the specific instance of France:

The Constitutional Council has first of all, permitted the alternance through the canalization of the stream of change, ensuring its regulation; and furthermore with its decisions has given a regularised authentic certification to the measures taken by the new majority. In the end, the legislation of the new majority has passed through some kind of filter, but once the dispositions have been filtered and sifted, its promulgation gave a definitive juridical force to the dispositions, and it is no longer possible to attack them [at least on the grounds of its conformity with the Constitution].[42]

In such situations, the existence of constitutional review of legislation has had the effect of avoiding any rapid breakdown in the constitutional balance, since the laws and reforms approved by the new majority must be submitted for review by the constitutional judges in order to determine which could be enacted according to the Constitution, and which laws and reforms required constitutional review. In these cases constitutional review may mean a restraint on the possibilities for action open to the majority with respect to the proposed reforms. But on the other hand, if these reforms are brought into question before a constitutional judge, and his verdict declares them to be in accordance with the Constitution, the acts enjoy a supplementary authority.[43]

Finally, the essential part of the *état de droit* and one of the basic arguments used to defend the legitimacy of judicial review, is with regard to the guarantee of fundamental rights and liberties. In effect, constitutional justice and judicial review of the constitutionality of legislation are bound up with the effective establishment of fundamental rights. When there are entrenched declarations of fundamental rights and liberties linked with the constitutional values of a given society, judicial review must necessarily exist as an integral part of the protection of these values.

Although entrenched fundamental rights had historical antecedents in Europe, with the exception of Austria and Czechoslovakia in the 1920s, no effective means existed for enforcing them. This changed after the Second World War. It is not by chance that it happened first in Italy and Germany where, for the first time in their constitutional history, the validity of the rights of man and the need to organize mechanisms for their defence was affirmed. Among these defences was the review of constitutionality of legislation.

What must be concluded is that if written constitutional systems pretend to have a supreme, obligatory and enforceable law, they must establish means for the defence and guarantee of the Constitution. As Hans Kelsen said:

A Constitution without guarantees against unconstitutional acts, is not completely obligatory in its technical sense... A Constitution in which unconstitutional acts and particularly, unconstitutional laws, remains valid because its unconstitutionality cannot lead to its annulment, is more or less, equivalent from a juridical point of view, to a desire without obligatory force.[44]

The judicial guarantees of the Constitution, that is to say, the power given to ordinary judges or special Constitutional Courts to declare the unconstitutionality of state acts issued in violation of the Constitution, or to annul those acts with general effects, is therefore an essential part of the *état de droit*. Their duty is to ensure that all state organs are submitted to the rule of law and that they will respect the limits imposed upon them by the Constitution.[45]

# Part IV

# THE DIFFUSE SYSTEMS OF JUDICIAL REVIEW

# 11

## GENERAL CHARACTERISTICS
## OF THE DIFFUSE SYSTEM

The diffuse system of judicial review empowers all the judges and courts of a given country to act as constitutional judges. Thus, when a dispute which depends upon a particular law is before them, the courts are permitted to consider the validity of the law and to apply it or reject it depending upon whether they consider that law is constitutional or unconstitutional.

### (a) The logic of the system

From a logical and rational point of view, this general power of all judges and courts to act as constitutional judges is the obvious consequence of the principle of the supremacy of the Constitution. If the Constitution is the supreme law of the land, in cases of conflict between a law and the Constitution, the latter must prevail and it is the duty of the judiciary to determine the issues in each case. As Justice William Paterson stated in *Vanhorne's Lessee* v. *Dorrance* (1795):

if a legislative act oppugns a constitutional principle the former must give way, and be rejected on the score of repugnance. I hold it to a position equally clear and sound, that, in such case, it will be the duty of the court to adhere to the Constitution, and to declare the act null and void.[1]

Thus, supremacy of the Constitution and judicial review, as the power of all judges to defend the Constitution and to control the constitutionality of legislation, are essentially linked. That is why a supremacy clause was established in the Constitution of the United States. This clause, in Article 6, section 2 states:

This Constitution, and the laws of the United States which shall be made in pursuance thereof; and all Treaties made, or which shall be made, under the Authority of the United States, shall be the supreme law of the land; and the judges in every State shall be bound thereby, anything in the Constitution or laws of the State to the contrary notwithstanding.

127

This supremacy clause was extended to federal laws in *Marbury* v. *Madison* (1803) through a logical and rational interpretation and application of the principle of the supremacy of the Constitution, and has been expressly established in a general sense, as a positive rule in other countries. In this respect, for example, Article 215 of the Colombian Constitution has established that 'In all cases of incompatibility between the Constitution and the law, the constitutional dispositions will preferably be applied.'[2] Similarly, the Venezuelan Civil Procedural Code, originally established in 1897, states in Article 20 that 'When a law in force whose application is required, collides with any constitutional disposition, the courts will preferably apply the latter.'[3]

### (b) The compatibility of the system with all legal systems

The diffuse system of judicial review of constitutionality of legislation is not a system peculiar to the common law system of law. It has existed since the last century in most Latin American countries, all of which belong to the roman law family of legal systems.

This is the case in Mexico, Argentina and Brazil, which followed the American model, and also of the mixed systems in Colombia and Venezuela. It has also existed in Europe in countries with a civil law tradition, like Switzerland, Portugal and Greece. In Switzerland, the diffuse system of judicial review was first established in the 1874 Constitution, although in a limited way. The Swiss system also currently allows the courts to review legislative acts of the Cantons on constitutional grounds, although this does not apply to federal laws.[4] In the mixed system of Greece, the 1975 Constitution entrusts all courts with the power not to apply legal dispositions whose contents they consider to be contrary to the Constitution.[5] In particular, Article 95 establishes that 'The courts shall be bound not to apply laws, the contents of which are contrary to the Constitution.' Although certain authors have commented on the suitability of a diffused system of judicial review to civil law systems, it appears as if the determining factor is not the system of law but the acceptance of constitutional supremacy.

If the principle of constitutional supremacy is adopted the logical and necessary consequence is that the courts must have the power to decide which norm is to be applied when a contradiction exists between a particular law and the Constitution. Regardless of whether the legal system of the country is the common law or roman law system, the courts are obliged to give priority to the Constitution.

Nevertheless, other criticisms have been made with regard to the practical effects of a diffuse system method of judicial review in a civil law system. For example, Hans Kelsen referred to the problems raised by the diffuse system for justifying the 'centralization of the power to examine the regularity of general norms', stressing 'the absence of unity in the solutions' and 'the legal uncertainty' that results when a court 'abstains from applying a regulation and even a law as irregular, while another court does the contrary'.[6] The argument is as follows:

Under the Anglo-American doctrine of *stare decisis*, a decision by the highest court in any jurisdiction is binding on all lower courts in the same jurisdiction, and thus as soon as the court has declared a law unconstitutional, no other court can apply it. The court does not need a specific grant of the power to declare a law invalid, nor must it decide anything beyond the applicability of the law in question to the concrete case; *stare decisis* does the rest by requiring other courts to follow the precedent in all succeeding cases. Thus, although the unconstitutional statute may remain on the book, it is a dead law ... *Stare decisis,* however, is not normally part of the Roman Law systems, and thus in these systems, the courts are not generally bound even by the decisions of the highest court.[7]

Where the essence of the criticism is that the conflicting decisions of a diffuse system will result in uncertainty, the situation will be the same in common law or civil law countries. If it is true that the doctrine of *stare decisis* may be a correction of the problem, such correction will not be absolute since even in common law systems not all cases in which constitutional matters are decided upon by lower courts can go before a Supreme Court. In fact, that court usually has discretionary power to control the cases which may be brought to it on appeal.

Alternatively, although *stare decisis* is a common law concept, certain roman law countries have a related concept. For instance, the Mexican Constitution has adopted the principle that with regard to the particular law of *amparo*, the *jurisprudencia* or the precedents derived from previous decisions of the federal courts are to be considered obligatory for lower courts.[8] This happens only after five consecutive decisions to the same effect, uninterrupted by any incompatible ruling, have been rendered. The effects of the *jurisprudencia* have been considered equivalent to those resulting from the rule of *stare decisis*.

Similarly, in Argentina and Brazil an institution called the 'extraordinary recourse of unconstitutionality' has been developed which can be brought before the Supreme Court against judicial decisions adopted at the last instance, when a federal law is considered as unconstitutional and inapplicable by a court.[9] In these cases, the decision adopted by the Supreme Court has *in casu et inter partes* effects but, being adopted by the highest court, has factual binding effects upon inferior courts.[10]

In the same sense, in some European countries with a roman law tradition but which have adopted the diffuse system of judicial review, special judicial mechanisms have been established to overcome the problems deriving from contradictory decisions of different courts on constitutional issues. This is the case in Greece under the 1975 Constitution where a Special Highest Court has powers to decide upon the unconstitutionality of laws when contradictory decisions on the matter have been adopted by the State Council, the Court of Cassation or the Auditory Court. In such cases, the decisions of the Special Highest Court have absolute and general effect regarding the constitutionality of laws.[11]

Finally, in other countries with a roman law tradition, the corrections to the problems of uncertainty and conflictiveness have been established by adopting a mixed model of judicial review, that is to say, by having the diffuse and concentrated systems operate in parallel. This is the case in Guatemala,[12] Colombia and Venezuela. Through the functioning of the concentrated system of judicial review, the Supreme Court is empowered to formally annul any law, on the grounds of unconstitutionality, with *erga omnes* effects.[13] The action is usually initiated through a popular action which allows any inhabitant of the country to bring the constitutionality issue before the Supreme Court.

In the same sense, other European countries with a roman law tradition and a diffuse system of judicial review, have mixed certain features of the concentrated systems so as to give their Supreme Court the power to annul unconstitutional laws. This is the case with Switzerland with regard to the issue of constitutionality of Canton laws in cases of violations of fundamental rights.[14]

Therefore, in order to resolve the problems of uncertainty and the possible conflictive character of judicial decisions taken by different courts upon the unconstitutionality of laws which the diffuse system of judicial review could bring about, some countries with a roman law tradition and a diffuse system of judicial review have developed various particular legal solutions, either by giving obligatory character to precedents or by granting the necessary powers to declare the unconstitutionality of statutes to their Supreme Court, in some cases even with general and binding effects.

The problems posed by the diffuse control of constitutionality of legislation, therefore, are common to countries with either common or roman law systems. This cannot of itself result in a conclusion that the diffuse system of judicial review and the civil or roman law system of law are incompatible. The compatibility which is consistent is that when the principle of the supremacy of the Constitution exists, the logical consequence is that all judges, who are charged with applying the law must have the power to decide upon the applicability of legislation to the Constitution.

While European countries with a roman law system have manifested their traditional distrust of judicial power with the establishment of the concentrated system of judicial review, this is merely a method of constitutional supremacy by other means. Yet this cannot lead one to consider the diffuse control of the constitutionality of legislation as being incompatible with the roman law legal system.

### (c) The rationality of the system

As indicated earlier, the essence of the diffuse system of judicial review is the very notion of constitutional supremacy: if the Constitution is to be the supreme law of the land, prevailing over all other laws, no state act contrary to the Constitution can be an effective law. In the words of Chief Justice Marshall, if the Constitution is 'the fundamental and paramount law of the nation... an act of the legislature, repugnant to the Constitution, is void'.[15] In this respect, the effective guarantee of the supremacy of the Constitution is that acts repugnant to it are in fact null and void, and as such have to be considered by the courts that are the state organs called upon to apply the laws.

### (i) The nullity of the unconstitutional state act

The first aspect that shows the rationality of the diffuse system is the principle of the nullity of state acts and particularly of legislation repugnant to the Constitution.

In principle, the nullity of a state act means that an act that pretends to be a juridical state act, objectively is not, because it does not correspond to the conditions established for its enactment by a norm of a superior rank. This was what Hans Kelsen called an 'objective guarantee' of the Constitution,[16] and it means that a state act that is null and void cannot produce any effect, and does not need another state act to be produced to

131

withdraw its usurped quality of state act. If another state act were needed, then the guarantee would not be the nullity of the state act, but its annullability.

In strict logic, the supremacy of the Constitution means that all state acts that violate the Constitution are null and void. Theoretically, all public authorities and individuals could be entitled to inspect the irregularity of state acts and to consider whether the act is valid and obligatory. Since this would lead to juridical anarchy, positive law normally reserves this power to the judges. Therefore, state acts which violate the Constitution can only be examined by the courts and only the courts have the power to declare them to be null and void.

Although only courts may declare state acts to be null, this fact does not mean that the guarantee of the Constitution ceases to be the nullity of the state act and is converted into one of annullability. Instead, the nullity of the unconstitutional state act persists but with the limitation deriving from the legal reserve granted to the judges to declare its nullity.

Thus, up to that moment, the irregular state act must be considered by other public authorities, particularly administrative authorities and by individuals, as being effective and obligatory; but once a judge declares it unconstitutional in relation to a particular process, then the act becomes null and void regarding that process.

In conclusion, in the diffuse systems of judicial review, it is the duty of all judges and courts to examine the constitutionality of laws and to declare, when necessary, that a particular law or statute is unconstitutional and therefore must be considered null and void.

### (ii) The power of all courts

Within the diffuse system of judicial review, all judges have the power to declare the unconstitutionality of legislation. This ability logically stems from the acceptance of the supremacy of the Constitution.

Thus, whenever a court is presented with an issue which involves some aspect of the law, they must decide the case 'conformably to the Constitution, disregarding the unconstitutional law' this being 'of the very essence of judicial duty'.[17] In the diffuse system of judicial review this role is exercised by all courts and not only by one particular court or tribunal, the difference with the concentrated system is that it results not from the conferral of power but from a duty inherent in their existence.[18]

### (iii) The incidental character of the system

This duty of the courts can only be accomplished *incidenter tantum*, through a particular process that has been brought before them, and where the constitutionality of a particular law is neither the issue nor the principal issue in the process.

Therefore, a non-constitutional process must be initiated before a court on any matter or subject whatsoever, before the diffuse system of judicial review of constitutionality can operate. The question of the unconstitutionality of a law and of its inapplicability may be raised in such an instance so long as the issue of the validity of the law is considered to be, by the judge, relevant to the decision in the case.

### (iv) The initiative power of the courts

If it is a duty of the judges to apply the Constitution in a concrete decision, and therefore to consider the constitutionality of the law, the rationality of the diffuse system must allow the judge to consider the constitutional question even on his own initiative, even when none of the parties in the particular process have raised the question of the constitutionality of the law before the judge. This is the direct consequence of the guarantee of the Constitution, established as an objective guarantee which means the nullity of laws contrary to its norms.

Although this aspect of the rationality of the diffuse system of judicial review is followed in many countries, as in the case of Venezuela and Greece,[19] procedural rules in most countries forbid the courts to consider, on their own initiative, any questions of the constitutionality of laws.[20]

### (v) The *inter partes* effects of the court decision

The fifth and final aspect of the rationality of the diffuse system of judicial review concerns the effects of the decision adopted by the court in regard to the constitutionality or applicability of the law in the concrete process; and this aspect of the effect of the judicial decision refers to two questions: first, who does the decision affect? and, second, when do the effects of the decision begin?

In relation to the first question, the rationality of the diffuse system of judicial review is that the decision adopted by the court only has *in casu et inter partes* effects; that is, restricted to the concrete parties and the concrete process in which the decision is adopted. This is a direct consequence of the aspect previously mentioned regarding the incidental character of the diffuse system of review as raised in a concrete process. Thus, if a law is considered unconstitutional in a judicial decision, this does not mean that the law has been invalidated and that it is not enforceable or applicable elsewhere. It only means that concerning the particular process and parties in which the inapplicability of the law has been decided by the court, the law must be considered unconstitutional. Nevertheless, to avoid the uncertainty of the legal order and of contradictions in relation to the value of the laws, corrections have been made to these *inter partes* effects through the doctrine of *stare decisis* or through positive law, in instances when the decision has been given by a Supreme Court.

### (vi) The declarative effects of the court decision

These *inter partes* effects of the judicial decision in the diffuse system of judicial review are closely related to the time when the declaration of unconstitutionality is to be effective.

The first and foremost fundamental aspect of the rationality of the diffuse system of judicial review is that of the supremacy of the Constitution over all state acts. Thus since the Constitution provides the authority for all state acts, any act which is created without the authority of the Constitution has no validity whatsoever. Consequently when a court decides upon the constitutionality of a law and declares it unconstitutional, it is because it considers the law null and void as if it had never existed.

Since the law has never had any validity, the court need not do any positive act in order to invalidate the law. They need only to declare that the law is unconstitutional and consequently, that it has been unconstitutional ever since its enactment. This law is considered by the court as never having been valid and as always having been null and void. That is why it is said that the decision of the court, as it is a declarative one, has *ex tunc, pro-praeterito* or retroactive effects in the sense that they go back to the moment of the enactment of the statute considered unconstitutional.

### (d) Conclusion

In conclusion we can say that as a matter of principle the rationality of the diffuse system of judicial review works as follows.

The Constitution has a supreme character over the whole legal order so that acts contrary to the Constitution cannot have any effects and are considered null and void.

All courts have the power and duty of applying the Constitution and the laws, and therefore, to give preference to the Constitution over statutes which violate it, and to declare them unconstitutional and inapplicable to the concrete process developed before the court. This power and duty of the courts to consider a statute unconstitutional giving preference to the Constitution, can only be exercised in a particular process initiated by a party, where the constitutional question is only an incidental matter, and when its consideration is necessary to resolve the case. The court judgement regarding the unconstitutionality and inapplicability of a statute in a particular process can be taken by the judge on his own initiative because it is his duty to apply and respect the supremacy of the Constitution.

The decision adopted by the court concerning the unconstitutionality and inapplicability of a law only has *inter partes* effects regarding the concrete case in which it is made; and it is of a declarative effect in the sense that it only declares the *ab initio* nullity of the statute. Thus, when declaring the statute unconstitutional and inapplicable, in fact, the decision has *ex-tunc* and *pro praeterito* effects in the sense that they are retroactive to the moment of the enactment of the statute so that the statute is considered as not having produced any legal effect with regard to the concrete process and parties.

Of course, this logic of the diffuse system of judicial review is not always consistent. Each legal system has modified this pure form to its own particular specification.

# 12

## THE AMERICAN SYSTEM OF JUDICIAL REVIEW

The most important example of the diffuse system of judicial review is the one that has been developed in the United States of America. Since the diffuse system of judicial review is considered to have originated in the United States, this system of judicial review has become known as the American system.[1]

### (a) Judicial review and judicial supremacy

When Alexis de Tocqueville visited America and described the political system of the United States more than 150 years ago, he considered the way the Americans had organized their judicial power to be unique in the world.[2] His observations about the powers of the courts, which he considered, 'the most important power' of the country,[3] were directed toward the powers of judicial review. He specifically pointed out that 'that immense political power'[4] of the American courts 'lies in this one fact': 'The Americans have given their judges the right to base their decisions on the Constitution rather than on the laws. In other words, they allow them not to apply laws which they consider unconstitutional.'[5] Following the same idea, he said: 'if anyone invokes in an American Court a law which the judge considers contrary to the Constitution, he can refuse to apply it'.[6] This power of the American judges, de Tocqueville stressed, was 'the only power peculiar to an American judge';[7] yet today it is the power common to all judges in legal systems with a diffuse system of judicial review.

What was peculiar to this system was that the power of all courts to 'pass upon the constitutionality of legislative acts which fall within their normal jurisdiction to enforce and ... to refuse to enforce such as they find to be unconstitutional and hence void',[8] was not expressly established in the Constitution. It was deduced from the whole constitutional system by the Supreme Court in the case of *Marbury* v. *Madison* (1803).[9] The conclusions of that case were based on two main arguments, first, the supremacy of the Constitution as a fundamental law to which all other laws must be submitted; and second, the power and duty of the courts to interpret the laws and not to apply laws repugnant to the Constitution.[10]

This fundamental duty of the American courts has been clearly summarized by the Supreme Court in *United States* v. *Butler* (1936) with the following words:

The Constitution is the supreme law of the land ordained and established by the people. All legislation must conform to the principles it lays down. When an act of Congress is appropriately challenged in the Courts as not conforming to the constitutional mandate the judicial branch of the Government has only one duty – to lay the article of the Constitution which is invoked beside the Statute which is challenged and to decide whether the latter squares with the former. All the Court does, or can do, is to announce its considered judgment upon the question. The only power it has, if such it may be called, is the power of judgment. This Court neither approves nor condemns any legislative policy. Its delicate and difficult office is to ascertain and declare whether the legislation is in accordance with, or in contravention of, the provisions of the Constitution; and, having done that, its duty ends.[11]

According to this doctrine, the United States courts are considered the special custodians or guardians of the terms of the national Constitution as well as the Constitutions of the various states.

As result of the federal system, three branches of judicial review have been distinguished in the United States: a national judicial review, referring to the power of all courts to pass judgement upon the validity of acts of Congress under the United States Constitution; a federal judicial review, referring to the power and duty of all courts to prefer the United States Constitution over all conflicting state constitutional provisions and statutes; and a states' judicial review, referring to the power of state courts to pass judgement upon the validity of acts of the state legislatures under the respective state Constitutions.[12]

The national judicial review branch was the only one not expressly established in the Constitution, and was deduced from the constitutional system by the Supreme Court. The federal judicial review branch was expressly established in the supremacy clause of the Constitution;[13] and the state judicial review branch is generally regulated in the Constitutions of the states. Because of its importance, the following comments will be restricted to the national judicial review branch and the role of the Supreme Court.

However, it must be pointed out that this power of judicial review in the constitutional system of the United States can be exercised over all state acts and not only over legislative acts of the federal government.

Therefore, all Acts of Congress, Constitutions and statutes of the states, all acts of the government and of the administration and even of the judiciary are submitted to judicial review of constitutionality.[14] Although no treaty has ever been held to be unconstitutional,[15] in the case of *Missouri* v. *Holland* (1920) it was clearly expressed that the constitutional validity of treaties and legislation resting on treaties may appropriately be the subject of judicial inquiry.[16]

### (b) Judicial review as a power of all courts

In the United States there is no special judicial body empowered to decide upon the constitutionality of state acts. Thus, all the courts, state courts, federal courts and the Supreme Court have the power of judicial review of constitutionality, and none of them have their jurisdiction limited in any special way at all over the decision of constitutional questions. Constitutional matters or issues are always decided upon by the courts when they arise in the course of a concrete case, when they are necessary to the decision of the case.

The courts, organized in the pyramidal format usual in contemporary legal systems, have either original or appellate jurisdiction. General original jurisdiction in the federal judicial system in the United States is vested in the district courts which are a large number of tribunals of territorial competence located throughout the country, generally coinciding with the territories of the states. The jurisdiction of these district courts extends to numerous types of controversies: civil and criminal cases arising out of the laws of the United States; controversies between citizens of different states; cases in which the United States is a plaintiff or defendant; *habeas corpus* proceedings; and cases rising out of federal civil rights litigation originating from violations by state officers of the constitutional rights of the plaintiff seeking damages or other relief.[17] It is in the course of these controversies that constitutional issues may be raised.

Over the district courts are the United States courts of appeal. The federal judicial districts are organized into larger judicial units known as circuits, and in each of these there is one court of appeal. These courts of appeal do not have original jurisdiction and are strictly appellate tribunals, with very extensive jurisdiction derived from the fact that all the final decisions of the district courts may be appealed to them. The work of these courts of appeals is very important due to the fact that they perform the function of ultimate appellate courts, bearing in mind that only the most important cases can be taken from a court of appeal to the Supreme Court of the United States.

It must also be pointed out that various statutes have given these appeal courts appellate jurisdiction to review the decisions of some important federal administrative agencies, such as the National Labour Relations Board, Federal Power Commission, and special federal courts, like tax courts, in which constitutional issues frequently arise.

In other federal matters there are specialized courts with original and appellate jurisdiction separate from the general system of the district and circuit courts, as in the case of the Court of Customs and Patent Appeals, the Court of Military Appeals and the Court of Claims.[18]

At the apex of the federal judicial system is the United States Supreme Court, which has appellate and an original jurisdiction. This jurisdiction is established in the Constitution, so cannot be varied by Congress.[19] The original jurisdiction refers to 'cases affecting ambassadors, other public ministers and consuls, and those in which a State shall be party',[20] and it is classified by the United States Code, in Sec. 1251, title 28, as exclusive and non-exclusive jurisdiction, as follows:

The original and exclusive jurisdiction refers to all controversies between two or more states; and the original but not exclusive jurisdiction refers to all actions or proceedings brought by ambassadors or other public ministers of foreign states or to which consuls or vice consuls of foreign states are parties; all controversies between the United States and a state; and all actions or proceedings by a State against the citizen of another state or against aliens.

Because of the limited and less important nature of the original jurisdiction of the Supreme Court, it is evident that its most important activity, as interpreter of the Constitution and the laws and treaties of the United States, is developed through its appellate jurisdiction in which it operates as the court of last resort. In this respect, particularly in the field of constitutional matters, the Supreme Court appears as 'the most important tribunal in the American system'[21] with a very broad appellate jurisdiction regulated by Congress to ensure a final, authoritative, and uniform interpretation of the Constitution and of the laws and treaties of the United States.

Thus, the Supreme Court is authorized to review all the decisions of the United States Courts of Appeal,[22] which have the power to review the decisions of all the district courts. This appellate jurisdiction of the Supreme Court can be extended to all the cases originating in the federal court system.

In addition, the Supreme Court has appellate jurisdiction to review the decisions of the highest courts of the various states in all cases of federal laws, that is to say, cases that draw into question the validity of a federal statute or treaty or the validity of a state statute or where otherwise a claim of right under the Constitution, treaties or laws of the United States is involved.[23] Finally, the Supreme Court also has appellate jurisdiction to review the decisions of the specialized federal courts, like the Court of Claims, the Court of Customs and Patent Appeals and the Court of Military Appeals.[24]

Apart from this appellate jurisdiction, there are also cases in which the Supreme Court can act as an appellate court of last resort to review decisions of the federal district courts brought directly to the Supreme Court by means of an appeal. In this respect, the United States Code establishes a right to appeal to the Supreme Court from the decision of any federal court, including federal district courts, 'holding an Act of Congress unconstitutional in any civil action, suit, or proceeding to which the United States or any of its agencies, or any officer or employee thereof, as such officer or employee, is a party'.[25] Likewise the United States may appeal directly to the Supreme Court against any decision of a federal district court dismissing a criminal proceeding or setting aside a criminal conviction on the grounds of unconstitutionality of the federal criminal statute.[26] Finally, the United States Code allows any party to appeal directly 'to the Supreme Court from an order granting or denying, after notice and hearing, an interlocutory or permanent injunction in any civil action, suit or proceeding required by any Act of Congress to be heard and determined by a district court of three judges',[27] which is needed when either a federal or state statute is questioned on the grounds of its constitutionality.

### (c) The mandatory or discretionary power of the Supreme Court

As can be seen, the appellate jurisdiction of the Supreme Court is so enormous that the right to appeal to it must necessarily be restricted. Thus, the Supreme Court has been permitted to judge as to whether or not it would receive an appeal, basing this decision on whether it feels that the question involved is one of sufficient importance.

The appellate jurisdiction of the Supreme Court therefore, is twofold: mandatory and discretionary, the latter being the most important in the number of cases reviewed.

The main reform in this respect was taken by the 1925 Judiciary Act.[28] With the public interest in mind, the discretionary appellate jurisdiction was widened. This discretionary power to determine the cases to be heard by the Court, has altered the character of the Supreme Court as an ultimate appellate tribunal or an ordinary judicial body. As has been pointed out, the Supreme Court: 'is a Court of Special Resort for the settlement only of such questions as it deems to involve a substantial public concern, rather than the concerns only of private persons as such'.[29]

The distinction between the mandatory and the discretionary appellate jurisdiction of the Supreme Court, depends on the methods established in the United States Code through which cases may be reviewed by the Supreme Court. These three methods are the appeals, the petitions for writ of *certiorari* and the certifications.

### (i) Right to appeal and mandatory appellate jurisdiction

Obligatory or mandatory appellate jurisdiction exists when a right of appeal is granted to a party to bring a case before the Supreme Court, and this is restricted to the following cases, all related to constitutional justice:

(a) Cases in which a federal court, including district courts, has held an Act of Congress to be unconstitutional, so long as the federal government is a party.[30]

(b) Cases in which a federal court of appeal has held a state statute to be invalid as repugnant to the Constitution, treaties or laws of the United States.[31]

(c) Cases in which a State Supreme Court has drawn into question the validity of a treaty or statute of the United States [Act of Congress] and the decision is against its validity.[32]

(d) Cases in which a State Supreme Court has drawn into question the validity of a statute of any state on the grounds of its being repugnant to the Constitution, treaties or laws of the United States, and the decision is in favour of its validity.[33]

(e) Cases decided by special three judge federal district courts, bearing in mind that a special three judge federal court must be set up through the enlargement of the federal district court where normally only one judge sits to hear the case, when a proceeding is initiated to enjoin either a federal or state statute on the grounds of its constitutionality.[34]

Thus this right to appeal and the mandatory appellate jurisdiction of the Supreme Court is restricted to important constitutional issues.

## (ii) The discretionary appellate jurisdiction and the writ of *certiorari*

In all other cases, whether or not they involve constitutional issues, the United States Supreme Court is authorized to review all the decisions of the federal courts of appeals, of the specialized federal courts, and all the decisions of the Supreme Courts of the states involving issues of federal law. This jurisdiction is a discretionary one when the application is for a petition for a writ of *certiorari*.

In all cases in which there is no right of appeal established and where the mandatory appellate jurisdiction of the Supreme Court is not established, cases can reach the Supreme Court as petitions for *certiorari*, where a litigant who has lost in a lower court petitions the Supreme Court to review the case, setting out the reasons why review should be granted.[35] This method of seeking review by the Supreme Court is expressly established in the following cases:

(a) Cases decided by the federal court of appeals, granted upon the petition of any party to any civil or criminal case, before or after rendition of judgement or decree.[36]

(b) Cases decided in the Court of Claim granted on petition of the United States or the claimant.[37]

(c) Cases decided in the Court of Customs and Patent Appeals.[38]

(d) Cases decided by the Supreme Courts of the states where the validity of a treaty or statute of the United States is drawn into question or where the validity of a state statute is drawn into question on the grounds of its being repugnant to the Constitution, treaties or laws of the United States, or where any title, right, privilege or immunity is specially set up or claimed under the Constitution, Treaties or statutes of, or commission held or authority exercised under the United States.[39]

In all these cases, as the Supreme Court's Rule No. 17 establishes, when referring to the 'considerations governing review on *certiorari*': 'A review on writ of *certiorari* is not a matter of right, but of judicial discretion, and will be granted only when there are special and important reasons therefor.'[40]

The same Rule No. 17 adopted by the Supreme Court, lists the factors that might prompt the court to grant *certiorari* even though without 'controlling nor fully measuring the court's discretion', as follows:

(a) When a federal court of appeal has rendered a decision in conflict with the decision of another federal court of appeal on the same matter; or has decided a federal question in a way in conflict with a State court of last resort; or has so far departed from the accepted and usual course of judicial proceedings or has so far sanctioned such a departure by a lower court, as to call for an exercise of this Court's power of supervision;

(b) When a State court of last resort has decided a federal question in a way in conflict with the decision of another State court of last resort or of federal court of appeal;

(c) When a State court or a federal court of appeal has decided an important question of federal law which has not been, but should be, settled by this Court, or has decided a federal question in a way in conflict with applicable decisions of this Court.[41]

According to this rule, therefore, in order to promote uniformity and consistency in federal law, the following factors might prompt the Supreme Court to grant *certiorari*: (a) important questions of federal law on which the Court has not previously ruled; (b) conflicting interpretations of federal law by lower courts; (c) lower courts' decisions that conflict with previous Supreme Court decisions; and (d) lower court departures from the accepted and usual course of judicial proceedings.[42] Of course, review may be granted on the basis of other factors, or denied even if one or more of the above mentioned factors is present. The discretion of the Supreme Court is not limited, and it is the importance of the issue and the public interest viewed by the Court in a particular case, which leads the Court to grant *certiorari* and to review some cases.

### (iii) The jurisdiction of the Supreme Court in cases of certification

The appellate jurisdiction of the Supreme Court can also be exercised through the request of certification by a federal court of appeal or by the Court of Claims. This method is very rarely employed. The U.S. Code establishes in section 1254, as one of the methods through which the decisions of the courts of appeal may be reviewed by the Supreme Court, the following:

By certification at any time by a court of appeal of any question of law in any civil or criminal case as to which instructions are desired, and upon such certification the Supreme Court may give instructions or require the entire record to be sent up for decision of the entire matter in controversy.[43]

Therefore, certification is the procedure whereby a lower federal court requests instruction from the Supreme Court on a point of law, relevant to the case under consideration. In these cases of certified questions, the Supreme Court is obliged to consider and answer the questions put to it.[44] In this situation the Supreme Court does not normally deal with the whole case, but sends its instructions back to the court of appeal, although the Court is authorized to require the entire case to be brought before it.

### (d) The incidental character of judicial review
#### (i) Cases or controversies

Judicial review of legislation, whether exercised by lower courts or by the Supreme Court in its original or appellate jurisdiction, is always a power that can only be exercised by the courts within the context of a concrete adversary litigation, when the constitutional issue becomes relevant and necessary to be resolved in the decision of the case. In this respect there is no special type of proceeding required for raising constitutional issues in the courts. As one author has pointed out in his study on judicial review of constitutional issues in the United States:

The constitutional question, if relevant to the disposition of the case and if asserted by a proper party in interest in an adversary proceeding, may be raised regardless of the nature of the proceeding. Thus it may be raised in the course of a civil proceeding between private parties where damages or other relief are sought; as a defense in a criminal proceeding under the criminal laws of the United States, as the basis for an injunction sought by a party in a proceeding directed either against public authorities or private persons to restrain the enforcement of a statute or an administrative order or other administrative action, in a *mandamus* proceeding to compel the performance of a public duty, in a damage action brought against the United States to collect taxes or to enforce a federal administrative order or in a declaratory judgement proceeding designed to obtain a judicial declaration of rights between opposing parties.[45]

Thus, the incidental character of judicial review, essential to the diffuse system, is the main trend of the American system and has been developed by the Supreme Court by interpreting the terms 'cases' and 'controversies' used in Article 3, Section 2 of the Constitution. As a result, no abstract judicial review of the validity of legislation is authorized in the United States.[46] In this respect, the comment by Justice Sutherland in *Frothingham* v. *Mellon* (1923) is conclusive:

We have no power *per se* to review and annul acts of Congress on the grounds that they are unconstitutional. The question may be considered only when the justification for some direct injury suffered or threatened, presenting a justiciable issue, is made to rest upon such an act. Then, the power exercised is that of ascertaining and declaring the law applicable to the controversy.[47]

Consequently, the courts must not decide constitutional questions when they are convinced that the parties are acting in accord. 'It never was thought that, by means of a friendly suit, a party beaten in the legislature could transfer to the courts an inquiry as to the constitutionality of the legislative act.'[48]

The need for cases or controversies to seek judicial review of the constitutionality of legislation nevertheless does not prevent the possible questions of constitutionality from being raised in a declaratory judgement. Although discussed by the courts in applying state legislation, after the 1934 *Federal Declaratory Judgment Act* it has been definitively accepted that, provided all other jurisdictional requirements are satisfied, the federal courts are authorized to declare the rights of the parties in a case before them even though a specific form of remedy, such as a judgement for damages or an equitable decree, is not sought by the petitioner.[49] In any case, it has been pointed out that even though of declaratory character, these judgements are not mere advisory opinions, in the sense that to be accepted a genuinely adversary proceeding between parties asserting appropriate interests must exist.[50] Thus, declaratory judgements are considered cases or controversies, and can be used to obtain a judicial decision upon constitutional issues.[51]

Since judicial review is an inherent ability of all courts in any type of case and controversy, the United States is not always necessarily a party in the proceedings. Nevertheless, in all cases when the United States or any agency officer or employee thereof is not a party, and wherein the constitutionality of any Act of Congress affecting the public interest is drawn into question, the court shall certify such facts to the Attorney of evidence and for argument on the question of constitutionality. In such cases, the United States shall have all the rights of a party.[52]

However, even if the consideration of constitutional issues must be confined to cases or controversies, the invalidity of the legislation must be raised by a party with sufficient standing and its resolution must be necessary and indispensable for the resolution of the case. In this respect, the Supreme Court has developed a few rules that have been considered as 'self-restraint'[53] over its judicial review powers, particularly in three aspects specifically related to the incidental character of judicial review: the standing requirement and the evident and indispensable character of the constitutional question.

### (ii) Personal interest and the constitutional question

Once it has been established that the parties must be within a case or controversy, the Supreme Court has developed the principle that the constitutional issue can only be alleged by a proper party with a personal interest. As indicated earlier, in *Frothingham* v. *Mellon* (1923) the Court expressly established that the constitutional questions, 'may be considered only when the justification for some direct injury suffered or threatened, presenting a justiciable suit is made to rest upon such an act ...'[54] The party alleging the invalidity must show, 'not only that the statute is invalid, but that he has sustained or is immediately in danger of sustaining some direct injury as the result of its enforcement, and not merely that he suffers in some indefinite way in common with people generally'.[55] In this respect, when considering the standing of tax-payers to question the budget decisions of Congress,[56] Chief Justice Burger in *United States* v. *Richardson* (1974) referred to the 'basic principle that to invoke judicial power the claimant must have a "personal stake in the outcome"... or a "particular concrete injury"... "that he has sustained... a direct injury"... in short, something more than "generalized grievances"'.[57]

Therefore, not only is a case or a controversy needed for judicial review, but also the constitutional issue should be alleged by a party with the necessary standing by alleging a particular interest based on 'his own legal rights and interests' affected by the act whose validity is questioned.[58] Even in cases in which the Supreme Court allows persons or organizations or public authorities, not party to a case before it, to file a brief as *amicus curae*, this only happens when they have a special interest in the matter and have applied for standing to the Court or acted with the consent of the parties. In all such instances, their briefs are intended to support or supplement the arguments of the parties.[59]

If these restrictions were not imposed on the parties, it would mean that 'the courts would be called upon to decide abstract questions of wide public significance even though other governmental institutions may be more competent to address the questions and even though judicial intervention may be unnecessary to protect individual rights....'[60]

However, the requirement of standing to sue and to raise the constitutional question is not sufficient to be considered by the Court; the party that alleges the invalidity of a statute must demonstrate its invalidity. The Supreme Court has in this sense established that there is a presumption of constitutionality and validity in the statutes approved by Congress, unless the opposite is clearly demonstrated.[61] In this sense, the requirement that a party have standing and a particular interest in the law is not enough; he must also rebut the presumption of the legislation's validity.

### (iii) The evident and indispensable unconstitutionality

The presumption of constitutional validity of the statutes lead to the second of the self restraints developed by the Supreme Court, in the sense that it should declare an Act of Congress unconstitutional only when its invalidity is clear and undoubtedly demonstrated. This principle was established by Chief Justice Marshall in *Fletcher* v. *Peck* (1810) where he said:

The question whether a law be void for its repugnancy to the Constitution, is, at all times, a question of much delicacy, which ought seldom, if ever, to be decided in the affirmative, in a doubtful case ... But it is not on slight implication and vague conjecture that the legislature is to be pronounced to have transcended its powers, and its acts to be considered as void. The opposition between the Constitution and the law should be such that the judge feels a clear and strong conviction of their incompatibility with each other.[62]

The third self-restraint, developed by the Supreme Court upon its judicial review powers, also related to the need for a case or controversy where a constitutional issue can be raised, is that the invalidity of a statute may only be resolved by the court when the decision upon the constitutionality or unconstitutionality of an Act of Congress is 'absolutely necessary to the decision of the case'.[63] Consequently, the courts may not decide upon the constitutionality of a statute when that decision would not necessarily effect a definitive change over the rights of the parties. Thus the constitutional issue will not be determined when the question has insufficient relation with the controversy or when there are ways of satisfying the claim of a party without determining the constitutional issue. The rule was enunciated by Chief Justice Marshall in *Ex parte Randolph* (1833), when he said:

No questions can be brought before a judicial tribunal of greater delicacy than those which involve the constitutionality of a legislative act. If they become indispensably necessary to the case, the Court must meet and decide them; but if the case may be determined on other points, a just respect for the legislative requires that the obligation of its laws should not be unnecessarily and wantonly assailed;[64]

This restraint has led to the criteria developed by the Supreme Court that statutes must be constructed and interpreted, if possible, so as to avoid constitutional issues, and that the courts must draw interpretations in order to achieve this result.[65]

### (iv) The exception: political questions

Although all of the previous requirements have been satisfied, the Court still considers certain political questions, particularly those related to the separation of powers and 'the relationship between the judiciary and the co-ordinate branches of the Federal Government', as non-justiciable.[66]

The main issues considered to be political are those related to foreign affairs. This involves, as the Supreme Court stated in *Ware* v. *Hylton* (1796), 'considerations of policy, considerations of extreme magnitude, and certainly entirely incompetent to the examination and decision of a Court of Justice'.[67] Decisions concerning foreign relations therefore, as stated by Justice Jackson in *Chicago and Southern Air Lines* v. *Waterman Steamship Co.* (1948), 'are wholly confined by our Constitution to the political departments of the government ... They are decisions of a kind for which the judiciary has neither aptitude, facilities nor responsibility and which has long been held to belong in the domain of political power not subject to judicial intrusion or inquiry.'[68]

The Supreme Court has also considered certain matters relating to the government of internal affairs, like the decision as to whether a state must have a republican form of government, as political and therefore non-justiciable.[69] Yet although the Supreme Court may not decide political questions, it has retained the responsibility of determining when an issue is or is not a political question. 'Deciding whether a matter has in any measure been committed by the Constitution to another branch of government, or whether the action of that branch exceeds whatever authority has been committed, is itself a delicate exercise in constitutional interpretation, and is a responsibility of this Court as ultimate interpreter of the Constitution.'[70]

## (e) The decision upon the constitutionality of the statutes

Apart from the problems related to political questions considered as a possible and undesirable exception to the principle of legality,[71] once a judicial decision is adopted by the courts on a constitutional issue, the classic problem of the effects of the judicial decision must be resolved.

The general principle in this matter is that a judicial decision, in matters of control of constitutionality in a diffuse system of judicial review, has *in casu et inter partes* and *ex tunc* retroactive effects, that is to say, as a consequence of the decision, the act considered unconstitutional must be understood for the parties in the case to be null and void and as never having existed. This principle, however, has been modified in its concrete application as a result of the requirements of legal reliability and justice.

### (i) The *inter partes* effect and the *stare decisis* doctrine

In general, the decision adopted by a court of the United States, concerning a constitutional question, has relevancy only for the parties to the case. Thus the decision *per se* has no general effects or *erga omnes* effect. A statute declared unconstitutional is not annulled by the court nor repealed by it, since the legislature which enacted a statute is empowered to do so. Consequently the statute declared null and void by a court continues on the books notwithstanding the adverse decision on its validity.

Nevertheless, when a decision on the constitutionality of a statute is adopted by the Supreme Court, as far as the inferior courts are concerned, the rule *stare decisis et non quieta movere* (let the decision stand) applies and the inferior courts are bound by the decision of the superior court. In practice the statute may be considered as no longer enforceable since it may be supposed that after the Supreme Court decision, any other proceedings brought under the same statute will result in the same decision.[72]

This declaration from the United States Supreme Court has binding effects on all state bodies. This binding force of declarations was explained in *Cooper* v. *Aaron* (1958). In this case the Court reaffirmed the binding effects of its previous decision in the *Brown* v. *Board of Education of Topeka* (1954)[73] on segregation practices in education over all state executive, legislative and judicial bodies. In *Cooper* v. *Aaron* the Court said:

'Article VI of the Constitution makes the Constitution the supreme law of the land.' In 1803 Chief Justice Marshall, speaking for a unanimous Court referring to the Constitution as 'the fundamental and paramount law of the nation', declared in the notable case of *Marbury* v. *Madison* ... that:

it is emphatically the province and duty of the judicial department to say what the law is. This decision declared the basic principle that the federal judiciary is supreme in the exposition of the laws of the Constitution, and that principle has ever since been respected by this Court and the Country as a permanent and indispensable feature of our constitutional system. It follows that the interpretation of the Fourteenth Amendment enunciated by this Court in the Brown case is the supreme law of the land, and Art. VI of the Constitution makes it of binding effect on the states any thing in the Constitution or laws of any state to the contrary notwithstanding ...[74]

This binding effect of Supreme Court decisions over inferior courts, through the *stare decisis* principle, contributes to the uniformity of the interpretation of the Constitution thus tending to avoid contradictory decisions on constitutional issues.

However, the *stare decisis* rule is not absolute and in the United States it has less rigidity than in the British legal system,[75] particularly when the Supreme Court is involved. As Justice Brandeis said in *Burnet* v. *Coronado Oil and Gas Co.* (1972), *stare decisis*

is usually the wise policy, because in most matters it is more important that the applicable rule of law be settled than that it be settled right ... But in cases involving the Federal Constitution, where corrections, through legislative action are practically impossible, this Court has often overruled its earlier decisions. The Court bows to the lessons of experience and the force of better reasoning, recognising that the process of trial and error, so fruitful in the physical sciences, is appropriate also in the judicial function.[76]

In fact, over the last fifty years, one of the outstanding features of the Supreme Court of the United States has been the frequency with which it has repudiated its earlier attitude toward constitutional questions, not following decisions handed down by its predecessors and overruling a great many of its earlier decisions 'some of which had been regarded as settled in American law for the better part of a century'.[77] This attitude of the Supreme Court has been explained by Justice Reed, delivering the opinion of the Court in *Smith* v. *Allwright* (1944) in which a previous constitutional interpretation was overruled with the following words:

In reaching this conclusion we are not unmindful of the desirability of continuity of decisions in constitutional questions. However, when convinced of former error, this Court has never felt constrained to follow precedent. In constitutional questions, where corrections depend upon amendments and not upon legislative action this Court throughout its history has freely exercised its power to re-examine the basis of its constitutional decisions. This has long been accepted practice and this practice has continued to this day. This is particularly true when the decision believed erroneous is the application of a constitutional principle rather than an interpretation of the constitution to extract the principle itself.[78]

Although the binding force of Supreme Court judgements are accepted, it must be noted that the *stare decisis* principle operates differently depending on the contents of the decision. For instance in some situations a statute may be held to be invalid only in its application to the situation before the court and not invalid on its face in which case the statute may continue to have validity in its application to other situations.[79] The binding effect of the Supreme Court decision, therefore, will depend upon the nature of the attack on the statute: that is, whether the litigant is alleging the statute's invalidity or only its application to the party by reference to facts peculiar to it.

### (ii) The nullity of unconstitutional acts and the retroactive effects of the courts' decisions

In a diffuse system of judicial review such as that in the United States, the courts do not annul an unconstitutional statute but only declare its nullity. The implication is that decisions of the court on matters of constitutionality have *ex-tunc* and retroactive effects. This was the doctrine defined in the circuit Court case *Vanhorne's Lessee* v. *Dorrance* (1795) in which it was considered that a void act 'never had constitutional existence; it is a dead letter, and of no more virtue or avail, than if it never had been made ...'[80] A hundred years later, in *United States* v. *Reality* (1895), the Supreme Court expressed the same principle in a more conclusive way, by saying that an 'unconstitutional act of Congress is the same as if there were no act'.[81]

Nevertheless, because of the negative or unjust effects that could be produced by court decisions with regard to the effects already factually produced by the statute now considered invalid, the Supreme Court was able to lessen the rigidity of the doctrine. Thus the Court could establish, in each particular case, whether or not retroactive effects would apply. This was expressly established in *Linkletter* v. *Walker* (1965) where the Supreme Court applied new constitutional rules to cases finalized before the promulgation of other rules. The Court said:

Petitioner contends that our method of resolving those prior cases demonstrates that an absolute rule of retroaction prevails in the area of constitutional adjudication. However, we believe that the Constitution neither prohibits nor requires retrospective effect. As Justice Cardozo said, 'we think the federal Constitution has no voice upon the subject'.

Once the premise is accepted that we are neither required to apply, nor prohibited from applying a decision retrospectively, we must then weigh the merits and demerits in each case by looking to the prior history of the rule in question its purpose and effect and whether retrospective operation will further or retard its operation.[82]

Therefore, acknowledging that 'the past cannot always be erased by a new judicial decision',[83] the retroactive effects of the Supreme Court decisions in constitutional issues have been applied in a relative way. These questions, said the Supreme Court in *Chicot County Drainage District* v. *Baxter State Bank* (1940) 'are among the most difficult of those which have engaged the attention of courts, state and federal, and it is manifest from numerous decisions that an all-inclusive statement of a principle of absolute retroactive invalidity cannot be justified'.[84] In this modified system of retroactive declarations of validity, it is possible that 'an unconstitutional act may give rise to rights. It may impose duties. It may afford protection. It may even create an office. In short it may not be as inoperative as though it had never been passed.[85]

For instance, in criminal matters the Court has given full retroactive effects to its rules when they benefit the prosecuted. In particular it has given retroactive effects to decisions in the field of criminal liability permitting prisoners on application for *habeas corpus* to secure their release on the grounds that they are being held under authority of a statute which, subsequent to their conviction, was held to be unconstitutional.[86]

The Court has also given retroactive effects to its constitutional decisions when it considers the rules essential as a safeguard against the conviction of innocent persons, such as the requirement that counsel be furnished at the trial (*Gideon* v. *Wainwright* (1963) 327 U.S. 335) or when the accused is asked to plead (*Arsenault* v. *Massachusetts* (1968) 393 U.S. 5) or when it is sought to revoke the probation status of a convicted criminal because of his subsequent conduct (*McConnell* v. *Rhay* (1968) 393 U.S. 2) as well as the rule requiring proof beyond a reasonable doubt (*Ivan* v. *City of New York* (1972), 407 U.S. 203). Its ruling concerning the death penalty has also been made fully retroactive (*Witherspoon* v. *Illinois* (1968) 397 U.S. 510).[87]

Similarly, the Supreme Court has held that any change in the interpretation of the Constitution that has the effect of punishing acts which were innocent under the earlier interpretation cannot be applied retrospectively, since as it stated in *Marks* v. *United States* (1977), 'the notion that persons have a right to fair warning of that conduct which will give rise to criminal penalties, is fundamental to our concept of constitutional liberty'.[88]

Whenever the decision has not affected the 'fairness of a trial', but only the rights to privacy of a person, the Court has denied the retroactive effects of its ruling. Such was the case in *Linkletter* v. *Walker* (1965) where the Court stated:

> In ... the ... areas in which we have applied our rule retrospectively the principle that we applied went to the fairness of the trial, the very integrity of the fact-finding process. Here ... the fairness of the trial is not under attack. All that petitioner attacks is the admissibility of evidence [illegally seized], the reliability and relevancy of which is not questioned, and which may well have had no effect on the outcome ...[89]

Thus when the purpose is merely to protect the privacy of the individual or to improve police standards, as in the case of new rules as to searches through electronic surveillance (*Desist* v. *United States* (1969) 394 U.S. 244) or in connection with a lawful arrest (*Hill* v. *California* (1971) 401 U.S. 797), police questioning leading to confessions (*McMann* v. *Richardson* (1970), 397 U.S. 759) or the use of incriminating reports filed by the accused (*Mackey* v. *United States* (1971) 401 U.S. 667), the doctrine of non-retroactiveness adopted in *Stovall* v. *Denno* [90] has been applied.[91]

It must also be mentioned that even in cases of rules related to the idea of the type of trial necessary to guard against convicting the innocent, the rules established by the Supreme Court have been made wholly prospective when to give them retroactive effect would impose what the Court considers unreasonable burdens upon the government brought about at least in part by its reliance upon previous rulings of the Supreme Court. This happened in *De Stefano* v. *Woods* (1968), which established that state criminal trials must be by jury[92] and in *Adam* v. *Illinois* (1972), which established the right to counsel at the preliminary hearing whose retroactivity the courts said 'would seriously disrupt the administration of our criminal laws'.[93]

On the other hand, in civil cases it has been considered that the new rule established in a court decision on constitutional matters cannot disturb property rights or contracts previously made. In this respect the Supreme Court in *Gelpcke* v. *Dubuque* (1864) considered that a decision of the Supreme Court of Iowa was to be given prospective effect only by stating: 'The sound and true rule is that if the contract, when made, was valid by the laws of the state as then expounded ... and administered in its courts of justice, its validity and obligation cannot be impaired by any subsequent action of legislation, or decision of its courts altering the construction of the law.'[94]

This doctrine of prospectiveness was also developed and applied by

State Supreme Courts regarding liability for acts of dependents. For instance the Supreme Court of Illinois in 1958 considered 'unjust, unsupported by any valid reason, and [without] ... rightful place in modern day society' the rule previously established by the same Court (1898), that held that a school district cannot be held liable for the careless acts of the drivers of its school buses. In principle, the overruling of the 1898 decision could have led to its application retroactively; nevertheless bearing in mind that its full retroactivity might endanger the fiscal integrity of many small school districts, the Court stated:

retrospective application of our decision may result in great hardship to school districts which have relied on prior decisions upholding the doctrine of tort immunity of school districts. For this reason we feel justice best be served by holding that, except as to the plaintiff in the instant case, the rule herein established shall apply only to cases arising out of future occurrence.[95]

Finally it must also be stated that in administrative cases, the doctrine of *de facto* officers has lead to the adoption of the prospective rule effects of the decisions on judicial review. In this respect, in *State* v. *Carroll* (1871) the Supreme Court of Connecticut stated that a statute 'which creates an office and provides an officer to perform its duties, must have the force of law until set aside as unconstitutional by the courts'.[96] Thus the invalidity of the office could not affect the acts accomplished by the *de facto* officer.

### (iii) The practical effects of the decision on judicial review

As indicated, the constitutional question can be raised incidentally in any type of otherwise valid proceeding. Nevertheless, in the United States, particular types of proceedings and remedies that are usually used for raising constitutional issues have been traditionally identified. These are, apart from the declaratory judgement proceeding, the request for an injunction, for a writ of *mandamus* or for a writ of *habeas corpus*.[97] These result in concrete and particular effects with regard to constitutional justice.

For instance, the *injunction* against enforcement of a statute by a prosecutor or by public agencies is the most direct remedy available in a case raising constitutional issues. It is an equity proceeding of preventive and negative effects. It is an order of the Court which prohibits a subject from enforcing certain acts that could be prejudicial to other subjects. The effect of granting a prohibition would depend upon whether the decision holding a statute invalid considered the statute void in its face or invalid only in its application to factual circumstances peculiar to the person raising the issue. Thus, if an injunction is sought against the enforcement of a statute on the grounds that it is void on its face as an impairment of constitutional rights, the Court's decree may be broad enough to prevent further enforcement of the statute against any other person, with the practical effect of making the statute completely unenforceable.[98]

Another of the remedies commonly used for controlling the constitutionality of statutes is the request for a writ of *mandamus*. This consists of a judicial order directed to a public officer commanding him to perform certain acts regarding the petitioner which he is obliged to perform.[99]

Finally, another remedy that is also used to test the constitutionality of a statute is the request for a writ of *habeas corpus* through which a person, who is being held in custody on a charge of violating a criminal statute, alleges that statute's invalidity. If the claim in this proceeding is sustained, the Court orders the release of the petitioner from official custody.

# 13

## THE DIFFUSE SYSTEM OF JUDICIAL REVIEW
## IN LATIN AMERICA

The constitutional system of the United States influenced many of the Latin American systems to adopt, during the nineteenth century, the diffuse system of judicial review. Alexis de Tocqueville's influential *Democracy in America*,[1] has been considered as having played a fundamental role in this adoption, particularly concerning the Latin American countries with a federal form of state. This was the case in Mexico in 1857, Venezuela in 1858, Argentina in 1860 and Brazil in 1890. The system was also adopted in other countries like Colombia in 1850 which had a brief federal experience, and even without connection with the federal form of state, in the Dominican Republic in 1844 where it is still in force.[2]

In most of the Latin American countries, the systems of judicial review moved from the original diffuse system towards a mixed system. This was done by adding concentrated aspects of judicial review, or by adopting the mixed system from the beginning. The Argentinian system remained faithful to the American model,[3] although it created its own natural characteristics. The Mexican system also remained as a diffuse system but with the peculiarities of the *juicio de amparo* (trial for constitutional protection), which has produced a unique and complex institution.

### (a) The Argentinian system

#### (i) Judicial control of constitutionality as a power of all courts

The Constitution of the Republic of Argentina of 1860 established in Articles 31 and 100 the principles of constitutional supremacy and the role of the judiciary. Article 31, in similar terms to the supremacy clause of the Constitution of the United States, established:

This Constitution, the laws of the Nation that the Congress consequently approves and the treaties with foreign powers, are the supreme law of the Nation, and the authorities of each Province are obliged to conform to it, notwithstanding any contrary disposition which the provincial laws or Constitutions might contain.

Article 100, referring to judicial power, further established: 'The Supreme Court and the inferior Court of the Nation, are competent to try and decide all cases related to aspects ruled by the Constitution, by the laws of the Nation and by the Treaties with foreign nations.' Therefore, like the Constitution of the United States, the 1860 Argentinian Constitution did not establish any norm expressly conferring judicial review power upon the Supreme Court or the other courts. Judicial review in Argentina, therefore, became a creation of the Supreme Court, based on the principles of supremacy of the Constitution and judicial duty when applying the law. The first instance in which it was exercised regarding a federal statute was the *Sojo* case (1887) concerning the unconstitutionality of a law which tried to enlarge the original jurisdiction of the Supreme Court.[4]

The question of the powers of the judiciary to control the constitutionality of legislation had been a matter of discussion in the *Paraná Constitutional Convention* in 1857-58. There the predominant opinion on the subject was that: first, the Constitution was a supreme law and it was the duty of the courts to maintain that supremacy over the laws which infringed upon it; second, popular sovereignty imposed limits over the constituted powers through the Constitution, so that laws contrary to the principles embodied in the Constitution could not be binding on the courts; and third, that the judiciary was the branch of the state organs which ought to have enough power to interpret the Constitution regarding the other state powers.[5]

As a result of this convention and of judicial decisions of the courts, the Argentinian system of judicial review has been developed over the last century as a diffuse system.[6] Thus all the courts have the power to declare the unconstitutionality of legislative acts, treaties,[7] executive and administrative acts and judicial decisions, whether at national or provincial levels.[8] This power of judicial review is, of course, reserved to the courts and the executive cannot decide not to apply a statute on unconstitutional grounds.

As Argentina is a federal state, both a national and a provincial court system exists. The provincial courts have jurisdiction over all matters of ordinary law (*derecho común*), such as civil, commercial, criminal, labour, social security, mining law, and public provincial law (constitutional and administrative provincial law). In each province there are courts of first and second instances, and at their apex a Superior Provincial Court.

The national courts have jurisdiction over all matters regulated by federal law, particularly concerning constitutional and administrative law cases and in all cases in which the nation is a party or foreign diplomatic agents are involved. The organization of the national courts is as follows: National Courts with territorial jurisdiction in the first instance, National Chambers of Appeals and at the apex the Supreme Court of Justice.[9]

The Supreme Court of Justice is the only judicial body created in the Constitution and considers itself the 'final interpreter of the Constitution' or as the 'defender of the Constitution'.[10] The Court has two sorts of jurisdiction: original and appellate. The original jurisdiction is established in the Constitution, and therefore, is not enlargeable by statute, and concerns all matters related to ambassadors, ministers and foreign consuls and to actions in which the provinces are party.[11] In its appellate jurisdiction, the Supreme Court has jurisdiction through two sorts of appeals: ordinary and extraordinary. In its appellate jurisdiction through ordinary appeals, the Supreme Court has the power of reviewing the decisions of the National Chambers of Appeal in the following cases: (a) cases in which the nation is a party according to an amount fixed periodically; (b) cases concerning extradition of criminals sought by foreign countries; (c) cases concerning the seizure of ships in time of war and other cases concerning maritime law.[12] In these cases of appellate jurisdiction through ordinary appeal, the Supreme Court is a court of last resort, reviewing whole cases decided by the National Chambers of Appeals.

The extraordinary appeal is in fact an extraordinary recourse that the party in a case decided by the National Chambers of Appeals and by the superior courts of the provinces can bring before the Supreme Court in particular cases related to constitutional issues and under special conditions. This is the means by which the Supreme Court normally decides upon the final interpretation of the Constitution and consequently is the most important means for judicial review of state acts.

### (ii) The incidental character of judicial review

As it is a diffuse system of judicial review, the Argentinian process is essentially an incidental one in which the question of constitutionality is not the principal object. Yet the constitutional issue can be raised at any moment and at any stage of any proceeding. This incidental character has led to a consideration of the Argentinian system of judicial review as an indirect control system,[13] because the constitutional issue can only be raised in a judicial controversy, case or process, normally through an exception, at any moment before the decision is adopted by the court, and therefore not necessarily in the *litis contestatio* of the proceeding.[14]

The principal condition for raising constitutional questions is that they can only be raised in a judicial case or litigation between parties[15] and not as an abstract question before a court, and the courts cannot render declarative decisions upon unconstitutional matters.[16] It is also essential that the question be raised by a party in the process with due interest in the matter, that is to say, which alleges a particular injury in his own right caused by the statute considered invalid.[17] Consequently, constitutional issues cannot be raised by the court on its own volition even if the court is convinced of the unconstitutionality of a statute. In such a situation, the court is bound to apply the statute to the decision of the case.[18] Yet although this has been the judicial doctrine invariably applied by the courts, certain authors have considered that the constitutional questions can be decided by the courts without such questions being raised by a party, based on the principle of constitutional supremacy and the notion of public order.[19]

Perhaps within this context, one exemption has been established by the Supreme Court which allows the Court to consider constitutional questions on its own in matters concerning the jurisdiction of the courts themselves and their functional autonomy. Consequently the Supreme Court decided upon the unconstitutionality of a statute that enlarged the original constitutional jurisdiction of the Supreme Court of Justice although the issue had not been raised by a party.[20]

An additional pre-condition to the resolution of constitutional questions raised in a case is due to the presumption of constitutionality of all statutes.[21] Thus the determination of a constitutional issue must be of an unavoiding character, in the sense that its decision must be essential to the resolution of the case.[22] Moreover, the constitutional question must be clear and undoubted. Therefore the declaration of unconstitutionality, being considered an act of extreme gravity and the last *ratio* of the legal order, the court must abstain its consideration when there are doubts about these issues.[23] Thus when an interpretation of a statute avoiding the consideration of the constitutional question is possible the Court must follow this path.[24]

Finally it must be noted that although it is not expressly stated in the Constitution, the Supreme Court of Justice has developed the same exception to judicial review established in the United States concerning political questions.[25] These political questions are related to the acts of government or political acts doctrine developed in continental European law, and which include: the declaration of a state of siege; the declaration of federal intervention in the provinces; the declaration of public use for means of expropriation; the declaration of war; the declaration of emergency to approve certain direct tax contributions; acts concerning foreign relations; the recognition of new foreign states or new foreign governments; and the expulsion of aliens. These acts are exercised by the political arm of the state in accordance with powers exclusively and directly attributed in the Constitution.[26]

### (iii) The extraordinary recourse before the Supreme Court of Justice and judicial review

Although the extraordinary recourse has certain similarities to a writ of *certiorari*, its difference lies in the fact that the Supreme Court of Justice does not have discretionary powers in accepting extraordinary recourses. Thus the appellate jurisdiction of the Supreme Court, whether ordinary or extraordinary, is a mandatory jurisdiction and is exercised as a consequence of a right the parties have either to appeal or to introduce the extraordinary recourse.

The difference between these two judicial measures is that, although called extraordinary appeal this recourse is not properly an appeal. It is rather an autonomous recourse. When it is exercised, the Supreme Court does not act as an appeal court, in that the Court does not review the motives of the judicial decision under consideration, regarding the facts; its power of review is restricted to questions of law. Moreover, contrary to an appeal, the extraordinary recourse must be motivated and founded on constitutional grounds.[27] That is why it has been said that the Supreme Court, as a consequence of an extraordinary recourse, does not act *jure litigatoris* but *jure constitutionis*, does not judge a *questio facti*, but a *questio juris*.[28]

The exercise of this extraordinary recourse is submitted to various particular rules. First of all, as the extraordinary recourse can only be exercised in connection with constitutional matters, it can only be exercised in three cases:

(a) When in a case the question of validity of a treaty, an act of Congress or of another authority exercised in the Nation's name has been raised, and the judicial decision has been against the validity of the particular act.
(b) When the validity of an act or decree of the provincial authorities has

been questioned on the grounds of its repugnancy to the Constitution, treaties or Acts of Congress, and the judicial decision has been in favour of the validity of the particular act.

(c) When the interpretation of a clause of the Constitution, of a Treaty or of an Act of Congress or other national act has been questioned, and the judicial decision has been against the validity of a title, right, privilege or exemption founded in the said clause which has been a matter of the case.[29]

The Supreme Court of Justice has also consented to hear applications of extraordinary recourse against arbitrary judicial decisions when the right to defend oneself in a proceeding is said to have been violated. It has also been accepted in cases of institutional gravity and in cases when an effective deprivation of justice has been committed.[30] Secondly, extraordinary recourse is only permitted when the constitutional question has been discussed in the proceeding in the lower courts and considered in its decision.[31] Furthermore, the constitutional issue must have been maintained in the various judicial instances in the lower court and not abandoned by the interested party.[32]

Finally, all of the other aspects of the incidental character of judicial review already mentioned apply to the admissibility of the extraordinary recourse. Thus the recourse is only available to a party with direct interests in the matter, whose rights are affected by the decision regarding the invalidity of a statute when the solution of the constitutional question is unavoidable and necessary for the decision of the case. Regarding standing, it must be pointed out that it is expressly accepted that public bodies, whose acts have been questioned on the grounds of unconstitutionality, and the Public Prosecutor, have the standing of a party regarding the exercise of the extraordinary recourse.[33]

### (iv) The effects of the decision on judicial review

As the Argentinian system of judicial review is a pure diffuse system, all courts have the ability to give preference to the Constitution by not applying laws which are contrary to it. The courts do not have the power to annul or repeal a law as this power is reserved to the legislator. The only thing they can do is to refuse its application to the concrete case when they consider it unconstitutional,[34] in which case the law is considered null and void with *ex tunc, pro praeterito* effects.[35]

As a consequence of the diffuse character of the system, the decision has only *inter partes* effects. Thus the decision considering the nullity of a

161

statute has effect only in connection with the particular process where the question has been raised and between the parties which have intervened in it.[36]

Although the 1949 constitutional reform expressly established that the interpretation adopted by the Supreme Court of Justice of the articles of the Constitution would be considered binding on the national and provincial courts,[37] this article of the Constitution was later repealed and the situation today is the absolute power of all courts to render their judgement autonomously with their own constitutional interpretation. Thus even the decisions of the Supreme Court on constitutional issues are not obligatory for other or inferior courts, although its decisions have a definitive influence upon all the inferior courts particularly when a doctrine has been clearly and repeatedly established by the Court.[38]

### (v) The recourse for *amparo* and judicial review

A recourse for *amparo* (constitutional protection) brought before the courts for the protection of fundamental rights can also be considered to be a creation of the courts.[39] This began with the *Angel Siri* case (1957)[40] in which the competence of ordinary courts to protect the fundamental rights of citizens against violation by the actions of public authorities or by individuals was definitively accepted.[41]

Since its general acceptance, and despite the diffuse system of judicial review followed in Argentina, the Supreme Court has refused to permit the *amparo* judge to review the constitutionality of legislation, limiting his powers to decide only on acts or facts that could violate fundamental rights. The Supreme Court considered that the judicial decision in cases of recourse for *amparo* could not have declarative effects regarding the unconstitutionality of law, due to the summary nature of its proceeding.[42] Thus it was established that the *amparo* could not be granted when the complaint contained the allegation of the unconstitutionality of a law on which the said acts or facts were based. The Supreme Court's position was supported by Law 16.986 of 18 October 1966 in which it was expressly established that the 'action for constitutional protection will not be admissible when the decision upon the invalidity of the act will require ... the declaration of the unconstitutionality of laws, decrees or ordinances'.[43] Nevertheless, the Supreme Court reconsidered its position in the *Outon* case[44] when it decided not to apply Law 16.986 and accepted the criterion that when considering *amparo* cases, the courts have the power to review the unconstitutionality of legislation. This position had been previously supported by the leading constitutional law authors of the country.[45]

By adopting this new position on *amparo*, the Supreme Court has altered the Argentinian diffuse system of judicial review, where constitutional challenges are an incidental aspect of litigation, to a situation where the constitutionality of the laws has become a direct issue of the action itself. That is why it has been said that by accepting this feature of the action for protection, the Supreme Court has opened the way to a new direct means of judicial review of constitutionality of legislation.[46]

### (b) The Mexican system of judicial review of constitutionality of legislation

The 1847 Mexican Constitution[47] was influenced by the constitutional system of the United States as described by Alexis de Tocqueville.[48] As a result, a diffuse system of judicial review was created by assigning to the federal courts the duty to protect the rights and freedoms established in the Constitution, against any attack from the legislative and executive powers either of the federation or of the states. Article 25 of the Act of Reforms of 1847, established:

> The courts of the federation will protect [*ampararan*] any inhabitant of the Republic in the exercise and conservation of the rights granted to him in the Constitution and the constitutional laws, against any attack by the Legislative or Executive Powers, whether of the federation or of the States; the said courts being limited to give protection in the particular case to which the process refers, without making any general declaration regarding the statute or the act which brings it about.[49]

A similar article was later adopted in the 1857 Constitution. This produced a unique jurisdictional institution known as the *juicio de amparo* (trial for protection). Today this provision is based on the constitutional text published in 1982, following the lines established in the 1917 Constitution.

### (i) The trial of *amparo* and the diffuse system of judicial review

The present bases of the trial for *amparo* are established directly in the Constitution which, first of all, reserves the proceeding to the jurisdiction of the federal courts.[50] In this respect, Article 103 of the Constitution states:

The federal courts shall decide all controversies that arise:
i. Out of law or acts of the authorities that violate individual guarantees;
ii. Because of laws or acts of the federal authority restricting or encroaching on the sovereignty of the States;
iii. Because of laws or acts of State authorities that invade the sphere of federal authority.

The basic constitutional provisions related to this trial for *amparo* are established at the beginning of article 107 of the Constitution:
I. A trial for *amparo* shall always be held at the instance of the injured party.
II. The judgment shall always be such that it affects only private individuals being limited to affording them shelter [*ampararlos*] and protection in the special cases to which the complaint refers, without making any general declaration as to the law or act on which the complaint is based.

In accordance with the provisions of this article and of the regulations of the Amparo Law, the trial for *amparo* originally sought as a proceeding for the protection of constitutional rights and freedoms, today comprises five different aspects which in most civil law countries correspond to five different judicial proceedings. These five different aspects of the trial for *amparo* have been systematized[51] as follows:

The first aspect of the trial for *amparo* is the *amparo de la libertad* (protection of liberty) in which the *amparo* proceeding functions as a judicial means for the protection of fundamental rights established in the Constitution. In this respect the trial for *amparo* could be equivalent to the request for a writ of *habeas corpus* when it seeks the protection of personal liberty, but can also serve as the protection of all other fundamental rights established in Articles 1 to 29 when violated by an act of an authority.[52]

The second aspect is the *amparo judicial* or *amparo casación* which proceeds against judicial decisions[53] when it is alleged that they have incorrectly applied legal provisions. This is similar to the recourse of cassation that exists in civil and criminal procedural law in civil law countries, to control the legality of judicial decisions.

The third aspect of the trial for *amparo* is the *amparo administrativo* through which it is possible to impugn administrative acts that violate the Constitution or the statutes.[54] This aspect of the trial for *amparo* results in a means for judicial review of administrative action and is equivalent to the French *contentieux administratif*.

The fourth aspect of the trial for *amparo* is the *amparo agrario* which is set up for the protection of peasants against acts of the agrarian authorities which could affect their agrarian rights. These rights are regulated by the agrarian reform provisions and refer particularly to collective rural property.[55]

Finally there are the *amparo contra leyes* (*amparo* against laws). This can be used to impugn statutes which violate the Constitution and therefore provides the judiciary with a means of directly reviewing the constitutionality of legislation. This aspect of the trial for *amparo* has been considered as the most specific in constitutional justice aspects.[56]

The first four aspects of the trial for *amparo* can be used as a means for judicial review of legislation when a constitutional question, having been raised in a particular proceeding, is determined adversely to the interests of the party raising the issue. In such cases, the party who alleges that the basis of the judicial decision was an invalid statute and that his rights or interests were injured by the decision, can exercise a recourse of *amparo* against the judicial decision seeking judicial review of legislation.[57] In these cases, the recourse of *amparo*, being a review of a judicial decision, must be brought before a Collegiate Circuit Court or the Supreme Court of Justice, according to their respective jurisdictions.[58]

When cases of *amparo* are brought before the Collegiate Circuit Courts, they may only be reviewed by the Supreme Court when constitutional issues are involved. The Constitution states:

Decisions, in direct *amparo* rendered by a Collegiate Circuit Court are not reviewable unless the decision involves the unconstitutionality of a law or establishes a direct interpretation of a provision of the Constitution, in which case it may be taken to the Supreme Court of Justice, limited exclusively to the decision of actual constitutional questions.[59]

Nevertheless, the same constitutional provision states that decisions of the Collegiate Circuit Court in direct *amparo* are not reviewable if they are based 'on a precedent established by the Supreme Court of Justice as to the constitutionality of a law or the direct interpretation of a provision of the Constitution'.

Since in all these cases of *amparo* judicial review of legislation has an incidental character within a concrete judicial proceeding, the Mexican system of judicial review of legislation has the general characteristics of the diffuse systems of judicial review according to the American model.[60] However, a few very important particular features result from this unique judicial proceeding of *amparo*. First of all, as the jurisdiction for a trial for *amparo* is reserved to the federal courts, judicial review of the constitutionality of legislation in Mexico is not a power of all courts but attributed only to the federal courts. Secondly, *amparo* trials are always initiated against a public authority. This may be the judge who has dictated the judicial decision, the administrative authority which has produced the administrative act, or the legislative authorities which have approved the statute. Because the public authorities are a party from the beginning of the action, they continue to be the same throughout the action.[61]

### (ii) The *amparo* against laws

The peculiarity of the *amparo* against laws is that it is a proceeding initiated through a direct action brought before a federal district court,[62] against a particular statute. The defendants are the supreme organs of the state which intervened in the process of formation of the statute, namely, the Congress of the Union, or the state legislatures which produced it; the President of the Republic or the governors of the states which enacted it, and the Secretaries of State who countersigned it and ordered its publication.[63] In these cases, the federal district court's decisions are reviewable by the Supreme Court of Justice.[64]

The *amparo* against laws, therefore, is a direct action against a statute, the existence of a concrete administrative act or judicial decision for its enactment or its application not being necessary to the exercise of this action.[65] Nevertheless the constitutional question involved in this action is not an abstract one. Only statutes that inflict a direct injury on the plaintiff, without the necessity of any other intermediate or subsequent state act, can be the object of this action.[66] That is why, in principle, the action seeking the *amparo* against laws must be brought before the court within thirty days after their enactment. Nevertheless, the action can also be brought before the court within fifteen days after the first act of enactment of the said statute so as to protect the plaintiff's rights to sue.[67]

### (iii) The effects of the decision on judicial review

Since the institution of the trial for *amparo* in the middle of the last century, the Constitution has expressly established that the courts cannot 'make any general declaration as to the law or act on which the complaint is based', that judgments can affect 'only private individuals' and must be 'limited to affording them shelter and protection in a special case to which the complaint refers'.[68] Therefore, a decision in a trial for *amparo* in which judicial review of legislation is accomplished, can only have *inter partes* effects, and can never consist of general declarations with *erga omnes* effects. Consequently, the court decisions regarding the unconstitutionality of a statute do not annul or repeal that law. Instead, the statute remains in the books and can be applied by the courts in the future.

The decisions of *amparo* are only obligatory on other courts in cases of established *jurisprudencia*, that is to say, of obligatory precedent. The Constitution does not expressly establish when an obligatory precedent exists and refers to the special Organic Law of the Constitutional Trial to specify 'the terms and cases in which the *jurisprudencia* of the courts of the federal judicial power is binding, as well as the requirements for modifying it'.[69] According to that Organic Law *jurisprudencia* is established by the Supreme Court of Justice or by the Collegiate Circuit Courts when five consecutive decisions to the same effect, uninterrupted by any incompatible rulings, are rendered.[70] These can be modified when the respective court pronounces a contradictory judgement with a qualified majority of votes of its members.[71]

Nevertheless, as *jurisprudencia* can be established both by the federal Collegiate Circuit Courts and by the Supreme Court, contradictory interpretations of the Constitution having binding effect upon the lower courts can exist. In order to resolve these conflicts, the Constitution gives either the Supreme Court or the Collegiate Circuit Court the power to resolve the conflict when the contradiction is denounced by the Chambers of the Supreme Court or another Collegiate Circuit Court, by the Attorney General, or by any of the parties to the cases in which the *jurisprudencia* was established.[72] The resolution of the contradiction between judicial doctrines has the sole purpose of determining one single *jurisprudencia* on the matter and does not affect concrete juridical situations derived from the contradictory judicial decisions adopted in the respective trials.[73]

Finally, with regard to the practical effects of the trial for *amparo*, it must be noted that the Constitution establishes a particular preliminary remedy during the trial for *amparo*, which consists of the possible suspension of the application of the contested state act. In certain aspects this is similar to the *injunction* in the North American system but reduced to an *injunction pendente litis*. In this respect, Article 107 of the Constitution established that:

Contested acts may be subject to suspension in those cases and under conditions and guarantees specified by law, with respect to which account shall be taken of the nature of the alleged violation, the difficulty of remedying the damages that might be incurred by the aggrieved party by its performance, and the damages that the suspension might cause to third parties and the public interest.[74]

# 14

## THE DIFFUSE SYSTEM OF JUDICIAL REVIEW IN EUROPE AND OTHER CIVIL LAW COUNTRIES

### (a) The diffuse system of judicial review in Greece

As a result of the influence of the system in the United States, Greece adopted a diffuse system of judicial review which has been considered to be 'very similar to the United States' system of judicial review'.[1]

### (i) The general trends

Based on the principle of the supremacy of the Constitution, and on the rigid character of the 1844 and 1864 Constitutions, the notion of judicial review was originally formulated by the Supreme Court of Greece in 1847. This early power of judicial review was limited to determining whether a legislative act 'bears all the forms that are necessary, according to the Constitution, for the establishment of a legislative decision'.[2] In the same decision, the Court expressly stated that its jurisdiction did not include the examination of 'the contents of the legislative decision, because it cannot be assumed that the power, which represents the sovereignty of the state, is acting unlawfully'.[3] Later, in 1871 and 1879, the Supreme Court reversed this opinion and considered that judicial review could refer to a statute when it 'is in evident contradiction with a superior provision of the Constitution' in which case 'the court has the power not to apply it in the case that the court is hearing'.[4]

The first Constitution which expressly established judicial review powers of all courts was the 1927 Constitution. Article 5 was amended to include an interpretative clause, which in the Greek constitutional system has the same legal force as constitutional provisions, in which it was stated that 'the true sense' of the provision which declares that the 'judicial power is vested in independent courts subject only to the law'[5] 'is that the courts have the duty not to apply statutes, the contents of which are contrary to the constitution'.[6]

This express constitutional norm concerning judicial review continued to be applied by the Supreme Court and the Council of State as a matter of 'supplementary custom' of the Constitution despite the elimination of this express provision in 1935.[7]

On the basis of this judge-made law, and in the absence of the express constitutional provisions that had previously existed in the 1927 Constitution, scholars of public law supported the theory that the power of the courts to review the constitutionality of statutes and to deny applications of those statutory provisions they considered unconstitutional derived from a supplementary custom of the Constitution.[8]

The Constitution of 29 September 1968, published by the military dictatorship, re-established the constitutional basis for judicial review by stating in Article 118 that 'the courts have the duty not to apply provisions of statutes, legislative decrees and rules, which have been enacted in breach of the constitution or are contrary to its contents'.[9]

This principle was later established in the present 1975 Constitution, in which it is stated that '[t]he courts shall be bound not to apply laws, the contents of which are contrary to the Constitution'.[10] Along the same line of principles, Article 87 of the Constitution states that 'judges shall in the discharge of their duties be subject only to the Constitution and the laws; in no case whatsoever shall they be obliged to comply with provisions enacted in abolition of the Constitution'.[11] Thus, judicial review of legislation in the Greek constitutional system is an express constitutional duty for all judges.

Contrary to the general rule in the common law countries, in which the constitutional question must always be raised by a party in the proceeding, in the Greek system the courts have *ex officio* powers to review the constitutionality of legislation.[12] Of course, if a challenge is presented by a party with personal interests in the matter, the court must examine the constitutional issue.

Finally it must be noted that in accordance with the general trends of a diffuse system of judicial review, a declaration of a court that a statute is contrary to the Constitution results in the statute being considered null and void with regard to the concrete case. That is why, for instance, if the act held unconstitutional had abrogated or amended previous statutory provisions, the Council of State has considered that the abrogation or amendment never took place, and has applied the previous provision as if it were effective and unamended.[13]

Furthermore, the courts' decisions upon constitutional questions are not binding regarding the same or another court in other cases where the same statutory provision may be challenged. Thus the *stare decisis* doctrine does not apply in the Greek system. Therefore, if the decisions of the Supreme Court or of the Council of State are followed by the inferior courts of the judiciary, it is due to practical reasons derived from the factual influence of these superior courts.[14]

### (ii) Constitutional justice and conflicting judicial review adjudications: the Special Highest Court

The diffuse system of judicial review in Greece has an element within it which differentiates it from that of the United States. In effect, the basic judicial bodies in Greece are organized in two fundamental and separate branches, with some similarities to the French model: a civil and criminal judiciary with a Supreme Court at its apex, and an administrative judiciary with a Council of State at its apex.[15] Consequently, there are two supreme judicial bodies with final appellate jurisdiction. Additionally the Constitution establishes a third separate branch of the judicial power attributed to the Comptrollers Council, mainly concerned with public audit and financial matters.[16] All the courts of the three branches of the judicial powers have the power of judicial review, and therefore it is possible that the Supreme Court, the Council of State, or the Comptrollers Council, may render contradictory and conflicting judgements on constitutional issues.

To resolve possible conflicting decisions on constitutional matters between these judicial organisations, the 1968 Constitution established a Constitutional Court,[17] which the 1975 Constitution transformed into a Special Highest Court. The jurisdiction of this Special Highest Court has approximated the Greek system of judicial review to the mixed systems,[18] but since it owes its peculiar character to the existence of three separate judicial organisations, its functions are rather a corrective effort for the inconsistencies which the diffuse system could cause in the three branches of the judiciary.

This Special Highest Court, according to Article 100, has jurisdiction not only over constitutional aspects, but also over electoral matters and the settlement of controversies related to the designation of rules on international law.[19] Furthermore, it acts as a jurisdictional conflict court like the French Tribunal of Conflicts.[20] Yet its primary function is to act as the final resort court for the settlement of controversies on constitutional matters between the Supreme Courts. In this respect, the Constitution gives jurisdiction to this Special Highest Court, for the 'Settlement of controversies on whether a law enacted by Parliament is fundamentally unconstitutional, or on the interpretation of provisions of such law when conflicting judgements have been pronounced by the Council of State, the Supreme Court or the Comptrollers Council.'[21] This Special Highest Court is composed of the President of the Council of State, the President of the Supreme Court and the President of the Comptrollers Council, four Councillors of State and four members of the Supreme Court. When acting in the settlement of controversy on constitutional matters, its composition is expanded to include two ordinary law professors from the law schools.[22]

According to the special law or Statute no. 345 of 1978, which regulates the procedure to be followed by the Special Highest Court to settle controversies, a controversy arises when one of the supreme courts, when examining the constitutionality of a statute involved in the case, forms an opinion contrary to an opinion already expressed by another supreme court covering the same statute.[23] In that case, the controversy may be submitted to the Special Highest Court, in either an incidental or a principal way.

The first means of an incidental character allows the Supreme Court, whose opinion created the controversy, to refer a preliminary judgement concerning the question of constitutionality directly to the Special Highest Court. In this case, the final adjudication of other non-constitutional matters at issue are postponed. The second means of a principal character can be exercised when a supreme court concerned does not postpone its final adjudication but renders it. The constitutional question can be brought before the Special Highest Court through a petition by the Minister of Justice, the Public Prosecutor of the Supreme Court, the State Commissioner to the Comptrollers Council, the State Commissioner to the Administrative Justice or by any person who has a legally protected interest. This latter includes the party who has lost the case.[24]

The Special Highest Court can only examine the question of constitutionality referred or submitted to it, and the decision rendered on the matter has *erga omnes* effects.[25] According to Article 100 of the Constitution, 'provisions of law declared unconstitutional shall be invalid as of the date of publication of the respective judgement, or as of the date specified by the ruling'. Therefore, the decision of the Special Highest Court, in principle, annuls the unconstitutional act with *ex nunc* , prospective effects, but the Special Highest Court can give its decision retroactive effects.[26]

If, after a Special Highest Court decision, a lower court renders a decision with respect to the constitutionality of a statute contrary to the opinion of the Special Highest Court, the litigants have the right to make an appeal. If this decision is adopted by one of the supreme courts, the parties have the right to submit a petition for a new hearing.[27]

The immediate effects of the Special Highest Court decision vary depending upon whether the proceeding was initiated as an incidental or principal type. If the proceeding was an incidental one and the final adjudication was postponed in a Supreme Court, after the judgement of the Special Highest Court is pronounced, the Supreme Court must continue its proceeding consistent with the Special Highest Court ruling.[28]

But if the proceeding before the Special Highest Court was a principal one, and the Supreme Court concerned pronounced a final judgement prior to the Special Highest Court decision, that Special Highest Court decision does not automatically have an effect upon the Supreme Court's final adjudication. Instead, the litigants have the right within ninety days from the date on which the judgement of the Special Highest Court is pronounced to submit a special petition and demand a new hearing of the case by the Supreme Court, which then must apply the Special Highest Court ruling.

### (b) Judicial review in some of the Scandinavian countries

Most of the Nordic or Scandinavian countries, all of which have a parliamentary system of government and a unitarian form of state, have a diffuse system of judicial review with the general trends of the American model.[29]

According to Article 92 of the Finnish Constitution Act of 1919, 'if a provision in a decree is contrary to a constitutional or other law, it shall not be applied by a judge or other official'.[30] Accordingly, 'any official or authority is empowered, and is duty bound, not to apply any legal provision below the level of Acts of Parliament if he or it deems the provision to be contrary to the Constitution or any Act of Parliament.'[31] Nevertheless, due to the absence of court decisions, it can be concluded that 'the Finnish system does not recognize the judicial review of legislation in the most significant meaning of that expression, i.e. as exercised by courts in applying the law in a litigation'.[32] Instead, a system of control of legislation only exists prior to its enactment during the legislative process, in which judicial bodies can intervene. In effect, the President of the Republic can request an opinion on a bill before presenting it to Parliament, either from the Supreme Court or the Supreme Administrative Court or from both.[33] In fact, this is a form of pre-parliamentary control, and the decision of the courts in these cases is merely an advisory opinion. Nevertheless, this form of preventive control of the constitutionality of legislation, added to the political control developed over bills in Parliament, seems to occupy an important place in the system.[34]

There is also a preventive system of judicial review of bills in Sweden. In this respect Article 8:18 of the Constitution creates a Council of the Laws which is formed by members of the two highest courts of the country (Supreme Court and Supreme Administrative Court), which is in charge of giving advice, among other things, on the relations between a bill and the constitutional text, at the request of the government and of Parliament. This control only refers to bills drafted by the government and cannot be exercised regarding the laws finally adopted by Parliament. Moreover, the advisory opinion of the Council is not obligatory either for the government or for Parliament.[35] That is why it has not been considered in the strictest sense as a judicial review control.[36]

In Scandinavian countries other than Finland, a system of judicial control of the constitutionality of legislation exists. The common fundamental trends of the judicial control of the constitutionality of legislation in these Nordic countries, following the general features of the American system of judicial review, have been summarized as follows. First, the power of judicial review is attributed to all judges. Thus, there are not specialized judicial organs in charge of this control. Second, constitutional questions must be raised in cases or controversies in ordinary civil, criminal or administrative litigation by a party having personal interests to do so. Third, the constitutional issue raised in a particular process must only be decided upon if it is unavoidable for the resolution of the concrete case, and the judge has a certain criterion concerning the unconstitutionality of the act, which would depend on the degree of precision of the Constitution. Fourth, because constitutional questions must be considered in accordance with the normal procedural rules, the effect of the judicial decision on the matter only applies to the parties in the process. The judges do not annul the law but only limit their decisions to not applying the unconstitutional act to the concrete case, without *erga omnes* effects.[37]

Sweden has most recently recognized the power of judicial review in their 1974 Constitution. In Article 11:14 it states:

When a [judicial or administrative] court finds a [legislative or executive] disposition contrary to the Constitution or to other superior rules, or when it finds that the proceeding rules have not been observed in an essential point during the process of elaboration of the above mentioned disposition, it will be inapplicable.[38]

Although this article could be interpreted as permitting *ex officio* powers of the courts to declare an unconstitutional statute inapplicable, in practice it is accepted that only parties to the action can raise the constitutional issue in their particular process.[39] Moreover, although Article 11:14 is very broad, it restricts the power of judicial review by insisting that laws will only be considered to be inapplicable when the on record error is a manifest one.[40]

It is Norway which has 'at least in theory the most comprehensive power of judicial review found anywhere'.[41] In addition to the power of all courts to declare the invalidity of statutes contrary to the Constitution as an incidental aspect of a private law dispute, the Supreme Court of the country can also be requested by Parliament to give direct advisory opinions on the constitutionality of statutes.

### (c) The diffuse system of judicial review in Japan

Contrary to the tradition of the legal system of the country,[42] the 1946 Constitution of Japan, drafted under the overwhelming influence of the United States,[43] established the basis of the diffuse system of judicial review in the country. This is regulated only by Article 81, which states that 'the Supreme Court is the court of last resort with power to determine the constitutionality of any law, order, regulation or official act'.[44] In spite of the absence of any statutory regulation regarding its content,[45] the Supreme Court has commented that this power 'has been developed through interpretation of the American Constitution'.[46] Thus the Japanese courts have concluded that no direct or abstract action can be brought before the Supreme Court to challenge a statute. This was expressly resolved by the Supreme Court in a 1952 decision involving an action brought directly before the Court by the chairman of one of the main political parties for the declaration of unconstitutionality of a national police force. The Court dismissed the action and held that the judicial review power is part of the ordinary judicial power and its exercise is conditioned by the existence of a concrete case of litigation that must be started in an appropriate lower court.[47]

The object of control can be 'any law, order, regulation or official act', which includes of course, any normative state act. Discussions have been held regarding the reviewability of international treaties and although there has not been any decision by the Supreme Court considering the unconstitutionality of a treaty, the Court has not excluded, in principle, this possibility. In the *Sunagawa* case the Court commented upon this issue, saying that it was 'highly political' and that 'the unconstitutionality did not reveal itself in a clear and evident way'.[48] Yet the implications were that treaties were in principle subject to the Constitution and therefore to judicial review.

This position leads not only to the political questions doctrine but also to the rule of the presumption of constitutionality of statutes. This means that a constitutional issue must only be decided when unavoidable for the resolution of the case, and when there is no other way of interpreting the statute to avoid its unconstitutionality.[49]

The courts do not annul unconstitutional acts but only declare their inapplicability to the concrete case, with *inter partes* effects.[50] Discussions have taken place regarding the retroactive effects of the decision,[51] but because the Supreme Court's decisions upon the unconstitutionality of statutory provisions are widely accepted, so that those provisions are in general considered as being no longer in force,[52] the retroactive effects of the decision are usually evident.

Contrary to the system in the United States, the role of the Supreme Court of Japan has been considered as passive in the sense that in the forty years of enforcement of the Constitution, between 1973 and 1976, the Supreme Court has only held statutes unconstitutional in three cases.[53] Before 1973, the active character of judicial review referred mainly to statutory provisions no longer in force[54] or to the affirmation of the constitutionality of challenged statutes,[55] and it was only after 1973 that the Supreme Court declared the unconstitutionality of a few statutory provisions. First was an article of the Penal Code which prescribed a more severe penalty for murder of a close relative than for ordinary homicide. This was considered to have violated the equality under the law clause.[56] Later in 1975 the Supreme Court declared the unconstitutionality of a provision of the Pharmaceutical Affairs Act which prescribed that a newly opened pharmacy had to be not less than a certain distance from an existing one. This was held to have violated the right to choose one's occupation.[57] Finally, in 1976 the Supreme Court declared unconstitutional a provision of the Public Office Election Law which fixed the electorate for each election district and ignored the inequalities caused by the movement of population into cities. Thus this law was seen as violating the equality under the law clause of the Constitution.[58]

Finally it must be said that the doctrine of *stare decisis* has not been accepted in Japan.[59] Thus inferior courts are not legally bound by the decisions of higher courts, even by the decisions of the Supreme Court. Nevertheless, the authority of the Supreme Court produces *de facto* binding effects of its decisions upon the inferior courts.[60] Moreover, the Supreme Court is not bound by its own decisions, and has the power to override its previous decisions even on constitutional matters. This happened precisely in the *Patricide* case (1973) in which the Court overrode a previous 1950 decision in which it considered the constitutionality of Article 200 of the Penal Code which established the aggravation of the penalty for patricide.[61]

# 15

## SOME ASPECTS OF THE DIFFUSE SYSTEM OF JUDICIAL REVIEW IN COMMONWEALTH COUNTRIES

Contrary to the situation in the United Kingdom, the diffuse system of judicial review is a common constitutional practice in almost all the Commonwealth countries. Ironically the United Kingdom has played an important role in the establishment of this development.

In fact, all the Commonwealth countries with the single exception of New Zealand[1] have written Constitutions and, in general, entrenched declarations of fundamental rights. During the process of independence or in the process of reshaping the constitutional system, the Westminster Parliament has played a fundamental role in many of the countries.[2] These written Constitutions are considered as the supreme law of the land in each of the Commonwealth countries and this presupposed the establishment of limits upon state powers and particularly upon legislative power.

Consequently, the principle of the sovereignty of Parliament, considered as a constitutional law curiosity[3] peculiar to the British constitutional system, is not followed in most Commonwealth countries.[4] Instead the Constitutions are considered the supreme law of the land so that any state act contrary to their dispositions are considered null and void. For instance, this is expressly stated in the Constitutions of the West Indian countries,[5] and of Nigeria in which it is declared that 'if any law is inconsistent with the provisions of this Constitution, this Constitution shall prevail and that other law shall, to the extent of the inconsistency be void'.[6] Also concerning fundamental rights, the Indian Constitution states that 'the State shall not make any law which takes away or abridges the rights conferred by this Part [Part III, Fundamental Rights] and any law made in contravention of this clause shall, to the extent of the contravention, be void'.[7]

Constitutional supremacy was not the inevitable choice. In India, for example, the choice was between constitutional or parliamentary supremacy.

The framers of the Indian Constitution were inclined in favour of the British principle of Parliamentary supremacy, but although they adopted the English model of Parliamentary government and made Parliament the focus of political power in the country and the dominant machinery to realize the goal of social revolution, they did not make it a sovereign legislature in the same sense and to the same extent as the British Parliament was sovereign. They placed as much supremacy in the hands of the legislature as was possible within the bounds of a written Constitution with a federal distribution of powers and a bill of rights. In its turn, the judiciary has been assigned a superior position in relation to the legislature but only in certain respects. The Constitution endows the judiciary with the power of declaring a law as unconstitutional if that is beyond the competence of the legislature according to the distribution of powers provided by the Constitution, or if that is in contravention of the Fundamental Rights guaranteed by the Constitution.[8]

This Indian dilemma between parliamentary supremacy and judicial review was explained in *A. K. Goplan* v. *State of Madras* in which it was stated:

In India the position of the judiciary is somewhere in between the Courts in England and the United States. While in the main leaving our Parliament and the State Legislatures supreme in their respective legislative fields, our Constitution has, by some of the articles put upon the Legislature certain specified limitations ... in so far as there is any limitation on the legislative power, the Court must on a complaint being made to it, scrutinise and ascertain whether such limitation has been transgressed and if there has been any transgression the Court will courageously declare the law unconstitutional, for the Court is bound by its oath to uphold the Constitution. ... Our Constitution, unlike the English Constitution, recognizes the Courts supremacy over the legislative authority ... confined to the field where the legislative power is circumscribed by limitations put upon it by the Constitution itself. ... But our Constitution, unlike the American Constitution, does not recognize the absolute supremacy of the Court over the legislative authority in all respects, for outside the restricted field of constitutional limitations our Parliament and the State Legislatures are supreme in their respective legislative fields and in that wider field there is no scope for the Court in India to play the role of the Supreme Court of the United States.[9]

Another contribution made by the United Kingdom was in the role played by the Privy Council as the final appellate tribunal for the overseas Empire. This body exercised judicial review of the Constitutions of the self-governing members of the Commonwealth and had the concomitant power to strike down as invalid, those colonial laws which were contrary to the rules of the colonial Constitutions passed by the Imperial Parliament.[10] As E. McWhinney has pointed out:

the Privy Council was the highest appellate tribunal of the old British

Colonial Empire, and it exercised the right to scrutinize colonial legislation and ordinances and the administration thereof to ensure their conformance to the provisions of the Imperially granted constitution or charter of the colony concerned and ultimately to ensure their conformance to the principles of Imperial constitutional law as a whole.[11]

This jurisdiction of the Privy Council remained in force until as late as 1949, when it was generally swept away by legislation of the individual Commonwealth countries with a few exceptions (i.e. Australia, Trinidad and Tobago and New Zealand), in favour of the jurisdiction of the Supreme Courts of those countries. The Supreme Courts of these Commonwealth countries can be seen as the 'lineal successors to the Privy Council',[12] and that is why it has been said that 'after the abolition of the appeal to the Privy Council, the Canadian Supreme Court, for example, continues to exercise the power of judicial review in relation to legislation passed by the Canadian federal and provincial legislators'.[13] In a similar way, the High Court of Australia assumed the power to invalidate, on the grounds of unconstitutionality, legislation passed by the Australian Parliament on certain matters established in the Australian Constitution, and in respect of which, therefore, 'any appeal to the Privy Council was prohibited by the Constitution'.[14]

Although not always expressly established in the Constitutions of the Commonwealth countries, it has been accepted that judicial review of the constitutionality of legislation was influenced by the American system of judicial review.[15] Consequently, the system of judicial review in the Commonwealth countries follows the general trends of the diffuse system, but so that in all matters related to general law and of constitutional questions, the Supreme Courts of these Commonwealth countries have the final appeal jurisdiction.[16]

Some Commonwealth countries have expressly established in their Constitutions the jurisdiction of the courts to judge upon constitutional questions regarding legislation, and in particular, they have established the jurisdiction of their Supreme Court on the matter. For instance, in Trinidad and Tobago the High Court of Justice has wide ranging jurisdiction, including interpretation of the Constitution. The Appellate Division of the Supreme Court is vested in the Court of Appeal and there is an appeal as of right to it from decisions of the High Court on constitutional questions and fundamental rights. The peculiar regulation concerning Trinidad and Tobago is that when the question is one of interpretation of the Constitution from the Court of Appeal, there is an appeal to the Judicial Committee of the Privy Council.[17]

the Supreme Court [of Trinidad and Tobago] as guardian of the Constitution has the power to declare null and void Acts of Parliament which violate the provisions of chapter 1 or other entrenched provisions of the Constitution where the Act is not passed in the prescribed manner with the requisite majority for an alteration of those provisions.[18]

The Constitution of India distinguishes between an original and appellate jurisdiction of the Supreme Court. The original and exclusive jurisdiction of the Supreme Court extends to

any dispute between the Government of India and one or more States; or between the Government of India and any State or States on one side and one or more other States on the other; or between two or more States, if and in so far as the dispute involves any question on which the existence or extent of a legal right depends.[19]

The appellate jurisdiction of the Supreme Court in appeals from the High Court on constitutional matters, is established as follows:

an appeal shall lie to the Supreme Court from any judgement, decree or final order of a High Court in the territory of India, whether in a civil, criminal or other proceeding, if the High Court certifies that the case involves a substantial question of law as to the interpretation of this Constitution.[20]

Nevertheless, the Constitution states that the Supreme Court may grant special leave to appeal when 'the High Court has refused to give such a certificate' and 'it is satisfied that the case involves a substantial question of law as to the interpretation of this Constitution'.[21]

Other Commonwealth countries have established an exclusive jurisdiction of their Supreme Court on constitutional issues, which leads to the adoption of a concentrated system of judicial review.[22] Such is the case in Papua New Guinea whose Constitution gives the Supreme Court exclusive jurisdiction over questions of interpretation and application of constitutional law, subject to the Constitution. Consequently, when such a question arises in any court or tribunal it shall be referred to the Supreme Court.[23] Special jurisdiction is also given, to the Supreme Court and to the National Court,[24] to enforce the fundamental rights of the Constitution.

As the judicial review system followed in the Commonwealth countries is a diffuse system, it is traditional in these countries that courts *per se* do not initiate actions and that constitutional issues must be raised in a case or controversy by a litigant with personal interest in the matter.[25] Nevertheless, a few exceptions to this principle could be found. For instance, the Supreme Court of Canada has the ability to deliver rulings on abstract constitutional issues referred to it by the federal government.[26] In a similar way, the Constitution of India empowers the president to refer questions of law or fact of particular nature or importance to the Supreme Court to obtain opinion upon them and the Court may, after such hearing as it thinks fit, report to the president its opinion thereon.[27]

Finally, it must be noted that the *stare decisis* principle applies generally in the Commonwealth countries so that decisions on constitutional questions adopted by a Supreme Court, although of *inter partes* effects, have binding effects on inferior courts. That is expressly stated in the Constitution of India, where Article 141 establishes that 'the law declared by the Supreme Courts shall be binding on all courts within the territory of India'.[28] Nevertheless, regarding their own decisions, the principle has been interpreted in a flexible way. Thus various Supreme Court have pointed out that *stare decisis* is not an inflexible rule of law and cannot be allowed to perpetuate errors to the detriment of the general welfare of the people.[29]

Part V

# THE CONCENTRATED SYSTEMS OF JUDICIAL REVIEW

# 16

## GENERAL CHARACTERISTICS OF THE CONCENTRATED SYSTEM

The concentrated system of judicial review is characterised by the fact that the constitutional system empowers one single state organ of a given country to act as a constitutional judge. It is the only state organ to decide upon constitutional matters regarding legislative acts and other state acts with similar rank or value, in a jurisdictional way. This state body can be either the Supreme Court of Justice of the country, in its character as the highest court in the judicial hierarchy, or it can be a particular constitutional court, council or tribunal, specially created by the Constitution and organized outside the ordinary judicial hierarchy. In both cases the constitutional judges exercise a jurisdictional activity.

### (a) The logic of the system

From a logical and rational point of view, it can be said that this power assigned to one state organ with jurisdictional activity to act as constitutional judge is a consequence of the principle of the supremacy of the Constitution. As the Constitution is the supreme law of the land, in cases of conflict between a state act and the Constitution, the latter must prevail. But the constitutional system does not always empower all courts to act as constitutional judges, and in certain cases, it reserves the power to act as a constitutional judge to the Supreme Court of Justice or to a special Constitutional Court.

It can therefore be said that, similar to the diffuse systems, the logic of the system is based on the supremacy of the Constitution with a duty in the courts to say which law is applicable in a particular case,[1] but with a concrete limitation: the power to judge the unconstitutionality of legislative acts and other state acts of similar rank or value is reserved to the Supreme Court or to a Constitutional Court. Yet because of the concept of constitutional supremacy, all courts have a certain power to act as a constitutional judge and to decide upon the constitutionality of the other norms applicable to the case, although not with respect to statutes or acts adopted under the direct authority of the Constitution.[2]

Due to these limits which the system imposes on the duty and power of all judges to say which law is applicable, it is the Constitution as the supreme law of the land which can establish limits upon their general power and duty and assign that power and duty to a specific constitutional body. Therefore, contrary to the diffuse systems, a concentrated system of judicial review must be established and regulated expressly in the Constitution. State organs to which the Constitution reserves the power to act as constitutional judges are always constitutional bodies expressly created and regulated in the Constitution whether they be the Supreme Court of a given country or a specially created Constitutional Court, Tribunal or Council.

## (b) The compatibility of the system with all legal systems

The concentrated system should not be thought of as peculiar to the civil law system of law, and incompatible with the common law tradition. Instead, it must be considered in relation to its origin: a system that must be expressly established and regulated in a written Constitution. Accordingly, it can therefore indifferently exist in systems with a common law tradition or with a civil law basis, although it is most commonly found in civil law countries.

For instance, in Papua New Guinea, a country which gained its independence from Australia in 1975 and which therefore has a common law tradition, the Constitution gives the Supreme Court exclusive jurisdiction over questions of interpretation and application of constitutional law. Therefore, when such a question arises in any court or tribunal, it shall be referred to the Supreme Court.[3] In a similar sense, the 1966 Constitution of Uganda also established an exclusive jurisdiction of the High Court on constitutional matters. In this respect, Article 95 stated that

Where any question as to the interpretation of this Constitution arises in any proceedings in any court of law, other than a court-martial, and the court is of the opinion that the question involves a substantial question of law, the court may, and shall if any party to the proceedings so request, refer the question to the High Court consisting of a bench of no less than three judges of the High Court.

The same Article added:

Where any question is referred to the High Court in pursuance of this article, the High Court shall give its decision upon the question and the court in which the question arose, shall dispose of the case in accordance with that decision.[4]

Similarly, in the 1960, 1969 and 1979 Ghanaian Constitutions, the Supreme Court was vested with original and exclusive jurisdiction to exercise the power of judicial review. Article 42 of the 1960 Constitution and Article 106 of the 1969 Constitution stated:

The Supreme Court shall have original jurisdiction in all matters where a question arises whether an enactment was made in excess of the powers conferred on Parliament by or under the Constitution, and if any such question arises in the High Court or an inferior court, the hearing shall be adjourned and the question referred to the Supreme Court for decision.[5]

Additionally, Article 2 of the 1969 Constitution established a direct action that could be brought before the Supreme Court to seek judicial review, as follows:

A person who alleges that an enactment or anything contained in or done under the authority of that or any other enactment is inconsistent with, or in contravention of, any provision of this Constitution may bring an action in the Supreme Court for a declaration to that effect.[6]

For the purpose of that declaration, the Supreme Court shall 'make such orders and give such directions as it may consider appropriate for giving effect to or enabling effect to be given to the declarations so made'.[7] These provisions regarding judicial review were also adopted in the 1979 Constitution,[8] but since 1971 were interpreted by the Supreme Court to reduce the referral of certain cases to the Supreme Court and to avoid referrals of frivolous submissions.[9]

Although judicial review itself has not always functioned in some Commonwealth countries because of democratic instability,[10] the concentrated system of judicial review exists and has functioned in legal systems with a common law tradition. While it is true that common law 'practice has always been intolerant of the notion of specialised, expert, tribunals on the continental model',[11] this must be understood as referring to the specialised Constitutional Court as in the European model, and not to a system 'where jurisdiction is determined and limited in terms of subject matters'.[12]

The adoption of a system is always a constitutional option according to the concrete circumstances of each country. Many European countries have opted for Constitutional Courts, Tribunals or Councils for their exercise of the concentrated system of judicial review.[13] This can only be seen as a concrete consequence of a peculiar constitutional tradition regarding the principles of the supremacy of the law, the separation of powers and the traditional fear of the judges to control legislative acts.[14] Other countries with a civil law tradition have developed concentrated systems of judicial review by attributing the original and exclusive jurisdiction to annul statutes and other state acts with similar rank and effects to their Supreme Courts.

Three conclusions can be drawn from this: first, the concentrated system of judicial review can only exist when it is established *expressis verbis* in a Constitution, and it cannot be developed by interpretation of the principle of the supremacy of the Constitution; second, the concentrated system of judicial review is compatible with any legal system, whether common law or roman law legal systems; third, the concentrated system of judicial review does not imply the attribution of the functions of constitutional justice to a special Constitutional Court, Tribunal or Council created separate to the ordinary judicial organization. It may also exist when constitutional justice functions are attributed to the existing Supreme Court of the country, even though in the latter case the system generally tends to mix its trends with elements of the diffuse system of judicial review.

## (c) The rationality of the system

Just as in the diffuse system of judicial review, the essence of the concentrated system of judicial review is based on the notion of the supremacy of the Constitution: if the Constitution is the supreme law of the land prevailing over all other laws, no state act contrary to the Constitution can be an effective law. The main element that leads to the differentiation between both systems of judicial review is the type of guarantee adopted in the constitutional system to maintain that supremacy. As Hans Kelsen pointed out in 1928, these objective guarantees are the nullity or the annullability of the unconstitutional act. As he explained, nullity means the unconstitutional state act cannot be considered objectively as a juridical act. In principle, therefore, it is not necessary to take away its juridical qualities by means of another juridical act. Theoretically, everybody, public authorities or individuals, would have the right to examine the regularity of the acts and to consider such acts as non valid and non obligatory.[15]

### (i) The annullability of certain unconstitutional state acts

The first aspect that shows the rationality of the concentrated system of judicial review is the principle that when state acts are considered to be contrary to the Constitution, they may be annulled. This annullability of a state act, as an objective guarantee of the Constitution, means that a state act, even if it is irregular or unconstitutional, once issued by a public body it must be considered as valid and effective until it is repealed by the same organ which produced it or until it is annulled by another state organ with constitutional powers to do so. In the concentrated systems of judicial review, the Constitution assigns this power to annul unconstitutional state acts to only one state organ; either the existing Supreme Court or a special constitutional body created separately from the ordinary judiciary.

However, it must be born in mind, that in the concentrated systems of judicial review, the annullability of state acts is always accompanied by the nullity. In a certain way, annullability is a restriction to the nullity rule resulting from the violation of the Constitution. As indicated earlier, positive law limits the theoretical general power that public authorities and individuals have to declare the invalidity of an unconstitutional act, and reserves this power to the judges. This means that, in fact, the unconstitutional state act can only be examined by the courts and only the courts have the power to consider it null and void. Up until that moment, the irregular act must be considered by other public authorities and individuals as being effective and obligatory. In the diffuse system of judicial review, once the court declares the invalidity of the unconstitutional act in relation to a particular process, then the act becomes null and void regarding that process.

This same situation exists in constitutional systems with a concentrated system of judicial review regarding all other state acts different from those which can only be annulled by the Constitutional or the Supreme Court. In effect, with regard to state acts of lower levels in the hierarchy of norms, for instance administrative acts with normative effects, all judges in a concentrated system of judicial review normally have the power to consider them null and void when unconstitutional, with respect to the particular process in which they are questioned. In such cases, the guarantee of the Constitution is the nullity of the unconstitutional state act, even though only the courts can determine that.

What is peculiar to the concentrated system is that constitutional positive law establishes an additional limitation concerning the effects of the unconstitutionality of state acts. With regard to certain acts, the power to declare their unconstitutionality and invalidity has been exclusively reserved to one constitutional organ: the existing Supreme Court or a special Constitutional Court. In those cases, and regarding such certain acts, normally being legislative acts and other state acts enacted under the direct authority of the Constitution, the guarantee of the Constitution has been reduced to the annullability of unconstitutional state acts.

(ii) The power of a special constitutional body regarding the annulment of certain state acts on the grounds of unconstitutionality

The second aspect of the rationality of the concentrated system is that the power to declare the nullity of legislation is assigned to one single constitutional organ with jurisdictional functions. This modality of the concentrated system of judicial review, which consists of the establishment of a special constitutional body, has marked the development of constitutional law during the recent decades, since the first Constitutional Courts were established in Austria and Czechoslovakia in 1920. The system was later adopted in Germany and Italy, after the Second World War, and more recently in Spain and Portugal. It has also been adopted in some socialist countries (Yugoslavia, Czechoslovakia and Poland) and has been developed with particular trends in France. Under the influence of the European model, but in an incomplete way, the system was adopted in the early seventies in Chile where a Constitutional Tribunal was established, and more recently in Ecuador and Peru, where Constitutional Guarantees Tribunals have been created.

Although constitutionalism developed in the theory and practice of constitutional law since the beginning of the last century, a system of constitutional justice was not accepted in Europe until after the First World War, and then took place in two ways. One was established in the Weimar Constitution (1919), whereby Germany established a Tribunal entrusted with jurisdiction to settle disputes between the state constitutional powers and, more specifically, between the different territorial powers vertically distributed as a result of its federal organization. The second was the Austrian system, the personal masterpiece of Professor Hans Kelsen. This was first expressed in the 1920 Austrian Constitution and later perfected by the 1929 Constitutional Reform.

The incorporation of this system of constitutional justice in Europe was due to the influence of Hans Kelsen's pure theory of law, which conceived constitutional norms as the basis for the validity of all the norms of a given legal order. This basic concept had a fundamental corollary: the need for a state body to guarantee the Constitution, that is to say, to settle disputes over the consistency of all legal norms, both specific and general, with the superior hierarchy on which they are based, and in the last instance, with the Constitution.[16]

Kelsen himself established quite clearly that constitutional justice consisted of the guarantee of the consistency of an inferior norm to a superior norm from whence it arose and from whence its contents were determined. In the end constitutional justice was a guarantee of the Constitution resulting from the 'juridical pyramid' of the legal order whereby the unity and hierarchy of its different norms were established.

As a result of Kelsen's influence, Czechoslovakia also adopted a system of constitutional control in its Constitution of 29 February 1920.[17] The grounds for the establishment of the Czechoslovakian concentrated system of constitutional control are to be found in the existence of a constitutional norm which explicitly sets forth the supremacy of the Constitution over the rest of the legal order[18] and which explicitly prohibits the courts from the possibility of exercising diffuse control over the constitutionality of laws.[19] In addition, the Constitution established the obligation for all courts to consult with the Constitutional Tribunal in cases of the enforcement of a law thought to be in violation of the Constitution. Those elements led to the concentration of constitutional jurisdiction to judge the constitutionality of laws in a single body, the Constitutional Tribunal, which continued to exist until 1938.[20]

Kelsen's conception of the concentrated system of judicial review, contrary to the diffuse system which implies that all judges are entitled to abstain from enforcing laws they deem contrary to the Constitution, results in an attribution of an exclusive power to declare the unconstitutionality of a law to a single state body. In this system, ordinary courts lack the power to refrain from enforcing unconstitutional laws on their own.

In its original theoretical conception, this concentrated system was conceived by Kelsen as being 'a system of negative legislation'.[21] A Constitutional Court does not specifically decide upon the unconstitutionality of statutes on any assumption of a single fact; this is reserved for the *a quo* court raising the question of constitutionality. Its competence is normally limited to the purely abstract issue of the logical compatibility which must exist between the statute and the Constitution. As there is no real enforcement of the law in any specific case in this logical system, it was considered that it was not the case of jurisdictional activity which implied a concrete decision. This led Kelsen to maintain that when the Constitutional Tribunal declares a statute unconstitutional, the decision with *erga omnes* effects was a typical legislative action. Hence the common assumption that the Constitutional Tribunal's decision had the force of law. Consequently, until a decision is adopted, the statute is valid and the judges of ordinary courts are obliged to enforce it.[22]

This reasoning was developed by Kelsen in response to possible objections that the jurisdictional control of legislative action, based on the European concept of the supremacy of Parliament, could produce. By forbidding ordinary judges to abstain from enforcing the laws and granting the power to declare a statute unconstitutional with *erga omnes* effect to the Constitutional Court, the judiciary was subject to the laws adopted by Parliament and at the same time the primacy of the Constitution over Parliament could be maintained. In this way, it was considered that the Constitutional Tribunal became Parliament's logical complement. Its function was reduced to judging the validity of a statute with simple and rational logic, completely separate from the need to settle disputes in specific cases and acting as a negative legislator. In this way, legislative power was, for Kelsen, divided between two bodies: the first, Parliament, the holder of political initiative, the positive legislator; and the second, the Constitutional Tribunal, entrusted with the power to annul laws which violate the Constitution. Under this conception, of course, the Constitutional Court needed to be a constitutional body separate from all traditional state powers: thus it was not strictly a judicial body.[23]

### (iii) The principal and incidental character of the system

Under a concentrated system of judicial review, constitutional issues can be brought before the Constitutional Court either by virtue of a direct action or request or by referral from a lower court where the constitutional question has been raised in a concrete proceeding, either *ex officio* or through the initiative of a party. Thus the concentrated feature of the system does not imply that the constitutional question must only be raised either in a principal or in an incidental way. It can be either one form or the other, or through both in parallel, depending on the concrete positive law regulations. Consequently, the concentrated system of judicial review can not be identified by the principal character of the method of reviewing the constitutional question although this may have been true in the original Austrian system established in 1920.[24]

In the principal method, the constitutional issue regarding a statute is the only and principal question of the process initiated through the exercise of a direct action that can be brought before the Constitutional Court, either by someone through an *actio popularis* or within some *locus standi* rules or by specific public officials and authorities. In the incidental method the constitutional issue is raised before an ordinary court as an incidental question aspect of a process, or the court can raise it *ex officio*. This court is the one which must refer the constitutional question to the Constitutional Court, the suspension of the decision of the concrete case being necessary until the constitutional issue is resolved.

### (iv) The initiative power of judicial review

The Constitutional Court (including the Supreme Court) does not have any self-initiative to act as a constitutional judge.[25] Thus the principle *nemo iudex sine actore* applies. But once a constitutional question has reached the court as a result of an action or of a lower court referral, the principle *ne iudex iudicet ultra petitum partis* does not apply. That is to say, the constitutional judge, once required by a party or through incidental means, has *ex officio* powers to consider questions of constitutionality other than those already submitted.

Although the Constitutional Court cannot raise issues on its own initiative in the incidental method of concentrated judicial review, the lower courts that refer constitutional issues to the constitutional judge can. That is to say, the ordinary courts when raising constitutional issues in the incidental method are not always bound by the requirements of the parties or of the public prosecutor. Thus the judges may raise constitutional issues *ex officio* for referral to the Constitutional Court for its decision.

### (v) The *erga omnes* effects of the court decision

The final aspect of the rationality of the concentrated system of judicial review can be considered under two issues: first, who the decision affects; and second, when do the effects of the decision begin.

In relation to the first issue, the decision adopted by a Constitutional Court has general effects so that it applies *erga omnes*. This is particularly so when judicial review is sought by a direct action. In this case the process is objective with the object of the annulment of unconstitutional statutes. The effects must necessarily be *erga omnes*, and not *inter partes*, because of the absence of proper parties.

However, even when judicial review is sought by incidental methods, the decision of the Constitutional Court must be concentrated on aspects regarding law only and not facts. Since the court in this case is not limited to a concrete process or to the parties in which the constitutional question was originally raised, the effects must also be *erga omnes*.

Accordingly, the constitutional judge in the concentrated system does not decide a concrete case, but only a question of constitutionality of a statute. The logic of the system, therefore, is that the decision must apply to everybody and to all state organs, thus the *erga omnes* effects. Thus if a law is considered unconstitutional by the Constitutional Court, the law thereof is annulled and cannot be enforceable or applicable anywhere or in any case.

### (vi) The constitutive effects of the Constitutional Court decision

These *erga omnes* effects and the annullability aspect are closely related to the question as to when the declaration of unconstitutionality is to be effective. As indicated earlier, the fundamental aspect of the rationality of the concentrated system is that of the supremacy of the Constitution. In concentrated systems, the Constitution has restricted its own guarantee by reserving the appreciation and declaration of nullity of laws to only one single constitutional organ.

Consequently, when a constitutional judge decides upon the unconstitutionality of a law, the decision has a constitutive effect: it determines that the law is a nullity because of its unconstitutionality, the law having produced effects up to the moment in which its nullity is established. Thus the decision of the court has *ex-nunc, pro futuro* or prospective effects.

Nevertheless, this element of the logic of the concentrated system of judicial review is normally tempered by the constitutional system itself. Therefore a distinction is established between the absolute or relative nullity of the law. Thus certain constitutional errors may produce a statute with an absolute nullity, so that the decision of the court has *ex-tunc* effects, or the constitutional defects of the statute may be considered to be not so grave as to produce an absolute nullity but only a relative nullity. In this instance, the effects of the annulment of the statute are only *ex-nunc, pro futuro*.

# 17

## THE ORIGIN OF THE EUROPEAN MODEL OF JUDICIAL REVIEW AND THE AUSTRIAN SYSTEM OF THE CONSTITUTIONAL TRIBUNAL

### (a) The European antecedents

The concentrated system of judicial review through a Constitutional Court originated in Europe, and is basically a European institution. Its use became more common after the two World Wars,[1] and it has been called the European model[2] or the Austrian[3] system of judicial review.

The system is a result of Hans Kelsen's ideas and work related to the supremacy of the Constitution and to the need for a jurisdictional guarantee of that supremacy.[4] In this respect, the Austrian Constitution established a prohibition towards ordinary judges, to 'examine the validity of laws, decrees or international treaties duly enacted',[5] and the Czechoslovakian Constitution of 1920 reduced the powers of ordinary judges to verify that laws had been correctly published.[6] Consequently, the only means through which the supremacy of the Constitution could be guaranteed was by creating a constitutional organ, apart from the judicial power, in charge of controlling the constitutionality of legislation as a negative legislator.[7]

According to these fundamental ideas, the first Constitutional Tribunals were established in Czechoslovakia and Austria, in their Constitutions of 29 February and 1 October 1920 respectively. The Czechoslovakian Tribunal did not develop an effective control of constitutionality during its existence, and it disappeared in 1938,[8] although it was later re-established under the socialist system in 1968.[9] Nevertheless, as its original regulations can be considered to be the antecedent of the European model of judicial review, its general characteristics were as follows.

The Constitution expressly established the principle of its supremacy and ensured that all statutes which were contrary to its regulations and to the constitutional laws were to be considered invalid.[10] The monopoly for the appreciation of the unconstitutionality of statutes, whether of the national Parliament or of the legislatures of the autonomous territorial units, was attributed to a Constitutional Tribunal created in the Constitution[11] and regulated by a special law enacted immediately after the enactment of the Constitution.[12] This constitutional body had only constitutional judicial power with no other kind of attribution.[13]

The question of the unconstitutionality or invalidity of statutes could only be brought before the Constitutional Tribunal in an abstract way through a 'recourse of unconstitutionality of statutes'[14] without any relation to a particular case. Thus the method for seeking judicial review was a direct one exercised only by some legislative and judicial state organs: the Chambers of the National Assembly, the Supreme Court, the Supreme Administrative Court and the Electoral Tribunal.[15]

The Constitutional Tribunal did not have *ex-officio* powers on constitutional issues[16] and the action could only be brought before the Tribunal within a period of three years following the publication of the statute.[17] Finally, the effects of the decision of the Constitutional Tribunal were *erga omnes* and *ex-nunc*, *pro-futuro*, from the day of the publication of the decision.[18]

Because of its permanence and its re-establishment in 1945, however, the Austrian Constitutional Tribunal, first created by the 1920 Constitution, was to be the leading institution of the European concentrated system of judicial review. The original general characteristics of the institution, very similar to that of Czechoslovakia, were formulated by Hans Kelsen – himself a member of the Constitutional Tribunal until 1929. These original characteristics were reviewed by the constitutional amendments of 1925 and 1929. In 1929 the Constitution was amended to give the Tribunal the shape which has been embodied in the 1945 Constitutional Law and which has itself been amended many times.[19]

## (b) The Austrian Constitutional Tribunal

The Austrian Constitutional Tribunal is regulated in the 1945 Constitution[20] as a constitutional organ established separately from the judicial power. Its basic regulations are established in the special Federal Law of the Constitutional Tribunal of 1953 modified on various occasions[21] and in the Interior Rules of the Tribunal enacted by itself[22] in accordance with an auto-regulatory power which confirms its independence in the political system.

Although it is conceived of as a constitutional organ independent of the other organs of the state, its members are appointed by the executive power with the participation of the legislative power.[23] In accordance with

Article 147 of the Constitution, the Tribunal is composed of a President, a Vice-President, twelve members and six alternative members. The President, the Vice-President, six members and three alternative members are appointed by the President of the Republic following a proposal from the federal government, and they must be chosen from among magistrates, public officers and university law professors. The other six members and the other three alternative members are appointed by the President of the Republic following a proposal formulated by the legislative organs – the National Council and the Federal Council.

As the appointment of the members of the Tribunal follows the normal political rules of the country and the normal influence of the political parties,[24] there is a danger of political influence over the activities of the Tribunal. Yet Kelsen was aware of this when he commented that 'If this danger is particularly important, it is preferable to accept the legitimate participation of the political parties in the formation of the Tribunal, rather than its hidden and uncontrollable influence...'[25] Nevertheless, the Constitution has established various restrictions to secure the impartiality of the Tribunal,[26] members are forbidden to belong to the government or any of the legislative organs or to be leaders of the political parties. In particular, the President and Vice-President of the Tribunal must not have occupied a political position for at least four years previous to their appointment.[27]

Contrary to the Czechoslovakian example in which the Constitutional Tribunal was conceived exclusively as a constitutional judge, the Austrian Constitutional Tribunal combines its functions of judicial review with other powers related to political and organic matters. These other powers are the following:

In the first place, there exists a series of jurisdictional powers to settle controversies in which the political bodies of the federal state are involved. Some of these controversies are derived from the federal system and the vertical distribution of state power, for instance, the Constitutional Tribunal has jurisdiction regarding patrimonial actions against the Federation, the states (*Länder*), the districts, the municipalities or associations of municipalities when they cannot be resolved by an ordinary judicial procedure or by administrative resolution.[28] These actions are exceptional and regulated by public law.[29] The Constitutional Tribunal also has jurisdiction to resolve all conflicts between constitutional organs. This includes conflicts of jurisdiction between administrative and judicial authorities; conflicts of jurisdiction between courts; and, in particular, conflicts between the federation and the *Länder* or between the *Länder*.[30]

Regarding conflicts between the federation and member states, Article 138, Paragraph 2 of the Constitution attributes to the Constitutional Tribunal specific powers to determine when they will hear a request of the federal or states government before a concrete conflict has arisen. A decision in such a case prevents disputes over the vertical distribution of state power.[31] In addition, the Constitutional Tribunal can interpret agreements adopted between the different levels of the federal state, particularly between the federation and the *Länder* or between the *Länder*.[32]

Secondly, the Constitutional Tribunal has jurisdictional powers regarding elections and *referenda*. The Tribunal is empowered to decide upon actions that could be brought before it against the election of the President of the Federation, of the representatives to the Assemblies, of the representatives of the organs of the professional associations, and against the elections of government officials to the *Länder* and at municipal level. It also has jurisdiction to resolve the loss of the respective mandate of elected representatives[33] and to decide upon any claim against the result of a *referendum* directed to approve certain laws.[34]

Thirdly, the Constitutional Court has jurisdiction to decide upon accusations against the supreme organs of the federation or of the *Länder*, based on constitutional liability derived from illegalities.[35] The Court's decision in this instance could produce the loss of office and even the temporary loss of political rights.[36]

Finally, the Constitutional Tribunal is empowered to act as a constitutional judge controlling the constitutionality of laws, executive regulations and treaties and empowered to grant constitutional protection against the violation of fundamental rights.

## (c) The Constitutional Tribunal and judicial review

The Constitutional Tribunal is able to review legislative acts as well as treaties and executive regulations. Legislative acts include both federal and *Land* statutes.[37] The power of reviewing international treaties has only been conferred upon the Constitutional Tribunal since 1964.[38] Contrary to legislative acts and treaties adopted under direct authority of the Constitution,[39] regarding executive regulations, Professor Kelsen said:

Without doubt these executive regulations [*reglements*] are not acts immediately subordinate to the Constitution; their irregularity immediately consists of their illegality, and only in a mediate way, their constitutionality. If, in spite of that, we propose to extend the attributions of the constitutional jurisdiction to them, it is not due to the mentioned relativity of the opposition between direct and indirect constitutionality, but taking into consideration the natural boundary between general and particular juridical acts.[40]

Consequently, according to Kelsen, only administrative and judicial acts were to be excluded from constitutional jurisdiction.[41]

### (d) The methods of control and the *ex officio* powers of the Constitutional Tribunal

Although in its original 1920 version the only established method of seeking the jurisdiction of the Constitutional Tribunal was through a petition reserved only to certain political organs of the state,[42] there are now two basic methods for seeking the jurisdiction of the Constitutional Tribunal: through a direct petition or in an incidental way. The 1929 and 1975 constitutional reforms enlarged the standing requirements to interpose the direct petition, and in 1929 the incidental method of judicial review was also established. Additionally, the Constitutional Tribunal was empowered by the Constitution to raise constitutional issues *ex officio*. It is also possible to distinguish another indirect method of seeking judicial review as a consequence of the exercise of the constitutional protection actions regarding fundamental rights. Thus five different methods of seeking judicial review can be distinguished in the Austrian system.

#### (i) The direct petition for unconstitutionality

The first direct method is the petition for unconstitutionality of statutes that can be brought before the Constitutional Tribunal. This can be used to question the validity of federal statutes, at the request of the government of the *Länder* or of one third of the members of the National Council, or to question the validity of *Länder* statutes, at the request of the federal government. Also, the Constitutions of the *Länder* are authorized by the federal Constitution to give the right to petition to one third of the members of their legislatures.[43] It must be noted that by granting standing to interpose the direct petition to one third of the representatives in the legislative bodies, the 1975 constitutional reform has given the opposition a means of controlling the laws adopted by the majority.[44] This follows the trends developed in other European countries.

The direct petition of illegality can also be used by the governments of the *Länder* if the object of judicial review is a federal executive decree. If it is a decree of the *Länder* executive authorities, the petition can be brought by the federal government. If the *Land* executive decree is directed toward local government control,[45] then the municipalities have standing. The Constitution relies upon an analogous application of the previously mentioned rules in order to permit a differentiation between treaties approved by the National Council and those enacted by executive means.[46] This ensures that international treaties are subject to judicial review.

### (ii) The direct action of unconstitutionality

Since the 1975 constitutional reform, a direct action has also been granted to individuals, but only when they deem their rights have been directly violated by a statute or an executive regulation. It is necessary that the norm in question be directly applicable to them, without any other further judicial decision or individual administrative act.[47] In this case, the claimant must express in his action, how the statute, without any further judicial decision or administrative act, can affect his rights directly. Therefore, this form of constitutional complaint is not an *actio populuris*,[48] but an action submitted to specific requirement for standing.

This action cannot be brought before the Constitutional Tribunal against a statute if there have been judicial decisions or administrative acts enforced in application of the said statute. If such an administrative or judicial decision exists, a recourse must first be interposed against those decisions. In such cases, the constitutional issue could be raised in an incidental way or *ex officio* by the Constitutional Court.[49]

### (iii) The incidental method for judicial review

Since the 1929 constitutional reform an incidental method for judicial review has been established in Austria which was enlarged in 1975. According to this procedure, a constitutional question regarding statutes could reach the Constitutional Tribunal by a referral formulated by the Administrative Court, the Supreme Court of Justice, or any court of appeal when they must apply the law in a concrete proceeding.[50] If the issue concerns the validity of executive regulation, the constitutional question can be brought before the Constitutional Tribunal by any court.[51] In such cases, the incidental referral formulated before the Constitutional Tribunal has suspensive effects regarding the concrete proceeding in which the constitutional question has been raised, which can only be continued after the Constitutional Tribunal's judgement has been adopted.[52]

Even though the Supreme Courts and the Courts of Appeal do not have judicial review power, this incidental means for judicial review gives them not only the power but the duty 'not to apply laws whose constitutionality is in doubt, without having first heard the binding judgement of the Constitutional Court'.[53] This means that those courts have the power to appreciate the unconstitutionality of legislation, although not to annul these laws.

### (iv) The *ex officio* powers for constitutional review

The Constitution also empowers the Constitutional Tribunal to raise, on its own initiative, any constitutional question regarding statutes and executive regulations, in cases developed before the Tribunal, in which a statute or an executive regulation must be applied for resolution.[54] Nevertheless, the Constitution establishes that even though the Tribunal is convinced that a statute is unconstitutional, if the complete annulment of the statute would mean a manifest prejudice against the juridical interests of the individual claimant in a direct action, or of the plaintiff in the proceeding in which an incidental question was brought before the Tribunal, it must not annul the statute.[55]

### (v) The indirect means for judicial review and the protection of fundamental rights

The Constitution also establishes the right of individuals to bring before the Constitutional Tribunal recourses or complaints against administrative acts when the claimant alleges that they infringe a right guaranteed in a constitutional law.[56] But the relation between this recourse for protection of fundamental rights against administrative acts of particular effect and judicial review of constitutionality, is that it could also be based on the allegation that the administrative act prejudiced the claimant because it applied an illegal decree, an unconstitutional law or an international treaty contrary to the rule of law.[57] In these cases the Constitutional Tribunal must decide upon the constitutional issue.

### (e) The effects of judicial review

In all these five methods of judicial review of legislation, the decision of the Constitutional Tribunal has *erga omnes* effects.[58] The decision has also constitutive effects in the sense that it annuls the statute or the decree, *pro-*

*futuro, ex-nunc.* Nevertheless, the Tribunal has powers to annul statutes or decrees already repealed,[59] which, in principle, supposes the retroactive effects of the judicial review, this being an exception to the *ex-nunc* effects.

According to the general rule of prospectiveness, proposed as a matter of principle by Hans Kelsen,[60] the factual situations verified before the annulment of the statute or decree will continue to be submitted to its regulation, except in the case considered in the decision, unless the Tribunal decides otherwise.[61] Thus, the possible negative consequences of the *ex-nunc* rule, can be tempered by the Tribunal in its own decision.

In general, the effects of the Tribunal's decision only begin the day of the publication of the consequent repeal of the annulled act unless the Tribunal establishes a delay for the expiration of the effects of the annulled act[62] not in excess of one year. In such cases, and on a purely discretionary basis, the beginning of the *ex-nunc* effects due to the annulment of the statute, can be postponed by the Tribunal.

The annulment of statutes could bring about a situation in which other statutes previously repealed by the annulled one, will restart their validity beginning the day in which the annulment is effective, unless the Tribunal decides otherwise.[63] This confirms the *ex-nunc* effects.

The Constitutional Court has no power to annul treaties directly, but must only declare their unconstitutionality. This implies, first, that the treaty will not be applicable from the day in which the decision is made public by the state organ which is due to execute it, unless the Tribunal fixes a delay in which the treaty could continue to be applied.[64] Second, if the treaty is due to be applied by laws or decrees, any of these will cease to have effects.[65]

# 18

## JUDICIAL REVIEW IN THE FEDERAL REPUBLIC OF GERMANY: THE FEDERAL CONSTITUTIONAL TRIBUNAL

### (a) The Weimar antecedents

The basic elements for the development of a constitutional system of judicial review were established in Germany under the federal Weimar Constitution of 11 August 1919. These elements were dispersed among a set of courts and tribunals. In particular, a limited system of concentrated judicial review can be found within the powers attributed to the Tribunal of the Empire (*Reichsgericht*), the highest court in the ordinary judiciary, which had powers to resolve the compatibility of laws passed by member states of the Federation (the *Länder*) with Imperial legislation.[1] Another special court, the Tribunal of State Justice (*Staatsgerichthof*), had the special task of resolving constitutional litigation arising within any *Land* which lacked special courts to do so and of resolving public law conflicts arising between different *Länder* or between the Empire and a *Land*, when these cases fell outside the jurisdiction of any other court of justice of the Empire.[2] This Tribunal of State Justice was also empowered to try accusations against the President, the Chancellor and the Imperial Ministers, for infractions of the Constitution.[3]

Moreover, certain discussions occurred with regard to the powers of all courts to control the constitutionality of laws. In support of these discussions, certain judicial decisions were adopted in this respect by the Tribunal of the Empire. In the decision of the *Reichsgericht* of 4 November 1925, in accordance with Article 102 of the Constitution, the Tribunal stated

the submission of the judge to the law does not exclude the power of the judge to question the validity of statutes of the Empire or of certain of its dispositions when they are in opposition to other preeminent dispositions that must be observed by the judge. This is the case when a statute is in opposition to a juridical principle established in the Imperial Constitution...[4]

The Imperial Tribunal concluded:

The Imperial Constitution, not containing any disposition in accordance to which the decision upon the constitutionality of a statute of the Empire would have been taken away from the judges and transferred to another specific organ, the power and the duty of the judge to examine the constitutionality of statutes of the Empire must be recognised.[5]

Nevertheless, the situation of the system of judicial review up to 1933 was not completely clear so that judicial review of federal laws by all courts was not always accepted and was frequently criticized.[6] This led to an important change in the establishment of a system of constitutional justice in West Germany, in the Constitution of the Federal Republic of Germany of 23 May 1949.

### (b) The concentrated system of judicial review in West Germany and its co-existence with a limited diffuse system of review

The Constitution of 1949 created a Federal Constitutional Tribunal which, although considered part of the judicial power,[7] is the 'supreme guardian of the Constitution' [8] so that it has 'the last word on the construction of the Federal Constitution'.[9] To accomplish this role of constitutional judge, the Federal Constitutional Tribunal was organized in the federal law referred to in the Constitution,[10] as a constitutional organ of the federation, 'autonomous and independent regarding all other constitutional organs' [11] and with self-regulatory powers.[12]

The status of the Federal Constitutional Court, as a constitutional organ, is reflected in its composition. According to the Constitution, its members are elected by the fundamental politico-representative organs of the federation: the *Bundestag* (National Council) and the *Bundesrat* (Federal Council), in equal numbers in each case. Elected members may not be members of both Councils or of the federal government nor of any of the corresponding organs of a *Land*.[13] All the members of the Tribunal are considered to be federal judges, although only a proportion of them must be elected from active federal judges.[14]

Because of these constitutional provisions regarding the organization, composition and powers of the Federal Constitutional Court, it has been considered by one of its former presidents as a 'neutral power' within the state, with a constitutional pre-eminence over all other state organs. The various constitutional judicial review powers that the Constitution has assigned to it have been considered as 'not having been conferred to any other Constitutional Tribunal, or Supreme Court' in any other country.[15] This Tribunal, as the concentrated system's expression of judicial review, is established to 'protect the legislator against the ordinary judicial power'.[16]

The establishment of the Federal Constitutional Tribunal did not, however, completely eliminate the diffuse system of judicial review in West Germany. According to the general trend in all concentrated systems of judicial review, the concentration of the powers of constitutional justice in one single organ is only established regarding certain state acts, particularly legislative acts. As a result, all other state acts not specified in the concentrated powers are subject to the concept of the supremacy of the Constitution which allows all the other courts to control their constitutionality in a diffuse way. This general trend is followed in the West German system.

Since Article 93, Section 2 of the Federal Constitution gives the Federal Constitutional Tribunal the exclusive power to review the constitutionality of federal laws and laws of the *Länder*, statutes adopted before 1949 can be the object of judicial review in a diffuse system by all courts. Moreover, executive regulations or other normative decrees are not exclusively reserved to the Federal Constitutional Tribunal.[17] Nevertheless, pre-constitutional legislation can be constitutionally reviewed by the Federal Constitutional Tribunal but only by means of the direct action which leads to the abstract control of norms.[18] Consequently, the West German constitutional system has established a concentrated system of judicial review by attributing exclusive powers to the Federal Constitutional Tribunal to control the constitutionality of certain state acts while allowing the ordinary courts some power of review.

It must also be noted that each *Land* has its own constitutional court empowered to control the violations of the *Länder* Constitutions and to settle constitutional litigations within each *Land*.[19]

### (c) The Federal Constitutional Tribunal as a constitutional jurisdiction

At the federal level, however, the Federal Constitutional Tribunal as the supreme guardian of the Constitution has a monopoly of a very wide range of powers attributed to it in the Constitution.[20] These powers, all of a jurisdictional nature, can be classified into six groups of attributions through which the Tribunal guarantees the protection of the politico-constitutional order; the distribution of state powers; the electoral representative character of the political system; the protection of fundamental rights; the interpretation of the Constitution, and control of the constitutionality of all normative state acts.

The first group of jurisdictional powers of the Federal Constitutional Tribunal, relates to what may be called the protection of the politico-constitutional order embodied in the Constitution, or in other words, the protection of the state against actions taken by political parties, individuals or public officials. In relation to political parties, which in the constitutional system of the Federal Republic are the main means by which 'the political will of the people'[21] is formed, the Constitutional Tribunal is empowered to declare them unconstitutional, when 'by reason of their aims or the behaviour of their adherents [they] seek to impair or destroy the free democratic basic order or to endanger the existence of the Federal Republic of Germany'.[22]

The protection of the state against individuals is regulated in the Constitution particularly as a consequence of the abuse of certain freedoms and liberties, which could endanger the constitutional order. In this respect, the Federal Constitutional Tribunal is empowered[23] to decide upon the deprivation of the freedoms of speech, of the press, of education, of assembly, of association, of secrecy of mail, post and telecommunications, and the rights of property and of asylum, by those who abuse those rights in using them to fight against the fundamental and free democratic order and who consequently make themselves unworthy of those freedoms.[24] Regarding state officials, within the Constitutional Tribunal function as protector of the state, it is empowered to take cognizance of accusations brought against the Federal President by the *Bundestag* or the *Bundesrat* for voluntary infraction of the Constitution or of other federal laws[25] and also of accusations brought against federal judges who undermine the principles of the Constitution or the constitutional order of a *Land*.[26]

The second group of constitutional jurisdictional powers of the Federal Constitutional Tribunal relates to the institutional functioning of the state and empowers the Tribunal to resolve constitutional conflicts and litigations regarding the vertical and horizontal distribution of state powers.

With regard to the federal form of the state, the Tribunal has jurisdiction in cases of 'difference of opinion over the rights and duties of the Federation and the *Länder*, particularly in the execution of federal law by the *Länder* and in the exercise of federal supervision'.[27] It also has jurisdiction 'on other disputes involving public law, between the

Federation and the *Länder*, between different *Länder* or within a *Land*, unless recourse to another court exists'.[28]

With regard to the vertical distribution of powers, the Constitutional Tribunal has jurisdiction to resolve conflicts between the Federal and *Länder* powers and the municipalities, in the sense that it shall decide 'on the complaints of unconstitutionality, entered by municipalities or association of municipalities on the grounds that their right to self-government ... has been violated by a law other than a *Land* law open to complaint to the respective *Land* Constitutional Court'.[29] This competence leads directly to one of the means of judicial review of legislation.

Concerning the horizontal distribution of state power, the Federal Constitutional Tribunal shall decide upon the interpretation of the Constitution, 'in the event of disputes concerning the extent of the rights and duties of a highest federal organ or of other parties concerned who have been vested with rights of their own by the Constitution or by a regulation of the highest federal organ'.[30]

These 'highest federal organs' whose conflicts must be decided upon by the Tribunal, are the *Bundestag,* the *Bundesrat,* the President of the Federation, the Federal Government and the Permanent Commission of the *Bundestag*. The political parties have also been considered as having the right to allege violations to their rights as participants in constitutional life.[31]

The third group of constitutional jurisdictional powers attributed to the Federal Constitutional Tribunal concerns the electoral-representative basis of the political system. In relation to this the Tribunal must resolve 'the claims against the decisions of the *Bundestag* over the validity of an election or the acquisition or loss of the condition of representative to the *Bundestag*'[32] as well as recourses against referenda when a new division of the federal territory is adopted as a result of the modification of the boundaries of the *Länder*.[33]

The fourth group of constitutional jurisdictional powers assigned to the Constitutional Tribunal concerns the protection of fundamental rights and freedoms against the state. Specifically the Federal Constitution empowers the Tribunal to decide 'on complaints of unconstitutionality' which may be entered by any person who claims that one of his basic constitutional rights has been violated by public authority.[34] This power of the Constitutional Tribunal, established in the 1951 Statute of the Tribunal and regulated only in the 1969 amendment to the Constitution, has given rise to a very important recourse for the protection of fundamental rights against public authorities. Like the 'trial for *amparo*' developed in Latin American countries, the 'constitutional complaint' has contributed to the consideration of fundamental rights and freedoms as a limit upon the powers of the state.

The fifth group of constitutional jurisdictional powers of the Federal Constitutional Court related to constitutional justice, concerns the interpretation and application of the Constitution and of federal legislation. Two attributions of the Constitutional Tribunal can be distinguished regarding the interpretation of the Constitution: first, the power of the Tribunal to decide cases in which a Constitutional Court of a *Land* intends to deviate from a decision previously taken by the Federal Constitutional Tribunal or by the Constitutional Court of another *Land* when interpreting the Federal Constitution;[35] and second, the power of the Tribunal to resolve upon the continuity of the validity of a pre-constitutional law as federal law.[36]

Regarding the application of federal law, a third attribution of the Constitutional Tribunal may be distinguished with regard to international law which, in accordance with the Constitution, forms part of the federal law.[37] In this respect, if in the course of a litigation before a court, doubt exists as to whether a rule of public international law is an integral part of federal law and whether such a rule directly creates rights and duties for the individual, the court shall obtain a decision from the Federal Constitutional Court.[38]

Finally, the sixth group of constitutional jurisdictional powers attributed to the Federal Constitutional Tribunal are the powers to control the constitutionality of normative state acts. It is precisely this function of verifying the constitutionality of normative state acts, in which the character of the Tribunal reveals itself in full, as the constitutional organ laid down in the Constitution for the purpose of judicial review of legislation. In order to accomplish these functions, the constitutional questions regarding normative acts of the state can reach the Constitutional Tribunal by three methods: a direct request or complaint brought before the Tribunal; an incidental referral placed before the Tribunal by a lower court; or in an indirect way when the Constitutional Tribunal must decide upon the unconstitutionality of a state act, for the resolution of another of the constitutional jurisdictional proceedings different from the abstract or concrete control of normative acts of the state.

## (d) The constitutional control of normative state acts through direct requests or complains

The first method established in the Federal Constitution for the purpose of judicial review of state normative acts is through the exercise of a direct request, action, or complaint brought before the Federal Constitutional Tribunal. The purpose of this action is to seek a decision exclusively upon the unconstitutionality of a statute or other normative act of the state. This direct means for judicial review can be exercised through two specific actions: first, by a request formulated by some state organs, called the abstract control of norms; and second, by the exercise of a constitutional complaint brought by any person who claims that one of his fundamental rights has been violated by the specific statute or act, or by a municipality who claims that its right to self-government has been violated by a federal law.

### (i) The request for the abstract control of norms

The request for the abstract control of norms (*Die abstrakte Normenkontrolle*), that is to say, the exercise of judicial review powers by the Constitutional Tribunal without reference to a particular case or process, is established in Article 93, Section 1, No. 2 of the Constitution, when it states that the Constitutional Tribunal shall decide:

in case of differences of opinion or doubts on the formal and material compatibility of federal law or *Land* law with this Basic Law, or on the compatibility of *Land* law with other federal laws, at the request of the Federal Government, of a *Land* Government or of one third of the *Bundestag* members.[39]

This power attributed to the Constitutional Tribunal has led to the development of what may be called an 'objective' judicial review proceeding because it has as its only purpose the ensuring of the maintenance of the hierarchy of norms, in an abstract way.[40]

As indicated earlier, the Constitution gives the right to formulate the request only to the federal government, the government of a *Land* and to one third of the *Bundestag* members.[41] It also establishes that the representatives of the interested constitutional organs that have participated in the formation of the challenged normative act must be heard[42] by the Tribunal. Nevertheless, it must be said that in the proceeding there are no proper parties.[43] The request, in fact, is formulated against a state act, not against a state organ, and the Constitutional Tribunal must decide the constitutional question in an abstract way, being allowed moreover to raise other constitutional questions *ex officio* regarding the challenged act or any of its articles.[44]

The objective character of the proceeding and the powers of the Constitutional Tribunal as a guardian of the Constitution are furthermore confirmed by the fact that even when a request is withdrawn by the state organ, the Tribunal can continue the proceeding when it is justified as being in the general interest.[45]

On the other hand, it must be said that this objective proceeding for the abstract control of norms refers to all normative state acts. Thus, it is not a proceeding for the sole purpose of judicial review of legislative acts in its formal sense, but can be referred to any other normative act of the state, including pre-constitutional statutes, executive normative decrees and international treaties and even constitutional amendments.[46] In particular, all the statutes through which international treaties are approved are subject to judicial review. This has occurred, for example, in relation to state acts concerning the laws of the European Community.[47] With regard to treaties, the Constitutional Tribunal's decision upon the constitutionality of its approving statute must be adopted after its sanction but before the treaty comes into effect.[48]

### (ii) The constitutional complaint against statutes

The abstract control of norms can also be exercised by the Federal Constitutional Tribunal as a result of a constitutional complaint that any person can bring before the Tribunal when he claims that one of his basic or fundamental rights has been directly violated by a normative state act. This 'constitutional complaint', only constitutionalized in 1969, was originally established in the 1951 Federal Statute of the Constitutional Tribunal[49] and is conceived as a special judicial means for the protection of fundamental rights and freedoms against any action of the state organs which violates them. Therefore, it is not a specific action to obtain judicial review of legislation, but it can be used for that purpose when exercised against a statute. If the statute is contrary to the Constitution, it must be annulled.

The constitutional complaint after the 1969 constitutional amendment is expressly established in Article 93, Section 1, No. 4a of the Constitution when attributing the Federal Constitutional Tribunal power to decide 'on complaints of unconstitutionality, which may be entered by any person who claims that one of his basic rights or one of his rights under paragraph (4) of Article 20, under Articles 33, 38, 101, 103, or 104 has been violated by public authority'.[50] Therefore, the constitutional complaint can be brought before the Tribunal against any state act, whether legislative, executive or judicial, but in all cases, it can only be exercised once the ordinary judicial means for the protection of the fundamental rights have been exhausted.[51] The only exceptions are when the Constitutional Tribunal considers the matter as being of general importance or when it considers that the claimant is threatened by a grave and irremediable prejudice if it is sent to the ordinary judicial means for protection.[52]

The basic condition for the admissibility of constitutional complaints against laws is that the challenged statute or normative state act must personally affect the claimant's fundamental rights, in a direct and current way, without the need for any further administrative application of the norm. If a further administrative application is needed, the claimant must wait for the administrative execution of the statute and complain against it. This direct prejudice caused by the normative act on the rights of the claimant, as a basic element for the admissibility of the complaint, justifies the delay of one year after its publication established for the introduction of the action before the Tribunal.[53] It also explains the power of the Constitutional Tribunal to adopt provisional protective measures regarding the challenged statute, *pendente litis*, in the sense that the Tribunal can even theoretically suspend the application of the challenged law.[54]

With regard to this constitutional complaint, Article 93, Section 1, No. 4b of the Constitution empowers the Constitutional Tribunal to decide: 'on complaints of unconstitutionality, entered by communes [municipalities] or association of communes [municipalities] on the ground that their right to self-government under Article 28 has been violated by a law other than a *Land* law open to complaint to the respective *Land* constitutional court'. The direct constitutional complaint against laws, therefore, is not only attributed to individuals for the protection of their fundamental rights, but also to the local government entities for the protection of their autonomy and right to self government guaranteed in the Constitution. In these cases, it also results in a direct means of judicial review of legislation.

### (e) The incidental method of judicial review

Article 100 of the Constitution establishes an incidental method of judicial review called the concrete control of norms (*Konkrete Normenkontrolle*) as follows:

If a court considers unconstitutional a law the validity of which is relevant to its decision, the proceeding shall be stayed, and a decision shall be obtained from the *Land* court competent for constitutional disputes if the Constitution of a *Land* is held to be violated, or from the Federal Constitutional Court if this Basic Law is held to be violated. This shall also apply if this Basic Law is held to be violated by *Land* Law or if a *Land* Law is held to be incompatible with a federal law.[55]

Contrary to the abstract control of norms by direct petition, the concrete control of norms only refers to statutes in the sense of formal law.[56] In this incidental method of judicial review, the constitutional question of a statute always reaches the Constitutional Tribunal through the referral made by any court.[57] The referral is made as a result of a concrete proceeding before the court when a law is considered unconstitutional. So long as the validity of the law is relevant to its decision, the court must suspend the case and refer the constitutional question. The judge must be convinced of the unconstitutionality of the statute and lay the foundations of his referral to the Tribunal by explaining in which way his decision depends on the validity of the statute, and with which constitutional disposition the law is incompatible.[58] Once the Constitutional Tribunal decides upon the constitutional question, the lower court must resume the suspended proceedings and render a judgement consistent with that of the Constitutional Tribunal.[59]

While the courts do not have the power to declare statutes null, and do not have *ex officio* power to decide not to apply them, they do have the power to appreciate the unconstitutionality of the statutes[60] by formulating a referral of a constitutional question before the Constitutional Tribunal. This power can be exercised *ex officio*.[61]

The powers of the Constitutional Tribunal are limited to the consideration of the constitutional question raised in the referral. Thus the Constitutional Tribunal does not review the case on its merits and only decides the question of whether or not the statute which a lower court considers unconstitutional is repugnant to the Constitution. These restrictions make this proceeding an objective one.[62]

### (f) The indirect method of judicial review

This indirect method for judicial review of the unconstitutionality of statutes can be developed in the following principal situations. First, it can be developed as a consequence of a constitutional complaint for the protection of a fundamental right when exercised, not directly against a statute, but against a judicial decision which is considered to have violated the rights and freedoms of a person because it applied a statute which is alleged to have been unconstitutional.[63] In this case, the Constitutional Tribunal must decide upon the unconstitutionality of the statute indirectly challenged before it.

In the second place, according to Article 93, 1, 4, of the Constitution, the Constitutional Tribunal exercises its powers of judicial review when deciding upon conflicts between constitutional organs of the federation,[64] that is to say, disputes concerning the extent of the rights and duties of the highest federal organs established in the Constitution. These cases of conflict can lead to an indirect control of the constitutionality of statutes only when the act that causes prejudices to the rights and duties of a state organ is a statute. In this case, however, it is considered that the court does not have powers of annulment regarding the statute unless the abstract control of norms method is accumulated.[65]

### (g) The effects of the decisions of the Federal Constitutional Tribunal on judicial review and its *ex-officio* powers

When exercising its powers of judicial review of the constitutionality of normative state acts, the general rule is that the Tribunal declares the nullity of the unconstitutional provision of the statute or normative act. In this respect, Article 78 of the Federal Law of the Constitutional Tribunal establishes that: 'If the Constitutional Tribunal reaches the conviction that the federal law is incompatible with the Constitution, or that the law of a *Land* is incompatible with the Constitution or with another norm of federal law, it declares its nullity in its decision.' [66]

This decision can be in accordance with the contents of the petition, the constitutional complaint or the court referral, according to the method used for obtaining judicial review. However, in accepting jurisdiction the Constitutional Tribunal is not bound by the contents of the complaint, but has *ex officio* powers to raise another constitutional question and to decide *ultra petita*. That is why the same Article 78 of the Federal Law of the Constitutional Tribunal establishes that 'If other dispositions of the same statute are incompatible with the Constitution, or another norm of federal law, the Constitutional Tribunal can declare them null at the same time.'

The decisions of the Constitutional Tribunal are always obligatory for all constitutional organs of the Federation and of the *Länder*, as well as for all the authorities, the courts[67] and of course, for the individual. Thus, the court's decisions, have *erga omnes* effects, particularly in cases of abstract or concrete control of norms, and the decision has the same force as a statute[68] in the sense that its obligatory *erga omnes* character includes the Constitutional Court itself.[69]

Contrary to Hans Kelsen's conception of the effects of the decision of the constitutional judge,[70] yet in accordance with the German constitutional tradition[71] in cases of abstract and concrete control of norms, when the Constitutional Tribunal decides that a statute is contrary to the Constitution, it is understood that it is declared null and void *ab initio*, that is to say, the decision of the Tribunal has *ex-tunc*, retroactive effects.[72] This traditional doctrine is confirmed by the fact that the legislator, in the Federal Law of the Constitutional Tribunal, has expressly limited its scope by establishing that after a statute has been declared null because of its unconstitutionality, only criminal proceedings can be reviewed in cases in which the final judicial decision would have been based on the said statute declared null.[73] All other final and non-reviewable judgements and administrative acts resting on the statute declared null, will stand unchangeable, but their enforceability, if not yet made, would be illicit.[74]

Since a presumption of constitutionality of statutes[75] exists as a matter of principle, the Constitutional Tribunal has tended not to declare statutes null on the grounds of unconstitutionality if it is possible to interpret them as consistent with the Constitution. In this sense, the Constitutional Tribunal in many cases has followed the method of 'interpretation according to the Constitution' so as to avoid making a declaration of the nullity of a statute.[76]

In other cases, in order to avoid a possible vacuum in the legal order that could be produced by the nullity of the state act, the declaration of nullity is not adopted. Instead, the Tribunal only declares its 'simple unconstitutionality' and in some cases has referred the matter to the legislator to rectify the unconstitutional disposition.[77] Finally, in other cases, the Constitutional Tribunal, although considering a statute consistent with the Constitution, has nevertheless referred the matter to the legislator with indications for the rectification of the statute so as to convert it into being 'absolutely constitutional' and therefore avoiding any possible future declaration upon its unconstitutionality.[78]

# 19

## JUDICIAL REVIEW IN ITALY:
## THE CONSTITUTIONAL COURT

### (a) The constitutional compromise
### and the Constitutional Court as its guarantor

Immediately after the Second World War, yet before the creation of the Federal Constitutional Tribunal in the Federal Republic of Germany, the Constitution of the Italian Republic of 1 January 1948 created a Constitutional Court charged with controlling the constitutionality of statutes and other state acts with the same force. Nevertheless the system only started to function in 1956 when the Constitutional Court initiated its activities. Up to that year, the pre-1948 diffuse system of judicial review persisted according to which all ordinary courts had the power not to apply statutes they considered unconstitutional.[1]

The radical change in the system can be attributed to various factors, but primarily to a rigidity in the 1948 Constitution in contrast to the flexibility of the monarchical Fundamental Law (*Statuti Albertini*) of 1848.[2] Particularly after the totalitarian experiment of fascism, there was a need to protect the Constitution, and fundamental rights and freedoms, against legislative power.[3] The Constitutional Court, therefore, was conceived as the organ in charge of the guarantee of the 'constitutional compromise' embodied in the Constitution to establish a democratic regime in which the powers of the state organs were limited.[4] As a former member of the Constitutional Court said: 'The Court is the constitutional organ which secures the balance among the various powers of the state, preventing any one of them from trespassing the limits imposed by the Constitution, and thus ensures an orderly development of public life and the observance of the Constitutional rights of citizens.'[5]

As the Constitutional Court in Italy is the guarantor of the Constitution,[6] it was established as a 'constitutional organ'[7] independent from all other state organs, although in a less expressly positive law way than the Federal Constitutional Tribunal in West Germany[8] or the

Constitutional Tribunal in Spain.[9] Nevertheless, the position of the Constitutional Court as an independent and paritarian constitutional organ has been recognized, and is reflected in various aspects concerning the status of its members; its administrative and budgetary autonomy; the absence of any external control that could be exercised over it;[10] and its auto-regulatory powers.[11]

Furthermore, the independence of the Constitutional Court from the traditional organs of the state is guaranteed by Constitutional Law No. 1 of February 1948. This independence results from the paritarian form established for the appointment of its members, which is attributed not only to the politico-representative organs of the state as is the case in West Germany, but to the three traditional powers of the state: the President of the Republic, the Parliament and the judicial power. In accordance with the Constitution and Statute No. 87 (1953) concerning the Court,[12] the Constitutional Court is composed of fifteen members, appointed in the following manner: five are appointed by the ordinary and administrative judicial order, as follows: three by the Court of Cassation, one by the Council of State and one by the Court of Accounts, chosen from among members of the judiciary, even if they are retired members. The second five members are elected by Parliament, both chambers sitting in joint session, by a majority of three fifths of the members of the Assembly. They are chosen from among judges, ordinary professors of law in universities, or lawyers having practised twenty years or more before the supreme judicial organs of the Republic. The last five members are appointed by the President of the Republic.

Although the Constitutional Court is not a judicial organ, discussions were held at the beginning of its functioning regarding the nature of the powers it exercised. It was at this time that its judicial character was rejected, and Kelsen's idea of the negative legislator was initially accepted.[13] Today the jurisdictional character of the functions of the Court is the predominant thesis.[14] Thus, like the other European Constitutional Courts, particularly the Austrian and Spanish Tribunals, the Constitutional Court in Italy is conceived as a constitutional body, separate and independent from the judiciary,[15] and with the jurisdictional function of resolving and deciding upon conflicts regarding the constitutionality of state acts and the submission of all the activities of the state organs to the Constitution. As in Austria and the Federal Republic of Germany, the Italian Constitutional Court not only has powers of judicial review of legislation, but has power also to settle other constitutional disputes which arise as a result of the vertical and horizontal systems of distribution of state powers adopted in the Constitution.

## (b) The jurisdiction of the Constitutional Court

In effect, three main sets of competences of the Constitutional Court can be identified in accordance with the Constitution. The first general attribution of the Constitutional Court is related to the settlement of 'conflict of attribution' which may arise among the powers of the state. These conflicts of attributions or powers can derive from the vertical distribution of state powers, particularly regarding the Regions, and the horizontal distribution of state powers among the constitutional organs.

The Italian Republic has been constitutionally organized as a regional or decentralized state. Thus there is a basic distribution or political decentralization of state powers in the vertical sense, over territorially autonomous units, called Regions. Thus if the national state invades the sphere of regional authority or if a Region exceeds its own sphere[16] invading the national state power, or if the Regions invade each other's powers, the Constitutional Court has jurisdiction. The conflict, in such cases, arises as a consequence of administrative acts. Thus, when rendering a decision the Constitutional Court not only decides to which level of state powers the challenged attribution belongs, but has the power to annul the administrative act that brought it about[17] and to suspend *pendente litis* its effects, when serious reasons to do so exist.[18] These are the only cases in which the Italian Constitutional Court can declare the nullity of an administrative act.[19]

If the conflicts of attributions between the state and the Regions have their origin in legislative acts of the state, their resolution by the Constitutional Court is made through a direct means for judicial review of legislation exercised by the Regions.

Conflicts may also arise between the powers constitutionally assigned to the various national constitutional organs. In this respect, the Constitutional Court also has jurisdiction to resolve these conflicts 'for the delimitation of the sphere of attributions determined for the various powers by constitutional norms'.[20] These horizontal constitutional organs will include the Chamber of Deputies, the Senate, the President of the Republic and Parliament. Other state institutions are also included, for instance, the Superior Council of the Judiciature, the Court of Accounts, and the National Economic Council. In this respect a former Constitutional Court judge has said that the expression 'state powers' must be understood to comprise 'all the bodies of the state organization which, in accordance with the constitutional order, are in such a situation that its activities are not subject to any kind of external control by any other state organ [even constitutional state organs]'.[21]

In all these cases of conflicts of attributions between constitutional organs of the state, the Constitutional Court must resolve the sphere of attributions conferred upon the various state powers by constitutional norms,[22] and must declare to which state organ the challenged power belongs. When an act has been produced which infringes a constitutional norm, the Court must annul it.[23]

The second general competence of the Constitutional Court refers to cases of accusations against or impeachment of the President of the Republic for crimes of undermining the Constitution and high treason, and against the President of the Council of Ministers and the Ministers for crimes committed by them in the exercise of their functions.[24] The accusation in these cases can only be brought before the Court by Parliament, which must vote on it in a joint session of its two chambers.

The third jurisdictional power of the Constitutional Court refers to referenda, and the Constitution empowers the Court to judge upon the admissibility of derogatory referenda that can be presented for the abrogation of ordinary laws, exception being made of taxation and budget laws, laws granting amnesty and pardon, and laws authorizing the ratification of international treaties.[25] Nevertheless, the statute referred to in Article 75 of the Constitution, that must regulate the above mentioned admissibility conditions and modalities for the derogatory referenda, has not yet been approved.

Finally, the fourth set of jurisdictional powers of the Constitutional Court of Italy refers to judicial review of the constitutionality of legislation, that is to say, to statutes and other state acts with the same force. Thus, the Italian Court does not have jurisdiction over electoral matters and political parties[26] as the West German Federal Constitutional Tribunal has, and, more important, the Italian Constitutional Court does not have powers to act as a direct guarantor of fundamental rights and freedoms, not having attributions to decide upon constitutional complaints or recourses for constitutional protection as they exist in the West German, Austrian and Spanish systems of constitutional justice.[27] Nevertheless, the need for a direct action before the Constitutional Court was a matter of discussion during the drafting of the Constitution, and in one of the first drafts of the text the main form of judicial review of legislation was established. This was a direct recourse of unconstitutionality that could be brought before the Constitutional Court, as an *actio popularis*, accessible to all citizens without the need of an injury to be done to their subjective rights. The action needed to be exercised during a one year period after the publication of the statute.[28] This proposal for a popular action of unconstitutionality was later rejected, mainly due to political reasons,[29] so that the means for judicial review of legislation was reduced to an incidental system of judicial review concentrated in the Constitutional Court, combined with a limited principal means of review and a preventive system established only regarding certain state acts.

### (c) The scope of judicial review in the Italian system

As the Italian system of judicial review is a concentrated system, the Constitutional Court is the only state body to have exclusive jurisdiction to determine the conformity of legislation with the Constitution. The term 'legislation' comprises all statutes and other state acts with the force of law,[30] whether of the national state or of the Regions, as well as executive decrees[31] – laws enacted by virtue of parliamentary delegation or in time of urgency[32] and considered as being 'acts with force of law'. Moreover, the *interna corporis* of Parliament which are done under the direct authority of the Constitution are also subject to constitutional control.[33]

A few questions have been raised regarding the scope of judicial review concerning legislative acts. The first issue refers to whether the Constitutional Court has power to exercise control over laws which were passed before the enactment of the Constitution and which could be considered to have been tacitly repealed by it. However, this control is only exercised through the incidental method when an issue of constitutionality is raised before an ordinary judge in a concrete case and is then referred to the Constitutional Court.[34]

A second question is whether it is possible to raise the issue of constitutionality with respect to repealed laws which have already lost their force. The Italian Constitutional Court has repeatedly declared its competence to hear disputes concerning the constitutionality of these repealed laws, considering that they could have created situations, the persistence of which after their repeal, could have justified constitutional control.[35]

A third issue is concerned with the question of whether the Constitutional Court can only determine whether a statute is consistent with the Constitution in its normative contents or not, or whether it also has formal control over the procedures followed for its sanctioning, which has been accepted.[36]

Article 138 of the Constitution permits the enactment of constitutional laws in accordance with the Constitution. This creates a '*bloc* of constitutionality' composed of the Constitution, the principles which can be deduced from the constitutional text, and the 'constitutional laws'. Although the 'constitutional laws' are regulated by the Constitution which establishes their scope and possible contents, they can also be submitted to constitutional review by the Constitutional Court.[37]

Finally, discussions have arisen as a consequence of the terms used in Article 134 of the Constitution, indicating that the Constitutional Court has jurisdiction to settle disputes dealing with 'constitutional legitimacy' of laws and state acts with force of law.[38] Although this article could be interpreted as meaning that the Court could control the merits of legislative activities, the 1953 Statute No. 87 of the Constitutional Court expressly states: 'The Constitutional Court control over the legitimacy of laws or an act with force of law, excludes any value judgement of policy nature and any judgement upon the use Parliament makes of its discretionary power.' But even with a text of this clarity, the Constitutional Court has, since 1960, controlled the 'arbitrariness' of the legislator based on the principles of equality and non discrimination controlling the 'rationality' of the distinctions established in legislation.[39]

### (d) The incidental method of judicial review

The basic means for raising questions of constitutionality of legislation and undoubtedly the most important means for keeping statutes and legislative acts within the framework of the Constitution is the incidental method. This is expressly regulated in the 1948 Constitutional Statute No. 1, which contained the norms related to the trials of constitutional illegitimacy and to the independence guarantees of the Constitutional Court. Article 1 of that Constitutional Statute states:

The question of the constitutional illegitimacy of a law [statute] or of an act of the Republic with force of law, raised *ex officio* or alleged by one of the parties in the course of a trial, and not evidently considered unfounded by the judge, must be referred to the Constitutional Court for its consideration.

This incidental method of judicial review is regulated by the 1953 Statute No. 87 in which its fundamental provisions are to be found, and therein reinforces the concentrated-incidental character of the Italian system of judicial review.[40]

In accordance with this 1953 Statute No. 87, in the course of an independent process developed before a court, either party, or the Public Prosecutor, may raise the question of constitutional legitimacy in the form of a petition. This must allege, firstly the provisions of the law or the act with force of law of the state or of the Region which contains defects of 'constitutional illegitimacy'; and secondly, the provisions of the Constitution or of the 'constitutional laws' which have been violated.

If the judge considers that the issue of constitutionality has sufficient basis and its resolution is essential for the decision of the process, then he must decide upon the existence of both conditions and therefore refer the question to the Constitutional Court, sending with the referral the statement made by the parties or by the Public Prosecutor and the whole file of the case, whose proceedings must be suspended. The constitutional question alleged by the parties or by the Public Prosecutor can be rejected by the judge, in a motivated decision, when he considers that it has no relevance to the case or has no due foundation. However, this rejection does not prevent the parties from later raising the question in any stage of the proceedings.[41]

However the 1948 Constitutional Statute No. 1 and the 1953 Statute No. 87 state that the issue of constitutional legitimacy may also be raised, *ex officio*, by the judge hearing the case. In this event he must also take a decision in which he must include the precise indication of the provisions of the law, or of the acts with the force of law considered unconstitutional, as well as the norms of the Constitution or of the constitutional laws deemed to have been violated by the challenged statute. The judge must also justify in his decision the prejudicial character of the question and the reasons for considering the statute unconstitutional.

Furthermore, the Constitutional Court is not bound by the will of the parties to the original process in which the constitutional issue was raised. Accordingly, although the parties of the *a quo* process may be called upon and heard, as can the executive authority concerned (President of the Council of Ministers or of the Regional Board),[42] the proceeding developed before the Court is not an adversary one developed *inter partes*. Instead it is of a non adversary and objective nature, developed independent of the will of the parties so that even in cases of abandonment of action or when a voluntary dismissal of the case has taken place,[43] the court can continue to decide the constitutional issue.

The effectiveness of the incidental method of constitutional review of legislation has been criticized in the following manner in relation to statutes that could directly affect individual rights:

The inconvenience of this system results from the fact that certain statutes, particularly those called by the Mexican constitutional doctrine *auto-applicable* [auto-effective or auto-executive], could immediately infringe the juridical sphere of certain individuals, without the need of being 'concretized' by an executive or applicative act: thus, at least regarding these laws, the sole incidental control of constitutional legitimacy, could appear as insufficient.[44]

### (e) The direct method of judicial review and its regional scope

But in spite of its predominantly incidental-concentrated character, the Italian system of judicial review also allows a direct method of judicial review. This power is limited and relates very closely to the powers of the Court to resolve conflicts of attributions between state and Regions.

Article 2 of Constitutional Statute No. 1 of 9 February 1948 provides certain circumstances in which a constitutional question can be brought before the Constitutional Court by a direct action that can only be exercised by a Region against national legislation or statutes of other Regions. This article states the following:

When a Region deems that a statute or an act with force of law of the Republic invades the sphere of competences attributed to it in the Constitution, it can present before the Court, upon deliberation of the Regional Board, the question of constitutional illegitimacy within thirty days of the publication of the statute or of the act with force of law.[45]

This action cannot be brought before the Court by the Republic against the regional statutes. In these cases the question must be treated as a conflict of attributions in the sense already mentioned.[46]

Yet the direct action can also be brought by a Region against a statute or another act with force of law of another Region when it deems its competences have been violated by the other Region.[47] The proceedings in cases of direct action are considered more of an adversary process than the incidental method since in the direct action the will of the parties carries weight in the sense that the 'waiver of the action, if accepted by all parties, extinguishes the proceeding'.[48]

### (f) The preventive method of judicial review of regional legislation

The Constitution also establishes a preventive means of judicial review although limited to controlling only the constitutionality of regional legislation.[49] In these cases the Council of Ministers has the power to bring a direct action against regional statutes, before their enactment, within fifteen days following the formal information that the President of the Regional Board must send when a regional bill is approved in a second vote by the Regional Council.[50] In these cases, when the preventive judicial review request is brought before the Court, the enactment of the challenged regional statute must be suspended until a decision is adopted.[51] If it is unconstitutional, its promulgation is impossible.

### (g) The effects of the Constitutional Court decisions

In all cases of judicial review of the constitutionality of legislation, the Constitutional Court must decide, within the limits of the action or referral,[52] which are the norms considered illegitimate or unconstitutional. Thus, in accordance with the terms of Statute No. 87, it has been considered that the Constitutional Court does not have *ex officio* powers to consider other constitutional issues different from those submitted to it either by the incidental method or by the direct method. In this respect, the Court has powers only to declare 'which other legislative dispositions whose illegitimacy is a consequence of the decision adopted'.[53]

The Constitutional Court decision also has *erga omnes* effects so that the act 'cannot be applied onwards from the day following the publication of the decision'.[54] Therefore, it must be considered that the decision has a constitutive character[55] in the sense that it annuls the unconstitutional statute, its effect being *ex-nunc, pro futuro*. This rule has been widely discussed[56] and the Constitutional Court has interpreted the constitutional norm (Article 136) which states that the act declared unconstitutional cannot be applied onwards from the day after the publication of the Court decision, in the sense that

the decision upon the unconstitutionality, if it is true that it leaves out all the effects irrevocably produced by the norm declared unconstitutional, on the contrary it produces effects upon the juridical situations not yet exhausted, when they are still susceptible to being regulated in a different manner as a consequence of the decision. Thus the declaration of unconstitutionality of a statute produces its inapplicability to all the relations judicially controverted as and when they are still not the object of a decision with *res judicata* force, with the consequence that in all stages of the trial, the judge even *ex-officio* must take into account the said decision of constitutional illegitimacy when deciding the concrete juridical relation of a case, in the same way and to the same extent as if it were a *ius superveniens*.[57]

Nevertheless, retroactive effects are only applicable in criminal cases, when a judicial condemnation has been pronounced based on a statute declared unconstitutional. In these cases, the execution of the law and its penal effects must cease.[58] Another indirect exception of the *ex-nunc* effects of the decision results from the already mentioned possibility of annulment of statutes already repealed.[59]

The same cannot be said with regard to decisions which reject the question of unconstitutionality for lack of foundation. Initially Professor Calamandrei maintained that these decisions were to be considered authentic interpretations of the Constitution and so should have *erga omnes* effects to prevent future challenges.[60] Discussions have taken place regarding the matter and as a result the Constitutional Court has limited the effects, of its decisions declaring the lack of foundation of the unconstitutionality issue, to the principal process in which the issue was first raised.[61] To reach this conclusion, it has been considered that because the general norm of the Italian legal system is to limit the effects of judicial decisions to the case in dispute, the norm of Article 136 of the Constitution, which attributes *erga omnes* effects to declarations of unconstitutionality, has an exceptional character and cannot be the object of extensive interpretation. The result is that an *erga omnes* character cannot be applied to decisions which dismiss or reject issues of unconstitutionality.[62]

Another criterion that has been exposed is that of the preclusive effect of the Court decision, in the sense that the incidental question of constitutionality cannot be raised twice in the same process in its original form. Nevertheless, this does not preclude the possibility of it being raised in another process, or even, that the parties could raise new issues of unconstitutionality judged negatively by the Court on a previous occasion.[63]

# 20

## JUDICIAL REVIEW IN SPAIN:
## THE CONSTITUTIONAL TRIBUNAL

### (a) The Second Spanish Republic antecedents: the Constitutional Guarantees Tribunal

In the Second Spanish Republic, in accordance with the Constitution of 9 December 1931, a Tribunal of Constitutional Guarantees was created. The system established was a concentrated one under the direct influence of the Austrian experience and the ideas of Hans Kelsen,[1] although the historical antecedents in the projects of the First Republic in 1873[2] resulted in certain particular Spanish characteristics.

The 1931 judicial review system gave the Tribunal of Constitutional Guarantees exclusive powers to judge the constitutionality of statutes, through two methods: an incidental and a principal one. Additionally, the Constitution regulated a recourse of constitutional protection (*recurso de amparo*) which was to be exercised before the Tribunal for the protection of fundamental rights.

The incidental means for judicial review was established in Article 100 of the Constitution which stated that 'When a court of justice would have to apply a law which it deems to be contrary to the Constitution, it must suspend the proceeding and send a consultative request to the Tribunal of Constitutional Guarantees.' Additionally, the Constitution assigned competence to the Tribunal of Constitutional Guarantees to take cognizance of the 'recourse of unconstitutionality of laws'.[3] This was originally conceived as an autonomous action which could be exercised before the Tribunal by the public prosecutor, the government of the Republic, the Regions and by 'any individual or collective person even if it was not directly injured'.[4] Later this was converted into a popular action.

Although judicial review was broadly established in the 1931 Constitution in the sense of having both a direct and an indirect method, the methods of review were reduced in the Organic Law of the Tribunal enacted in 1933. There the 'recourse of unconstitutionality of laws' was

225

conceived only as an incidental means of judicial review, sought *ex officio* by a court or as a consequence of an exception raised in a concrete proceeding by the party whose rights could be affected by the application of the challenged statute, or by the public prosecutor.[5] In this way the system was distanced from the Austrian model. Following trends of the diffuse system of judicial review, the effects of the Tribunal decisions declaring the unconstitutionality of state acts were reduced from being *erga omnes* to applying only in 'the concrete case of the recourse or the consultation'. Thus, the statutes were not annulled by the Tribunal but only considered inapplicable to the concrete case.[6] The Organic Law of the Constitutional Guarantees Tribunal was broadly criticised for this restriction and was the first to be the object of an action of unconstitutionality.[7] In any case, less than five years after the promulgation of the Constitution it was repealed in 1936 and with it the system of judicial control of constitutionality was eliminated. It has only been with the publication of the new democratic Constitution of 27 December 1978 that a system of judicial review has been re-established in Spain. Similarly a Constitutional Tribunal was created and is now regulated in the Organic Law of the Constitutional Tribunal of 3 October 1979.[8]

### (b) The Constitutional Tribunal as a European model

Having been established after the consolidation of the main continental European experiences of constitutional justice, the Spanish judicial review system adopted the most important features of the West German, Italian and French systems. Prior to the creation of the Constitutional Tribunal in Spain, the Federal Constitutional Tribunal of West Germany had the widest jurisdiction on constitutional matters in the world;[9] after 1978 this assertion was no longer true[10] as the Constitutional Tribunal of Portugal established in the 1982 constitutional revision has succeeded that position.

Not only is the Constitutional Tribunal able to review the constitutionality of laws, but, as in other European countries, pre-constitutional legislation is reviewable in a diffuse way by all courts as well as by the Tribunal.[11] This is a result of Derogatory-Disposition No. 3 which states that 'all dispositions repugnant to what is established in this Constitution are repealed'.

As the Constitutional Tribunal is conceived in the Constitution as a constitutional organ, independent and separate from the judicial power but with jurisdictional functions as the guarantor of the constitutionality of state action,[12] the Spanish system is illustrative of a concentrated system of judicial review. In this respect, Article 1 of the Organic Law 2/1979 concerning the Tribunal expressly establishes that 'The Constitutional Tribunal, as the supreme interpreter of the Constitution, is independent from the other constitutional organs and it is only submitted to the Constitution and to this Organic Law.'

According to Article 159 of the Constitution, the Tribunal is composed of twelve members appointed from among magistrates and public prosecutors, university professors, public officials and qualified lawyers with over fifteen years in practice. The members of the Tribunal are appointed by the king, in the following manner: four are appointed on the proposal of a three fifths majority of the members of Congress; four on the proposal of the same majority of the Senate; two on the government's proposal; and two on the proposal of the General Council of the Judiciary. Thus, as in the Italian system, all the three traditional powers of the state intervene in the appointment of the members of the Tribunal.

As in the other European systems, the Constitution is quite explicit as to the political incompatibilities with respect to its members. It stipulates that the status of being a member of the Constitutional Tribunal is incompatible with any representative mandate, with political and administrative posts, with directive functions in a political party or trade union, or employment by them, with a judicial or public prosecutor career and with any other professional or commercial activity. It is also stipulated that the members of the Constitutional Tribunal have the same incompatibility as the members of the judiciary.

The competences of the Tribunal can be classified into three main groups: the resolution of constitutional conflicts between state powers; the decision of the recourses of constitutional protection (*recursos de amparo*) of fundamental rights; and the control of the constitutionality of legislation.

The first major group of powers assigned to the Constitutional Tribunal refer to the resolution of constitutional conflicts between state organs and is in accordance with the vertical and horizontal systems of distribution of state powers adopted by the Constitution. The Constitution has created various Regions as Autonomous Communities, in a similar way to the Regional state formula of the Italian Constitution.[13] The Constitutional Tribunal is therefore, empowered to resolve 'the conflicts of attributions between the state and the Autonomous Communities' and conflicts between the latter. Within this context the Constitutional Tribunal is also empowered to resolve those conflicts that confront 'the

Government with the Congress of Deputies, the Senate or the General Council of the Judiciary; or any of those constitutional organs between themselves'.[14]

The justification of the competence of the Constitutional Tribunal in conflicts between constitutional bodies, as in all the other European constitutional justice systems, seems evident. Any conflict between political entities is, in itself, a constitutional conflict, which questions the organic system established by the Constitution itself. Consequently, the Constitutional Tribunal is the only adequate body for the settlement of such conflicts.

The judgements pronounced in the settlement of conflicts of competence have *inter partes* effects and the content of these judgements consists of a declaration on the entitlement of the constitutional bodies to the competence in dispute.[15] However, when the declaration on entitlement implies the declaration of the nullity[16] of the normative provision issued by the body declared to be incompetent, the judgement must be published for it to have *erga omnes* effects.[17]

The second attribution of the Constitutional Tribunal relates to the decision of the *recursos de amparo* (recourse for constitutional protection) which can be brought directly by individuals to the Constitutional Tribunal. To sustain this action the individual's constitutional rights and liberties must have been violated by dispositions, juridical acts, or simple factual actions of the public powers of the state, the Autonomous Communities or other public territorial entities or by their officials.[18] Unlike the West German system, this recourse for the protection of fundamental rights cannot be exercised against statutes which violate fundamental rights in a direct way.[19] It can only be exercised against administrative or judicial acts and acts without force of law produced by the legislative authorities,[20] and only when the ordinary judicial means for the protection of fundamental rights have been exhausted.[21] Consequently, the recourse for *amparo* in general, results in a direct action against judicial acts[22] and can only indirectly lead to judicial review of legislation when the particular state act challenged by it is based on a statute considered unconstitutional.[23]

The third attribution of the Constitutional Tribunal refers to judicial review of legislation, which can be exercised through a direct action or in an incidental way. The power of judicial review can also be exercised by the Constitutional Court in an indirect way and, if it concerns certain state acts, in a preventive way. Therefore, four different means of judicial review of legislation can be distinguished in the Spanish system.

## (c) The direct control of the constitutionality of legislation

The first of the means through which judicial review powers can be exercised by the Constitutional Tribunal is through the 'recourse of unconstitutionality against laws and normative acts with force of law'.[24] Through this procedure 'the Constitutional Tribunal guarantees the primacy of the Constitution and judges the conformity or inconformity' of the laws and normative acts with force of law with it.[25]

Similarly to the Italian situation, the state acts which can be the object of this direct recourse of unconstitutionality are statutes and other state acts with the same force of laws. These include the Statutes of Autonomy approved by Parliament for the Autonomous Communities; the organic laws and the ordinary laws approved by Parliament;[26] international treaties;[27] the *interna corporis* regulations of the Chambers and Parliament;[28] other normative acts of the national state with force of law, including the decrees enacted by the government,[29] either through delegated legislation[30] or in cases of urgent and extraordinary necessity;[31] and normative regulations of the Legislative Assemblies of the Autonomous Communities.[32]

This direct action can be brought before the Constitutional Tribunal by the President of the government, the Peoples Defendant, fifty deputies or fifty senators,[33] and by the collegiate executive organ and the legislative of the Autonomous Communities when the challenged acts are laws or other state acts with similar force of law which affect their respective autonomy ambit.[34] In any case, the recourse can only be brought before the Tribunal within a delay of three months following the publication of the challenged act.[35]

The radical difference between the direct action or recourse of unconstitutionality established in Spain, and the Italian model in which, for instance, the ability of the government is limited to challenging only regional laws, may be noted. The standing in the Spanish system which is attributed to the various political organs, including the president of government, implies their right to challenge any law or state act with force of law on the grounds of unconstitutionality.[36]

With regard to the dispositions and decisions of the organs of the Autonomous Communities which can be challenged by the government, the Constitution establishes the suspensive character of the recourse in relation to the challenged acts.[37]

As in the West German system, the aim of this direct action is to exercise an abstract control over normative state acts, without reference to a particular conflict in which it would be necessary to elucidate the constitutional issue. Thus in these cases it is simply a question of an abstract discrepancy over the interpretation of the Constitution in relation to a particular law.[38] Although state organs whose normative acts are questioned may be called upon and heard,[39] the proceeding for the decision of this recourse of unconstitutionality is considered an objective one in which the political organs which initiated it and the representatives[40] of the state organs whose statutes and acts are challenged, do not have the strict procedural position of parties.[41] Consequently, the abandonment of the recourse is not possible.[42]

### (d) The incidental method of judicial review of legislation

The second method of judicial review in the Spanish system is the incidental one, established in article 163 of the Constitution as follows:

When a judicial organ considers in a process, that a norm with rank of law applicable to the case and on whose validity its decision depends, could be contrary to the Constitution, it must refer the question to the Constitutional Tribunal in the manner and with the effects established in the law, which in any case will be of a suspensive character.[43]

The first aspect that must be stressed regarding this means of judicial review, is that the judges can consider a constitutional question, either *ex officio* or on the instance of a party.[44] Therefore, although the parties can raise the constitutional question at any stage in the concrete process, it is the judge who must appreciate it in a non-appealable decision.[45] Only when he considers the specific norm contrary to the Constitution, can he refer the question to the Tribunal. Since the Organic Law stipulates that a constitutional question can be raised by the judge only once the concrete proceeding has concluded but before the decision, the issue does not have suspensive effects.[46]

The judge in his referral must describe the statute or norm with force of law whose constitutionality is questioned, the constitutional norm that is supposed to be infringed and justify to what extent the decision in the concrete proceeding depends on the validity of the norm in question. Before adopting his own decision on the matter, the judge must hear the Public Prosecutor and the parties regarding the constitutional issue.[47] Once the issue of unconstitutionality has been raised before the Constitutional Tribunal, the parties of the *a quo* proceeding have no right to intervene in the constitutional process. The Constitutional Tribunal need only notify the representatives of the organs whose acts have been challenged, in order to allow them to argue the constitutional issue before the Tribunal on the matter.[48]

It must be stressed that in Germany the incidental constitutional question can only be raised by a court before the Constitutional Tribunal when the judge is convinced of the unconstitutionality of the particular statute, whereas in the Spanish system it is sufficient for the judge to consider that the applicable norm 'could be contrary to the Constitution'. Thus the Spanish is closer to the Italian system in which the judge must raise the constitutional question only when he considers that it is not evidently unfounded.[49]

## (e) The indirect means of judicial review of legislation

Apart from the direct and incidental methods of judicial review, a constitutional question can be raised in other constitutional processes developed before the Tribunal whose objectives are not the direct review of legislation. This can happen in cases of conflicts of attributions between constitutional organs and in cases of recourses for constitutional protection (*amparo*) of fundamental rights.

In cases of conflicts regarding competences or attributions directly assigned by the Constitution, by the statutes of autonomy or by the Organic or ordinary Laws, the Constitutional Tribunal has concluded that, for instance, if the conflict arises from an executive regulation which is based on an unconstitutional statute, the constitutionality of the latter must be reviewed by the Tribunal.[50]

In cases of a recourse for the protection (*recurso de amparo*) of fundamental rights, an action can be brought against state acts of a non-legislative character by any person with direct interest in the matter.[51] If this recourse relies on the fact that the challenged state act is based on a statute that, at the same time, infringes fundamental rights or freedoms, the Tribunal must proceed to review its constitutionality through the procedural rules established for the direct action or recourse of unconstitutionality.[52] The Constitutional Tribunal has considered that the interpretation of the Organic Law, particularly its Article 52, 2,

compels one to understand that the unconstitutionality of a statute that violates fundamental rights and liberties could be alleged by the claimant, from which it can be deduced that a direct claim of unconstitutionality by individuals is admissible, although limited to the laws which violate or prejudice the rights and liberties established in the Constitution and to cases in which the claimant has suffered a concrete and actual injury in his own right and always that constitutional protection is irrescindable from the unconstitutionality of the statute.[53]

### (f) The preventive judicial review system of legislation

State laws and other acts with force of law, including international treaties, Organic Laws and Statutes of Autonomies of the Autonomous Communities, can also be the object of a preventive system of judicial review. This is an important innovation in the Spanish system as compared to the German and Italian models, and resembles that of the French system.[54]

In particular, the Spanish Constitution expressly establishes that the signing of international treaties containing dispositions which may be contrary to the Constitution permits the government, or either of the Chambers of Parliament, to request the Constitutional Tribunal to decide whether a contradiction exists or not.[55] The constitutional review system adopted is a preventive one which coexists with the direct, incidental and indirect means for judicial review of constitutionality. These means of review can be used severally or successively.[56] When the preventive means of control is requested, the Court must hear the representative of the state organs concerned.[57]

Although the preventive system of control was limited originally to international treaties,[58] the Organic Law 2/1979 has since extended preventive control of constitutionality to the Statute of Autonomy and to Organic Laws so that it is now possible to exercise 'a recourse of unconstitutionality, with previous character', by the same political organs that can exercise the direct recourse of constitutionality against them.[59] This preventive means of control is particularly important to the Statutes of Autonomy of the Autonomous Communities.[60] Although a direct recourse could be exercised against them, since the Statutes of Autonomy must be approved by referendum, a preventive control as established in the Organic Law could avoid political difficulties deriving from the possible annulment of a statute after its approval by referendum.

When it is an Organic Law directed for the approval of an international treaty,[61] because of the close link between the approval law and the treaty,[62] the preventive constitutional control produces an indirect preventive means of control of international treaties.

In cases of preventive control of constitutionality the effects vary regarding the act subject to control. If it is an international treaty not yet definitively consented to by the state, and the Tribunal declares that it contradicts the Constitution, the treaty's enactment could only be possible through a reform of the Constitution.[63] If it is a Statute of Autonomy or Organic Law, the declaration of the unconstitutionality of their dispositions has binding effects and implies that the procedure for their definitive adoption cannot continue unless they were suppressed by the respective state organ.[64] In this latter case, the decision of the Tribunal rejecting or declaring the unconstitutionality of dispositions of a Statute of Autonomy or of an Organic Law, does not prejudge the future decision that could be taken if direct recourses of unconstitutionality are exercised against them, after their enactment.[65]

### (g) The effects of the decision of the Constitutional Tribunal on judicial review

Regarding the effects of the decisions of the Constitutional Tribunal in matters of judicial review, the Spanish constitutional and legal system provides a few dispositions in which the different situations that can result are regulated.

The first positive law aspect refers to the power of the Constitutional Tribunal as supreme interpreter of the Constitution. While a question of unconstitutionality of a statute cannot be raised *ex officio* by the Tribunal, once the issue has been brought before it, the Tribunal has *ex-officio* powers to raise other unconstitutionality questions regarding the particular challenged norm and so to 'found the declaration of unconstitutionality in the violation of any other constitutional disposition, being invoked or not in the course of the process'.[66] The Tribunal can also extend the declaration of unconstitutionality to other dispositions of the statute, when a partial challenge has been made, in cases of connection or as a consequence of the declaration of the challenged dispositions.[67]

The second aspect established in the Constitution relates to the force attributed to Constitutional Court decisions, as supreme interpreter of the Constitution. Since these decisions 'have the value of *res judicata* from the day following its publication', and as it is not possible to exercise any recourse against such decisions,[68] the decisions adopted by the Constitutional Court in any proceeding of judicial review are 'obligatory regarding all public powers and have general effects from the date of their publication in the Official Journal of the state'.[69]

The third aspect, expressly regulated in the Constitution and the Organic Law of the Tribunal, concerns the effects of the decision, to whom they apply, and when they begin. In this aspect an important distinction is made between the decision that declares the unconstitutionality of a norm and those decisions that reject the alleged unconstitutionality.

With regard to decisions that declare the unconstitutionality of a statute or other norms with force of law, all of the methods of judicial review result in *erga omnes* effects.[70] In cases of incidental means of judicial review, the Constitutional Court must immediately inform the respective court which must decide the process, which in its turn must notify the parties to the conflict. In this case, the Organic Law of the Tribunal states that 'the judge or court would be subject to the decision from when it learns about it, and the parties from when they are notified'.[71]

According to the provisions of the Constitution, the 'declaration of unconstitutionality' or 'declaration of nullity' of a statute means annulment, the guarantee of the Constitution being the annullability of the unconstitutional state acts rather than their nullity. Consequently, the statute declared unconstitutional is annulled, the declaration having *ex-nunc, pro futuro* effects.[72] That is why the Constitution expressly establishes that 'the decisions already adopted in judicial proceedings will not lose their *res iudicata* value'[73] and the Organic Law of the Tribunal also establishes that 'The decisions which declare the unconstitutionality of statutes, dispositions or acts with force of law, will not allow the review of judicial proceedings ended by decisions with *res judicata* force in which the unconstitutional act would have been applied.'[74]

As is the trend in the concentrated system of judicial review in Europe, however, there is an exception to the *ex-nunc* effects with regard to criminal cases. Here a limited retroactive effect is permitted. This has been extended to administrative justice decisions in cases of administrative sanction cases. Article 40, 2 of the Organic Law of the Tribunal in this respect establishes the possibility of review of judicial processes, in cases of 'penal or administrative justice processes concerning sanctioning proceedings in which, as a consequence of the nullity of the applied norm, a reduction of the penalty or sanction results, or an exclusion, exemption or limitation of liability also results'.

Finally, constitutional review of legislation can be exercised as a consequence of an indirect question that can be raised in a proceeding of a recourse for protection (*amparo*) of fundamental rights or in cases of conflict of attributions between constitutional organs or between the state and the Autonomous Communities. In the first case, the declaration of unconstitutionality of a statute considered unconstitutional applied in a particular act that affects the fundamental rights of an individual is possible, and its effects are the same as already mentioned.[75] In cases of conflict of attributions, the Organic Law of the Tribunal authorizes it to annul the acts which originate the conflicts and to decide what might be necessary in consequence of the annulled acts.[76]

The Organic Law of the Constitutional Tribunal also expressly regulates the effects of the decisions in cases of rejection of the question raised before the Tribunal. Two consequences have been given depending on the nature of the rejection. If it is a rejection based on the constitutional question in its substantive aspect, the decision of rejection will prevent any other future allegation of the constitutional question 'through the same means', founded in the violation of the same constitutional norm.[77]

In cases of recourses of unconstitutionality against statutes or dispositions or acts with force of law, if the rejection was based on formal reasons, the decision will not prevent the same statute, disposition or act being the object of a constitutional question raised when applied in other processes,[78] and of course of another recourse in which the formal questions would have been corrected.

# 21

## CONSTITUTIONAL JUSTICE IN THE SOCIALIST EUROPEAN COUNTRIES

The European model of judicial review, with one constitutional organ able to control the constitutionality of statutes and other legislative acts, has been followed in some socialist countries.

One of the basic principles of the constitutional systems of the socialist countries, principally derived from the influence of Soviet constitutionalism, is the principle of the unity of state powers based on the assignment of all legislative and executive powers of state to its representative democratic body. This representative political organ is the supreme organ of state power and the only one able to create law and control the activities of all other state organs.[1] This concept necessarily implies the rejection of any form of separation of state powers[2] and, with regard to the legislative body, of the difference between the constituent and the constituted bodies of the state. The Constitutions of the socialist countries have a pre-eminent character over the whole legal order,[3] but at the same time the organ that can control the submission to constitutional rule and can modify the Constitution is the supreme organ of the state. Consequently, an essential incompatibility exists between the principle of the unity of state power which results in the supremacy and sovereignty of the constituted organs as representatives of the popular will, with any sort of judicial control of the constitutionality of statutes.[4]

Nevertheless, three socialist countries, Yugoslavia, Czechoslovakia and Poland, have developed advanced systems of constitutional justice. This may be seen as a sign of departure from the principle of the unity of state power, although this conclusion is commonly rejected by socialist authors who see those experiences more as a departure from the Soviet interpretation of the principle than from the principle itself. For instance, referring to the Yugoslav theory and system, a former President of the Constitutional Court of the Socialist Republic of Slovenia said, that it 'represents no departure from the principle of the unity of powers, but a departure from the rigid, formalistic, strictly dogmatic, bureaucratic-Stalinist conception of the unity of authority with its wrong ideas about the function of legality and the status of the judicature under the socialist order'.[5]

The adoption of a concentrated system of judicial review in these socialist countries is based on a principle of vertical distribution of state powers, normally with a federal form which 'calls, *ipso facto*, for an agency whose independent and authoritative status and competencies would enable it to deal with possible disputes between the republics and between the republics and the federal authority'.[6] It is also based on the limitations imposed upon the politico-representative organ of the state in the Constitution, regarding other state bodies. Additionally, the declaration of fundamental and self-government rights has justified the establishment of an extra-parliamentary and independent state organ for controlling the constitutionality of statutes and other normative acts of the state organs.[7]

The first socialist country to establish a Constitutional Court was Yugoslavia in 1963 and, more recently, Czechoslovakia followed in 1968. In Poland the 1982 Constitution has established a limited jurisdictional control of constitutionality of statutes in the sense that the Constitutional Court created does not decide definitively upon their unconstitutionality, but must only refer its appreciation to the decision of the legislative organ in its character as the supreme organ of power.[8] Thus, only in the Yugoslav and Czech systems is it possible to distinguish a jurisdictional organ with powers to annul legislative acts.

## (a) Judicial review in Yugoslavia: the Constitutional Court

The Constitution of Yugoslavia and the Constitutions of her Socialist Republics, promulgated in April 1963 and reformed in 1975, established an advanced concentrated system of judicial review. The intent was 'to prevent violations of the system laid down by the Constitution and usurpation of rights to the prejudice of citizens or self-governing bodies, as well as to enforce respect for law and the Constitution by all, the highest social organisms and state officials included'.[9] The system brought about the establishment of a Constitutional Court of Yugoslavia, regulated by a special statute enacted in the same year, as well as the establishment of Constitutional Courts in the six republics of the federation.[10]

## (i) The jurisdiction of the Constitutional Court

The Constitutional Court is conceived as an 'independent Federal organ' whose main function is to 'ensure protection of constitutionality and legality on the basis of the Constitution acting within its rights and duties as laid down by the Constitution'.[11] This is accomplished through three basic sets of attributions concerning the settling of disputes between the socio-political communities, the protection of fundamental rights and liberties, and judicial review of constitutionality.

The first set of attributions confers on the Constitutional Court powers to 'settle disputes involving rights and duties between the Federal authority and a Republic, between the Republics, and between other socio-political communities from the territory of different Republics'.[12] This power is a direct consequence of the establishment in the Federal Socialist Republic of Yugoslavia, of a series of autonomous solutions to its fundamental political, economic and social aims which separate it from the Soviet model.[13] The Court also has competence to settle all 'conflicts of jurisdiction that may arise between courts of law and Federal authorities, and also between courts of law and other state authorities from the territory of different Republics'.[14]

When resolving the former of these conflicts, the Court has the power to fix a particular obligation for a socio-political community and to order the elimination of the consequences brought about by the act or action which caused the violation or interference of attributions.[15]

The second set of attributions of the Constitutional Court relates to the protection of self-governing rights and other fundamental rights and liberties granted by the Constitution where they have been violated by a particular act or action on the part of federal or central authorities.[16] This power of the Court can only be exercised when the ordinary recourse for the protection of such rights and liberties has already been exhausted.[17] The proposal for protection can be presented 'by any one who had his right of self-government or other fundamental rights or liberties as granted by the Constitution, violated', as well as by a socio-political organization on behalf of their members.[18]

As the proposal for protection can only be used against a 'particular act or action of an authority or organization',[19] and as the ruling of the Court must consist, subject to the circumstances of the case, of the abolition of the act and of the elimination of the consequences brought about by such an act,[20] the proposal is not possible against normative acts.

Finally, the Constitutional Court is empowered to review 'the constitutionality and legality of prescriptions and other general acts' with binding authority.[21] This attribution is conceived as a power of the Court that can be exercised *ex officio*, or when hearing a request for constitutional review presented by state organs or by individuals. This power allows the Court to make rulings concerning the compatibility of laws with the Constitution; the compatibility of a republican law with federal law and the compatibility of other dispositions and general acts made by authorities and organizations with the Constitution, with federal law and with other federal dispositions.[22]

### (ii) The *ex-officio* powers of the Constitutional Court

The Constitutional Court is empowered, by the law which regulates its functioning, to 'initiate the procedure for judging the constitutionality and legality of a disposition or other general acts on its own initiative'. Thus any member of the Court may request such a procedure to be initiated and a decision to be taken thereupon.[23]

The Court can also, on its own initiative, give its opinion concerning the compatibility of the Constitution of a republic with the Constitution of Yugoslavia to the Federal Assembly.[24] It can also 'offer opinions and proposals to the Federal Assembly for the enactment and amendment of laws, for the provision of authentic interpretation and for taking measures to ensure constitutionality and legality, and protect the self-governing rights and the other rights and liberties of citizens and organizations'.[25] These *ex-officio* powers of the Yugoslav Constitutional Court are the most distinguishable feature of the Yugoslav system.

### (iii) The request for judicial review and popular action

The powers of judicial review are more commonly exercised by the Constitutional Court of Yugoslavia, when a request is presented before the Court by some state organs, or by any person through a popular action. In the first case, when the request is presented by 'authorities of organizations specified under the Constitution' or by an assembly of a commune, a district or an autonomous province, or by Federal Secretaries or Republican Secretaries, or by authorities of a socio-political community,[26] the Court is obliged to initiate the procedure 'for considering the constitutionality' of legislation.[27] When a popular action is exercised by individuals, the Court shall itself decide whether to initiate the procedure or not. When a request has been made, the Constitutional Court is not bound by the points raised in the proposal concerned but may also examine the constitutionality of other dispositions or acts not challenged by the proponent as unconstitutional.[28]

It is important to notice that this popular action which authorizes 'any one' to request the Constitutional Court to initiate a procedure for judicial review of legislation,[29] is exceptional in European countries, even though in such cases the Court is not obliged to initiate it, which confirms its own powers in the matter.

### (iv) The decision of the Constitutional Court on judicial review

Contrary to the situation in other European countries, a decision of unconstitutionality by the Yugoslav Court does not cause the immediate annulment of the normative act. Instead, three different stages can be distinguished in the proceeding.

First, prior to taking a decision, the Constitutional Court may give an opportunity to the representative body or other authority or organization concerned to eliminate the incompatibility of a disposition or other general act with the Constitution and/or federal law.[30] In this way, the Court avoids declaring an act unconstitutional and allows the state organ to make the necessary corrections to it. In this stage and concerning the challenge of the law of a republic when incompatible with the Constitution or with federal law or in cases of incompatibility between the law of the republic with federal laws which the Court finds contrary to the Constitution, the Court can rule that the dispositions of the republican law or of the federal law are not to be applicable pending the issue of its final decision.[31]

Secondly, in cases of incompatibility between federal law and the Constitution, or between republican law and the Constitution or federal law, the Constitutional Court does not annul the act immediately. Instead it must announce its ruling to the parties concerned and notify the federal or the republican assemblies concerned, allowing them to bring the challenged act into conformity with the Constitution or the federal law.

Thirdly, the law of the Court establishes that if the public authority does not correct the unconstitutional act within six months from the date when the Constitutional Court announced its decision, then 'the Court shall issue a ruling establishing that the law involved has ceased to have effect'.[32] In cases of incompatibility between the republican law and the Constitution or with federal law, the Court may 'abolish such republican law if it involves a manifest violation of the prerogative of the federal

240

authorities'.[33] These decisions, of course, have binding authority[34] and *erga omnes* effects.

Even though the law of the Court uses two expressions for the qualification of its decisions upon unconstitutionality of normative acts, abrogation or abolishment of the unconstitutional challenged act, the general effect of the decision in time is equivalent to the annulment of the act *ex-nunc, pro futuro*. The annulled act 'shall not be applicable as from the date of publication of the Court's ruling in the official gazette of the federation',[35] and neither the dispositions nor other general acts serving for the enforcement of the unconstitutional statute, shall be applicable if the ruling of the Court implies that such acts are contrary to the Constitution.[36] Additionally, the Court can give its opinion as to which legal rules are to be applicable pending the issue of a new statute conforming to the Constitution to replace the one invalidated.[37]

Although the particular relations may have been created by a statute declared unconstitutional before the date of publication of the Court's decision, the unconstitutional act shall not be applicable to them if a valid settlement of the relations is still pending on that date.[38]

The law of the Tribunal establishes a general difference with regard to final and valid acts issued in particular cases in application of the unconstitutional law. When the normative act has been abolished, the law of the Tribunal, in a general exception to the *ex-nunc* effects, assigns to any one who may have had a right of his violated by a valid particular act issued in application of the unconstitutional normative act, the right to seek review of such act by the court of law or other authority that issued it; and they must do so within a delay of six months after the publication of the Court decision.[39]

Additionally, the Court can also rule that a court of law or other competent authority concerned is to be bound to review all acts or certain categories of acts produced based on the unconstitutional statute on the demand of citizens or organizations whose rights were violated.[40]

In relation to all other decisions of the Court on constitutional review matters, the law of the Court establishes a few exceptions to the *ex-nunc* effects, and allows for the retroactive applicability of the annulment. This is particularly so in criminal cases and where self-governing rights have been violated.[41] In particular, in criminal cases, the law of the Constitutional Court gives the right to whoever had penal sanctions imposed upon him to seek the review of such act by the court of law or other competent authority that imposed the sanction.[42]

Finally, it must be noted that the powers of the Constitutional Court are also very significant in the interpretation of the Constitution in cases where it merely considers that a practical application of an otherwise valid law has been constructed in a manner contrary to the Constitution. In such cases, the Court may lay down, through a decision, the significance thereof corresponding to the Constitution and the situation to be observed when enforcing such law or other normative act.[43]

### (b) The control of constitutionality in Czechoslovakia: the Federal Constitutional Court

After the Second World War, the Czech Constitution of 1948 followed the Soviet model so that there was no longer a form of judicial review of constitutionality. It has only been in the Constitution of 27 October 1968, where a federal form of state was adopted, and following the Yugoslav model, that a concentrated system of judicial review was established.[44] Thus, there is a federal Constitutional Court and two Constitutional Courts in each of the republics of the Czech federation.

Judicial review power of the Czech Federal Constitutional Court relates to all laws enacted by the Federal Assembly and by the Czech National Councils, as well as to all the general provisions of the administrative bodies, both of the federation and of the federal republics.[45]

As with the Yugoslav Constitutional Federal Court, the decisions of the Czech Court do not imply the immediate cessation of the effects of the challenged act, but only the obligation, following the publication of the decision, for the bodies that passed the provisions to redraft them and make them consistent with the Constitution. They have six months to carry out this task. The challenged dispositions only cease to be effective when this time period has elapsed.[46]

The Czech Federal Constitutional Court is also empowered to settle disputes of competences between the bodies of the federal republic and those of one or other of the two federal republics, or between the internal organs of the latter.[47]

Lastly, the Constitutional Federal Court of Czechoslovakia has the ability to protect rights and freedoms established in the Constitution against their violation by provisions or acts of the federal authorities, when the ordinary law does not establish any other jurisdictional safeguard.[48]

# 22

## THE CONCENTRATED SYSTEM OF JUDICIAL REVIEW IN LATIN AMERICA

Judicial review has a long tradition in Latin America, and over the course of more than a century it has been adopted in one way or another in all Latin American countries. While some have adopted the diffuse system, as in Argentina and Mexico, in most countries a mixed system is followed in which the diffuse system functions in parallel with the concentrated system of judicial review. Yet examples can also be found of a pure concentrated system in which the powers of judicial review of constitutionality of legislation have been exclusively attributed to the Supreme Court of Justice of the country or to a specially created constitutional court.

### (a) The Supreme Court as a concentrated organ for judicial review: Panama, Uruguay, Paraguay

The Constitution of Panama gave the Supreme Court the duty to 'guard the integrity of the Constitution',[1] and to control the constitutionality of legislation, by two means: a direct action or an incidental referral from a lower court.

The direct action is a popular action (*acción pública*) which can be brought before the Supreme Court by any person who challenges the constitutionality of laws, decrees, decisions, or acts whether on a substantive or formal basis. In this instance, a decision cannot be adopted by the Court until it has heard the Solicitor General of the nation.[2]

The Constitution also establishes that when, in an ordinary judicial process the judge, *ex officio* or at the request of any of the parties, notices that the legal or executive normative act applicable to the case is unconstitutional, he must submit the question of unconstitutionality to the Supreme Court. In this instance he is allowed to continue the proceeding of the case until the decision stage.[3] In both cases, the decision of the Supreme Court is obligatory,[4] with *erga omnes* and *ex-nunc* effects, and non reviewable.[5]

In the Uruguayan system, the Constitution[6] gives the Supreme Court exclusive and original jurisdiction to declare the unconstitutionality of statutes and other state acts with force of law. Unconstitutionality can be based on substantive or formal reasons.[7] In accordance with the Constitution, a declaration of unconstitutionality can be requested from the Supreme Court by all who deem their direct, personal and legitimate interests have been injured.[8] Thus a requirement of standing, very similar to the one established regarding judicial review of administrative action, is established.

The competence of the Supreme Court on judicial review, can be sought either through a direct action, when there is no judicial proceeding pending of decision or through an incidental means when a referral is made before the Supreme Court by a lower court.

This second method can be exercised *ex officio* by the lower court or as a consequence of an exception raised by any party.[9] In this case, the judge must refer a briefing of the question to the Supreme Court and should continue with the proceeding up to the stage of deciding upon the case. After the Supreme Court has adopted its decision, the court must make its own decision in the case in conformity with the latter.[10]

In both cases the effects of the Supreme Court decisions are restricted to the concrete case, so that it only has effect in the proceedings in which it was adopted.[11] While this disposition may be satisfactory in the incidental means of judicial review, in cases of a direct action, it is not. In this case, the Statute 13,747 of 1969[12] establishes that a Supreme Court decision declaring a norm unconstitutional is effective to prevent the applicability of the unconstitutional norm to the successful party. This inapplicability can be opposed by the successful party in any judicial proceeding, including the judicial review of administrative action.[13]

In Paraguay, the Constitution empowers the Supreme Court to decide upon actions and exceptions in order to declare the 'unconstitutionality and inapplicability of dispositions contrary to the Constitution'.[14] The proceeding can be initiated through an action or an exception, and in the latter case, the proceeding in the concrete case must continue until the decision stage. In any case, the decision of the Supreme Court only has effects regarding the concrete case or the petitioner.[15]

### (b) The parallel concentrated system of judicial review: Chile and Ecuador

The constitutional systems of Chile and Ecuador have established a concentrated system of judicial review in which two separate organs exercise constitutional control: the Supreme Court of Justice, through incidental means, and a Constitutional Tribunal, through direct means.

## (i) The Chilean experience

*The Supreme Court of Justice and the incidental method of judicial review*

Since the 1925 constitutional reform in Chile, the second paragraph of Article 86 authorizes the Supreme Court of Justice to declare the inapplicability of a law in force, on the grounds of unconstitutionality. This reform substantially modified the previous situation, in which the courts could not declare the inapplicability of an unconstitutional law as there was no constitutional provision granting them that power. Consequently, the 1925 reform represented an important step towards the control of the constitutionality of law.[16] This norm of the Constitution still in force states as follows:

The Supreme Court, in the concrete cases which it is conducting or in cases which were raised before it through recourses originated in proceedings developed before other courts, can declare any legal disposition contrary to the Constitution inapplicable to that case. This recourse can be exercised in any stage of the proceeding, without its suspension.

Consequently, a concentrated system of judicial review of incidental character is established through this institution called the 'recourse of inapplicability of statutes'.[17]

But this system of judicial review did not resolve constitutional conflicts between state organs, many of which originated in questions of unconstitutionality of statutes and other norms of equal force. The continuous conflict between those organs was the main factor that contributed to the establishment of a constitutional organ other than the Supreme Court.[18] Thus, the constitutional reform of 21 January 1970 created a Constitutional Tribunal with a variety of functions all related to the settlement of conflicts of attributions between the state organs.

In 1973 the Tribunal was dissolved as a result of a military coup that dissolved the Congress. Since the main function of the Constitutional Court was to settle conflicts between the executive and the legislature, and since the National Congress had been dissolved, the existence of the Court was no longer justified. Thus the Court ceased to function.[19] The Constitutional Court was later re-established by Articles 81 and 83 of the political Constitution approved by referendum on 11 September 1980 and drawn up by the Military Junta, in the exercise of its constituent power. The Court was assigned attributions similar to those established by the Fundamental Charter of 1970, and its functioning is regulated in the Organic Constitutional Law of 12 May 1981 passed by the government Junta.[20]

## The Constitutional Tribunal and its powers

In accordance with these new regulations, the attributions of the Tribunal are the following:[21] first, it is competent to judge upon the constitutionality of organic laws prior to their promulgation, or of any law which interprets a particular precept of the Fundamental Charter. It is also authorized, by means of a request, to exercise preventive control over any issues which may arise during the processing of ordinary bills of law, or constitutional amendments, as well as international treaties submitted for the approval of Congress.

It is also competent to resolve executive issues of constitutionality such as claims against the President of the Republic when he fails to promulgate a law which he is required to do, or when he promulgates a different text, or issues unconstitutional decrees or regulates subjects reserved to formal law. The Court can also decide upon conflicts when the office of the General Comptroller refuses to register decrees or resolutions issued by the President of the Republic.

Secondly, the Court is authorized to settle issues as to the constitutionality of the calling of plebiscites as well as questions relating to an individual's constitutional or legal eligibility for appointment to the office of Minister of State.

These powers of the Constitutional Court were originally established in 1970. However, the 1980 Constitutional amendment gave the Court the competence to judge the constitutionality of organizations and political parties or movements, and the responsibility to determine who had transgressed the constitutional order of the Republic.[22] These powers are consistent with the existence of a military regime.

In the area of judicial review, the Chilean Constitutional Tribunal is able to review the constitutionality of legislation in two specific ways: a preventive control and a limited *a posteriori* control.

## The preventive control of constitutionality of legislation

In the first place, the Constitution permits the Tribunal to resolve constitutional questions that arise during discussions of Organic Constitutional Laws, of statutes intended to interpret a constitutional disposition, of any bill or project of constitutional amendment and of international treaties submitted to Congress for approval.[23] As in the French model, this control is a preventive one, and can be obligatory or exercised through a petition. In the case of Organic Constitutional Laws and of statutes that interpret a constitutional disposition, the preventive control of the Tribunal is obligatory, in the sense that such texts must always be sent to the Tribunal by the President of the corresponding Chamber of Congress within five days of being sanctioned. The proceedings are not adversarial, as the Tribunal has *ex officio* powers to consider constitutional issues. If one or more of the text dispositions are considered to be unconstitutional, they are sent back to the corresponding Chamber where its President, in his turn, must send the text to the President of the Republic for promulgation without the dispositions considered unconstitutional.

In the case of other bills, projects of constitutional amendments or international treaties, exercise of the preventive control is only possible when a petition is formulated before the promulgation of the text, and during the discussion of the project, by the President of the Republic or by any of the Congress Chambers or by a quarter of their members. In this case the petition does not have suspensive effects over the legislative procedure and the proceeding before the Tribunal is an adversary one: the Tribunal must notify the interested constitutional organs and hear their arguments. The decision of the Tribunal considering unconstitutional dispositions of a project of a statute or a treaty prevents its promulgation.[24]

### *The judicial review powers of the Constitutional Tribunal through direct means*

The *a posteriori* powers of judicial review are only exercised against executive decrees with force of law, that is to say, those issued by the President of the Republic by virtue of powers delegated by Congress, and against the powers of the President for promulgating statutes. Thus substantive judicial review does not proceed against statutes once in force.

One of the traditional functions of the General Comptrollers Office has been the control of executive decrees, through their registration or rejection. As a consequence, when the Office of the General Comptroller raises objections concerning the incompatibility of decrees with the

Constitution, controversies can arise as to their constitutionality. Prior to the existence of the Tribunal, these controversies were settled by the executive, which could insist, with the backing of the signatures of all the ministers,[25] on the registration of the decrees. This situation was changed after the 1970 constitutional reform, which stipulated that if a decree was rejected by the General Comptrollers Office, the President of the Republic could no longer insist on it being registered. Instead, within a time limit of thirty days after the rejection, the President could raise the question before the Constitutional Tribunal, which has the last word on the matter of constitutionality. However, if the General Comptroller registers a decree, either of the Chambers of Congress or more than one-third of their active members is authorized to raise the issue of its unconstitutionality before the Tribunal, also within a time limit of thirty days from the publication of the decree.

The procedure in such cases is of an adversary character, so that any declaration has binding effects on the lower courts. In the event that the Tribunal declares the decree to be constitutional, the Supreme Court of Justice cannot later declare it inapplicable when exercising its concentrated diffuse powers of judicial review.[26]

The *a posteriori* judicial review powers of the Constitutional Tribunal can also be exercised regarding statutes but only in relation to the formalities of their promulgation by the President of the Republic. Thus the Constitution gives the Tribunal power to resolve claims that can only be exercised by the Chambers of Congress, in cases in which the President of the Republic does not promulgate a statute when he should, or when he promulgates a text other than the one that proceeds constitutionally.[27] In such cases, the constitutional review control does not refer to the substantive aspects of the statutes, but only to the way the President of the Republic exercises his power when promulgating statutes, the decision of the Tribunal being directed to the correction of the promulgation.

### (ii) The parallel concentrated system of judicial review in Ecuador and the Tribunal of Constitutional Guarantees

In Ecuador the Supreme Court of Justice has exclusive power to judge the constitutionality of legislation through a diffuse system, while the Tribunal of Constitutional Guarantees is empowered to exercise judicial review of legislation in a concentrated way. Both systems of judicial review are based on the principle of the supremacy of the Constitution expressly established as follows:

The Constitution is the supreme law of the state. The secondary norms and all others of inferior hierarchy must maintain their conformity with the constitutional dispositions. The laws [statutes], decrees, ordinances, dispositions, international treaties or accords which, in any way, would be in contradiction with the Constitution or alter its disposition, will have no value.[28]

In accordance with this proclaimed constitutional supremacy, the Constitution of 1978, reformed in 1983, assigned a diffuse power to exercise judicial review power to the Chambers of the Supreme Court of Justice, to the Tax Tribunal and to the Administrative Justice Tribunal by attributing them competences to declare 'in concrete cases taken over from a lower court, the inapplicability of any legal norm contrary to the Constitution'.[29] As this decision 'does not have obligatory force but only in the concrete case in which it is pronounced' its effects are *inter partes*.

The same 1978 Constitution also established the Tribunal of Constitutional Guarantees assigned the duty of controlling the application of laws being issued under the authority of the Constitution, by requesting action from authorities and public officials.[30] The Tribunal was originally empowered to formulate observations regarding decrees, accords, regulations or resolutions issued in violation of the Constitution or the statutes. In these proceedings the authority which created the law in dispute would be heard. If the Tribunal's observations were not followed, it was authorized to publish those observations in the press and notify the National Chamber of Representatives to allow them to make a resolution.[31]

This Tribunal of Constitutional Guarantees was also empowered to take notice of complaints of citizens that the Constitution had been violated. In such cases, the Tribunal could prepare the accusation against the public official involved, and send it to the National Chamber of Representatives for their prosecution.[32]

Moreover, in what can be considered a concentrated system of judicial review, the Tribunal of Constitutional Guarantees has also been given the exclusive power to suspend the effects of unconstitutional legislative acts. Until the constitutional reform of 1983,[33] this power had been attributed to the Supreme Court of Justice.

Since 1984 when this amendment came into force, the Tribunal of Constitutional Guarantees has had the exclusive power to 'suspend totally or partially, at any moment, *ex officio* or following a party's petition, the effects of laws [statutes], ordinances or decrees that were unconstitutional whether in substance or in form'.[34] This suspension of the effects of legislation is an important judicial review remedy regarding unconstitutional acts, although the Tribunal must submit its decision to the National Chamber of Representatives for its resolution. In accordance with the Constitution, neither the decision of the Tribunal nor the resolution of the National Chamber of Representatives has retroactive effects,[35] although they have *erga omnes* effects. This can be deduced, particularly regarding the Tribunal's suspensive decision, from what is established in the Constitution regarding the inapplicability of legislation by the Chambers of the Supreme Court, the Tax Court or the Administrative Justice Court, with *inter partes* effects in processes developed before them. In these latter cases, the courts must notify their decisions to the Supreme Court in Pleno which, if it accepts the criterion, must inform the Tribunal of Constitutional Guarantees which could exercise its powers to suspend the effects of the challenged act.[36]

# 23

# PREVENTIVE JUDICIAL REVIEW IN FRANCE: THE CONSTITUTIONAL COUNCIL

All the concentrated systems of judicial review that follow the European model can be characterized by the establishment of various means of controlling legislation once in force. Only in an exceptional way do some European concentrated systems allow for a preventive means of control regarding certain state acts.

The basis for the existence of an *a posteriori* judicial review system has been the overcoming of the dogma of the sovereignty of Parliament, and therefore of its laws, and of the rigidity of the separation of powers principle. Judicial review implies the existence of a written and rigid Constitution through which limits are imposed upon all constitutional organs so that their activities conform to its text.

While these principles have been of particular importance in the development of the French constitutional system, the contemporary trends of constitutionalism have affected this traditional basis by the establishment of a preventive system of judicial review. This preventive system of judicial review, and the activity developed by the French Constitutional Council, have been considered of revolutionary character[1] because they mean the acceptance of the principle of constitutionality and the submission of the legislator to constitutional limits.[2] Yet if it is compared with the system of judicial review adopted in the other European countries, it must be concluded that the French judicial review system is a limited one[3] since the statutes in force are not subject to constitutional judicial control.

## (a) Historical background

The French preventive system of judicial review of legislation was established in the Constitution of 5 October 1958 wherein the Constitutional Council was given[4] the power to judge the legislation's 'conformity with the Constitution ... before its promulgation'.[5] This institutional innovation was the result of a reaction against at least two of the traditional bases of the French constitutional system: the absolutism of the law and the rejection of any judicial interference regarding other state powers, particularly of the legislative branch.

One of the most important political results of the French Revolution was the legislator's mistrust of judges. In pre-revolutionary France, Parliaments, as higher courts, examined laws and decrees to ensure they did not contain 'anything contrary to the fundamental laws of the Kingdom'. This gave them an important conservative political power *vis-à-vis* the pre-revolutionary regime, which resulted in this deep mistrust that the revolutionary legislator had regarding judges. Thus, after the Revolution, they were denied any possibility of controlling the other state powers, particularly the legislative and the executive powers.

Even the interpretation of the laws was reserved to the legislators, who exercised these powers at the request of the judges through the *référé législatif*.[6] Judges were *la bouche de la loi*, that is to say, 'the mouth that pronounces the words of the law, mere passive beings, incapable of moderating either its force or rigour'.[7]

Before the creation of the Constitutional Council in 1958, a special political body was given the function of guaranteeing the Constitution. This happened with the Conservative Senate of the Constitution of the Year VIII of the 22 Frimaire, and with the attributions of the Senate in the Constitutional Charter of 1852.[8] This was repeated in the 1946 Constitution which gave the power to a political body called the Comité Constitutionnel. As this body only determined if a legislative enactment required a previous amendment of the organic part of the Constitution, it was a very limited system of constitutional control. If the Committee deemed that the law was in fact contrary to the Constitution, it was returned to the Assembly for reconsideration, and if the Assembly confirmed its first decision, it was then necessary to proceed to reform the Constitution. However, the law could not be enacted until the reform had been concluded.[9]

### (b) The Constitutional Council and its jurisdiction

The 1958 Constitution created the Constitutional Council,[10] which was a kind of 'supreme political jurisdiction' entrusted with power to control the constitutionality of the law and the regularity of presidential and parliamentary elections. The term 'political jurisdiction' expresses the rather atypical[11] and ambiguous[12] nature of the institution: it has been assigned the role of a judge, but must exercise its activities in the political arena and, more important, with political motivations. Its members enjoy the independence of all magistrates and judges, but are politically recruited and appointed. Consequently, discussions have arisen in France regarding the jurisdictional character of the Constitutional Council[13] and these have given rise to a distinction between the judicial power and a more broad jurisdictional power, the latter understood to include other than ordinary judiciary and administrative justice functions, the constitutional justice attributions of the Constitutional Council.[14]

The Constitutional Council is composed of nine members, other than *ex officio* members who are the former Presidents of the Republic, appointed in a paritarian way: three by the President of the Republic; three by the President of the National Assembly; and three by the President of the Senate.[15]

The functions of the Council members are incompatible with being a member of government, of Parliament or of the Economic and Social Council.[16] Council members cannot be appointed to any public office[17] during their term, nor are they allowed to take political stands on issues which have been or could be susceptible to a decision by the Council.[18] They are also prohibited from accepting positions of responsibility or administrative posts in any political party or group, nor can they mention their post in any document which could lend itself to publication on any public or private activity.[19]

The Constitutional Council, in addition to its consultative powers, in the area of judicial review is also the judge of the constitutionality of legislation and of electoral and referendum disputes. The first of these competences refers to the exercise of a series of functions of a consultative nature, and indeed, of political importance. Thus the Council can determine when the President of the Republic is not fit to perform his functions,[20] and give its opinion regarding the situations and measures to be taken in cases of extraordinary circumstances.[21]

The Constitution does not define the notion of being 'unfit to perform' (*empechement*) so as to limit it to a physical disability or unfitness resulting from sickness or accident. Thus the power of appreciation of the Constitutional Council is practically unlimited. If the Constitutional Council declares the unfitness or disability of the President to be of a definitive nature, it must call new elections between twenty and fifty days following its decision. Nevertheless, the Constitutional Council can confirm the existence of a *force majeure* preventing it from calling the election, in which case, as would occur in the event of temporary incapacity, the President of the Republic would be replaced by the

President of the Senate, who is empowered to exercise all of the former's attributions, with the exception of the right to dissolve the Assembly, or to call a referendum.[22]

The Constitutional Council can also give an opinion when consulted by the President of the Republic regarding the situation and the measures that must be taken when a serious and immediate threat against the institutions of the Republic, the independence of the nation, the integrity of its territory or the execution of international accords exists, or when the regular functioning of the constitutional public powers is interrupted. In order to adopt the necessary measures in the circumstances, the President must also consult the Prime Minister and the President of the Assemblies. In this case the opinion must be published.[23] If the Constitutional Council is consulted on any measures which the President of the Republic intends to take under Article 16 of the Constitution, the opinion of the Constitutional Council would not be published.[24]

In its role as Supreme Electoral Tribunal, the Constitutional Council can judge parliamentary elections, presidential elections and referenda.[25] Regarding parliamentary elections, the Constitutional Council has constitutional powers to decide upon the regularity of elections of deputies and senators[26] and as a result the Council can annul any election or can amend its reported results, and is even empowered to declare another candidate as having been regularly elected.[27] To this end, every parliamentary election can be challenged before the Tribunal, within a ten day period, by any elector of the respective electoral circumscription, following a contradictory procedure in which the contested parliamentary assembly and the candidate whose election is under question are entitled to make observations.[28]

Regarding the control of presidential elections,[29] the powers of the Constitutional Council are not restricted to reviewing the regularity of an election if contested, but to actively searching for irregularity in elections. To this effect, the Constitutional Council is entrusted with the task of adopting and proclaiming the final results of the electoral process.[30] Moreover, the Constitutional Council *ex officio*, when it has evidence of serious irregularities which could prevent the sincerity of the election and affect its overall result, can pronounce the nullity of the election. In this case the government must fix a date for a new election.[31] Only the prefects or heads of the respective territories may exercise a recourse before the Constitutional Council within the forty-eight hours following the closure of the ballot count.[32]

The Constitutional Council can also participate in the electoral process when the government deems it necessary to replace the normal vote counting procedure, carried out at the level of the heads of departments and of the territories, by a centralized vote count taken in Paris. However, the Council must agree to their participation.[33]

With regard to referenda, the Council must first be consulted on the organization of the operations of the referendum, that is to say, its technical application. Second, it must supervise both the operations and the final vote count, and then proclaim the results.[34] Third, in the case of disputes relating to the referendum, the Constitutional Council also examines and decides on every claim raised before it.[35] The Organic Law of the Constitutional Council does not clearly establish who is entitled to make such claims, but, in view of the nature of a referendum, that is to say, a popular consultation via direct votes, it could be considered that every elector has the right to request a decision from the Constitutional Council.[36] If the Council confirmed irregularities, it would then have to decide whether to maintain the operation of the referendum or to change it, making a statement on its partial annulment.[37]

Finally, the Constitutional Council can control the constitutionality of legislation. This is conceived as a means of preventing encroachment of competences between the constitutional organs of the state, but particularly to keep Parliament within its constitutional boundaries.[38] The control only proceeds against statutes sanctioned by the Assemblies but not yet promulgated by the President, and it is precisely this aspect which brings about the great difference between the French system and the other European systems.

Thus judicial review powers of the Constitutional Council can be classified into two groups: the preventive control of the constitutionality of non promulgated legislation; and the preventive control over the distribution of normative powers between the law and the executive regulations.

## (c) The preventive control of the constitutionality of non-promulgated legislation

The preventive control of the constitutionality of non-promulgated legislation is exercised by the Constitutional Council in two ways: in a compulsory way regarding parliamentary regulations, and Organic Laws, and in a facultative way regarding ordinary laws and international treaties.

### (i) The obligatory control of the constitutionality of Organic Law and parliamentary regulations

In accordance with Article 61 of the Constitution, Organic Laws and the internal regulations of parliamentary assemblies must be submitted to the Constitutional Council before they are promulgated, for its decision as to whether they are consistent with the Constitution.

In the case of Organic Laws, they must be submitted to the Constitutional Council by the Prime Minister who must state, when appropriate, if the decision is urgent. In the case of parliamentary regulations or modifications to the regulations adopted by one of the assemblies, they must be submitted to the Constitutional Council by the President of the Assembly.[39]

### (ii) The facultative control of the constitutionality of ordinary laws and of international treaties

Ordinary laws can also be submitted to the Constitutional Council, by the President of the Republic, the Prime Minister or the President of one of the Assemblies, before their enactment. Moreover, the 1974 Constitutional reform allows sixty representatives or senators to submit the question of constitutionality regarding ordinary laws to the Constitutional Council.[40] This gives minorities the means to challenge majority decisions.

This facultative control of constitutionality also applies to international treaties and, in this case, the Constitutional Council must decide whether an international treaty contains clauses contrary to the Constitution, when requested by the President of the Republic, the Prime Minister or the President of one of the Assemblies. In this case the authorization for its signing or for its approval could only be possible after a constitutional reform takes place.[41]

The authority that submits an international treaty or a law to the Constitutional Council for constitutional control must immediately notify such action to the other authorities entitled to require a decision of the Constitutional Council.[42]

### (iii) The suspensive effects of the recourses and the decisions of the Council

In any case in which the Constitutional Council is requested to exercise control of constitutionality before the enactment of Organic Laws, parliamentary regulations, ordinary laws and international treaties, as soon as the Council hears the request, the promulgation of the normative text under challenge is suspended.[43] The Council has a month in which to make a decision, although in an urgent case the government may request that this term be reduced to eight days.[44] The decision of the Council, that must be motivated and published in the *Official Journal*,[45] can be to declare that the challenged statute is not contrary to the Constitution. In this case the suspensive delay of its promulgation ends.[46] If the Constitutional Council declares the normative text unconstitutional, the text can neither be promulgated nor enforced.[47] If the Constitutional Council decides that an international treaty contains a clause contrary to the Constitution, the authorization to ratify or approve it must be postponed until the Constitution has been amended.[48]

If the Constitutional Council deems that an unconstitutional provision of a statute is inseparable from the rest of the text, the full text of the law cannot be promulgated.[49] If the Council deems that the unconstitutional provisions can be separated from the text, the President of the Republic can either enact the incomplete text, or call for a second discussion by the Chambers.[50] In any case, the decision of the Constitutional Council is not reviewable and has binding effects on all public powers and administrative and jurisdictional authorities.[51]

### (d) The preventive control of the distribution of normative competences

The 1958 French Constitution deviated from the parliamentary tradition of modern states, and as a result of an obvious anti-parliamentary reaction, established a system for the distribution of competences between Parliament and government based on an assignment to Parliament of power over matters expressly enumerated in the Constitution. This resulted in an extreme restriction of parliamentary powers. Consequently, Article 34 of the Constitution enumerated an exclusive list of subjects whose regulation is attributed to the competence of Parliament; and Article 37 says that in all other matters, outside those that form the domain of the law (statute), the regulatory powers upon them are attributed to the executive.

This system of distributing normative state powers causes innumerable disputes between the law and the executive regulations which the Constitutional Council must settle. To resolve conflicts, the Council must intervene, although without examining the definitive normative text to ensure the compliance of constitutional provisions. The intervention is at the time of drafting the respective texts, and the Council can authorize or prohibit their continuation until the final version of the text is ready. This competence of the Council is exercised in two aspects with regard to statutes and to the exercise of the executive regulatory power.

### (i) The preventive control of bills

In the first aspect, the intervention of the Council concerns the procedure for the drafting of statutes and their reforms. For instance, the government may be opposed to the continuation of the discussion of a bill by the Assembly because it considers that it includes matters which are not under the domain reserved to the law in Article 34 of the Constitution.[52] It is possible in this case for the President of the Assembly to come to an agreement with the government whereby neither the proposal nor the reform is discussed. If no agreement can be reached, the Constitutional Council is called upon to settle the conflict by any of the interested organs and must adopt a decision within an eight day period. In that case, the discussion of the law or of the legislative amendment is immediately suspended.[53] In addition, the authority that requests the intervention of the Constitutional Council in the conflict, must notify all other authorities with the same competence to request a decision from the Constitutional Council.[54]

### (ii) Constitutional control of statutes regarding executive regulations

The Constitutional Council can also intervene when the government attempts to modify statutes. This can occur either when the statute in question has been adopted before the delimitation of the legislative domain in the 1958 Constitution but the matters concerned enter within the executive normative powers or, when statutes which come within the executive normative powers have been adopted after the 1958 delimitation but were not submitted to the control of the Constitutional Council before enactment.

Under the first possibility, the government is free to modify the existing pre-constitutional statutes. In such cases, the government is only obliged to adopt the corresponding decree after it has requested and obtained a consultative opinion from the Council of State.[55]

The second possibility deals with the exercise of executive regulatory

258

power to modify statutes adopted by Parliament after the 1958 Constitution. In such cases, the government is empowered to pass the respective regulatory decree only when the Constitutional Council has declared the executive regulatory nature of the matter.[56] In this way, if a government, through neglect or by deliberate political will, does not submit a non-promulgated statute which falls outside the domain reserved for the legislative power to the Constitutional Council before its enactment, successive governments are not bound by this decision and can submit the statute in question to the Constitutional Council. If the Council declares it to be subject to the executive, the government can modify it by decree.[57]

### (e) The substantive control of constitutionality of legislation and the principle of constitutionality

The French Constitution does not have an express declaration or enumeration of fundamental rights. The only declaration of the Constitution concerning fundamental rights of individuals is in its Preamble, which states that: 'The French people solemnly proclaim their adherence to the Rights of Man and to the principles of national sovereignty as have been defined in the Declaration of 1789, confirmed and completed by the Preamble of the 1946 Constitution.'

A similar preamble was established in the 1946 Constitution, which the then Constitutional Committee considered as not being directly enforceable.[58] Nevertheless, no special provision in this respect was established in the 1958 Constitution.

This approach changed on 16 July 1971 when a statute, sanctioned by Parliament, was declared unconstitutional by the Constitutional Council as being contrary to the freedom of association.[59] The Council based itself on the Preamble and through it on the 'fundamental principles recognised by the laws of the Republic and the Declaration of the Rights of Man and the Citizen of 1789'. With this incorporation of the Preamble, the '*bloc* of constitutionality' was enlarged by the Constitutional Council and the Council has become the guardian of rights and freedoms.[60] As a result, the Constitutional Council has created for itself the power and duty to control the conformity of non-promulgated statutes, not only to what is established in Articles 34 and 37 of the Constitution, but to the general principles as they arise from the Universal Declaration and from the Preamble, and the fundamental rights of individuals. Later decisions of the Council, such as in the nationalization case,[61] further enlarged the *bloc* of constitutionality to comprise the 'principles and rules of constitutional value'[62] to which the legislator is also submitted.

Finally, it must be noted that the control of constitutionality of legislation has also been enlarged through the work of the other main jurisdictional organs in France, the Council of State and the Court of Cassation.

In particular the Council of State, since its decision *Syndicat Général des Ingénieurs-Conseils* (1959),[63] has exercised constitutional control over executive normative acts (decree laws) adopted in accordance with the powers attributed to the executive in Article 37 of the Constitution. This control does not refer to the submission of executive regulations to statutes sanctioned by Parliament, but to the Constitution, and extends to 'the general principles of law which result basically from the Preamble of the Constitution' which 'are imposed on the regulatory executive authority, even in the absence of a legislative disposition'.[64]

The Court of Cassation, in *Administration des Douanes* v. *Société Cafés Jacques Varbre S.A.* (1975),[65] led the way to the exercise of a diffuse system of judicial review in France by establishing the power of courts to refuse to apply statutes which were contrary to the Treaties of the European Economic Community.[66] This possibility of a diffuse system of judicial review could lead to a general examination of statutes to test their conformity with fundamental rights. This may occur partly because the European Convention of Human Rights is part of French law,[67] but also because of the express acceptance by the Constitutional Council of the constitutional rank, value and character of the fundamental rights contained in the 1789 Declaration. Of course, to that end, the reluctance of the courts to control the constitutionality of statutes so traditional in France must be overcome. That is a fundamental task they have in the future.

# 24

# THE LIMITED CONCENTRATED SYSTEM OF JUDICIAL REVIEW IN BELGIUM: THE ARBITRATION COURT

In Belgium there is a decentralised political form of state. Its establishment can be traced back to the 1970 constitutional reform although it was not actually established until the 1980 constitutional reform.[1] The regions and communities which resulted from this are based upon the linguistic and ethnic divisions in the country. Consequently, there is a need for an independent constitutional organ to resolve conflicts between the various political entities. This was brought about by the creation of an Arbitration Court in the same 1980 amendment to the Constitution.[2]

The Court of Arbitration is composed of twelve members: six French speaking members, who form the French language part of the Court, and six Flemish speaking members who represent Flemish speaking communities. The members of the Court are appointed by the King for life from a list with twice the number. This list is submitted by the Senate who have already adopted it by a two thirds majority of its members present. The candidates who must be over forty years of age, must either have held posts for five years as judicial or administrative magistrates, or be professors of law, or they must have been members of the Senate or of the Chamber of Deputies for at least eight years. Each linguistic group must share an equal distribution of the two above mentioned categories.[3]

The Court of Arbitration has only a limited competence to judge the conformity of laws and decrees with the Constitution.[4] These judicial review powers are applicable only to certain disputes of competences between state bodies.

The powers of the Arbitration Court can be exercised through direct or incidental means. The direct recourse is brought before the Court by the Council of Ministers or by the executive body of the communities or the regions. They can request the annulment of any legislative act on the grounds that it infringes the vertical distribution of powers established in the Constitution. This right may also permit the Presidents of the legislative assemblies to bring matters before the Court at the request of two thirds of their members. In any case, the recourse must be presented before the Court within the period of one year following the publication of the challenged act,[5] and the Court can decide, when demanded by a party, to suspend the application of the challenged statute or decree. In the case of a suspended law, the Court must decide the recourse within a period of three months.[6]

The final Court decisions on the matter can declare the nullity of the unconstitutional act, 'having absolute *res judicata* authority from its publication in the *Moniteur Belge*'.[7] This means that they have *erga omnes* effects. Additionally, it has been considered that such decisions have retroactive effects,[8] thus, *ex-tunc, pro praeterito*.

The second method through which a constitutional question can reach the Court of Arbitration is the incidental one, when the issue is referred to the Court by any ordinary court.[9] The ordinary courts do not have *ex officio* powers to refer constitutional questions to the Court, but have an important appreciation power when considering the issue raised by a party in the case.[10] The decision of the Court of Arbitration in these incidental judicial review cases has binding effects, not only upon the ordinary court that has referred the question, but also upon all other courts that must intervene in the same case.[11]

# Part VI

## THE MIXED SYSTEM OF JUDICIAL REVIEW

As has been seen, both the concentrated and the diffuse systems of judicial review have, as their basic principle, the supremacy of the Constitution. Moreover, it may be noted that either of these systems can exist and function in countries with either a common or roman law tradition. Moreover, they can co-exist in a particular country. This latter phenomenon gives rise to a mixed system of judicial review in which the maximum protection of the Constitution is established. In Europe, a mixed system of judicial review exists in Portugal and in a more limited way in Switzerland. In Latin America countries such as Colombia, Venezuela, Guatemala, Peru and Brazil follow a mixed system.

# 25

## THE CONTROL OF THE CONSTITUTIONALITY OF LEGISLATION IN THE PORTUGUESE REPUBLIC

The Constitution of the Republic of Portugal, approved by a Constituent Assembly in April 1976, established the basis of a mixed system of judicial review of the constitutionality of legislation. This mixed system was maintained in the First Revision of the Constitution approved by the Constitutional Law No. 1/82 of 30 September 1982.[1] This system, in which the Council of the Revolution, its Constitutional Commission and the ordinary courts played a very important role,[2] is the most complete system of judicial review in Europe and includes the basic elements of the European model and the French system in parallel with elements of the diffuse system of judicial review.

### (a) The principle of constitutional supremacy and its consequences

The 1982 Constitution is not only a written and rigid Constitution,[3] but is expressly conceived as the supreme law of the land, to which all other state acts must be submitted. In this respect, Article 3 of the Constitution states: 'The State shall be subject to the Constitution and based on democratic legality ... The validity of the laws and other State acts of the autonomous regions and local authorities shall depend on their being in accordance with the Constitution.'

The consequence of this supremacy clause is also expressly established in the text of the Constitution in which Article 277 states: 'Provisions of law that infringe a provision of the Constitution or the principles laid down therein are unconstitutional.' Of course, the consequence of this assertion is the establishment of a complex system of judicial review in which a diffuse system exists in parallel with a concentrated system attributed to a Constitutional Court.

The Constitutional Court was created by the Constitution, within the judicial power,[4] as a constitutional organ 'competent to judge whether acts are unconstitutional and illegal' in accordance with the provisions[5] of the

Constitution. It is also competent to judge questions related to the exercise of Presidential functions and electoral matters.[6] The Constitutional Court is composed of thirteen judges, ten being named by the Assembly of the Republic and three co-opted.[7]

### (b) The diffuse system of judicial review and the direct appeal before the Constitutional Court

In accordance with Article 207 of the Constitution 'The Courts shall not apply unconstitutional provisions or principles to matters brought before them.' This constitutional provision authorizes all the courts of the country not to apply unconstitutional provisions or principles. Thus statutes, decrees, executive regulations, regional or any other normative state acts, and international treaties are subject to the review of the courts. As the ability is given in terms of a duty, the courts have an *ex officio* power to raise constitutional questions. Issues can also be raised by the party in the concrete case or by the Public Prosecutor.

When the courts consider that a norm is unconstitutional, the norm is considered invalid regarding the concrete case, that is to say, with *inter partes* effects as well as *ex-tunc, pro praeterito* effects.

The most interesting feature of this diffuse system is the direct appeal established before the Constitutional Court against judicial decisions. This permits constitutional questions to be decided in a similar way to the extraordinary recourse of unconstitutionality, in the Argentinian and Brazilian systems, or to the direct appeals before the Supreme Court in the United States.

Under the 'concrete scrutiny for the constitutionality' Article 280 of the Portuguese Constitution establishes the right to appeal before the Constitutional Court against any court decisions when they, firstly, refuse to apply any provision of law on the grounds that it is unconstitutional or, secondly, when they apply a provision of a law the unconstitutionality of which has been raised during the proceedings.[8]

This appeal must be compulsorily exercised by the Department of the Public Prosecutor in cases in which a court of justice refuses to apply any provision of an international convention, a legislative act or a regulative decree on the grounds that it is unconstitutional.[9] In cases in which a court applies a provision of law, the unconstitutionality of which has been raised by a party during the proceeding, only that party has the right to appeal before the Constitutional Court.[10]

The Constitutional Court also has the ability to hear appeals against lower court decisions in the following cases: first, when the courts refuse to apply a provision of a regional instrument because it violates the statute of the autonomous regions or general law of the Republic; second, when the courts refuse to apply a provision of an instrument emanating from an organ of supreme authority on the grounds that it violates the statutes of an autonomous region; and thirdly, when the court applies a provision the illegality of which has been raised during the proceedings on the grounds of violating regional autonomies. In this latter case, only the interested party which raised the question has the right of appeal.[11] On the other hand, the Public Prosecutor is obliged to appeal against court decisions in which a provision of law, previously judged unconstitutional or illegal by the Constitutional Court itself, is applied.[12]

In any of these cases of appeals before the Constitutional Court, they shall be restricted to the question of unconstitutionality or illegality depending on the case.[13] The Court does not review the case on its facts, its judicial review powers being limited to the constitutional question. Moreover, in these cases the decisions of the Court have effects only regarding the concrete case. Only when the Constitutional Court has judged any provision of law unconstitutional in three concrete cases, can it judge and rule with generally binding validity on the unconstitutionality of the law.[14]

### (c) The concentrated system of judicial review and the powers of the Constitutional Court

In parallel with the diffuse system of judicial review, the Constitution of the Portuguese Republic has also established a concentrated system which can review both enacted and proposed legislation.

### (i) The preventive control of constitutionality

The Constitutional Court can exercise a preventive control of constitutionality, with regard to international treaties and agreements, formal laws and decree laws, when requested by the President of the Republic. It can review proposed regional legislative decrees or executive normative acts, when requested by the Ministers of the Republic. In the first case, Article 278, 1 of the Constitution establishes:

The President of the Republic may request the Constitutional Court to judge preventively the constitutionality of any provision of an international treaty that has been submitted to him for ratification, and acts sent to him for promulgation as a law or decree law or an international agreement the act of approval of which has been sent to him for signature.[15]

In such cases, if the Constitutional Court rules that a provision of any act or international agreement is unconstitutional, the act must be vetoed by the President of the Republic or by the Minister concerned, and must be sent back to the organ that approved it.[16] In principle, the act must not be promulgated or signed unless the organ that approved it expurgates the provision judged unconstitutional.[17] In such cases the possibility of requesting another preventive control of constitutionality of the reformulated act is expressly authorized.[18]

In cases in which the Assembly does not expurgate the unconstitutional provision of an international treaty, it could be ratified if the Assembly approves it by a two thirds majority of the members present.[19] Similarly, this may be done with regard to formal laws when their unconstitutionality has been determined by the Court.

## (ii) The abstract control of constitutionality \

The constitutionality of legislation can, however, also be the object of an abstract scrutiny by the Constitutional Court, exercised through a direct means or action. This abstract scrutiny permits enacted legislation to be reviewed without the requirement of an ordinary issue in law depending upon the validity of the legislation. Thus the unconstitutionality of any provision of law can be the object of a request formulated before the Constitutional Court by the President of the Republic, the President of the Assembly of the Republic, the Prime Minister, the Ombudsman, the Attorney General, or one-tenth of the members of the Assembly of the Republic.[20] Additionally, the regional assemblies or the chairmen of the regional governments can also exercise the direct request of unconstitutionality against laws, on the grounds that the rights of the autonomous regions have been violated.[21] Moreover, since the Constitution also permits a direct request on the basis that the statute of a region or the general law of the Republic has been violated, the Minister of the Republic in the autonomous region is entitled to formulate it.[22]

The effects of the Constitutional Court decisions in these cases are expressly regulated in the Constitution. The Court's decision, in cases of direct request of unconstitutionality, has generally binding effects 'as from the entry into force of the provision ruled unconstitutional or illegal and shall determine the restoration with retroactive effects, of the provisions that it may have revoked'.[23] If the legislation was enacted prior to the constitutional norm, the ruling of the Court shall produce effects only as from the entry into force of the new constitutional provision.[24]

These two express dispositions of the Constitution lead to the consideration that the general rule existing in the Portuguese system of judicial review is that decisions declaring the unconstitutionality of a state act, have *ex-tunc, pro praeterito* effects, except in 'cases already judged' which, in principle, 'shall be safeguarded, except if the Constitutional Court decides otherwise when the provision concerns penal or disciplinary matters or illegal acts in violation of mere social rules and is less favourable to the accused'.[25]

However, the powers of the Court in this respect are very wide, and the Constitution expressly establishes that 'when required by legal security, reasons of equity or public interest of exceptional importance, which shall be justified, the Constitutional Court may fix the effects of unconstitutionality or illegality in a more restrictive way'.[26] Thus it is possible to correct the inconvenient effects that could be produced by the rigidity of the retroactive general effects of the decisions.

### (d) The unconstitutionality by omission

Finally, the Constitution assigns the Constitutional Court powers to control 'unconstitutionality by omission'. The Constitution establishes that at

the request of the President of the Republic, the Ombudsman or, on the grounds that the rights of the autonomous regions have been violated, the President of the regional assemblies, the Constitutional Court shall judge and verify failure to comply with the Constitution by omission on the part of the legislative acts necessary to implement the provisions of the Constitution.

When the Constitutional Court verifies the existence of unconstitutionality by omission, it shall communicate the fact to the competent legislative organ.

This exceptional power attributed to the Constitutional Court was originally established in the 1976 Constitution as the result of the negotiations carried out by the Council of the Revolution in 1975, on behalf of the Armed Forces Movement, and the political parties, with a view to establishing a certain number of principles which were to be compulsorily observed and maintained by the respective parliamentary groups in the Constituent Assembly.[27]

Up to the sanctioning of the 1982 First Revision of the Constitution, in which this 'constitutional control by omission' was maintained, it was exercised on two occasions by the then Council of the Revolution. In 1977, the Council recommended the adoption of legislative measures to enforce the norms of Article 46 of the 1976 Constitution whereby, among other aspects, organizations with a fascist ideology were banned. In making its recommendation, the Council spelled out the necessary conditions for the existence of 'legislative omission'. This established that certain constitutional norms could not be self-applicable. Further, it indicated that an omission occurred when the competent body to adopt the legislative measures violated its obligation to dictate norms to a degree that the observance of the constitutional norm was obstructed by the very ones for whom the legal mandate was intended. Thus, if the legal order contained any prescriptions which made the constitutional norm applicable, an omission had not occurred.[28]

In a second case, in 1978, the Council of the Revolution recommended the adoption of legislative measures for guaranteeing the applicability of Article 53 of the Constitution to domestic servants. This article conferred upon workers the right to rest and recreation, by limiting the length of the working day, establishing the weekly rest period as well as periodic paid holidays. On this second occasion, the essential contribution of the Council lay in their extensive interpretation of the initiative to request control by omission.[29]

# 26

## THE LIMITED MIXED SYSTEM OF CONSTITUTIONAL
## JUDICIAL REVIEW IN SWITZERLAND

Although Switzerland has a mixed system of judicial review with regard to cantonal laws and federal executive regulations, their system of review must be considered to be limited because it is not permitted with respect to federal legislation.

### (a) The absence of judicial review over federal legislation

Since the main constitutional reform of 1874, in which the judicial federal courts were organized, the Federal Tribunal was vested with the task of ensuring that the Constitution and federal laws were observed.[1] In particular, the following clause was inserted in Article 113 of the Constitution: 'In all cases above mentioned the Federal Tribunal shall administer the laws passed by the Federal Assembly, and such ordinances of that Assembly as are of general application. It shall likewise act in accordance with treaties ratified by the Federal Assembly.'[2] Although this clause was initially limited to cases of public law, that is to say cases arising from conflicts between the confederation and the cantons or between cantons themselves, it was soon interpreted by the Federal Tribunal as being applicable to all other cases. This was a consequence of the fact that the Federal Tribunal was always bound to apply the laws as enacted by the federal legislature without having any power to review or control their constitutionality.[3] Thus the democratic idea which demands the recognition of the will of the people's representatives was responsible for the supremacy of Parliament and its laws over all other state organs and acts. That is why in a decision adopted in 1876, the Federal Tribunal stated:

It must be recognised as a principle of ... the Swiss federal and cantonal constitutional law that the authority of the legislative powers is supreme, and the Courts are not empowered to deny the validity and applicability of a law or decree enacted by the legislative authorities on the grounds that their content is repugnant to the Constitution; it belongs to them only to check formally whether they really face a law enacted in a way conforming to the Constitution.[4]

In spite of efforts to modify it, this doctrine is the one still prevailing in Switzerland.[5] Thus a clause similar to Article 113 was inserted in the 1912 constitutional amendment, in which it was stated that '[t]he administrative court shall apply federal legislation and treaties approved by the Federal Assembly'.[6] As a result, no judicial review is permitted either by the Federal Tribunal or by any other court in the country, regarding federal laws and other acts of general effects of the federal legislature.[7] The same principle applies to executive decrees with force of federal law adopted by the Federal Council executing extraordinary powers.[8] Thus, only cantonal laws and executive regulations at federal level can be reviewed by the courts, and this can be done either in a diffuse or a concentrated way.

## (b) The limited diffuse system of judicial review

All courts have the power to control the constitutionality of cantonal and federal executive regulations. This verification of the constitutionality of state acts is only of an incidental and pre-judicial character, as it is motivated by the need to apply a particular cantonal norm in a concrete case. A provision, which is considered to have violated the Constitution or federal law, can not be annulled by the judge. He can only declares it not applicable to the resolution of the case.[9] Moreover, although no judicial review of federal legislation is permitted, all courts have the power to verify whether a statute has or has not been duly published.[10]

## (c) The limited concentrated system of judicial review

In parallel with the limited diffuse system of judicial review, a limited concentrated system of judicial review exists. This may be exercised by means of a direct action called the recourse of public law.

Since the Federal Tribunal is the supreme judicial organ of the country, it is the final appeal in all judicial cases. As a result, it is divided into various sections. One of these sections is the public law and administrative law section, and through this section the Federal Tribunal acts as the court of last resort, in all administrative justice cases, and as a constitutional court.[11]

In its constitutional character, the Federal Tribunal is empowered to resolve and settle conflicts of competences resulting from the distribution of state powers within the federal system, and to decide any public law recourses that can be brought before it on constitutional matters. In the settlement of conflicts of attributions, the Tribunal is in charge of resolving conflicts of attributions which may arise between federal and cantonal authorities, as well as those that may arise between cantons themselves in connection with the delimitation of the legal domain attributed to them.[12]

The recourse of public law, conceived as the means for controlling normative and other acts of the cantonal legislature[13] with federal law, can be exercised by any interested individual or corporation, for the following reasons: (1) Violation of any of the citizens' constitutional rights; (2) violation of *concordats* or public law agreements between cantons; (3) violation of international treaties, except in cases of infringement of civil or criminal law provisions contained in some treaties by decision of the cantonal authorities; and (4) violation of federal law dispositions relating to the delimitation of areas of competence of the authorities.[14] Also considered as public law recourses, are those concerning the citizens' right to vote, and those relating to cantonal elections and voting, regardless of the cantonal constitutional or federal law provisions applicable.[15]

These public law recourses before the Swiss Federal Tribunal are essentially of a subsidiary nature, that is to say, they are only admissible when the alleged violation of the right cannot be brought before any other judicial authority through other legal means established either under federal or cantonal law.[16] Consequently, the action cannot be admitted unless all existing cantonal remedies have been exhausted. Nevertheless, this réquisite of previous exhaustion of ordinary legal procedures does not apply to actions relating to the violation of freedom of establishment, the prohibition of double taxation in fiscal matters, the citizen's right to appear before his natural judge, and the right to legal aid,[17] which can be brought before the Federal Tribunal in a principal way.

Citizens and corporations whose rights are violated by cantonal acts or provisions of general binding effect or who, even in the absence of any such violation, are personally affected by the said acts or provisions, are entitled to bring a public law recourse.[18] The term 'corporation' is understood by law to mean private law entities, which includes companies and professional associations.[19]

Exceptionally, a public law action could also be brought before the Tribunal by public law entities, to protect their sphere of autonomous action *vis-à-vis* administrative bodies of higher rank. In this respect, for example, a municipality can impugn acts of the canton of which it is a dependency by means of a public law recourse brought on the grounds of violation of municipal autonomy.[20]

In general, the Tribunal does not have *ex officio* powers to consider constitutional questions other than those raised by the claimant, and in the past the Tribunal has refused to consider facts not alleged in the ordinary judicial proceeding previously exhausted.[21] When the Federal Tribunal considers that a cantonal act is unconstitutional, it annuls the act with *erga omnes* effects.[22]

# 27

## THE MIXED SYSTEM OF JUDICIAL REVIEW IN VENEZUELA

### (a) Constitutional supremacy and judicial review

The Venezuelan constitutional system is based on the principle of constitutional supremacy, the Constitution being considered as a normative charter not only organizing the exercise of public power but also establishing the fundamental rights of citizens. Thus, it is considered an embodiment of positive norms directly applicable to individuals, a characteristic which has developed from the very beginning of the constitutional process in 1811.[1] This principle of the supremacy of the Constitution inevitably led, more than a hundred years ago,[2] to the development of a system of judicial review of constitutionality of state acts. The system was explained by the Supreme Court of Justice in 1962, when deciding a popular action brought before it against the law of approval of the extradition treaty signed with the United States of America, as follows:

The existence of a judicial control of the constitutionality of state acts exercised by the Highest Tribunal of the Republic, has been traditional in Venezuela, and is indispensable in any regime which pretends to subsist as a state submitted to the rule of law (*Estado de Derecho*). The unconstitutional is always anti-juridical and contrary to the principle that compels the public power, in all of its branches, to subject itself to the constitutional and legal norms which define its attributions. The unconstitutional is an outrage against the citizens rights and against the legal order in general, which have their supreme guarantees in the Fundamental Law of the state. In countries ruled freely, all private or governmental activities must necessarily be maintained within the limits established in the Fundamental Charter, which prescriptions, as the solemn expression of the popular will in the public law sphere, are norms of inescapable observance for those who govern and those who are governed, from the most humble of citizens up to the highest powers of the state. From the principles established in the Constitution, from the norms drawn up by it, whether in its organic or in its dogmatic parts, the laws and all dispositions enacted after must be simple developments; and as unconstitutional and thus, improper they would be considered if they exceed that character, as unconstitutional and also improper as would be any other act of the public powers which openly contravenes what is established in the fundamental law.[3]

As a consequence of this principle of constitutional supremacy, the 1961 Venezuelan Constitution, following a constitutional tradition that can be traced back to the 1858 Constitution,[4] established in Article 215 the competence of the Supreme Court of Justice to review the constitutionality of laws and other normative acts of the national, member states or municipal deliberative bodies, of executive regulations and acts of government adopted by the President of the Republic. Thus it provides for judicial review of the constitutionality of all state acts including judicial and administrative acts.

In particular, at the national level this includes laws and other acts with the same rank or force of law (other acts of parliament without the form of law, and decree laws and other government acts), and executive regulations adopted by the national executive. At the member state level, judicial review applies to laws issued by the Legislative Assemblies and, at the municipal level, to Municipal Ordinances adopted by the Municipal Councils. This review power of the constitutionality of state acts allows the Supreme Court of Justice to declare laws null and void when they violate the Constitution. It thus constitutes a concentrated system of control of the constitutionality of laws and other state acts.

However Article 20 of the Civil Proceedings Code allows all courts and tribunals of the Republic to declare all normative state acts inapplicable in a given case, when they consider them unconstitutional. Thus a diffuse system of judicial review is established. Therefore, as in the Portuguese system, the Venezuelan system is one of the most extensive systems of judicial review.[5]

With respect to this mixed character of the Venezuelan system, the Supreme Court has stated that judicial review is the responsibility

not only of the Supreme Court of the Republic, but also of the judges in general, whatever their rank and standing may be. It is sufficient for an official to form part of the judiciary for him to be a custodian of the Constitution and, consequently, to apply its ruling preferentially over those of ordinary laws ... Nonetheless, the application of the fundamental rules by the judges, only has effects in the concrete case at issue and, for that very reason, only affects the interested parties to the conflict. In contrast, when constitutional illegitimacy in a law is declared by the Supreme Court when exercising its sovereign function, as the interpreter of the Constitution, and in response to the pertinent action, the effects of the decision extend *erga omnes* and have the force of law. In the first case, the review is incidental and special, and in the second, principal and general. When this happens –

that is to say when the recourse is autonomous – the control is either formal or material, depending on whether the nullity has to do with an irregularity relating to the process of drafting the law, or whether – despite the legislation having been correct from the formalist point of view – the intrinsic content of the ruling suffers from substantial defects.[6]

## (b) The diffuse system of judicial review

Since Article 20 of the Civil Proceedings Code allows any judge to decide not to apply a law which conflicts with any provision of the Constitution, the principle of the supremacy of the Constitution is recognized.[7] According to this power, the diffuse system of judicial review in Venezuela can be characterised by the following trends.

### (i) The pre-eminence of the Constitution and the nullity of unconstitutional acts

Since the diffuse system is a consequence of the supremacy of the Constitution, judges are bound by the Constitution and have a duty to apply it. This has been the basic principle ever since the 1811 Constitution in which Article 227 stated:

The present Constitution, the laws to be adopted in its execution and the Treaties to be subscribed under the authority of the Union Government will be the supreme law of the state in the whole Confederation, and the authorities and inhabitants of the provinces are bound to religiously obey and observe them without excuse or pretext; but the laws enacted against the text of the Constitution will have no value unless they fulfil all the required conditions for a just and legitimate revision and sanction.[8]

According to this norm, as in the American model, unconstitutional laws were considered null and void and with no effect whatsoever. The guarantee of the Constitution in that case was the nullity of the unconstitutional act, and not its annullability and the judges had the duty not to 'obey or execute orders evidently contrary to the Constitution or the laws'.[9]

The same principles have been applicable, since the 1811 Constitution, with regard to fundamental rights and freedoms.[10] That is why the present 1961 Constitution expressly establishes in Article 46 that: 'Every act of the public power which violates or impairs the rights guaranteed by this Constitution is void, and the public officials and employees who order or execute it shall be held criminally, civilly or administratively liable, as the case may be, and orders of superiors manifestly contrary to the Constitution and the laws may not serve as an excuse.'

## (ii) The incidental character of the system
## and the *ex officio* powers of the judges

Following the general trends of all diffuse systems of judicial review, the Venezuelan system also has an incidental character, that is the courts can review the constitutionality of a law when deciding a concrete case. This power can only be exercised within a concrete adversary litigation when a constitutional issue is relevant to the case and necessary to the resolution of the decision. Moreover, as was stated in the 1901 Constitution,[11] the constitutional issue can be raised *ex officio* by the judge when deciding the concrete case.

## (iii) The effects of the judicial decision
## and the absence of extraordinary means of appeals or recourses

As the nullity of unconstitutional laws, particularly those which violate fundamental rights, are the guarantee of the Constitution, the decision of the courts in the diffuse system of constitutional control has declarative effects. Thus, when a judge decides not to apply a law in a concrete case by declaring it unconstitutional, it is considered to have been invalid ever since its enactment (*ab initio*). This decision evidently has *ex-tunc* and *pro praeterito* or retroactive effects, preventing the unconstitutional and inapplicable law from having any effect.

Of course, these declarative and *ex-tunc* effects of the decision only bind the parties within the concrete process in which the decision is adopted.[12] This is a consequence of the incidental character (*incidenter tantum*) of the diffuse control and of the Constitution which reserves the declaratory power of nullity exclusively to the Supreme Court.[13] Therefore, the fact that a law is declared inapplicable by reason of unconstitutionality by a judge in a particular case does not affect its validity nor is it equivalent to a declaration of nullity. The law as such continues to be valid, and will only lose its general effects if repealed by another law[14] or if annulled by the Supreme Court of Justice.[15]

Because *stare decisis* has no application, decisions regarding the inapplicability of a law have no binding effects on the same judge, who may change his legal opinion in other cases, nor regarding other judges or courts. Unlike the American or Argentinian systems, there are no extraordinary means of appeal or recourses against judicial decisions in which constitutional questions are involved. The judges' decisions are only subject to the ordinary means of appeal and to the recourse of cassation, following the general rules established in the Civil Procedural Code. It was only in the 1901 Constitution that the Federal Court was assigned the power to establish general criteria in constitutional matters referred to by lower courts, when a constitutional issue was raised in concrete judicial cases, which power was eliminated in the subsequent constitutional reform of 1904. In effect, Article 106, 8 of the 1901 Constitution established as an attribution of the Federal Court, to

declare in the shortest possible delay which disposition must prevail in the special case which is referred to it *motu proprio* or at the instance of the interested party by the judicial authority which is due to apply the law, in the delay established for adopting its decision, when the said judicial authority considers that a collision exists between the Federal or state Laws with the Constitution of the Republic.[16]

Notwithstanding this consultative power of the Federal Court, when a referral was made before it, it had no suspensive effect in the concrete process. Instead, if it was time to render a decision and the lower court had not yet received the Federal Court's opinion, the lower court was to decide by itself, reviewing the constitutionality of the legislation.

Any possible contradictions that could arise between different court decisions on constitutional matters have been corrected since 1858 with the establishment, in parallel with the diffuse system of judicial review, of a concentrated system of constitutional control assigned to the Supreme Court of Justice.

### (c) The concentrated system of judicial review

#### (i) Historical antecedents

The 1858 Constitution attributed competence to the Supreme Court to 'Declare the nullity of legislative acts sanctioned by the Provincial Legislatures, when petitioned by any citizen, when they are contrary to the Constitution.'[17] Thus, in 1858 a popular action was established to seek the control of the constitutionality of legislative acts adopted at provincial level. It was a limited concentrated judicial review system, which did not refer to the national legislative act, but it can be considered the direct antecedent of the current popular action established after 1893. Yet because it was originally intended to protect the invasions by the Provinces of the competences of the central power, in the 1864 Constitution that consolidated the federal form of the state, the principle of protection limited the invasions of the competences and rights of the member states by the federal level. In this sense, the 1864 Constitution expressly established in Article 92 that 'Any act of Congress or of the National Executive which violates the rights of the Member states guaranteed by the Constitution or which harm its independence, must be declared null by the High Court, when the majority of the legislatures demand it.'[18]

Although the 1864 Constitution eliminated the popular action and limited the standing to seek judicial review of legislation to the legislatures of the state members of the federation, the Federal High Court was given power to declare which law was in force when collisions existed among national laws, between those laws and legislation of the member states, and between the laws of the various member states.[19] Thus some form of judicial review remained.

This situation stood invariable until 1893, when the constitutional reform of that year extended the powers of judicial review of legislation of the Supreme Court to a point very similar to the present one. The 1893 Constitution gave the Federal High Court power to 'Declare which is the law, decree or resolution in force when a collision exists between the national acts, or those with one of the states, or between the acts of the states, and any of those acts with the Constitution.'[20] In this way the Supreme Court powers of judicial review of constitutionality were re-established, extended not only to laws, but also to decrees and resolutions, and maintaining the protective norm of the rights of the member states against the invasions of their competences by the federal or national power.[21] Moreover, in the same 1893 Constitution the guarantee of the fundamental rights of citizens was also established in an express form, by stating that, 'The rights recognised and established in the Constitution will not be harmed or damaged by the laws which regulate their exercise, and those which do so will be considered unconstitutional and will have no effects.'[22]

Finally the 1893 Constitution gave the Federal High Court powers to declare the nullity of all state acts which could be dictated by a usurped authority or as a consequence of a direct or indirect request by force or by a subversive people's gathering.[23]

The scheme of the 1893 Constitution, with the exception of a short period of three years between 1901 and 1904,[24] has more or less been maintained in all subsequent constitutional texts and reforms although the means of control has been increased. In 1925 the possibility of declaring the nullity of any Municipal Ordinances which violated the Constitution was added to the powers of the Supreme Court and,[25] in 1936, Executive Regulations were added to the list of acts submitted to constitutional judicial review.[26] It was in this 1936 Constitution, adopted after the end of a thirty-five year dictatorship, that the Constitution assigned to the Supreme Court, then the Federal and Cassation Court, power to declare the nullity of all acts of the Public Powers which violated the Constitution.[27]

In parallel with the regulations of judicial review of the constitutionality of legislation, the system of judicial review of administrative action was also expressly established. This was done by giving an administrative jurisdiction to the judiciary.[28] Constitutional jurisdiction however, was reserved to the Supreme Court.

In this respect, the 1961 Constitution in force today, establishes, as a competence of the Supreme Court of Justice, the power to declare, first, the total or partial nullity of national laws and other acts of the legislative bodies that are in conflict with the Constitution; second, the total or partial nullity of member state laws, municipal ordinances and other acts of the deliberative bodies of the states and municipalities that are in conflict with the Constitution; and third, the nullity of regulations and other acts of the national executive when they violate the Constitution.[29]

These attributions have been developed by the Organic Law of the Supreme Court of Justice of 1976[30] in which, it can be said, all state acts of a normative character (legislation of the three territorial levels and executive regulations) and all other state acts issued under direct authority of the Constitution are submitted to judicial review of constitutionality by means of a direct popular action.[31] This action is exercised through *a posteriori* judicial review. An *a priori* judicial review, particularly of national legislation, can also be exercised by the Supreme Court at the request of the President of the Republic, before the promulgation of the laws. Therefore, the concentrated system of judicial review can be both preventive and *a posteriori*.

### (ii) The preventive control of the constitutionality of laws

Since 1945 the Venezuelan Constitution has expressly established the possibility of a judicial preventive control of the constitutionality of national laws. This control is exercised by the Supreme Court of Justice, at the request of the President of the Republic as a consequence of its powers of veto regarding legislation approved by Congress.[32] The present 1961 Constitution in Article 173 establishes the procedure for the enactment of laws and, in particular, the possibility of the presidential veto to legislation in the following way.

The President of the Republic shall promulgate the law within ten days after the date of receipt, but within that period, with the approval of the Council of Ministers, he may ask Congress for its reconsideration, giving an explanation with reasons, in order to amend certain provisions or withdraw its sanction of all or part of the law. The Chambers in joint session shall decide on the points raised by the President of the Republic and may write a new text for the provisions objected to and those connected therewith.

When a decision has been adopted by two thirds of those present, the President of the Republic shall proceed with the promulgation of the law within five days following its receipt, and he may not offer new objections. But when the decision has been reached by a simple majority, the President of the Republic may choose between promulgating the law or returning it again to Congress within the same five day period for a new and final reconsideration. In this latter case the decision of the Chambers in joint session is definitive, even by a simple majority, and promulgation of the law must be made within five days following its receipt.

In any case, if the objection is based on unconstitutionality, the President of the Republic may, within the period fixed for the promulgation of a law, that is to say, within five days following the receipt of the law after Congress' reconsideration, have recourse to the Supreme Court of Justice, requesting its decision as to the alleged unconstitutionality.[33] The Court shall decide within a period of ten days, counted from the date of receipt of the communication from the President of the Republic. Nevertheless, if the Court denies the complaint of unconstitutionality, or does not decide within the aforementioned period, the President of the Republic must promulgate the law within five days after the decision of the Court or the expiration of the period indicated.[34]

If the Court accepts the allegation of unconstitutionality, it must decide the case and that will prevent the sanctioned law from being promulgated.[35] Although the Constitution does not deal with the possibility and the consequences of the Court not giving its decision as to the constitutionality of a law within ten days, after a request by the President, it can be considered that the expiry of that delay and the subsequent compulsory promulgation of the law, do not prevent the Court from the possibility of declaring the nullity of the law once in effect, based on its concentrated powers of judicial review of promulgated legislation.

### (iii) The direct control of constitutionality

In addition to the diffuse and preventive systems of judicial review, the control of the constitutionality of legislation can be exercised in a concentrated way by the Supreme Court of Justice at the request of any body, through a popular action.

## The popular action and the principal character of the process

The fundamental characteristic of the judicial review powers of the Supreme Court to control the constitutionality of legislation is that it has been set up as a consequence of a popular action, that is to say, of a recourse open to any inhabitant of the Republic in full possession of his rights.[36] For this reason, the popular action in Venezuela is open to:

any member of the general public [and] is intended to defend a public interest which is, at the same time, the simple interest of the petitioner who, for this reason alone, need not be vested with any other standing or juridical interest. [It is instituted to] contest the validity of an act by the public power, which by virtue of its normative and general character, acts *erga omnes* and thus its validity affects, and is of interest to, all equally.[37]

From this stems one of the great differences between the popular action of unconstitutionality and actions seeking judicial review of administrative acts. The former requires no special standing; a simple interest in legality is sufficient. By contrast, if an administrative act with individual effects is contested in the administrative jurisdiction, it is required that the petitioner is entitled to some subjective right, or has a personal, legitimate and direct interest in the legality of the act.[38]

It must be pointed out that the popularity of the popular action, traditionally wider than the other remedies, has since 1976 been restricted by the Organic Law of the Supreme Court of Justice. That law requires that the challenged law must violate 'the rights and interests of the petitioner' in some way.[39] This restriction can be considered reasonable, and can only affect standing in extreme cases: for instance, if the challenged law is a law of a member state, at least it is required that the petitioner is a resident of the said state or has some particular interest located in that state.[40]

Yet doubts about the extent of the restriction to the popularity of the action have been clarified by the Supreme Court, which has considered that the legal reference to the need that the challenged law affected 'the rights and interests' of the petitioner does not mean that the popular action has been eliminated, and that a special standing requirement has been established to bring such action before the Court. The object of the popular action, the Court has said, is the 'objective defence of the majesty of the Constitution and its supremacy', and if it is true that the Organic Law of the Supreme Court requires that the petitioner be affected in his rights or interests, this expression must be interpreted in a restrictive way. Thus the Court has concluded that when the popular action is exercised against legislative acts, 'a presumption exists that at least relatively, the challenged act of general effects, affects the rights or interests of the petitioner in his condition as a Venezuelan citizen in some way, unless the contrary shows itself evident from the text of the complaint'.[41]

Another difference is that because unconstitutionality refers to legislative acts, the popular action is not subject to any expiry period; it is unextinguishable.[42] However, judicial actions against administrative acts, when referred to acts with particular effects, must be exercised within a delay of six months.[43] After this period they expire.

In relation to the popular nature of the action of unconstitutionality, because it is open to any person whose rights and interests have been violated, the fact that deficiencies may exist in the petitioner's legal representation is no impediment to acceptance of the recourse;[44] the legal representative could equally well bring the action in his personal capacity. On the other hand, not only individuals and public corporations have standing to bring a popular action of unconstitutionality before the Supreme Court, but any public officer is entitled to do so.[45] Thus, even the President of the Republic has been recognized by the Supreme Court as having standing to bring a popular action against legislative acts before the Court.[46]

### The objective character of the process

The direct consequence of the popular character of the action is the objective character of the process developed before the Court. The action is not presented against a state organ, but only against a state act: the law. Thus, there are no parties to the process in the strictest sense. The petitioner is not a plaintiff and there is no defendant. The process is a judicial process against a state act which can be initiated by any individual or corporation, or by any public official, even a member of the Supreme Court in his personal capacity.

As there are no defendants in the process, it is not required that any person be summoned,[47] and only the head of the legislative body and the Prosecutor General are notified if they are not already the petitioner.[48] The Court must order the publishing of a notice requesting the intervention of any interested person in the process. Thus, in the same way that any citizen whose rights and interests have been prejudiced may exercise the action of unconstitutionality of laws and other state acts of legislative rank, so any citizen with the same simple interest has the right to present writs and briefs to the Court, against or in defence of the law or act being challenged.[49]

The popular action of unconstitutionality must be brought before the Supreme Court by means of a petition for remedy in which the petitioner must clearly state the act which he is impugning[50] and indicate precisely the breach of the Constitution denounced.[51] However, given that this is a popular action in which the validity of a law and the supremacy of the Constitution are at stake, the Court might be able to raise and consider defects not alleged by the petitioner.[52] Therefore while the popular action can be brought before the Court by a petitioner,[53] the Supreme Court is not totally subject to his will, and if the petitioner abandons the action, the Court is empowered to continue with the hearing.[54]

### Grounds for the action

The only grounds that can be claimed for the action of unconstitutionality are violations or collisions with the Constitution; that is to say, grounds of unconstitutionality,[55] whether of a substantive or of a formal or adjective character.

The Supreme Court of Justice, however, has maintained that not all constitutional rules, when violated, provide grounds for the exercise of judicial review. It has frequently been required that a directly operative rule is at issue, and the Court has not annulled a law when violations of a programmatic rule have been alleged.[56] This does not mean, however, that judicial review of legislation cannot be exercised based on constitutional principles. For instance, Article 50 of the Constitution expressly establishes that: 'The enunciation of rights and guarantees contained in this Constitution must not be construed as a denial of others which, being inherent in the human person, are not expressly mentioned herein. The lack of a law regulating these rights does not impair the exercise thereof.' Thus the Supreme Court of Justice could exercise judicial review control of legislation on the grounds of violations of rights inherent in the human person, not enunciated expressly in the Constitution.

The complaint of unconstitutionality must necessarily involve a 'logical link by way of a serious and necessary motivation between the act contested and the rule which is said to have been broken by it'.[57] For this reason, the Court has considered complaints of infractions of constitutional rules to be formally insufficient when such a link does not appear in the petition. Yet it is clear that the act which is challenged may constitute a breach of the Constitution when it contradicts the spirit and purpose of a constitutional rule,[58] and not only when there is a literal contradiction between the rules and the challenged act.

### Content of the Court's decision

According to the provisions of the Organic Law of the Supreme Court of Justice, once the grounds on which the action has been founded have been examined, the Court shall declare the nullity of the challenged act or of its articles when accepted.[59]

Accordingly, the Court is under an obligation to examine all the grounds on which the action is founded. But since the Organic Law does not limit this appraisal solely to those grounds alleged by the petitioner, and in view of the issue of unconstitutionality involved, the procedure must be in the nature of an inquiry so that the Court is able to assess grounds for unconstitutionality which are not alleged by the petitioner. In this regard the Supreme Court pointed out in 1966 that:

It is the function of the Court, when exercising its power to review the constitutionality of acts of the legislative bodies, to declare the nullity of the act which is challenged if it is in any way in conflict with the precepts of the Constitution, and as a consequence of that declaration, to proclaim the legal annulment or, alternatively, to sustain it in full force instead of the assumptions which were advanced.[60]

In 1976, however, the Organic Law of the Supreme Court of Justice included Article 131 after insisting that 'In its final decision, the Court shall declare whether or not the nullity of the act which is being contested is admitted, and shall determine the effects of its decision over time'[61] and then added: 'Also, according to the terms of the corresponding petition, the Court may order the payment of sums of money and the restitution of damages, for whose origin the administration has responsibility and may also make the necessary provisions for re-establishing the subjective legal situations prejudiced by the activity of the administration.'

The placing of this rule might lead one to think that the Court's verdict may have a condemnatory content. However, the references the article makes to the administration and to administrative activity would make it inapplicable to any supposed responsibility of the state for a legislative act. This shows the legislature's intention of confining the damages claimed only to cases of judicial review of administrative action.

Finally, the Supreme Court decision can also be that of rejecting the action when it is without grounds and, in particular, if the Court considers that the action was rash and obviously unfounded, it can impose a fine on the petitioner.[62] Through these responses the possible inconveniences that can be produced by the popular character of the action can be overcome.

### (d) Effects of concentrated control decisions

As noted, the Court may either accept a petition and declare the nullity of the unconstitutional challenged law or it can reject the action. The effects of those decisions are, of course, different.

#### (i) The effect of the dismissal decisions

In cases in which the Court's decision is to declare the action unjustified, the effects of the decision are *erga omnes* with respect to the constitutionality of the law, at least as far as it concerns the challenged articles and the defects reported.[63] Moreover, in relation to these rejected defects, the decision has the force of *res judicata*. Naturally this does not extend to other similar legislative acts which may be contested for the same defects. In this respect, the Civil Cassation Chamber of the Supreme Court of Justice has analysed this problem when considering the effects of a decision of the Politico-Administrative Chamber of the same Supreme Court in which a Municipal Ordinance was annulled on the grounds of unconstitutionality. The situation was as follows: the Politico-Administrative Chamber of the Supreme Court, in a previous decision, had dismissed a popular action against a Municipal Ordinance of the Bocono District. In a civil and different procedure in which a Municipal Ordinance of the Valera District had to be applied, a party alleged its unconstitutionality, bringing before the Cassation Chamber of the Supreme Court the previous decision of the Politico-Administrative Chamber. In this respect the Cassation Chamber stated that:

It is to be observed that, although the said decision produces *res judicata erga omnes,* this is limited strictly to the matter itself which was decided on, that is, the constitutionality of the Ordinance of the Bocono District, and there can be no question of extending it to that of the Valera District, nor to any other, despite the fact that they deal with the same matter and that their regulations are, by chance, similar.

In this case, the question of the constitutionality of the Valera District Ordinance was raised, both as incidental and as an exception, and the lower courts which decided in this case were completely at liberty to consider and decide, under Article 7 of the Civil Procedures Code, whether or not the Ordinance brought before them was unconstitutional, without being bound to any *res judicata* whatever, because there was no such thing. They found that the Ordinance in question is not unconstitutional, and ordered that it be complied with.

The same occurs with this Civil, Mercantile and Labour Cassation Chamber, which is not bound in the least by the *res judicata* pronounced in some different matter, in which a decision was reached on the constitutionality of an Ordinance, different from the one which is required to be complied with here. Had the decision of the Political and Administrative Chamber dealt with the Valera District Ordinance, then for this Chamber – as for all – the constitutionality of that Ordinance would have been beyond discussion, as it would have been covered by *res judicata*.

As it is not precisely that Ordinance which is at issue, but another different one, this Chamber has the full and absolute jurisdiction, liberty and discretion to decide, for the purposes of these proceedings, whether the Ordinance which is in question here is in conflict with the National Constitution or not, in terms of the infractions of which the challenged judicial decision is accused, as a result of the lower judge having complied with the provisions of that Ordinance which, according to the appellant, are unconstitutional.

The criteria established by that Politico-Administrative Chamber when setting out the grounds for its decision, merits the greatest respect and attention from this Civil Cassation Chamber when reaching verdicts on similar matters, but does not bind it – in the same way that its own criteria on matters decided previously does not bind it – if it finds sufficient reasons to modify it. [64]

A few basic principles can be deduced from this Supreme Court decision of 1963. First, the absolute powers of all judges to control the constitutionality of legislation through the diffuse system of judicial review. Second, the power of the Supreme Court to control the constitutionality of legislation in a concentrated way, the decisions in this case having *erga omnes* effects. Third, the *res judicata* effects of constitutional decisions of the Supreme Court, either when a legislative act is annulled or when a popular action of unconstitutionality is dismissed, only refers to the particular and specific law challenged before the Court and cannot be extended to other legislative acts.

In another decision of the Civil, Mercantile and Labour Cassation Chamber of the Supreme Court of Justice of 1971, the Court was even clearer in establishing that a decision by the Politico-Administrative Chamber of the Court, in which it dismissed a popular action of unconstitutionality, should necessarily be applied by the Cassation Chamber, as well as by all other courts, as it was a pronouncement with *erga omnes* force. As a consequence, the Cassation Chamber allowed a remedy for cassation with regard to a lower court decision which had not applied a previous Politico-Administrative Chamber's decision.[65]

### (ii) The effects of decisions declaring the nullity of the legislative act

When the Supreme Court declares a challenged legislative act to be annulled, either totally or with respect to those of its articles against which action is lodged, it produces cessation of the effects of the act. The Court is also authorized to declare null all other acts carried out on the basis of the act which is declared null.[66] In such cases, the effects of the Court's decisions are of *erga omnes* effects. For instance, in 1938, the former Federal and Cassation Court sustained the following:

> The Federal and Cassation Court is the highest level in the judicial hierarchy; *res judicata* established by it, even supposing it were mistaken doctrinally, is the last word by the Judiciary, against which nothing and nobody can prevail in law, neither the Court itself, nor the other two powers [of the state]. As it is a federal institution with exclusive power to annul *erga omnes* the laws and acts of the Public Power which are in violation of the Constitution, it thus constitutes the sovereign interpreter of the constitutional text and of ordinary laws, and the sole judge of acts by the Public Powers and high officials of state. Any official, however high-ranking he may be, or any of the other Public Powers which seek their own interpretation of the Law to prevail over the interpretation and application established by the Court when reaching decisions and verdicts on the same matter, usurps power and violates the Constitution and the laws of the Republic.[67]

In this respect, the same former Federal and Cassation Court described its decisions in 1939 as 'provisions complementary to the Constitution and Laws of the Republic, which produce *erga omnes* effects';[68] and in a decision in 1949 it indicated that its decisions 'come to form a special legislation, arising from the secondary Constitutive Power which this High Court exercises in these matters'.[69] The former Federal Court that followed the latter as the constitutional body for judicial review of legislation agreed with this criterium, and in 1953 indicated that as its decisions have *erga omnes* effects, they 'take on force of law'.[70]

More recently, the Civil, Mercantile and Labour Cassation Chamber of the Supreme Court of Justice was precise in this respect in a decision on 12 December, 1963:

Absolute review of constitutionality is exercised firstly by the full-court session of the Supreme Court of Justice [Pleno Court] when it declares the nullity of a national law by reason of its unconstitutionality. This decision deprives the law, or that part of it which is annulled, of effect, and has the force of *res judicata, erga omnes*. This nullity is declared as a result of what is known as a popular action.

A similar power is exercised by the Politico-Administrative Division of this Supreme Court, also by popular action – but only with respect to state laws and Municipal Ordinances – and its verdict also produces *res judicata, erga omnes*.

This is to say that the declaration of the constitutionality or unconstitutionality of a law by principal [popular] action is definitive and produces effects against everyone, since that supposed law ceases to be such from the moment it is declared unconstitutional. The same occurs with state Laws and Municipal Ordinances which are pronounced unconstitutional.[71]

Consequently, according to the doctrine established by the Court, the verdict declaring the unconstitutionality of a law, and thereby annulling it, has *erga omnes* effects and an absolute character as *res judicata*.

### (e) The question of the temporal effects of concentrated constitutional review

Is the law which is declared null considered to have produced effects until declared null by the Court, or is it considered never to have produced effects? In other words, does the Court's decision take effect from the moment it is published, or are its effects retroactive to the moment the act which has been annulled was first published?

The Organic Law of the Supreme Court of Justice of 1976 does not resolve the question and only establishes that, in its decision, the Supreme Court must 'determine the effects of its decision in time'.[72] With two systems of judicial review, the diffuse and the concentrated systems, existing in parallel in the Venezuelan constitutional system, confusion about the judicial review decision effects in each case has been frequent.

In order to examine this problem accurately, it is necessary to distinguish the effects of the diffuse system of judicial review from the concentrated system of judicial review.

### (i) The principles common to both systems of judicial review

Under the diffuse system of judicial review, any judge in a concrete case may appraise the constitutionality of a law and determine its constitutionality. This decision has *inter partes* effects. A concentrated system of judicial review also exists and in this role the supreme interpreter[73] and defender[74] of the Constitution is responsible for being the balancing point in the application of the principle of the separation of powers.[75]

The effects of constitutional review thus differ in the two cases, and in the absence of a law specifically governing constitutional jurisdiction,[76] solutions must be found in comparative law. But of course it is neither appropriate nor possible to apply the characteristics of constitutional review of laws in the American model, which is exclusively diffuse in nature, to constitutional review of laws as exercised by the Supreme Court of Justice of Venezuela, which is a concentrated one.

In the diffuse system of judicial review, the decision declaring the unconstitutionality of a law in a concrete case does not affect its general validity; it has only a declarative, *inter partes*, and *pro praeterito* effect. Similarly, in an analysis of the North American constitutional system, it has been said that:

The law is neither repealed nor annulled. It is purely and simply not recognized, as if it were not a law, but rather, it could be said, a simple appearance of law, and the rights of the parties are regulated as if it had never been approved ... The Court is limited, purely and simply, to ignore the law ... From [which] ... stems the retroactive effect of the declaration of unconstitutionality.[77]

Consequently the retroactivity of the declaration of inapplicability of a law only makes sense when one bears in mind that the judge considers it never to have produced effects, in which case the declaration of unconstitutionality operates *ex tunc*.

These effects are quite different from those of the concentrated system of judicial review. In the concentrated system of judicial review, as exercised by the Supreme Court of Venezuela, the Court declares the nullity of the law,[78] that is to say, annuls it. Up to the moment when the Court's decision is published, the law must be considered valid and effective, producing all its effects despite its unconstitutionality. Thus, as Professor Cappelletti indicated when he emphasized the difference between the concentrated and diffuse methods of constitutional review:

it can be said that, while the United States' system of judicial review of constitutionality of laws has a purely *declaratory character*, conversely, the Austrian system has the nature of a *constitutive* control of invalidity, and consequent inefficacy of laws contrary to the Constitution. From this, it is quite coherent to conclude that while in the first system, the effects (purely declarative) operate *ex tunc* that is, retroactively – it is, in effect, a simple declaration of a pre-existing nullity – in the Austrian system, on the contrary, the effects of the decision of unconstitutionality (which are constitutive, that is to say, of annulment), operate *ex nunc*, and thus *pro futuro*, which excludes retroactive effects of the annulation.[79]

Another fundamental difference must be added – in the concentrated systems, decisions do operate *erga omnes*. [80] Thus, in general most systems of concentrated constitutional judicial review of laws attribute general effects to the past (that is, *ex tunc, pro praeterito*) to all decisions in which unconstitutionality and nullity of laws is declared. Hence those decisions are not merely declaratory, nor do they have retroactive effects, but are solely constitutive. In systems, such as in Italy and Germany, although certain effects are retroactive, these are usually restricted to criminal matters. This situation is a compromise between a desire to maintain juridical stability, by not having retroactive effects, and justice in criminal cases where it would be considered unjust if decisions passed under a law which is subsequently annulled were not affected by its annulment.

This conflict between juridical stability and criminal decisions has lead the North American Supreme Court to establish exceptions to the opposite principle. We have seen that constitutional review being diffuse in character in the United States, the effects of decisions declaring laws unconstitutional are merely declaratory and thus retroactive in nature. Despite this, however, case law has extended this retroactive nature only to criminal cases.[81]

As the constitutional judicial review power which the 1961 Venezuelan Constitution attributes to the Supreme Court of Justice[82] is similar to concentrated systems, in the absence of any constitutional or legal positive rule, the effects of the declaration of nullity of a law on the grounds of its unconstitutionality can only be produced *erga omnes*, but towards the future. That is to say, in principle, the Supreme Court decisions are constitutive, *pro futuro* with *ex nunc* effects. This criterion has been followed by authors on constitutional law[83] and by decisions of the Supreme Court of Justice.

The Supreme Court of Justice in Venezuela is divided into three Chambers: the Politico-Administrative, the Civil Cassation and the Criminal Cassation Chambers, which can act in Pleno or Plenary session. According to the Constitution the concentrated system of judicial review is exercised only in Pleno and by the Politico-Administrative Chambers. These bodies sustain the criteria of the constitutive effects of their decisions. The Civil Cassation Chamber, which does not have powers of concentrated judicial review, has contradicted these criteria when it has interpreted the effects of the decisions of the former.

### (ii) The criteria of the constitutional organs with powers to annul laws: the Supreme Court in Pleno and its Politico-Administrative Chamber

The Supreme Court has expressly maintained that:'Laws are made to be executed, and should thus be accomplished even when, contingently, they may be declared constitutionally null as the result of a sufficient action. They are only rendered invalid by the definitive decision declaring their nullity.'[84]

In other words, it limits itself to proclaiming the juridical annulment of the law to which objection is made. That is to say, the Supreme Court has maintained that laws produce all their effects until they are annulled since, as it indicated in another decision, 'acts which are annullable are valid and, once passed, fully produce all their effects until they are declared null'.[85] While the effects of decisions declaring nullity by reason of unconstitutionality are general and *erga omnes* in nature,[86] when it declares a law to be null, the Supreme Court's decision comes to form part, *mutatis mutandis* of 'a special legislation arising from the secondary Constitutive Power which this High Court exercises'.[87] Such decisions 'are [a] complementary provisions of the Constitution and laws of the Republic'.[88]

Thus if a law is declared null on the grounds of its unconstitutionality, it is as if it had been abrogated by a later law. Therefore, it is clear then that just as that later law cannot have retroactive effects so neither can the decision declaring the law's nullity which is deemed to have 'force of law'. This affirmation is so logical that, in some Latin American constitutional systems, the classic principle of the lack of retroactivity of laws[89] has been expressly extended to decisions of the Supreme Court or of the Tribunal of Constitutional Guarantees.[90]

This principle, that the effects of the Supreme Court's decisions declaring the nullity of laws are not retroactive, stems from the constitutive rather than the declaratory nature of the decisions. This was expressly recognized by the Politico-Administrative Chamber of the Supreme Court when, in 1965, it decided to declare the nullity of a Municipal Ordinance which created a tax contravening a prohibition contained in paragraph 4 of Article 18 of the Constitution.[91] The petitioner's request 'that the Municipality be ordered to repay the sums of money which it had received by collecting the contribution under discussion ...' was rejected as unfounded.[92] In this way, the Court acknowledged the nature of its decision to annul the Ordinance, as being constitutive and having effects towards the future. If it had considered the effects of the decision to be merely declaratory, *ex tunc*, it would have proceeded to order the Municipality to repay as requested.

Later, in 1968, the Court emphasized the presumption of the constitutionality of laws when it pointed out that 'national legislative acts, once passed and published, keep their effectiveness and validity until such time as they are repealed by the body which passed them or are annulled by the Court and, meanwhile, their legitimacy also extends to actions taken by other authorities under powers which the laws attribute to them'.[93] In the same year, the Supreme Court incidentally recognized that its decisions were constitutive and not declaratory, when it maintained that:

The effects of the decisions passed by the Court when performing its function of judicial review of the constitutionality of laws, only extend for the duration of the validity of the constitutional rule on which ... [the Court's decisions] are based. Consequently, it is possible that a legal provision which is annulled because it is unconstitutional – but which in fact has continued to form a part of some legal instrument which has not been so repealed, recover legal force with the coming into effect of some other norm which repeals the constitutional rule on which the Court had founded its decision to declare the law null, or one which radically changes the previous legal system.[94]

If this situation is possible, it is precisely because the effects produced by the law remain intact as a result of its constitutive effect. If the decisions of the Court in which it exercises constitutional review of laws were retroactive, not only would those acts performed under the law declared null be rendered without effect, but if the unconstitutional law were non-existent, this would leave no room for the possible case in which it recovers its validity if the Constitution under which it was declared unconstitutional were modified.

There is thus no doubt, therefore, that in Venezuela the aims of the constitutional review powers exercised by the Supreme Court of Justice under paragraphs 3 and 4 of Article 215 of the Constitution, as a concentrated system of judicial review, are to annul laws; the Constitution says 'declare the nullity', and not 'declare the unconstitutionality'. This annulment is performed with *erga omnes* effects which extend *ex nunc* (*pro futuro* ) by means of a constitutive decision rather than a declaratory one,[95] except in cases of absolute nullity under some express constitutional provisions.

### (iii) The contradicting criteria of the Civil Cassation Chamber of the Supreme Court

However, this criterion has been contradicted by the Civil, Commercial and Labour Cassation Chamber of the same Supreme Court of Justice, in a decision of 10 August 1978. The Cassation Chamber decision was adopted after a Pleno Court decision declared the nullity of an article of a law approving a contract for fulfilment of the National Treasury auxiliary service, signed between the Republic and a private bank. The article in question exonerated the bank from paying municipal taxes. Once the article was annulled, the Federal District Municipality brought a civil suit against the private bank for payment of taxes incurred during the ten years previous to the Court's decision – which is the expiry period for claims for municipal taxes – interpreting the decision in which the annulment was declared, as producing *ex tunc* effects, that is, declaratory and retroactive. The bank alleged that these were constitutive in nature. When the Civil, Commercial and Labour Cassation Chamber of the Supreme Court heard the case for the cassation of the decision taken by a civil court, which had ordered the bank to pay the taxes as required, it applied 'its own doctrine' as follows:

Laws are constitutional or unconstitutional. The former are so because they conform to the rules of the National Constitution. The latter are unconstitutional when they include violations or breaches which would contradict the content of constitutional rules. Until such time as they are declared unconstitutional, they are rendered obligatory by a presumption of their legitimacy. If so declared however, – that presumption is removed by the declaration of nullity and everything they meant in the past is erased. That is to say that the decision declaring nullity is declaratory in nature, and its effects are, in principle, backwards to the past; retroactive, *ex tunc*. This conclusion follows freely from logical principles, since the declaration of nullity seeks to re-establish the legal order disturbed by an unconstitutional law. This Chamber does not hesitate to follow this doctrine, which is upheld by leading authorities, both national and foreign. Thus the decision which is being appealed against is correct in considering as declaratory the decision passed by the Supreme Court of Justice on 15 March, 1962, in which it annulled Article 23 of the Law approving the extension of the contract signed between the Federal Executive and the Banco de Venezuela, as being unconstitutional. As that Law was contested by means of a principal and direct action of unconstitutionality, the annulment pronounced by the Supreme Court is without question absolutely declaratory in nature, and thus its effects extend both backwards to the past [*ex tunc*] and towards the future [*ex nunc*]. Leading authorities indicate that 'that law which is declared unconstitutional should be regarded, to all intents and purposes, as if it had never possessed legal force'. This doctrine stems from precise constitutional texts which endow the Supreme Court with power to 'declare the total or partial nullity of national laws', without indicating therein what the nature or character of such nullity is. Within this doctrine, however, one must accept the possible existence of limiting cases, such as when considerations of higher justice or overriding public interest make it advisable to temper the rigour of its effects. Among the cases in which this occurs is the immutability of the *res judicata* arising from firm, final verdicts, which should, in principle, be maintained. In the case in question, however, this exceptional situation does not arise, since the interest at issue is eminently private by nature. Thus, as the decision of 15 March 1962 in which the Supreme Court of Justice declared the nullity on the grounds of unconstitutionality of Article 20 of the above law approving the contract signed between the National Executive and the Banco de Venezuela, is declaratory in nature, its *ex tunc* effects are correct and normal to this type of decision. The appellated decision thus did not violate the legal provisions mentioned in the petition when it ordered the bank to pay the taxes which had been demanded.[96]

Thus, as a result of decisions by its component Chambers, the Supreme Court of Justice has itself established contradictory criteria. In Pleno Court, and in the Politico-Administrative Chamber, it has maintained the constitutive nature *pro futuro* and *ex nunc* effects of its decisions to annul on the grounds of unconstitutionality, laws and other state acts with general effect. By contrast, the Civil, Commercial and Labour Cassation Chamber, which only has a reduced competence for hearing recourses of cassation, attributed to the Pleno Court and the Politico Administrative Chamber decision, different effects from those accepted by themselves. The Cassation Chamber decided that those decisions were declaratory in nature (not constitutive) with *pro praeterito* and *ex tunc* effects.

This is an inadmissible contradiction. Not only is the Civil, Commercial and Labour Cassation Chamber of the Supreme Court not competent to declare the nullity of laws, but it has erroneously attributed *ex tunc* effects to the decisions of another Chamber and to those of the Pleno Court contrary to their own criteria. The Cassation Chamber resorted to doctrinal criteria which relate to the diffuse systems of judicial review and which are inapplicable to the concentrated systems of judicial review.

In any case, since 1976, Article 131 of the Organic Law of the Supreme Court of Justice endows both the Pleno Court and the Politico

Administrative Chamber with power to establish 'the effects of their decisions with time'. Thus, despite the fact that the effects of their decisions declaring the nullity of laws on the grounds of unconstitutionality should, in principle, continue to be constitutive, *pro futuro ex nunc*,[97] the Court may correct the unfavourable effects which may be produced by the rigidity of this principle and give its decision retroactive *pro praeterito, ex tunc* effects.

With regard to constitutional rights and guarantees, the problem of the rigidity of the principle of the *ex tunc, pro futuro* effects of decisions annulling laws is resolved since the Constitution itself guarantees against this situation. It declares the absolute nullity of 'acts by the Public Power which prejudice constitutional rights and guarantees'.[98]

Thus it is the absolute nullity of certain acts, as provided for in the Constitution, which allows certain decisions in which the Court declares the nullity of a law to have retroactive effects, backwards to the past, and for them to be considered declaratory and *ex tunc* in nature.

### (iv) The objective guarantee of the Constitution: absolute or relative nullity

When the Supreme Court of Justice declares the nullity of a law which violates the Constitution, does the Court adopt its decision based on the annullability or relative nullity of the unconstitutional law, or does it annul the law based on the grounds of absolute nullity because the Constitution provides for cases of absolute nullity? To resolve this dilemma it is necessary to determine whether all unconstitutional laws are annullable acts or whether the possibility exists of unconstitutional acts with defects such that they are considered by the legal order as null and void acts.[99]

The general rule in Venezuela is that Supreme Court decisions declaring the nullity of laws are constitutive, so that unconstitutional laws are, in principle, state acts liable to relative annulment. There are two possible exceptions to the rule.

Despite the power legally attributed to the Supreme Court to determine the effects with time of its decisions, the Venezuelan Constitution implies that certain Supreme Court decisions which declare the nullity of a law, have *per se* the character of a declaratory judgement so as to produce full retroactive effects. In such cases the Constitution itself declares a law or state act as null and void or without effects. This possibility is provided for only in Articles 46 and 119 of the Constitution. Article 46 of the Constitution establishes the following:

All acts of the Public Power which violate or impair the rights guaranteed by this Constitution are null, and public officials and employees who order or execute them shall be held criminally, civilly and administratively liable, as the case may be, and orders from their superiors evidently contrary to the Constitution and the laws may not serve as an excuse.

According to this first express exception, a law which establishes a discrimination based on 'race, creed, sex or social status', expressly violates the right to equality guaranteed in Article 61 of the Constitution, and is 'null' under the text of Article 46. The defect is such that the nullity is absolute, and the act can produce no legal effect and should not even be applied by any authority, the contrary originating responsibility. In such cases, the Court's decision declaring the nullity of the law on the grounds of its being unconstitutional can be no more than merely declaratory, by virtue of the express text of the Constitution. It is only a question of certifying a nullity already established in the Constitution which extinguishes the law. In the possible cases in which rights guaranteed by the Constitution are at stake, and which are regulated by Article 46 of the Constitution, Supreme Court decisions cannot have constitutive effects so as to leave the effects produced by an unconstitutional law.

The second exception to the principle is expressly regulated by Article 119 of the Constitution which establishes that 'all usurped authority is without effect, and its acts are null'. By usurpation of authority should be understood 'the defects accompanying all acts decreed by a person totally lacking authority',[100] that is to say, the usurper is he who exercises authority and puts it into effect without any type of investiture, either regular or established. Since the Constitution states that usurped authority is without effects and its acts are null, if the Supreme Court declares the nullity 'of a law of a government organised by force',[101] it can only have the effect of declaring a nullity already expressly established in the Constitution.

Apart from these two express provisions of the Constitution by which the text of the Constitution itself declares a law absolutely null, and apart from the power of the Supreme Court to provide a retroactive effect to certain laws, when the Supreme Court of Justice declares the nullity of an unconstitutional law, it is generally considered to be a constitutive declaration of nullity.

Lastly it should be pointed out that whatever the temporal effects of a law being declared null on the grounds of its being unconstitutional, it is evident that the effects towards the future continue for as long as the Constitution, which gave rise to the annulment, is in force. Thus, if an annulment is declared on the basis of the violation of a particular constitutional rule, if that rule were to lapse as the result of constitutional reform, it would cause the decision declaring unconstitutionality to lose its *erga omnes* effects, and the law declared unconstitutional would regain its validity. The Supreme Court has expressly accepted this possibility.[102]

### (f) Judicial review and the fundamental right to constitutional protection (*derecho de amparo*)

One of the most important democratic innovations in all Venezuelan constitutional history was the establishment of the right to protection (*amparo*) in Article 49 of the 1961 Constitution. This extended the previous system for the protection of fundamental rights and liberties, which had been established in an incomplete form in previous constitutional texts[103] – the writ of *habeas corpus* [104] as a protection for personal liberty through the creation of a special institution. This right to protection presents peculiarities which distinguish it from similar contemporary institutions for the protection of constitutional rights and guarantees established both in Europe and in Latin America.[105]

#### (i) The constitutional basis of the right to protection

In effect, Article 49 of the Constitution declares the following:

According to the law, the Courts will protect all inhabitants of the Republic in the enjoyment and exercise of the rights and guarantees established in the Constitution. The procedure will be brief and summary, and the competent judge will be empowered to immediately re-establish the infringed legal situation.

The 1960 document which explained the motives of the constitutional project limited its comments on the matter by saying that 'with respect to protection, only the general principles were established, which the law must regulate; but so as not to suspend its effects until the respective law is passed, the right of *habeas corpus* was sanctioned in the constitutional Temporary Provisions, thus regulating it provisionally'. The Fifth Temporary Provision of the Constitution was then adopted. This established the rules of procedure for 'the protection of personal liberty, until such time as the special law regulating it is passed, as stipulated in Article 49 of the Constitution'.[106]

According to these rules, the 1961 Venezuelan Constitution sanctioned the right to protection as a fundamental right which is concerned with protecting all constitutional rights and guarantees, including that of personal liberty, so as to ensure that they are enjoyed and exercised by all inhabitants of the Republic. The 1960 document which explained the motives of the Project of Constitution thus described the right of *habeas corpus* as a specific means of the broader right to protection.

According to the Constitution, the *amparo* has been consequently sanctioned as a constitutional right of the inhabitants of the country. It enables them to require all of the courts within their own jurisdiction to protect and ensure the enjoyment and exercise of all the rights and guarantees established by the Constitution or inherent in the human person against any distress, whether by public authorities or individuals. The means by which this is done should be brief and summary so as to allow a judge to restore the infringed legal situation immediately.[107]

The Constitution does not establish only one action or writ of protection but rather a right to protection as a fundamental right which can be, and in fact is, exercised through a variety of legal actions and recourses, including a direct action for protection of a subsidiary nature.

Thus, Article 49 does not establish a particular objective guarantee of constitutional rank, but rather a true constitutional right; the right of everyone to be protected by the courts in the enjoyment and exercise of their constitutional rights and guarantees. This character of the *amparo*, as a constitutional right, is the basic element which identifies the Venezuelan institution[108] and which leads to its consideration not as a single action or complaint, but as a right.


### (ii) The *amparo* as a right to judicial means for protection

Since the Constitution does not identify the right of protection with any specific means, *amparo* is neither an action nor a remedy. Thus protection (*amparo*) may take the form of a recourse in the strict sense of the review of judicial or administrative decisions, or it may take the form of an autonomous action which does not necessarily entail the review of a given state act.

Moreover, Article 49 establishes a right of the inhabitants of the Republic to be protected as well as a duty on the Courts to protect all inhabitants of the Republic in the enjoyment and exercise of such rights and guarantees. For this reason, Article 49 begins by stating, 'the Courts shall protect ...' The Constitution is sufficiently broad and flexible to allow the legislator to organize a variety of legal means for the defence of civil rights and guarantees, whether these be by means of ordinary legal actions, or, in cases where these do not allow adequate protection of rights through the general and subsidiary means, action for protection.

But despite the several means for the legal protection of constitutional rights and guarantees which ensure the right to protection contemplated in the Constitution, there is a subsidiary action for protection which must be identified, and accepted, but only if those other ordinary legal means that can serve for the protection of constitutional rights and guarantees, formally established by law, are insufficient.

As the right to protection can be ensured by a variety of existing legal means, the right to protection is not identified with any specific legal action. Since the action for protection is admissible only when there is no other means of protection or relief formally provided for in the legal system, it is differentiated from other means for the legal protection of rights and guarantees and for the defence of the Constitution itself.

This leads to a consideration of the substantial difference which exists between the Venezuelan right to protection and action for protection and the Mexican trial for *amparo*. The Mexican actions covered by the heading *juicio de amparo* are: firstly, the protection of personal liberty, which is basically the remedy of *habeas corpus* ; secondly, what is known as the *amparo* against laws, which substitutes the direct action of unconstitutionality of laws; thirdly, the *amparo* of cassation, which is really the same as the recourse of cassation; fourthly, an administrative protection, which leads to judicial review of administrative acts; and fifthly, an agrarian *amparo* for the protection of the rights of peasants.[109]

By contrast, the right to protection contemplated in Article 49 of the Venezuelan Constitution ensures the possibility of protection by means of the action of unconstitutionality of laws (popular action), or through the decision of any judge not to apply a law in the diffuse system of judicial review of constitutionality; by means of the recourse of cassation with respect to judicial decisions; and by means of the administrative remedies against administrative actions. Additionally, it ensures the possibility of protection of fundamental rights against infringement by other individuals through ordinary judicial means.

### (iii) The action for protection as a subsidiary means

The right to protection gives rise to a subsidiary judicial means which appears in the legal system as completely different from the popular action of unconstitutionality of laws, the recourse of cassation, and from actions for judicial review of administrative actions. Thus this action can be resorted to when no other legal action is available or sufficient.

One of the characteristics of this autonomous subsidiary legal action is that it does not presuppose that other, previous legal means have to be exhausted before it can be exercised. This differentiates the institution of the action for protection in Venezuela from the recourse of protection or the constitutional complaint which has recently developed in Europe, particularly in Germany and in Spain. In these countries, the protective remedy is really an authentic recourse which is brought, in principle, against judicial decisions. For example, to bring a constitutional complaint for the protection of constitutional rights before the Federal Constitutional Tribunal of West Germany, the available ordinary judicial means need to be previously exhausted, although in exceptional cases a direct complaint for protection may be allowed.[110] In Spain, all legal recourses need to be exhausted in order to bring a *recurso de amparo* of constitutional rights before the Constitutional Tribunal, and, particularly when dealing with protection against administrative activities, the ordinary means for judicial review of administrative decisions must be exhausted.[111]

In many legal systems of Europe, particularly in Germany or in Spain, it is required that an action for protection be brought before one, particular court.[112] Because the right in Venezuela is expressed in several legal judicial means, it may be brought before any of the courts.

### (iv) The protection of all constitutional rights and guarantees

The right to protection, as expressed in the Constitution, is to protect all the rights and guarantees established by the Constitution. In support of this, it is sufficient to mention that Article 49 is placed under Chapter 1 containing the general provisions of Title III, which refers to 'Constitutional duties, rights and guarantees'. The remaining five chapters separately regulate: duties, and individual, social, economic and political rights.

This leads to the assertion that the right to protection and the subsidiary action for protection are means for protecting, not only those rights and guarantees listed in Articles 43 to 116 of the Constitution, but also all the rights inherent in the human person, even when not specified in the Constitution, and in this respect Article 50 of the Constitution provides that:

The declaration of rights and guarantees contained in the Constitution is not to be taken to mean the negation of others which, as they are inherent in the human being, do not figure expressly therein. The lack of a law regulating these rights does not prejudice its exercise.

Since the action for protection also protects therefore all those rights which are inherent in the human being but which do not appear expressly in the Constitution, it is not necessary to pass a law to guarantee their exercise. One result of the provisions of Article 50 is to give substantial importance to the series of human rights listed in the United Nations Universal Declaration of the Rights of Man, and in the International Conventions such as those of the American Human Rights Convention, and the International Pacts on Civil and Political, and Economic and Social Rights. These are, moreover, laws of the Republic because they have been approved in Congress by special laws.[113]

This protection thus constitutes a fundamental guarantee of human rights, which in turn entails certain implications. Since the objective of the right is to protect the enjoyment and exercise of constitutional rights and guarantees, it applies not only to individuals as holders of such rights but also to cases in which these rights are exercised by companies or corporations. Where Article 49 declares the right to protection, the expression 'all the inhabitants' must be understood to refer to all entities or organizations, since the rights established in the Constitution belong to collective entities as well as to individuals.

Moreover, while it is clear that the action is available to protect constitutional rights and guarantees from the interference of public actions in the Venezuelan system, the action is also available to protect constitutional rights from disruptions which may originate from private individuals. This is possible because the Constitution makes no distinction in this respect.

This also differentiates the Venezuelan system from that which exists in other systems. In Mexico or Spain, the action for protection is solely conceived against public actions.[114] Because the protection can be used to prevent interference from public authorities, it is admissible against all state acts as well as against any other action by public officials.

Additionally, the subsidiary action for protection is admissible against any action by the administration, even when this does not constitute a formal administrative act which would be open to actions before the administrative courts. That is to say, it would be admissible against material acts by the Administration; its *de facto* methods; its failure to act or to fulfil an obligation; in short against any action or omission by the Administration.

The subsidiary action for protection may also be admissible against actions by the legislative body against which there are no legal means for objection, and against judicial decisions, against which no legal means of appeal exist or the recourse of cassation cannot be exercised.

If the *amparo* in Latin America is analysed comparatively, the following criteria can, in general, be identified: a system which identify *amparo* with judicial protection from arbitrary detention, *habeas corpus*, where a writ is required which shows that a person detained be produced to the court. This was the practice in Chile. There are also systems which identify *amparo* as a means for the protection of all rights, except that of personal liberty which is protected by *habeas corpus*. This system distinguishes between the two types of action, the action for protection and the writ of *habeas corpus*, and is typical of the Argentinian and Brazilian systems.

Finally, *amparo* can also be seen as a means for the protection of all rights and guarantees enshrined in the Constitution. This is the system of Central America, and particularly of Guatemala, Honduras and Nicaragua, and can be contrasted with the situation in Europe in which the remedy is established for the protection of certain rights only.[115] This is the case in Spain, where the recourse of protection is reserved for the protection of a limited group of constitutional rights only.[116]

In Venezuela, *amparo* is conceived as the right to a legal means (action or remedy) for the protection of all constitutional rights and guarantees. This includes individual rights as well as social, political and economic rights. *Amparo* is also intended for the protection of what is elsewhere known as the right of *habeas corpus*. This is made clear by the regulation in the Fifth Temporary Provision of the Constitution, which provides that 'until such time as the special law is passed, according to Article 49, protection of the right to personal liberty shall proceed according to …' a series of procedural rules laid down therein, aimed at protecting individuals against the loss of or restriction to their liberty, in violation of their constitutional rights. When this Temporary Provision speaks of 'protection for personal liberty' and refers to Article 49, it is simply affirming that the right to protection expressed in Article 49 is also intended to protect personal liberty, and that a special temporary procedure is established in this provision.

### (v) The meaning of violation of the rights and guarantees protected by the right to *amparo*

The objective protected by the right to protection is the enjoyment and exercise of constitutional rights and guarantees. This protection is available either when there is a direct violation of a constitutional rule or when there is a violation of the legal rules which regulate the enjoyment and exercise of such rights.[117]

It must be noted that the regulation of constitutional rights and guarantees in Venezuela is not uniform, and that the manner in which they are embodied in the Constitution gives rise to differing effects.[118] One may identify the absolute rights, among which are the right to life, the right not to be held incommunicado, not to be subjected to torture or other procedures which cause moral or physical suffering and the right not to be condemned to prison for life, or to punishments which are defamatory or which restrict personal liberty for more than thirty years.[119] These rights can not be limited nor regulated by the legislator, nor can they be restricted or suspended by executive decision even in cases of emergency or disturbances which may disrupt the peace of the Republic. By contrast, all other rights and guarantees are liable to limitation or regulation by the legislator and may be subject to measures for their restriction or suspension.[120]

A second type of constitutional right comprises those whose exercise may be restricted or suspended by the President of the Republic, even though, in principle, they may not be limited by the legislator. This stems from the manner in which the Constitution expresses the rights, for example, to protection of honour, reputation and privacy; the right not to take an oath or to make self-incriminating statements; not to remain imprisoned once officially released from jail; not to be punished twice for the same crime; the right to equality and freedom from discrimination; the right to religious freedom and to freedom of thought; the right to petition and to receive timely response; the right to be judged by one's ordinary judges; the right to defence; the right of association; the right to health protection; the rights to education and to work; and the right to vote.[121]

A third category is composed of those rights which may be limited by the legislator in a limited way. This category includes prisoner's rights to be heard before being sentenced, 'as indicated by the law'; the right to inviolability of the home, except in cases of search 'according to the law and the decision of the courts'; the right to inviolability of correspondence, except in cases of inspection or fiscal supervision of accounting documents 'according to the law'; the right to take public office, with the only restrictions being conditions of aptitude 'required by law'.[122]

The fourth category comprises a series of constitutional rights that can be regulated and limited by the legislator in a wider form. Among such rights would be, the right not to be detained unless caught *in flagranti* 'in the cases and with the formalities established in the law'; the right not to be conscripted 'but within the terms established by law'; the freedom of movement 'with the condition established by law'; the right to follow a cult under the 'supreme inspection of the National Executive according to the law'; the right to carry on economic activities with no other limitations than those established by law by reasons of security, health or other social interests; the right to property, submitted to the 'contributions, restrictions and obligations established by law based on public or social interests'; the right to political association and to public demonstration 'according to the formalities established by law'.[123] In all such cases, the exercise of rights is subject to legislative stipulations within considerable margins.

The fifth and final category of constitutional rights and guarantees is formed by those established in such a manner that their exercise is subject to legal regulation. Among such rights would be, for example, that of using the organs for the administration of justice 'under the terms and conditions established by the law'; that of joining associations 'according to the law'; the right to strike 'under the conditions set by the law', and in the public services, 'in those cases permitted by the law'.[124] In all such cases, the manner in which the Constitution expresses the rights and guarantees requires that they be regulated by the law so as to be exercised at all.

It is evident that in these groups of rights and guarantees, the right can be modified or limited by law. Thus, if the protection is to be limited to those applications when the Constitution is directly violated, since many rights are not only embodied in the Constitution, but rather, exist by virtue of the Constitution itself, the protection itself would be severely limited. Consequently, it has been concluded that the right to protection is admissible against violations of laws which regulate the enjoyment and exercise of rights.

### (vi) The object of the right to protection: the enjoyment and exercise of constitutional rights and guarantees

Because the Constitution has the goal of ensuring the enjoyment and exercise of constitutional rights and guarantees, it grants the power to immediately 're-establish the infringed juridical situation' to the competent judge and also provides that 'the procedure should be brief and summary'. This goal entails that the judge has power to adopt preventive and cautionary measures, bearing in mind that the legal means of protection, and even the subsidiary action for protection, are not necessarily exhausted thereby.

In other words, the protection for the enjoyment and exercise of constitutional rights and guarantees does not only require the adoption of some immediate measure, by means of a brief and summary proceeding which re-establishes the infringed legal situation. Instead, the action for protection requires that the judge in the case of *amparo* decides on the substantive issue and gives a verdict as to the legality and legitimacy of the 'violation' of the right in question, without prejudice to the fact that, by means of brief and summary mechanisms, decisions may be adopted during the proceedings to immediately re-establish the infringed legal situation.

### (vii) The *amparo* as a right and not as a recourse or action, and its consequences

After analysis of the constitutional text, the following conclusions can be formed: first, the Constitution provides a right to protection, and not any particular action or remedy before a particular court. This right is established as a fundamental right of individuals and collective persons.

Second, the right to protection implies an obligation of all courts to protection according to the law, against disturbances of the enjoyment and exercise of rights and guarantees. Thus, what the legislator may, and has done, with this right to protection may take the form of pre-existing actions or remedies or it may consist of an autonomous action for protection.

Third, the right to protection may thus be guaranteed by means of actions and recourses contemplated in the legal order (the popular action of unconstitutionality; the power of all judges to decide not to apply a law considered unconstitutional; actions for judicial review of administrative actions; the provisional system of *habeas corpus*), or by means of the subsidiary and autonomous action for protection, whose development by the courts has recently begun,[125] and that can be brought before any court according to its subject of attributions.

Fourth, the right of protection is admissible to guarantee the enjoyment and exercise of all constitutional rights and guarantees. It may thus be put into effect with respect to disturbances of individual rights, as well as those of social, economic and political rights.

Fifth, the right to protection seeks to assure protection of constitutional rights and guarantees against any disturbance in their enjoyment and exercise, whether this be originated by private individuals or by public authorities. In the case of disturbance by public authorities, the right of protection is admissible against legislative, administrative and judicial acts, by means of the actions and recourses contemplated in the legal order (the action of unconstitutionality, the recourse of cassation, or actions for judicial review of administrative actions) when they allow a legal situation which has been infringed to be re-established by means of a brief and summary procedure, or by means of the subsidiary autonomous action for protection. Moreover, this action for protection is admissible against material acts or courses of action of the administration, therefore it is not then admissible against administrative acts only.

Sixth, by virtue of the different means in the Constitution for regulating fundamental rights, the right to protection can be exercised to protect the enjoyment and exercise of constitutional rights and guarantees, not only when there has been some direct violation of the Constitution, but also when what has been violated are the legal developments which, by virtue of the Constitution, regulate, limit and even allow the exercise of such rights. Of course, protection must be exercised against an activity which directly violates a fundamental right established in the Constitution, whether it be regulated by law or not, and whether or not the violation is contrary to what the law developing the right establishes.

Seventh, the decision of the judge as a consequence of the exercise of this right to protection, whether this be by means of pre-existing actions or recourses, or by means of the subsidiary and autonomous action for protection, should not limit himself to precautionary or preventive measures, but should re-establish the infringed legal situation, and to this end he should make a pronouncement on the substantive issue brought before him, namely the legality and legitimacy or otherwise of the disturbance of the constitutional right or guarantee which has been reported as infringed.

Eighth, as we have seen, the Venezuelan system of judicial review, being a mixed one, in which the diffuse system of judicial review has been fully developed, that is to say, it can be exercised by all courts in whatever kind of judicial proceeding, it is obvious that judicial review of legislation is a power that can be exercised by the courts as a consequence of any action or recourse for protection of fundamental rights and, of course, when deciding an autonomous action for protection of fundamental rights when, for instance, their violation is infringed by a public authority act based on a law deemed unconstitutional. In such cases, if the judge gives the protection requested through an order similar to the writs of *mandamus* or to the injunctions, he must previously declare the law based on which the challenged action was taken, inapplicable on the grounds of it being unconstitutional. In such cases, therefore, judicial review of the constitutionality of legislation is also exercised when an action for protection of fundamental rights is exercised as a consequence of the diffuse system of judicial review.[126]

# 28

## THE MIXED SYSTEM OF JUDICIAL REVIEW IN COLOMBIA

Since 1910, all courts in Colombia have been given the power to declare the inapplicability of laws they deem contrary to the Constitution. This system operates in parallel with a concentrated system of judicial review attributed to the Supreme Court.[1] Although this mixture has been qualified as non-systematic, disperse and incongruous,[2] when it is analysed in comparative law, it can be considered, like the Venezuelan, one of the most complete constitutionally established systems of judicial review.

Yet even before the constitutional reform of 1910, however, there existed the basis of the diffuse system of judicial review. This had been established by legislation. Article 5 of Law No. 57 of 1887 prescribed, in a very similar way to the present Article 215 of the Constitution, that 'when there was incompatibility between a constitutional provision and a legal one, the former will be preferred'.[3]

In the 1910 Constitutional Reform, the principle of the supremacy of the Constitution was expressly adopted with the consequent jurisdictional control of the constitutionality of laws assigned to the Supreme Court of Justice.[4] It was in the 1910 Constitution that the Supreme Court of Justice was first assigned the role of 'guardian of the integrity of the Constitution'. It is still referred to in the same manner in the fundamental text. It was also in the 1910 Constitution that the principle of the diffuse system of judicial review acquired constitutional rank. Today that principle is contained in Article 215 of the Constitution, which states: 'In all cases of incompatibility between the Constitution and a law, the Constitution rule must be applied in preference.' Within this mixed system there are two mechanisms of control: a preventive one, as a consequence of the veto powers of legislation given to the President of the Republic, and an obligatory one, concerning executive acts adopted in a state of emergency.

## (a) The diffuse system of judicial review through the 'exception of unconstitutionality'

Article 215 of the present Colombian Constitution provides the basis of the diffuse system of judicial review. According to this article, all judges have the power to decide not to apply a law in a concrete process when they deem it contrary to the Constitution. Because this article has been conceived as an exception of unconstitutionality, the system functions entirely according to the American model.

While Article 215 does not exclude the possibility of judicial *ex officio* powers to raise constitutional issues, the constitutional question must be raised in a process by one of the parties through an exception regarding the applicability of a law,[5] and that party must show a personal and direct interest in the non-application of the law in the concrete case.[6]

Because the system is one of diffuse constitutional control, the judges cannot annul the law or declare its unconstitutionality, nor can the effects of their decision be extended or generalized. Instead, as in other diffuse judicial review systems, the court must limit itself to the concrete case, so that the decision only has effects concerning the parties to the case. Therefore, as in similar systems, law whose application has been denied in a concrete case, continues to be in force and other judges can continue to apply it. Even the judge who choses not to apply it in a concrete case, can change his mind in a subsequent process.[7]

## (b) The direct control of constitutionality of legislation through a popular action

In addition to the diffuse system, the Colombian Constitution also provides for a concentrated system of judicial review attributed to the Supreme Court of Justice. In this respect, Article 214 of the Constitution establishes under Title XX related to 'Constitutional jurisdiction', the following:

The guarding of the integrity of the Constitution is assigned to the Supreme Court of Justice. Consequently, in addition to the attributions assigned to it in this Constitution and the laws, it shall have the following: ...

To definitively decide the unconstitutionality [*inexequibilidad*] of all laws and decrees enacted by the government according to the attributions referred to in articles 76, paragraphs 11 and 12, and 80 of the Constitution [decrees with the force of law], when denounced before it as unconstitutional by any citizen...[8]

This concentrated system of judicial review is attributed to the Supreme Court of Justice and can be exercised when an action is brought before it by any citizen, that is to say, through a popular action, that can be based on any grounds of unconstitutionality, whether substantive or formal.

### (i) The objective character of the process

Because the action of unconstitutionality can be exercised by any citizen without any particular requirement of standing, the subsequent process developed before the Supreme Court can be considered as an objective one: it is not the result of an action brought before the court against the state or any state organ, but against a law or a state act with the force of law. This means that any citizen can intervene in the procedure whether aiding the petitioner's position or as defender of the challenged law.[9] Also, the Attorney General of the nation may intervene as head of the Public Prosecutor's office.[10] The objective character of this process means that the Supreme Court of Justice has *ex officio* power to consider any defects of a constitutional nature and is not limited to the one denounced by the petitioner. Moreover, a withdrawal of the action by the petitioner has no effect, and the Court must continue its constitutional examination.[11]

Finally, there are no time periods in which the popular action must be exercised. It is unextinguishable because it has been considered a political right of the citizens.[12] Nevertheless, the constitutional reform of 1979, later ineffective, sought to establish that when the grounds of the action were based on procedural or formal defects of the challenged law, the action could only be brought before a court within a delay of one year after its enactment.[13]

### (ii) The object of the concentrated judicial review system

The popular action recognized by Article 215 of the Constitution, is available against 'all the laws' and decrees with force of law. This includes, therefore, those issued by the executive as a consequence of any extraordinary powers or special legislative authorizations by Congress,[14] and also those issued by the executive on matters concerning the economic, social and public works plans when Congress fails to sanction them within a particular delay.[15] It has also been determined that this action is available against legislative acts attempting constitutional reform.[16]

Nevertheless, in spite of the very wide constitutional review powers assigned to the Supreme Court concerning 'all the laws' of the nation, the Court itself has restricted the scope of its review powers and has excluded certain laws from being examined on the grounds of unconstitutionality. This is so with regard to laws of approval of other state acts, such as administrative contracts and international treaties. In these cases, the

Supreme Court has limited its judicial review powers and has abstained from exercising constitutional control over those laws.[17] In particular, concerning international treaties and contrary to the general trend, for instance in continental Europe, the Colombian Supreme Court has considered that to control the constitutionality of a law of approval of an international treaty would mean to break the international obligations of the state. This is consistent with the practice of Colombia which has traditionally regarded international treaties to be superior to internal public law.[18]

### (iii) The compulsory judicial review of executive emergency decrees

If the President of the Republic declares a state of siege as a consequence of an external war or of internal commotion or when the economic and social order of the country is gravely altered, the Colombian Constitution requires there to be a judicial review proceeding. In this process, the day following the enactment of the decree, the President of the Republic must submit it to the Supreme Court, which must then decide upon its constitutionality.[19] Any citizen is allowed to participate, whether in defence of or in the attack on the constitutionality of such decrees.[20] Once the Court has pronounced its decision, it has *erga omnes* effects and the value of *res judicata*; thus no further action of unconstitutionality can be exercised against those acts.[21]

### (iv) The role of the Constitutional Chamber of the Supreme Court

Although the powers to control the constitutionality of state acts have been assigned to the Supreme Court of Justice, which is exercised in Pleno Court,[22] because of the influence of the European model of judicial review, attempts were made in the 1960s to create a special Constitutional Court.[23] The project was rejected, and in the 1968 constitutional reform a Constitutional Chamber or Division of the Supreme Court of Justice was created instead. This is composed of four members of the Court specialising in public law[24] and they have the special task of studying previous cases of unconstitutionality and proposing projects or resolutions to it.[25] The Chamber is merely an advisory body and has no power of decision on constitutional questions.

It must be mentioned that the constitutional reform adopted by the Legislative Act No. 1 of 1979 tended to give the Constitutional Chamber self decision powers in almost all matters of unconstitutionality, except those regarding the unconstitutionality of constitutional reforms due to formal defects and that of executive decrees issued in cases of state of siege or economic emergency.[26] Nevertheless, Legislative Act No. 1 of 1979 was itself declared unconstitutional by the Supreme Court in 1981,[27] and consequently the 1979 constitutional reform ceased to be effective.

### (v) The effects of the Supreme Court decision on judicial review

As in all concentrated systems of judicial review, the Supreme Court declarations of unconstitutionality have general and *erga omnes* effects.[28] Additionally, the decision has *res judicata* value. This applies to declarations that a law is valid, as well as declarations that it is invalid and unconstitutional. Accordingly, ordinary courts cannot declare the inapplicability of the law on the same grounds of constitutionality rejected by the Supreme Court.[29]

Because of the presumption of constitutionality, laws are effective until their annulment is declared by the Court. This has been the opinion of the majority of academics. Nevertheless, any juridical situations which were originated by the law prior to its annulment can be submitted to review through ordinary judicial means.[30]

In the situation of legislative acts containing constitutional reforms, if the legislation is itself declared unconstitutional, the constitutional rules revoked or amended by the constitutional reform are revived,[31] thereby returning to the constitutional system in force prior to the enactment of the annulled reform.

### (c) The preventive judicial review of legislation

Since 1886 Colombia has established a preventive judicial review method of laws. This is as a consequence of the veto powers of legislation assigned to the President of the Republic.[32]

When a law is vetoed based on substantive or procedural constitutional issues, if the Legislative Chambers insist on its promulgation, the President of the Republic must send the proposed law to the Supreme Court and the Court must make its decision within six days. In the event of the Supreme Court declaring the bill unconstitutional, the proposed law is not enacted. But, if the Supreme Court rejects the constitutional objections raised by the President, then he is obliged to promulgate it.[33]

# 29

## THE MIXED SYSTEM OF JUDICIAL REVIEW IN BRAZIL

Like the Argentinian system, the Brazilian system of judicial review has closely followed the model of the United States.[1] However, after the establishment in the 1934 Constitution of a direct action of unconstitutionality that can be brought before the Supreme Court of Justice to impugn laws, it must now be thought of as a mixed system.

### (a) Historical background

The Federal Constitution of 1891 gave the Supreme Federal Tribunal an extraordinary power to review federal and state court[2] decisions in which the validity or the application of the treaties or federal laws had been questioned and the courts had found them invalid. Also, the Supreme Federal Tribunal had the power to review decisions in which laws or government acts of the states had been found to be contrary to the Constitution or to the federal laws.[3] As a consequence of this express constitutional attribution, the Federal Law 221 of 1894[4] assigned the power to judge obviously unconstitutional laws and executive regulations to all federal judges. Thus, the diffuse system of judicial review of legislation was established in Brazil. It was amended through subsequent constitutional reforms in 1926, 1934, 1937, 1946 and 1967.[5]

A concentrated system of review was established in the 1934 Constitution by giving power to the Supreme Federal Tribunal to declare the constitutions of member states or laws (state laws) unconstitutional. This power was to be used only when required to do so by the Attorney General of the Republic.[6] Thus a direct action of unconstitutionality was established to defend federal constitutional principles against member state acts.[7] This was later developed in subsequent constitutions,[8] up to its extension after the 1965 Constitutional Amendment, to control all normative acts of state, whether federal or of the member states.[9]

Since the diffuse system of judicial review operates in combination with a concentrated system, the Brazilian system can be considered to be a mixed one.[10]

# The mixed systems of judicial review

## (b) The diffuse system of judicial review

Contrary to the American model and to the Argentinian experience, in which the powers of the courts to control the constitutionality of legislation was derived from the principle of constitutional supremacy, the Brazilian diffuse system of judicial review arose from express provisions in the 1891 Constitution,[11] and is still based on constitutional norms. In this respect, the present Constitution establishes the competence of the Supreme Federal Tribunal to judge, through extraordinary recourses, cases decided in the last resort by other courts or judges, when the challenged judicial decisions, firstly were against any disposition of the Constitution or denied the enforcement of a treaty or federal law, secondly, when they declared the unconstitutionality of a treaty or of a federal law, and, thirdly, when they deemed a law or other local government act challenging the Constitution or a federal law valid.[12]

According to this norm, not only is the diffuse system of judicial review established, but the power of the Supreme Tribunal to intervene in all processes in which constitutional questions have been resolved is also established.

### (i) The incidental character of the system and the exception of unconstitutionality

Since the diffuse system of judicial review in Brazil follows the general trends of the United States and Argentinian models, all courts of first instance have the power not to apply laws (federal, state or municipal laws) they deem to be unconstitutional. Thus, the judges have no *ex officio* power to judge the constitutionality of the laws, and can only exercise it when the question of constitutionality has been raised by the interested party as an exception or defence in the process.[13] The constitutional question, once raised, has a preliminary character regarding the final decision of the case, which the judge must decide beforehand. Of course, the decision of the courts on constitutional matters has *in casu et inter partes* effects, and the unapplied law is considered null and void *ab initio*. Thus, the decision has *ex tunc* retroactive effects.[14]

The constitutional question can also be considered through the normal appeals process, in which case, when the court of appeal is a collegiate court, the decision upon matters of unconstitutionality of legislation must be adopted by a majority vote decision of its members.[15]

## (ii) The extraordinary recourse before the Supreme Federal Tribunal

Ever since the establishment of the constitutional review judicial system in 1891, the Brazilian Constitution has always expressly regulated the power of the Supreme Court to review the decisions of lower courts on matters of constitutionality. The review can be effected through an extraordinary recourse by the party to the process who has lost the case.[16]

This extraordinary recourse of unconstitutionality proceeds only when the Superior Courts of Appeal have taken decisions that are considered contrary to the Constitution or which deny the validity of a treaty or federal law; when the decisions declare the unconstitutionality of a treaty or of a federal law; and when they deem a local government law or act, which has been challenged as unconstitutional or contrary to a federal law, valid.[17]

Because it is the law which is the object of the proceeding before the Supreme Federal Tribunal, the Attorney General can always intervene. He can also intervene in any process pending decision, to raise constitutional questions.[18]

When deciding constitutional questions, the Supreme Federal Tribunal must adopt its decision with the vote of the majority of its members.[19] The declaration of the unconstitutionality of a law, has *inter partes* and *ex tunc* effects.[20] The Tribunal recognises the *ab initio* unconstitutionality of the law but does not annul or repeal the law, which continues to be in force and applicable.

Once adopted by the Tribunal, the decision must be sent to the Federal Senate which has the power, according to the Constitution, to 'suspend the execution of all or part of a law or decree' declared unconstitutional by the Supreme Federal Tribunal through a definitive decision.[21] In such case, the effects of the Senate decisions have *erga omnes* and *ex nunc* effects.[22]

As in the United States, a presumption of constitutionality exists regarding laws and other state acts. Consequently, only when the unconstitutionality of a law appears to be without doubt, can the Tribunal declare its unconstitutionality. In cases of doubt, it must reject the question and consider the law constitutional and applicable in the concrete case.[23]

## (c) The concentrated system of judicial review

Since 1934 Brazil has also had a concentrated system of review attributed to the Supreme Federal Tribunal. Actions can be initiated in this system through a direct action that can be brought before the Tribunal only by the Attorney General of the Republic. This direct action of unconstitutionality can be of two types: the interventive direct action and the generic direct action.

The interventive direct action was originally established in the 1934 Constitution as a means for the protection of the federal constitutional principles regarding state legislation.[24] The Constitution established the possibility for the federal government to intervene in the member states in order to secure the observance of the following principles: republican form of government; independence and harmony of powers; temporal character of electoral functions; non re-election of governors for the next term; municipal autonomy; submission of administrative accounts; and guarantees of the judicial power.[25]

When any of these principles are violated by a member state, the federal power can intervene. But previous to that intervention the Attorney General must submit the question of unconstitutionality of the member state's act for examination by the Supreme Federal Tribunal.[26] If the final decision of the Tribunal is to declare the unconstitutionality of the challenged member state's law, it must be published and sent to the President of the Republic for suspension and if necessary, to order federal intervention in the member state.[27] Only when the act is declared unconstitutional by the Tribunal, therefore, can federal intervention take place.[28] In this case, the effects of the Tribunal decision are considered to be declarative[29] and with *erga omnes* effects.[30]

In the 1946 Constitution a generic direct action of unconstitutionality was established.[31] This action differs from the one already mentioned by the fact that it is intended to protect, not only certain constitutional principles regarding member state's laws and acts only, but any of the dispositions of the Constitution. The Constitution gives the Supreme Federal Tribunal power to decide, at the request of the Attorney General of the Republic, upon the unconstitutionality of any law or act of a normative character, either federal or of a member state.[32] In this case, if the Supreme Federal Tribunal declares the unconstitutionality of the federal or state law or normative act, a copy of the decision must be sent to the Federal Senate. The Senate has the power to 'suspend the execution of all or part of the law or decree declared unconstitutional by a definitive decision of the Supreme Federal Tribunal'.[33]

Discussions have taken place among Brazilian constitutional law authors regarding the effects of the Supreme Federal Tribunal decision declaring the unconstitutionality of a law, as a consequence of a generic direct action. Because the Constitution assigns this power to the Federal Senate, it has been considered that its decisions do not have, in themselves, *erga omnes* effects,[34] their contents being only to verify the existence or not of a defect of unconstitutionality in the challenged act.[35] Thus, it has been thought to have declarative effects with *ex tunc* repercussions.[36] Only the Senate decision of suspension of the execution of the law is considered to have *erga omnes* effects.[37]

## (d) The indirect means for judicial review of legislation

An indirect means for judicial review also exists through the exercise of actions for protection of fundamental rights and liberties and of a popular action for the protection of public assets.

### (i) The *mandato de segurança* and *habeas corpus* actions and judicial review

Since 1934[38] the Constitution of Brazil has expressly established the *mandato de segurança*. This is a special means for the protection of fundamental rights, other than personal liberty, which is protected by *habeas corpus*. These two special actions for the constitutional protection of fundamental rights, the *mandato de segurança* and the *habeas corpus* actions, exist in parallel.

The *mandato de segurança* is intended to protect actual individual rights whoever the authority responsible for the illegality or abuse of powers may be.[39] Nevertheless, it has been traditionally considered that the laws or any other normative act of state cannot be the object of an action requesting either *habeas corpus* or a *mandato de segurança*.[40]

In this respect the abstract control of the constitutionality of laws is not possible through the exercise of the actions for a *mandato de segurança*, or *habeas corpus*, in other words no direct action against laws can be exercised through these actions, even if they are what the Mexican system calls auto-applicative or self-executing laws.[41] Nevertheless, such actions can serve as an indirect means of judicial review, according to the diffuse system, when they are exercised against an act of any authority, when executed based on a law deemed unconstitutional.

### (ii) The popular action for the protection of public assets and judicial review

Since the 1934 Constitution[42] a popular action has existed as a special means devoted to invalidate illegal acts which could affect the assets of public entities.[43] This is an action open to any citizen. Because it is principally directed to impugn administrative acts, it cannot be used to impugn, in a direct way, laws or normative acts on the grounds of being unconstitutional. Nevertheless, the popular action can be an indirect means of judicial review of legislation, if the concrete administrative act which causes damage to the assets of any public entity is based on a law deemed unconstitutional. Nonetheless, it has been considered a direct means of judicial review of legislation, in cases in which damage to the assets of public entities is directly caused by the law or decree.[44] In such cases the power of review of legislation exercised by the judges follows the general pattern of the diffuse system of review.

# 30

## THE MIXED SYSTEM OF JUDICIAL REVIEW IN GUATEMALA AND PERU

### (a) The Guatemalan system

Basing its system on the principle of the supremacy of the Constitution,[1] the 1921 Guatemalan Constitution established the power of the Court to declare in their decisions the inapplicability of any law or disposition of the other state powers when contrary to the norms contained in the Constitution of the Republic.[2] This diffuse power of the courts was maintained in all constitutional texts up to the present Constitution of 1965. At that time a concentrated system of review, attributed to a specially created Constitutional Court, was established in addition to the diffuse system. Thus, the Guatemalan system of judicial review can also be considered a mixed one.

### (i) The diffuse system of judicial review

The 1965 Constitution expressly establishes the principle of the supremacy of the Constitution and the subsequent nullity of all state acts contrary to it. In particular, Article 77 establishes the general rule by stating that: 'The laws, government dispositions, and any other order which regulates the exercise of the rights guaranteed in the Constitution shall be *ipso jure* null if they diminish, restrict or distort them.'[3] Additionally, Article 246 establishes: 'The Courts of Justice will always observe the principle that the Constitution must prevail over any law or international treaty.'

Thus, according to these norms, the judicial review power attributed to all courts of justice is conceived in the Constitution as a duty of the judges. Consequently, their power of judicial review can be exercised *ex officio* .[4] Nevertheless, when a party to the case raises a constitutional question regarding a law or a part of it, the judges must decide upon the question.[5] Because of the purely incidental character of this review, Article 246 of the Constitution states: 'If the unconstitutionality of a law is declared, the decision must limit itself to establishing that the legal disposition is inapplicable to the case and the question must be sent to Congress.'

Constitutional questions can be brought before the ordinary courts either through the concrete claim or as an exception in the process. In any case, prior to the judge's decision on the case the judge must hear the parties and the Public Prosecutor.[6]

As in all diffuse systems of judicial review, the judge's decision when declaring the inapplicability of a law on the grounds of unconstitutionality, has declarative effects, in the sense that it establishes a pre-existent nullity with retroactive or *ex tunc* effects, but exclusively related to the parties to the case (*in casu et inter partes*).[7]

(ii) The concentrated system of judicial review<br>and the Constitutional Court

Following the European model, the 1965 Constitution established a concentrated system by assigning the exclusive power to declare the unconstitutionality of laws, and thus to annul them with *erga omnes* effects, to a Constitutional Court.[8]

This Constitutional Court, although created in the Constitution,[9] is not conceived as a permanent organ. Instead it only functions when required to exercise judicial review. It has twelve members, appointed as follows: four by the Supreme Court of Justice, and the rest designated by the Supreme Court of Justice by a draw from within the members of the Court of Appeals and the Administrative Justice Tribunal. The President of the Constitutional Court is the President of the Supreme Court of Justice.[10]

The judicial review powers of the Constitutional Court are exercised when requested through a recourse of unconstitutionality. This is conceived as a direct action[11] that can be exercised against 'laws and governmental dispositions of general effects when considered to be totally or partially unconstitutional'.[12]

The standing to bring the action before the Constitutional Court is a specific one, thus differing from the popular action that can be brought before the Supreme Courts of Venezuela and Colombia. In particular, this recourse of unconstitutionality can only be brought before the Court by the following: the Council of State, conceived in the Guatemalan constitutional system as a consultative institution; the Public Prosecutor, when requested to do so by the President in a decision adopted in the Council of Ministers; and finally, by any individual or entity directly affected by the unconstitutionality of the law or the challenged governmental act, assisted by ten lawyers.[13] Thus, the standing has been considered extremely limited.[14]

If the Public Prosecutor does not bring the action before the Court, he must be notified and, in principle, he must defend the constitutionality of the challenged act although he can express his conformity with the alleged unconstitutionality.[15]

The effects of the challenged law or executive act can be provisionally suspended by the Court during the process, when the unconstitutionality is notorious and could produce irreparable damage. This decision of suspension of the effects of the law or executive act of general contents, has general effects and an *erga omnes* character and must be published in the Official Journal.[16]

The final decision of the Court, if it declares the unconstitutionality of the law, has also *erga omnes* effects but, as in all concentrated systems of judicial review, with *ex nunc* effects. Thus, the decision has a constitutive character, with *pro futuro* consequences, and without any effect back towards the past.[17] Only when a temporal suspension of the effects of the law has been decided by the Court during the procedure, can the final decision declaring the unconstitutionality of the law have *ex tunc* effects, but back to the date of the suspensive decision of the effects of the challenged law.[18]

### (iii) Judicial review and the constitutional protection (*amparo*)

Finally, it must also be mentioned that a special judicial means for constitutional protection (*amparo*) of the fundamental rights established in the Constitution, following the Mexican model,[19] has been established.

The main purpose of this *amparo* is to seek 'the maintenance of or the restitution to the aggrieved person of the enjoyment of the rights and guarantees established in the Constitution'.[20] Nevertheless, according to the Guatemalan Constitution the *amparo* is also admissible in order 'to declare, in concrete cases that a law, an executive regulation or any other act of an authority is not obligatory for the petitioner, because it contravenes or it restricts any of the rights guaranteed in the Constitution'.[21] Thus, through the *amparo* action, the judge can exercise his powers of judicial review, in an incidental way (*incidenter tantum*) and declare a law unconstitutional.

The concrete effect of the judge's decision granting *amparo* to the petitioner is to suspend the application of the law or executive regulation regarding the petitioner and restore him, when necessary, to his previous position.[22]

### (b) The Peruvian system

The Constitution of Peru of 12 July 1979,[23] in force since 28 July 1980,[24] followed a long tradition and established in Article 236 the diffuse system of judicial review as follows: 'In case of incompatibility between a constitutional norm and an ordinary legal one, the judge must prefer the former. In a similar way, he must prefer the legal norm above any other inferior norm.'

According to this constitutional disposition, all judges can exercise their power of judicial review of legislation, deciding not to apply a law which they deem unconstitutional. This must be done in an incidental way, when required by a party to the case and with *inter partes* effects.[25] This power of judicial review can be considered a diffuse one, even though not commonly exercised by the courts.[26]

In addition to the diffuse system of judicial review, a concentrated system of judicial review has also been in existence since 1980. The Tribunal of Constitutional Guarantees was created by the Peruvian Constitution of 1979 as a 'control organ of the Constitution'. It is made up of nine members appointed in a paritarian way (three each) by the Congress, the Executive Power and the Supreme Court of Justice.[27] Its functioning has been regulated by the Organic Law of the Tribunal of Constitutional Guarantees of 19 May 1982.[28]

This Tribunal of Constitutional Guarantees, with jurisdiction throughout the territory of the Republic, is competent in two basic aspects relating to constitutional supremacy: first, it has jurisdictional power to control the constitutionality of legislation; and second, it is competent to decide, as a Cassation Court, recourses regarding lower courts decisions on *habeas corpus* and *amparo*.[29] As a jurisdictional organ for judicial review, the Tribunal of Constitutional Guarantees is competent 'To declare, on the petition of a party, the partial or total unconstitutionality of laws, legislative decrees, regional norms of a general character, and municipal ordinances which contravene the Constitution as a matter of form or substance.'[30]

The parties who are authorized to interpose an action of unconstitutionality are the following: the President of the Republic, the Supreme Court of Justice, the Public Prosecutor of the Republic, sixty Members of Parliament, twenty senators, or 50,000 petitioning citizens whose signatures must be certified by the National Electoral Board.

The Tribunal has *ex-officio* powers to exceed the arguments of the parties and to declare dispositions, other than the challenged ones, unconstitutional so long as the ruling is a consequence or is in connection with the action's contents.[31]

In the case of statutes, the effects of the ruling upon its unconstitutionality are not immediate. Similar to the Yugoslavian situation, once the decision is adopted it must be communicated to the President of the Congress so that the latter may pass a law repealing the provision contrary to the Constitution. When forty-five days have elapsed without the new derogatory rule having been promulgated, the unconstitutional provision is understood to have been nullified and the Tribunal must publish the decision in the Official Gazette. When the ruling of unconstitutionality, however, relates to other normative state acts, different from formal laws, the Tribunal must order the publication of the ruling in the Official Gazette, and it becomes effective the day following publication.[32]

In both cases, the Tribunal decision declaring the unconstitutionality of a statute or other normative state acts, once published, has *erga omnes* effects, and in accordance with an express provision of the Constitution, they 'do not have retroactive effects'.[33] They are thus only *ex-nunc, pro futuro*. Accordingly, the Organic Law of the Tribunal establishes that decisions declaring the unconstitutionality of a normative state act cannot serve as support to review judicial processes already concluded in which the unconstitutional norms were applied. Nevertheless, in accordance with the general exception principle of the possible retroactivity of statutes in criminal, labour or taxation cases,[34] the Organic Law allows the retroactive applicability of the Tribunal decision in proceedings in which its effect could be favourable to the convicted person, the worker or the taxpayer.[35]

The 1980 Constitution also establishes the actions of *habeas corpus* and *amparo*, as special means for the protection of fundamental rights: the former, directed to protect personal liberty and the latter, as a means for the protection of all other fundamental rights recognised in the Constitution.[36] Through the exercise of these two actions the ordinary judge can also exercise judicial review powers when the alleged violation of the fundamental right is based on a norm incompatible with the Constitution. In such cases, the judge can declare the said norm inapplicable.[37] Thus, a diffuse system can also be distinguished in Peru, as a consequence of the exercise of the actions for protection of fundamental rights, and which performs in parallel with the concentrated system.

The decisions of the ordinary courts on matters of constitutional protection (*habeas corpus* and *amparo*) are subject to ordinary appeals before the superior courts and, against the decisions of the latter, a recourse based on reasons of nullity which can be exercised before the Supreme Court. The decisions of the latter can additionally be the object of a recourse of cassation before the Tribunal of Constitutional Guarantees in order to examine whether or not the Supreme Court has violated or erroneously applied the law.[38]

# Notes

## Introduction

1   E.S. Corwin, 'Judicial Review', *Encyclopaedia of the Social Sciences*, Vol. VIII, London, 1932, p. 457.
2   D.G.T. Williams, 'The Constitution of the United Kingdom' (1972) 31 *Cambridge Law Journal*, p. 277.
3   A.V. Dicey, *England's Case against Home Rule*, 3rd edn., London, 1887, p.168.
4   T.R.S. Allan, 'Legislative Supremacy and the Rule of Law: Democracy and Constitutionalism' (1985) 44 *Cambridge Law Journal*, p. 116.
5   1974 A.C. 765. See the text in O. Hood Phillips, *Leading Cases in Constitutional and Administrative Law*, London, 1979, pp. 1–6. See also the comments in P. Allott, 'The Courts and Parliament: Who whom?' (1979) 38 *Cambridge Law Journal*, pp. 80–1.
6   J.A.C. Grant, 'El control jurisdiccional de la constitucionalidad de las leyes: una contribución de las Américas a la Ciencia Política', *Revista de la Facultad de Derecho de México*, 45, 1962, pp. 417–37.

## 2   The limitation of power as a guarantee of liberty

1   Lord Hailsham, *Elective Dictatorship*, London, 1976, quoted by P. Allott, 'The Courts and Parliament: Who whom?' (1979) 38 *Cambridge Law Journal*, p. 115. Lord Hailsham said that Parliament had become 'virtually an elective dictatorship. The party system makes the supremacy of a government like the present, automatic and almost unquestioned,' quoted by M. Zander, *A Bill of Rights?*, London, 1980, p. 5.
2   J. Locke, *Two Treatises of Government*, Peter Laslett, ed., Cambridge, 1967, p. 324.
3   Ibid., p. 211.
4   Ibid., p. 371.
5   Ibid., paragraphs 134, 149, 150, pp. 384, 385. Peter Laslett commentaries, 'Introduction', p. 117.
6   Ibid., p. 117.

7    Ibid, p. 383. Locke comments in relation to the name given by him to this power: 'if any one pleases. So the thing be understood, I am indifferent as to the name.'

8    Ibid., 'Introduction', p. 118.

9    Ibid., pp. 117–18.

10   'Balancing the power of government by placing several parts of it in different hands,' ibid., pp. 107–350.

11   Ibid., p. 118.

12   M.J.C. Vile, *Constitutionalism and the Separation of Powers*, Oxford, 1967, p. 36. (Locke: 'There can be one supreme power, which is the legislative, to which all the rest are and must be subordinated ... for what can give laws to another, must need be superior to him,' ch. 13, pp. 149–50).

13   A. Passerin d'Entrèves, *The Notion of the State. An Introduction to Political Theory*, Oxford, 1967, p. 120.

14   Montesquieu, *De L'Esprit des lois*, G. Truc, ed., Paris, 1949, Vol.1, Book XI ch. 4, pp. 162–3.

15   Ibid., Vol. I, pp. 163–4.

16   Ibid., Vol. I, p. 164. In the same, Book XI, ch. 6, Montesquieu added that 'Were the judicial power joined with the legislative, the life and liberty of the subject would be exposed to arbitrary control; for the judge would be then the legislator. Were it joined to the executive power, the judge might behave with violence and oppression.' Cf. C.H. McIlwain, *The High Court of Parliament and its Supremacy*, Yale, 1910, pp. 322–3.

17   Montesquieu, op.cit, Vol. I, p. 165.

18   Ibid., Vol. I, Book XI, Ch. III, p. 162.

19   Ibid., Vol. I, p. 166.

20   Ibid., Vol. I, p. 172.

21   Passerin d'Entrèves, op. cit., p. 121.

22   J.J. Rousseau, *Du contrat social*, ed., Ronald Grimsley, Oxford, 1972, Book I, ch. IV, p. 114.

23   Ibid., Book I, ch. VIII, p. 119.

24   Ibid., Book II, ch. V, p. 134.

25   Ibid., p. 136.

26   Ibid., p. 153.

27   R. Grimsley, 'Introduction', in Rousseau, op. cit., p. 35.

28   Ibid., Book III, ch. VI.

29   Montesquieu, op. cit., Book XI, ch. III, p. 162.

30   J. Madison, *The Federalist*, B.F. Wright, ed., Cambridge, Mass.,1961, p. 336.

31   Art. XXX. *Massachusetts General Law Annotated*, St Paul, Minn., Vol. 1–A, p. 582. In 1776, the Constitution of Virginia also had a declaration on separation of powers, considered as 'the most precise statement of the doctrine which had at that time appeared'. Vile, op. cit., p. 118. Article III of that Constitution stated: 'The Legislative, Executive and Judiciary departments, shall be separate and distinct, so that neither exercise the powers properly belonging to the others; nor

shall any person exercise the powers of more than one of them at the same time, except that the Justice of the County Courts shall be eligible to either House of Assembly.'

32  J. Rivero, *Droit administratif*, Paris, 1973, p. 129; J. M. Auby and R. Drago, *Traité de contentieux administratif*, Paris, 1984, Vol. I, p. 379.

33  Rivero, op. cit., p. 129.

34  M. García-Pelayo, *Derecho constitucional comparado*, Madrid, 1957, p. 283; Cf. G. Marshall, *Constitutional Theory*, Oxford, 1971, p. 97.

35  P. Allott, 'The Courts and Parliament: Who whom?' (1979) 38 *Cambridge Law Journal*, p. 115.

36  For example, T.R.S. Allan has noted that 'the political consequence of the legal arrangement [that perceives the constitution as a legal order subject to, and dominated by, an unrestrained and all-powerful sovereign: the Parliament] is the overwhelming authority of a government with a majority of seats in the House of Commons'. and that 'It is this concentration of power which is seen as a threat to fundamental rights and liberties. Constitutional restraints are therefore needed to protect such rights from irresponsible legislative encroachment; the need is to counteract the "helplessness of the law in face of the legislative sovereignty of Parliament"' [Sir Leslie Scarman], in 'Legislative Supremacy and the Rule of Law: Democracy and Constitutionalism' (1985) 44 *Cambridge Law Journal*, pp. 111–12; Sir Leslie Scarman quoted from *English Law. The New Dimension*, Hamlyn Lectures, series 26, p. 15.

37  E.C.S. Wade and G. Godfrey Phillips, *Constitutional and Administrative Law*, 9th edn, by A.W. Bradley, London, 1985, p. 53.

38  Ibid., pp. 49, 564.

39  Allan, op. cit. p. 122.

40  H.W.R. Wade, *Administrative Law*, 5th edn, Oxford, 1984, p. 27. See also Sir Ivor Jennings, *The Law and the Constitution*, London, 1972 p. 147, where he says 'Parliament may remodel the British Constitution, prolong its own life, legislate ex-post facto, legalise illegalities, provide for individual cases, interfere with contracts and authorize the seizure of property, give dictatorial powers to the Government, dissolve the United Kingdom or the British Commonwealth, introduce communism or socialism, or individualism or fascism, entirely without legal restriction.'

41  A.V. Dicey, *An Introduction to the Study of the Law of the Constitution*, 'Introduction', by E.C.S. Wade, 10th edn, London, 1973, pp. 39–40.

42  O. Hood Phillips, *Leading Cases in Constitutional and Administrative Law*, London, 1979, pp. 2–5.

43  Ibid., p. 28. That is why George Winterton said that 'the rule of law comes to mean rule of law as enacted by Parliament, and not the rule of the ancient common law', 'The British Grundnorm: Parliamentary Supremacy Re-examined' (1976) 92 *Law Quarterly Review*, p. 596.

44  Allan, op. cit., p. 129. Also see Wade and Godfrey Phillips, op. cit., pp. 61–2.

45  Wade, op. cit. p. 28.

46  Ibid., p. 28. See also Winterton, op. cit., p. 597.

47  D.G.T. Williams, 'The Constitution of the United Kingdom', 31 *Cambridge Law Journal*, p. 179.

48  Winterton, op. cit., p. 599.


*3   The submission of the state to the law*


1   I. Jennings, *Magna Carta*, London, 1965, p. 9.

2   H.L.A. Hart, *The Concept of Law*, Oxford, 1961, p. 70. On p. 65 the auhor asserts: 'in every society where there is law there is a sovereign ... everywhere the existence of law implies the existence of such a sovereign'.

3   C.H. McIlwain, *Constitutionalism and the Changing World*, Cambridge, 1939, p. 31.

4   J. Austin, *The Province of Jurisprudence Determined*, H.L.A. Hart, ed., London, 1954, Lec. VI, pp. 230, 231, 251, quoted in Hart, op. cit. p. 72.

5   McIlwain, op. cit., p. 31

6   Hart, op. cit., p. 65.

7   That is why this sovereign, says Hart, 'makes law for his subjects and makes it from a position outside any law'. Therefore 'there are, and can be, no legal limits on his law-creating powers'. He concludes by saying that 'the legally unlimited power of the sovereign is his definition', op. cit., pp. 64–5.

8   Hart, op. cit., p. 72

9   Ibid.

10  Ibid., p. 73.

11  Ibid.

12  G.Winterton, 'The British *Grundnorm*: Parliamentary Supremacy Re-examined' (1976) 92 *Law Quarterly Review*, p. 596.

13  Ibid.

14  I. Jennings, *Parliaments*, Cambridge, 1961, p. 2.

15  J.D.B. Mitchell, *Constitutional Law*, Edinburgh, 1968, pp. 69–75.

16  Ibid., pp. 56, 66, 67.

17  Section 4 of the *Statute of Westminster* provides 'No act of Parliament of the United Kingdom passed after the commencement of this Act shall extend, or be deemed to extend, to a Dominion as part of the law of that Dominion, unless it is expressly declared in that Act that that Dominion has requested, and consented to, the enactment thereof.' Cf. C. Turpin, *British Government and the Constitution*, London, 1985, p. 27. In a contrary sense, Hamish R. Gray says that 'The general tendency of constitutional lawyers is to reject the interpretation of section 4 which requires Parliament as a matter of law to act in a particular way for any particular purpose.' 'The Sovereignty of the Imperial Parliament' (1960) 23 *Modern Law Review*, p. 647.

18  For example, *The Zimbabwe Act*, 1979, section I(2) provides: 'On and after Independence Day her Majesty's Government in the United Kingdom shall have no responsibility for the government of Zimbabwe; and no Act of the Parliament of the United Kingdom passed on or after that day shall extend, or be deemed to extend to Zimbabwe as part of its law.' Cf. Turpin, op. cit., p. 27.

19  Cf. F.A. Trinade, 'Parliamentary Sovereignty and the Primacy of European Community Law' (1972) 35 *Modern Law Review*, pp. 375–402; S.A. De Smith, 'The Constitution and the Common Market: a tentative appraisal' (1971) 34 *Modern Law Review*, pp. 597–614; H.W.R. Wade, 'Sovereignty and the European Communities' (1972) 88 *Law Quarterly Review*, pp. 1–5.

20  A.L. Goodhart, 'Legal Procedure and Democracy' (1964) *Cambridge Law Journal*, 22, p. 52. Cf. Mitchell, op. cit., p. 13.

21  Mitchell, op. cit., p. 66.

22  T.R.S. Allan, 'Legislative Supremacy and the Rule of Law: Democracy and Constitutionalism' (1985) 44 *Cambridge Law Journal*, p. 135 where the author states 'A common law presumption which commands the loyalty of the judges is as powerful an instrument for interpreting legislation so as to safeguard individual liberties as an enacted Bill of Rights.'

23  J.M. Snee (SJ), 'Leviathan at the Bar of Justice', in A.E. Sutherland, ed., *Government under the Law*, Cambridge, Mass., 1956, pp. 106–7.

24  With the exception of the United Kingdom, New Zealand and Israel, all countries in the world have written Constitutions. Cf. O. Hood Phillips, *Reform of the Constitution*, London, 1970, p. 4; F.M. Auburn, 'Trends in Comparative Constitutional Law' (1972) 35 *Modern Law Review*, p. 129.

25  J. Locke, *Two Treatises of Government*, Peter Laslett, ed., Cambridge, 1967, ch. 4.

26  J.J. Rousseau, *Du contrat social*, ed. Ronald Grimsley, Oxford, 1972, Book II, ch. V., p. 136; Book III, ch. IV, p. 163. This concept continued to the last century: R. Carré de Malberg, *La Loi, expression de la volonté générale*, 1932, quoted by M. Letourneur and R. Drago, 'The Rule of Law As Understood in France' (1958) 7 *American Journal of Comparative Law*, p. 148.

27  See W. Laqueur and B. Rubin, *The Human Rights Reader*, New York, 1979, p. 119. Cf. G. de Ruggeiro, *The History of European Liberalism*, Boston, 1967, p. 67.

28  E. García de Enterría, *Revolución francesa y administración contemporánea*, Madrid 1972, p. 16.

29  Arts. 2 and 4, Laqueur and Rubin, op. cit., pp. 118–19.

30  C. Eisenmann, 'Le Droit administratif et le principé de légalité', *Etudes et documents*, Conseil d'Etat No. 11, Paris, 1957, pp. 25–40; Letourneur and Drago, op. cit., p. 149. Other authors followed the broader sense of law, as 'legal order' in the definition of the principle of legality, A. de Laubadère, *Traité élémentaire de Droit Administratif*, Paris, 1962, p. 369.

31  A. Tunc, 'Government under Law: a Civilian View', in Sutherland, ed., *Government under Law*, p. 43.

32  G. MacCormack, 'Law and legal system' (1979) 42 *Modern Law Review*, pp. 285–90: 'Legal system understood as a collection of rules of law that have in common their interrelation in a particular order, mainly hierarchical.'

33  C.H. McIlwain, *Constitutionalism and the Changing World*, Cambridge, 1939, p. 73.

34  H. Kelsen, *General Theory of Law and State*, trans. Wedberg, Cambridge, Mass., 1945, p. 110, quoted by MacCormack, op. cit., p. 286.

35  H. Kelsen, *Pure Theory of Law*, trans. Max Knight, Berkeley, 1967, ch. IX; Spanish edition, *Teoría pura del derecho*, Buenos Aires, 1981, p. 135.

36  H. Kelsen, *Teoría pura*, p. 147.

37  'The law is today an amalgam of common law and statute law of such an interdependent kind that it is often difficult to say whether a particular result is determined by the statute or by ordinary case law.' P.S. Atiyah, 'Common Law and Statute Law' (1985) 48 *Modern Law Review*, p. 5.

38  A. Tunc, op. cit., pp. 46–7.

39  A.R. Brewer-Carías, *El derecho administrativo y la ley orgánica de procedimientos administrativos*, Caracas, 1982, pp. 379–414.

40  Ibid., pp. 112–18.

41  See, in general, P. Jackson, *Natural Justice*, London, 1979, p. 224.

42  W. Holdsworth, *A History of English Law*, London, 1972, Vol. II, p. 121. Cf. E.C.S. Wade, 'Introduction', A.V. Dicey, *An Introduction to the Study of the Law of the Constitution*, London, 1973, p. xcii.

43  Wade, op. cit., p. xcii.

44  Mitchell, op. cit., p. 53.

45  Dicey, op. cit., p. 188.

46  Ibid. p. 202. In this concept, regular law is understood to mean statute law and common law, but the former has supremacy over the latter.

47  I. Jennings, *The Law and the Constitution*, London, 1972, pp. 57–8.

48  Dicey, op. cit., p. 193.

49  Ibid., pp. 202–3.

50  Ibid., p. 203.

51  Ibid., pp. 336–7. 'An individual in his dealing with the State does not, according to French ideas, stand on anything like the same footing as that on which he stands in dealing with his neighbour.' p. 337.

52  H.W.R. Wade, *Administrative Law*, Oxford, 1984, p. 25.

53  Mitchell, op. cit., p. 58.

54  H.W.R. Wade, op. cit., p. 24.

55  I.L. Jaffe and E.G. Henderson 'Judicial Review and the Rule of Law: Historical Origins', *Law Quarterly Review*, 72, 1965, pp. 345–64. See, in general, B. Schwartz and H.W.R. Wade, *Legal Control of Government*, Oxford, 1978, p. 350.

56  Dicey, op. cit., p. 195.

57  Ibid., p. 203.

58 E.C.S. Wade and G. Godfrey Phillips, *Constitutional and Administrative Law*, London, 1982, p. 89.
59 Mitchell, op. cit., pp. 54–5.
60 H.W.R. Wade, op. cit., pp. 22, 24.
61 J. Raz, 'The Rule of Law and its Virtue' (1977) 93 *Law Quarterly Review*, pp. 198–202.

## 4 *The declaration of fundamental rights and liberties*

1 J. Locke, *Two Treatises of Government*, quoted in W. Laqueur and B. Rubin, eds., *The Human Rights Reader*, New York, 1979, p. 64.
2 Ibid., p. 65.
3 Ibid., p. 66.
4 Ibid., p. 67.
5 J.J. Rousseau, *The Social Contract*, quoted in Laqueur and Rubin, eds., op. cit., p. 70.
6 Montesquieu, *The Spirit of Laws*, quoted in Laqueur and Rubin, eds., op. cit., pp. 68–9.
7 K. Minogue, 'The History of the Idea of Human Rights', in Laqueur and Rubin, eds., op. cit., p. 6.
8 W. Holdsworth, *A History of English Law*, Vol. II, London, 1971, pp. 207–8. Cf. F.W. Maitland, *The Constitutional History of England*, Cambridge, 1968, p. 67.
9 Maitland, op. cit., p. 67.
10 Holdsworth, op. cit., Vol. II, p. 209.
11 Ibid., p. 212.
12 Ibid.
13 'A common and useful way of describing the change from the medieval to the modern world is to say that the idea of duty gave way to the idea of right.' Minogue, op. cit., p. 5.
14 Holdsworth, op. cit., Vol. IX, 1966, p. 104.
15 L.G. Schwoerer, *The Declaration of Rights, 1689*, Baltimore, 1981, pp. 19.
16 Schwoerer, op. cit., p. 283.
17 See the text in J. Hervada and J.M. Zumaquero, *Textos internacionales de derechos humanos*, Pamplona, 1978, p. 25.
18 Ibid., pp. 27–9.
19 Ibid., p. 37.
20 See the text in Laqueur and Rubin, eds., op. cit., pp. 106–18. Cf. A.H. Robertson, *Human Rights in the World*, Manchester, 1982, p. 7.
21 J. Rivero, *Les Libertés publiques*, Paris, 1973, Vol. I, p. 45; Robertson, *op cit.*, p. 7; G. Jellinek, *La Déclaration des droits de l'homme et du citoyen*, trad. G. Favioles, Paris, 1902.
22 Rivero, op. cit., pp. 42–3.
23 See the text in Hervada and Zumaquero, op. cit., pp. 39–40; Laqueur and Rubin, eds., op. cit., p. 118.

24  Ibid., pp. 41–9 and pp. 118–19.
25  See the text in A.R. Brewer-Carías, *Las Constituciones de Venezuela*. Madrid, 1985, pp. 175–7.
26  Ibid., pp. 196–200.
27  I. Jennings, *The Law and the Constitution*, London, 1972, pp. 40., 259.
28  M. García Pelayo, *Derecho constitucional comparado*, Madrid, 1957, p. 278.
29  Wade and Godfrey Phillips, op. cit., p. 441.
30  Jennings, op. cit., pp. 41, 262. 'It asserts the principle of legality, that everything is legal that is not illegal.' Therefore, the essence of the provisions related to fundamental rights regulation in Britain, is founded upon who can establish unlawful actions or prohibit them. Naturally, these limits must be found primarily in legislation, that is to say, in Acts of Parliament. Delegated legislation in relation to fundamental rights, in principle, is only possible in cases of state of emergency in accordance with the Emergency Powers Act, 1920. Wade and Godfrey Phillips, op. cit., p. 567.
31  A.V. Dicey, *An Introduction to the Study of the Law of the Constitution*, with an introduction by E.C.S. Wade, 1973, pp. 195, 196, 203. See also Wade's comments, p. cxviii.
32  J.D.B. Mitchell, *Constitutional Law*, Edinburgh, 1968, p. 55.
33  P.S. Atiyah, *Law and Modern Society*, Oxford, 1983, p. 109.
34  Ibid., p. 111.
35  M. Zander, *A Bill of Rights?*, London, 1985, p. 106.
36  Ibid., pp. 43–4.
37  Ibid., p. 45.
38  A.Z. Drzemczewski, *European Human Rights Convention in Domestic Law. A Comparative Study*, Oxford, 1985, p. 178.
39  Zander, op. cit., p. 45.
40  A. Lester, 'Fundamental Rights: the United Kingdom Isolated?' (1984) *Public Law*, p. 65.
41  H.W.R. Wade, *Constitutional Fundamentals*, London, 1980, p. 25. Cf. Hood Phillips, op. cit., pp. 11, 12; Lester, op. cit., p. 71; Zander, op. cit., p. 70.
42  D.G.T. Williams, 'The Constitution of the United Kingdom' (1972) 31 *Cambridge Law Journal*, p. 277. 'An entrenched Bill of Rights would, of course, involve the exercise of judicial review by English and other courts of the United Kingdom' so as to give domestic courts a 'blank cheque to protect certain fundamental freedoms even against the legislature itself'.
43  Lester, op. cit., p. 66.
44  Zander, op. cit., pp. 83–9.
45  J. Jaconelli, *Enacting a Bill of Rights. The Legal Problems*, Oxford, 1980, pp. 270–7.

# Notes

## 5. The written constitutional process

1 M.C. Wheare, *Modern Constitutions*, Oxford, 1966, pp. 1, 2.
2 See, in general, I. Jennings, *Magna Carta*, London, 1965, p. 9.
3 W. Holdsworth, *A History of English Law*, London, 1971, Vol. II, pp. 207, 219.
4 C. Schmidt, *Teoría de la constitución*, Spanish edn, Mexico, 1961, pp. 52–3.
5 C.H. McIlwain, *The High Court of Parliament and its Supremacy*, Yale, 1919, pp. 64–5.
6 Holdsworth, op. cit., Vol. II, p. 219.
7 Wheare, p. 9. Cf. J.D.B. Mitchell, *Constitutional Law*, Edinburgh, 1968, p. 27.
8 Cf. Holdsworth, op. cit., Vol. VI, p. 146; M. Ashley, *England in the Seventeenth Century*, London, 1967, pp. 91–2.
9 Holdsworth, op. cit., p. 146; Ashley, op. cit., p. 106.
10 Holdsworth, op. cit., pp. 154–5.
11 Holdsworth, op. cit., p. 147; Ashley, op. cit., p. 102.
12 Ibid., p. 165.
13 I. Jennings, *The Law and the Constitution*, London, 1972, p. 7; Wheare, op. cit., p. 10. 'Those who speak of an unbroken line of development in the history of English government ... have a good deal of truth on their side. There was a break and an attempt to make a fresh start with a Constitution, but it failed, and the former order was restored.'
14 Holdsworth, op. cit., p. 157.
15 R.L. Perry, ed., *Sources of our Liberties. Documentary Origin of Individual Liberties in the United States Constitution and Bill of Rights*, New York, 1952, p. 261.
16 Quoted by M. García-Pelayo, *Derecho constitucional comparado*, Madrid, 1957, p. 325.
17 Perry, ed., op. cit., p. 270.
18 C.F. Adams, ed., *The Works of John Adams*, Boston, 1850, Vol. II, p. 374, quoted by Perry, op. cit., p. 275.
19 Perry, ed., op. cit., p. 287.
20 Ibid., p. 317.
21 Ibid., p. 319.
22 R.B. Morris, 'Creating and Ratifying the Constitution', *National Forum, Towards the Bicentennial of the Constitution*, Autumn 1984, p. 9.
23 A.C. McLaughlin, *A Constitutional History of the United States*, New York, 1936, p. 131.
24 Ibid., p. 137; Perry, ed., op. cit., p. 399.
25 Perry, ed., op. cit., p. 401.
26 García-Pelayo, op. cit., pp. 336–7.
27 Morris, op. cit., pp. 12, 13; García-Pelayo, op. cit., p. 336; McLaughlin, op. cit., p. 163.

28 Morris, op. cit., p. 10; García-Pelayo, op. cit., p. 336; McLaughlin, op. cit., p. 179.

29 Morris, op. cit., p. 11; McLaughlin, op. cit., p. 185.

30 See the text in Perry, ed., op. cit., pp. 432–3.

31 A. de Tocqueville, *The Ancien Régime and the French Revolution*, trans. S. Gilbert, London, 1971.

32 García-Pelayo, op. cit., p. 463.

33 J. Rivero, *Les Libertés publiques*, Vol. I, Paris, 1973, pp. 38–42.

34 de Tocqueville, op. cit., quoted in Y. Madiot, *Droits de l'homme et libertés publiques*, Paris, 1976, p. 46.

35 H. Berthélemy and P. Duez, *Traité élémentaire de droit constitutionnel*, Paris, 1933, p. 74, quoted by García-Pelayo, op. cit., p. 461.

36 E. Sieyès, *Qu'est-ce que le tiers Etat?*, R. Zappeti, ed., Geneva, 1970, p. 121.

37 Ibid., p. 135.

38 'The people – the not privileged – of course were the ones that supported the Third Estate, that is to say, the bourgeoisie, because they did not have other alternatives, in the sense that they could not support the nobility or the clergy, who represented the privileged.' G. De Ruggiero, *The History of European Liberalism*, Boston, 1967, p. 74.

39 Ibid., pp. 75, 77.

40 J.L. Aranguren, *Etica y política*, Madrid, 1963, pp. 293, 297, quoted by E. Díaz, *Estado de derecho y sociedad democrática*, Madrid, 1966, p. 80.

41 Art. 3.

42 Under the influence of Sieyès, the Constitution established two categories of citizens: active citizens and passive citizens. G. Lepointe, *Histoire des institutions du droit public français au XIX siècle, 1789–1914*, Paris, 1953, p. 44.

43 'Il n'y a point en France d'autorité supérieur à celle de la loi.' García-Pelayo, op. cit., pp. 465–6.

44 Art. 4, ch. II, section 1.

45 Lepointe, op. cit., p. 44.

46 Art. 16.

47 Lepointe, op. cit., pp. 45, 49.

48 J.A. Hawgood, *Modern Constitutions since 1787*, London, 1939, p. 51.

49 P. Grases, ed., *Derechos del hombre y del ciudadano*, Caracas, 1959, pp. 105–21.

50 See the texts in A. R. Brewer-Carías, ed., *Las Constituciones de Venezuela*, Madrid, 1985.

51 S. Bolívar, 'Carta de Jamaica (1815)', in S. Bolívar, *Escritos fundamentales*, Caracas, 1982, p. 97.

52 S. Bolívar, 'Discurso de Angostura (1819)', in ibid., p. 120.

53 Ibid.

54 S. Bolívar (letter to D.F. O'Leary), in Bolívar, *Escritos Fundamentales*, pp. 200, 201.

## 6    *General trends of contemporary constitutionalism*

1    A. de Tocqueville, *Democracy in America*, J. P. Mayer and M. Lerner, eds., London, 1968, p. 50.
2    Ibid., p. 17.
3    Ibid., p. 285.
4    W.H. Hamilton, 'Constitutionalism', *Encyclopaedia of the Social Sciences*, Vol. IV, London, 1931, p. 255.
5    De Tocqueville, op. cit., p. 123.
6    Ibid., p. 124.
7    *Marbury* v. *Madison*, 5 U. S. (1 Cranch) 137; (1880) 2 L. Ed. 60. See the text in R. A. Rossum and G. Alan Tarr, *American Constitutional Law. Cases and Interpretation*, New York, 1983, p. 70.
8    Ibid., p. 70.
9    De Tocqueville, op. cit., Vol. I, p. 68.
10   Ibid., p. 78.
11   Ibid., p. 68.
12   Ibid., p. 69.
13   Ibid.
14   Ibid., pp. 78-9.
15   Ibid., p. 216.
16   Ibid., p. 213.
17   Title of ch. IX of 2nd part, op. cit., p. 342.
18   Ibid., p. 354.
19   Ibid., p. 86.
20   Ibid., p. 87.
21   Ibid., p. 51.   'In most European nations political existence started in the higher ranks of society and has been gradually but always incompletely, communicated to the various members of the body social. Contrariwise, in America, one may say that the local community was organized before the county, the county before the States; and the States before the Union.'
22   Ibid., p. 74.
23   Ibid., p. 75.
24   Ibid.
25   Ibid., p. 79.
26   Ibid., p. 192.   Cf. M. García-Pelayo, *Derecho constitucional comparado*, Madrid, 1957, pp. 215, 341.
27   De Tocqueville, op. cit., p. 194.
28   Ibid., p. 203.
29   Ibid., p. 204.
30   Ibid., p. 110.
31   Ibid., pp. 113, 115.
32   Ibid., pp. 148, 149.
33   Ibid., p. 155.
34   Ibid., p. 156.
35   Ibid., p. 120.

36  Ibid., pp. 122, 124.
37  Ibid., p. 120.
38  Ibid., p. 122.
39  Ibid., p. 184.
40  Ibid., p. 184.
41  Ibid., p. 185.
42  Ibid., p. 123.
43  Ibid., p. 124.
44  Ibid., pp. 222, 232.
45  Ibid., p. 222.

7  *The* état de droit *and judicial review*

1  *Marbury* v. *Madison*, 5 U.S. (1 Cranch) 137. See the text in R.A. Rossum and G.A. Tarr, *American Constitutional Law. Cases and Interpretations*, New York, 1983, p. 70.
2  See, in general, H. Kelsen, 'La Garantie juridictionnelle de la Constitution (La Justice constitutionnelle)', *Revue du Droit Public et de la Science Politique en France et à l'Etranger*, Paris, 1928, pp. 197–257.
3  Kelsen, op. cit., p. 201.
4  J.D.B. Mitchell, *Constitutional Law*, Edinburgh, 1968, p. 13.
5  Ibid., p. 13.
6  M. Cappelletti, *Judicial Review in the Contemporary World*, Indianapolis, 1971, p. vii.
7  (1803), 5 U.S. (1 Cranch) 137.

8  *The limited state organs and judicial review*

1  P. Duez, 'Le Contrôle juridictionnel de la constitutionnalité des lois en France', *Mélanges Hauriou*, Paris, 1929, p. 214.
2  Ibid.
3  Ibid., p. 215.
4  Ibid.
5  Cf. H. Kelsen, 'La Garantie juridictionnelle de la Constitution [la justice constitutionnelle]', *Revue du Droit Public et de la Science Politique en France et à l'Etranger*, Paris, 1928, pp. 197–257.
6  See, for example, M. Cappelletti, *Judicial Review in the Contemporary World*, Indianapolis, 1971, p. vii.
7  Cf. Kelsen, op. cit., p. 228.
8  Ibid., p. 229.
9  See P. Duez, *Les Actes de gouvernement*, Paris, 1953.
10  Cf. Kelsen, op. cit., p. 230.
11  Ibid., p. 231.

12  See, in general, Cappelletti, op. cit., p. 45, and M. Cappelletti and J.C. Adams, 'Judicial Review of Legislation: European Antecedents and Adaptations' (1966) 79 *Harvard Law Review* , p. 1207.

13  M. Cappelletti, 'El control judicial de la constitucionalidad de las leyes en el derecho comparado', *Revista de la Facultad de Derecho de Mexico*, 61, 1966, p. 28.

14  P. Lucas Murillo de la Cueva, 'El examen de la constitucionalidad de las leyes y la soberanía parlamentaria', *Revista de Estudios Políticos*, 7, Madrid, 1979, p. 200.

15  E.S. Corwin, 'The "Higher Law" Background of American Constitutional Law', 1955, p. 53 (reprinted from (1928–9) 42 *Harvard Law Review*, pp. 149–85 and 365–409).

16  Alexander Hamilton, *The Federalist*, ed., B.F. Wright, Cambridge, Mass., 1961, p. 491.

17  J. Rivero, 'Rapport de synthèse', in L. Favoreu, ed., *Cours constitutionnelles européennes et droits fondamentaux*, Aix-en-Provence, 1982, p. 519.

18  M. Cappelletti, 'Necessité et légitimité de la justice constitutionnelle', in L. Favoreu, ed., op. cit., p. 483, also reproduced in *Revue Internationale de Droit Comparé*, 2, Paris, 1981. p. 647.

9    *The Constitution and its supremacy*

1    M. García-Pelayo, 'El 'status' del Tribunal Constitucional', *Revista Española de Derecho Constitucional*, 1, Madrid, 1981, p. 18. The supremacy of the Constitution implies 'that the Constitution as a fundamental positive norm, links all the public powers, including Parliament, and thus, consequently, the law cannot be contrary to constitutional precepts, to those principles which arise or are to be inferred from them, and to the values which it aspires to put into practice. This is the essence of the *état de droit* .'

2    M. Cappelletti, 'Judicial Review of Legislation and its Legitimacy. Recent Development', *General Report*, International Association of Legal Sciences, Uppsala, 1984 (mimeo), p. 20; also published as the 'Rapport Général', in L. Favoreu and J.A. Jolowicz, ed., *Le Contrôle juridictionnel des lois. Légitimité, effectivité et développements récents*, Paris, 1986, pp. 285–300.

3    E. García de Enterría, *La Constitución como norma y el Tribunal Constitucional*, Madrid, 1985, pp. 33, 39, 66, 71, 177, 187.

4    (1958), 356 U.S. 86.

5    J. Rivero, *Les Libertés publiques*, Vol. I, Paris, 1973, p. 70.

6    L. Favoreu, 'Le Principe de constitutionalité. Essai de définition d'après la jurisprudence du Conseil Constitutionnel', in *Recueil d'études en hommage à Charles Eisenmann*, Paris, 1977, p. 33.

7    L. Favoreu, 'Le Contrôle juridictionnel des lois et sa légitimité. Développements récents en Europe Occidentale', International

Association of Legal Science, Colloquium, Uppsala, 1984 (mimeo), p. 8; also published in Favoreu and Jolowicz, eds., op. cit., pp. 17–68; J. Rivero, 'Rapport de synthèse' in L. Favoreu, ed., *Cours constitutionnelles européennes et droit fondamentaux*, Aix-en-Provence, 1982, p. 520.

8    E. García de Enterría, op. cit., pp. 37, 69. Cf. P. Biscaretti di Ruffia and S. Rozmaryn, *La Constitution comme loi fondamentale dans les états de l'Europe Occidentale et dans les états socialistes*, Turin, 1966, p. 39.

9    E. Corwin, 'The "Higher Law" Background of American Constitutional Law', New York, 1955 (reprinted from (1928–9) 42 *Harvard Law Review* pp. 149–85 and 365–409).

10    M. Cappelletti, *Judicial Review in the Contemporary World*, Indianapolis, 1971, pp. 36–7.

11    E. Coke quoted by Corwin, op. cit., p. 38. Regarding the inconsistency of Coke's views see W. Holdsworth, *A History of English Law*, Vol. V, London, 1966, p. 475.

12    See the quotation and its comments in C.H. McIlwain, *The High Court of Parliament and its Supremacy*, Yale, 1910, pp. 286–301. See the criticisms of Lord Coke's concepts in L.B. Boudin, *Government by Judiciary*, New York, 1932, Vol. I, pp. 485–517.

13    Corwin, op. cit., p. 52.

14    Ibid., pp. 54–5.

15    Ibid., p. 52.

16    McIlwain, op. cit., p. 307.

17    C.P. Patterson, 'The development and evaluation of Judicial Review', (1938) 13 *Washington Law Review*, pp. 75, 171, 353.

18    M. Cappelletti, *Judicial Review in the Contemporary World*, pp. 38–40. 'The principle of parliamentary supremacy – and hence the supremacy of positive law – which was introduced in England following the Glorious Revolution of 1688, produced quite different results in America than in England. In England the result was to remove every control over the validity of legislation from the judges, despite the early successes of Lord Coke's doctrine. In America, on the contrary, the result was to empower the colonial judges to disregard local legislation not in conformity with the English Law. Thus the apparent paradox has been explained: how the English principle of the uncontrolled supremacy of the Legislature helped, rather than hindered, the formation in America of an opposite system.' Ibid., p. 40. Cf. Corwin, op. cit., p. 53.

19    W.J. Wagner, *The Federal States and their Judiciary*, The Hague, 1959, pp. 87–8.

20    Article VI, paragraph 2 of the Constitution states: 'This Constitution, and the Laws of the United States which shall be made in pursuance thereof; and all Treaties made, or which shall be made, under the Authority of the United States, shall be the Supreme Law of the Land; and the Judges in every State shall be bound thereby, anything in the Constitution or Laws of any State to the contrary notwithstanding.'

21    *The Federalist*, B.F. Wright, ed., Cambridge, Mass., 1961, pp. 491–3.

22  Wagner, op. cit., pp. 90–1.
23  (1795), 2 Dallas 304. See the text in S.I. Kutler, ed., *The Supreme Court and the Constitution. Readings in American Constitutional History*, New York, 1984, pp. 7–13.
24  5 U.S. (1 Cranch) 137. In relation to this case see E.S. Corwin, *The Doctrine of Judicial Review. Its Legal and Historical Basis and Other Essays*, Princeton, 1914, pp. 1–78.
25  H. Kelsen, 'La Guarantie juridictionnelle de la Constitution (la justice constitutionnelle)', *Revue du Droit Public et de la Science Politique en France et à l'Etranger*, Paris, 1928, p. 214.
26  The Venezuelan Constitution, 1961, for example, in Article 46, establishes: 'Every Act of the Public Power which violates or impairs the rights guaranteed by this Constitution is void...'
27  Constitution of Uganda (Art. 1), Kenya (Art. 3), Nigeria (Art. 1), Swaziland (Art. 2). Cf. B.O. Nwabueze, 'Judicial Control of Legislative Action and its Legitimacy – Recent Developments', *African Regional Report*, International Association of Legal Science, Uppsala Colloquium, 1984 (mimeo), p. 2. Also published in Favoreu and Jolowicz, eds., op. cit., pp. 193–222.
28  Ibid., p. 2.
29  L. Favoreu, op. cit., p. 23.
30  J. Bryce, *Constituciones flexibles y constituciones rígidas*, Madrid, 1962, p. 19.
31  See, on the contrary, G. Trujillo Fernández, *Dos estudios sobre la constitucionalidad de las leyes*, La Laguna, 1970, pp. 11, 17.
32  P. de Vega García, 'Jurisdicción constitucional y crisis de la Constitución', *Revista de Estudios Políticos*, 7, Madrid, 1979, p. 94.
33  Trujillo Fernández, op. cit., pp. 17, 18.
34  P. Lucas Murillo de la Cueva, 'El examen de la constitucionalidad de las leyes y la soberanía parlamentaria', *Revista de Estudios Políticos*, 7, Madrid, 1979, p. 206.
35  A. Shapira, 'The Constitution and its Defense in Israel: Fundamentals, Guarantees, Emergency Powers and Reform', International Congress on the Constitution and its Defense, U.N.A.M., Mexico, 1982, (mimeo), pp. 2–5. See the Spanish version in *La constitución y su defensa*, U.N.A.M., Mexico, 1984, pp. 433–89. See also, A. Shapira, 'Judicial Review without a Constitution: the Israeli Paradox' (1983) 56 *Temple Law Quarterly*, p. 405.
36  Shapira, 'The Constitution', p. 8.
37  Ibid., p. 9.
38  (1969), 23 P. D. 693. See the references in J. D. Whyte, 'Judicial Review of Legislation and its Legitimacy: Developments in the Common Law World', International Association of Legal Sciences, Uppsala Colloquium, 1984 (mimeo) p. 57; A. Shapira, 'The Constitution', pp. 9–13.
39  Whyte, op. cit., p. 58.
40  Shapira, 'The Constitution', op. cit., p. 10.
41  Ibid., p. 11.

42 Favoreu, 'Rapport général introductif', in Favoreu, ed., *Cours constitutionnelles*, p. 45.

43 J.H. Ely, *Democracy and Distrust. A Theory of Judicial Review*, Cambridge, Mass., 1980, pp. 1–2; T. Grey, 'Do We Have an Unwritten Constitution?' (1975) 27 *Stanford Law Review*, p. 703; T. Grey, 'Origins of the Unwritten Constitution: Fundamental Law in American Revolutionary Thought' (1978) 30 *Stanford Law Review*, pp. 843–7; García de Enterría, op. cit., pp. 210–21; M. Cappelletti, 'El formidable problema del control judicial y la contribución del análisis comparado', *Revista de Estudios Políticos*, 13, Madrid, 1980, pp. 68–9, 'The Mighty Problem of Judicial Review and the Contribution of Comparative Analysis', 1980 *Southern California Law Review*, p. 409; B. Caine, 'Judicial Review: Democracy versus Constitutionality' (1973) 56 *Temple Law Quarterly*, p. 298.

44 Grey, 'Origins', op. cit., p. 844.

45 See, in particular, *Brown v. Board of Education of Topeka* (1954), 347 U. S. 483. See the text in Kutler, ed., op. cit., pp. 548–52. Cf. Ely, op. cit., pp. 79–90; García de Enterría, op. cit., pp. 216–17. See also R. Berger, *Government by Judiciary. The Transformation of the Fourteenth Amendment*, Cambridge, Mass., 1977.

46 Ely, op. cit., p. 13; García de Enterría, op. cit., p. 211.

47 T. Ohlinger, 'Objet et portée de la protection des droits fondamentaux: cours constitutionnelle autrichienne', in L. Favoreu, ed., *Cours constitutionnelles*, pp. 335–6.

48 Ibid., p. 346.

49 Cappelletti, 'El formidable problema', p. 69, note 20.

50 L. Hamon, 'Contrôle de constitutionnalité et protection des droits individuels. A propos de trois décisions récents du Conseil Constitutionnel', *Recueil Dalloz Sirey 1974*, Chronique XVI, p. 85.

51 See the 16 July 1971 Constitutional Council decision in L. Favoreu and L. Philip, *Les Grands décisions du Conseil Constitutionnel*, Paris, 1984, p. 222. See the comments on the 16 July 1971 decisions in J. Rivero, 'Note', in *L'Actualité juridique. Droit administratif*, Paris, 1971, p. 537; J. Rivero, 'Principes fondamentaux reconnus par les lois de la Republique; une nouvelle categorie constitutionnelle?', *Dalloz 1974*, Chroniques, p. 265; and J.E. Beardsley, 'The Constitutional Council and Constitutional Liberties in France' (1972) 20 *The American Journal of Comparative Law*, pp. 431–52; B. Nicholas, 'Fundamental Rights and Judicial Review in France', *Public Law*, 1978, p. 83.

52 J. Rivero, 'Les Garanties constitutionnelles des droits de l'homme en droit français', IX, *Journées juridiques franco-latino-americaines*, Bayonne, 21–23 May, 1976 (mimeo), p. 11: 'the liberty of association, which is not expressly established either in the Declaration or by the particularly needed principles of our times, but which is only recognized by a Statute of 1 July 1901, has been recognized by the Constitutional Council decision, as having a constitutional character, not only as a principle, but in relation to the modalities of its exercise'.

53    Nicholas, op. cit., p. 89.
54    Decisions of 8 November 1976; 2 December, 1976; 20 July 1977; 19 January 1981; 20 January 1981. Cf. the quotations in F. Luchaire, 'Procedures et techniques de protection des droits fondamentaux. Conseil Constitutionnel français', in L. Favoreu, ed., *Cours constitutionnelles,* pp. 69, 70, 83.
55    L. Favoreu and L. Philip, *Les Grandes Décisions du Conseil Constitutionnel,* Paris, 1984, pp. 490, 517.
56    Cf. D.G. Lavroff, 'El Consejo Constitucional francés y la garantía de las libertades públicas', *Revista Española de Derecho Constitucional,* 1 (3), 1981, pp. 54–5; L. Favoreu and L. Philip, *Les Grandes Décisions,* p. 213.
57    L. Favoreu, 'Les Décisions du Conseil Constitutionnel dans l'affaire des nationalisations', *Revue du Droit Public et de la Science Politique en France et à l'Etranger,* 98 (2), Paris, 1982, p. 401.
58    L. Favoreu, 'L'Application directe et l'effet indirecte des normes Constitutionnelles', French Report to the XI International Congress of Comparative Law, Caracas, 1982 (mimeo), p. 4.
59    M. Cappelletti, 'Necessité et légitimité de la justice constitutionnelle', in Favoreu, ed., *Cours constitutionnelles,* p. 474. Also published in *Revue International de Droit Comparé,* Paris, 1981, pp. 639–47.
60    'If it is true that precision has a place of honor in the writing of a governmental decision, it is mortal when it refers to a Constitution which wants to be a lively body.' S. M. Hufstedles, 'In the Name of Justice' (1979) 14 *Stanford Lawyers,* pp. 3–4, quoted by M. Cappelletti, 'Necessité et légitimité', p. 474. See the references in García de Enterría, op. cit., p. 229; Favoreu, 'Le Contrôle juridictionnel', p. 32.
61    F. Sainz Moreno, *Conceptos jurídicos, interpretación y descrecionalidad administrativa,* Madrid, 1976; E. García de Enterría, *La lucha contra las inmunidades de poder en el derecho administrativo,* Madrid, 1980, p. 32.
62    F. Luchaire, 'Procédures et techniques de protection de droits fondamentaux Conseil Constitutionnel français', in Favoreu, ed., *Cours constitutionnelle,* p. 83.
63    M. Cappelletti, 'El formidable problema', op. cit., p. 78.
64    (1954) 347 U.S. 483. See the text in Kutler, ed., op. cit., p. 550.
65    See Favoreu and Philip, *Les Grandes Décisions,* pp. 525–62.
66    Favoreu, 'Le Contrôle juridictionnel', p. 32.
67    Favoreu and Philip. *Les Grandes Décisions,* p. 526. Cf. Favoreu, 'Les Décisions du Conseil Constitutionnel dans l'affaire des nationalisations', p. 406.

*10   The judicial guarantee of the Constitution*

1   H. Kelsen, 'La Garantie juridictionelle de la Constitution (la justice constitutionnelle)', *Revue du Droit Public et de la Science Politique en France et à l'Etranger*, Paris, 1928, p. 206.

2   P. Biscaretti di Ruffia, 'Les Constitutions Européennes: notions introductives', in P. Biscaretti di Ruffia and S. Rozmaryn, *L a Constitution comme loi fondamentale dans les Etats de l'Europe Occidentale et dans les Etats Socialistes*, Turin, 1966, p. 70.

3   P. Nikolic, 'Le Contrôle juridictionnel des lois et sa légitimité. Développements récents dans les pays socialistes', International Association of Legal Sciences, Uppsala Colloquium, 1984 (mimeo), p. 14. Also published in L. Favoreu and J.A. Jolowicz, eds., *Le Contrôle juridictionnel des lois. Légitimité, effectivité et développements récents*, Paris, 1986, pp. 71–115.

4   Ibid., p. 17. P. Nikolic says in his report to the Uppsala Colloquium that the introduction of this judicial control of the constitutionality of legislation in some socialist countries does not mean the introduction of important elements of the separation of powers in the assembly's government system (p. 19), but in explaining the suitability of that judicial control says that it is exercised by an authority known and recognised separately and differently from the legislative power, because it is precisely its legislative activity that it must control and evaluate (p. 21).

5   E. García de Enterría, *La Constitución como norma y el Tribunal Constitucional*, Madrid, 1981, p. 164.

6   Quoted by C. H. McIlwain, *The High Court of Parliament and its Supremacy*, Yale, 1910, p. 323.

7   Quoted by García de Enterría, op. cit., p. 164, note 88.

8   P. Lucas Murillo de la Cueva, 'El examen de la constitucionalidad de las leyes y la soberanía parlamentaria', *Revista de Estudios Políticos*, 7, Madrid, 1979, p. 212.

9   L. Favoreu, 'Le Contrôle juridictionnel des lois et sa légitimité Développements récents en Europe occidentale', International Association of Legal Sciences, Uppsala Colloquium, 1984 (mimeo), p. 22. Published as 'Actualité et légitimité du contrôle juridictionnel des lois en Europe occidentale', *Revue du Droit Public et de la Science Politique en France et à l'Etranger*, Paris, 1984, pp. 1147 and 1201. Also published in Favoreu and Jolowicz, eds., *Le Contrôle juridictionnel des lois.*, pp. 17–68.

10   M. Cappelletti, 'Judicial Review of Legislation and its Legitimacy. Recent Developments', *General Report*, International Association of Legal Science, Uppsala Colloquium, 1982 (mimeo), p. 19. Also published in Favoreu and Jolowicz, eds., *Le Contrôle juridictionnel des lois*, pp. 285–300.

11  J. Rivero, 'Rapport de synthèse', in L. Favoreu, ed., *Cours Constitutionnelles européennes et droits fondamentaux*, Aix-en-Provence, 1982, p. 519.

12  Favoreu, 'Le Contrôle juridictionnel', p. 22.

13  Ibid., p. 23. Cf. L. Favoreu, 'Les Décisions du Conseil Constitutionnel dans l'affaire des nationalisations', *Revue du Droit Public et de la Science Politique en France et à l'Etranger*, 98 (2), Paris, 1982, p. 400.

14  Cappelletti, op. cit., p. 20.

15  Rivero, 'Fin d'un absolutism', *Pouvoirs*, 13, Paris, 1980, pp. 5–15.

16  Rivero, 'Rapport de synthèse', p. 519.

17  A. Bickel, *The Least Dangerous Branch. The Supreme Court at the Bar of Politics,* Indianapolis, 1962.

18  M. Cappelletti, 'El formidable problema del control judicial y la contribución del analisis comparado', *Revista de Estudios Políticos*, 13, Madrid, 1980, pp. 651–3; 'The Mighty Problem of Judicial Review and the Contribution of Comparative Analysis', 1980 *Southern California Law Review*, p. 409. M. Cappelletti, 'Judicial Review of Legislation and its Legitimacy', pp. 24–32.

19  'An efficient system of judicial review is totally incompatible with any antilibertarian, absolute, dictatorial regime, as is amply proven by historical experience and comparative study'; M. Cappelletti, 'Judicial Review of Legislation and its Legitimacy', p. 11. 'Judicial review cannot be practised efficiently where the Judiciary has no guarantee of its independence,' J. Carpizo and H. Fix-Zumudio, 'The Necessity for the Legitimacy of the Judicial Review of the Constitutionality of the Laws in Latin America. Recent Developments', International Association of Legal Sciences, Uppsala Colloquium, 1984 (mimeo), p. 22. Published in Spanish as, 'La necesidad y la legitimidad de la revisión judicial en Américan Latina. Desarrollo reciente', *Boletín Mexicano de Derecho Comparado*, 52, 1985, pp. 31–64.

20  E.V. Rostow, 'The Democratic Character of Judicial Review' (1952) 66 *Harvard Law Review*, pp. 193–224.

21  J. Rivero, 'Rapport de synthèse', pp. 535–6. Cf. Cappelletti, 'Judicial Review of Legislation and Its Legitimacy', p. 32.

22  García de Enterría, op. cit., p. 190.

23  Kelsen, op. cit., p. 253.

24  W.J. Wagner, *The Federal States and their Judiciary*, The Hague, 1959, p. 85.

25  In this sense, Hans Kelsen said in 1928 that 'it is in Federal States where the constitutional justice acquired the most considerable importance. It is not excessive to affirm that the political idea of the Federal State is not entirely realized without the institution of a Constitutional Tribunal', op. cit., p. 23. Cf. Favoreu, 'Le Contrôle juridictionnel des lois et sa légitimité', p. 35; B.O. Nwabueze, 'Judicial Control of Legislative Action and its Legitimacy – Recent Developments', *African Regional Report*, International Association of Legal Sciences, Uppsala Colloquium, 1984 (mimeo), p. 23. Also

published in Favoreu and Jolowicz, eds., *Le Contrôle juridictionnel des lois*, pp. 193–222.

26 Cappelletti, 'Judicial Review of Legislation and its Legitimacy', p. 26; Favoreu, 'Actualité et légitimité du contrôle juridictionnel des lois en Europe occidental', p. 1149.

27 Art. 1. Ley Orgánica del Tribunal Constitucional Oct. 1979, *Boletín Oficial del Estado*, No. 239.

28 G. Leibholz, *Problemas fundamentales de la democracia*, Madrid, 1971, p. 148.

29 García de Enterría, op. cit., p. 198.

30 M. García Pelayo, 'El "status" del Tribunal Constitucional', *Revista Española de Derecho Constitucional*, 1, Madrid, 1981, p. 15.

31 Ibid., p. 20.

32 Kelsen, op. cit., pp. 224, 226.

33 A. Pérez Gordo, *El Tribunal Constitucional y sus funciones*, Barcelona, 1982, p. 41.

34 H. Kelsen eventually accepted this view, op. cit., p. 226.

35 Cf. the argument in a contrary sense of Nwabueze, op. cit., p. 3.

36 García de Enterría, op. cit., p. 192.

37 Favoreu, 'Le Contrôle juridictionnel des lois et sa légitimité', p. 36.

38 Ibid., p. 36.

39 L. Favoreu, 'Les Décisions du Conseil Constitutionnel dans l'affaire des nationalisations', p. 377; 'Décentralisation et Constitution', *Revue du Droit Public et de la Science Politique en france et à l'Etranger*, Paris, 1982, pp. 1259–95; and L. Favoreu, ed., *Nationalisations et Constitution*, Paris, Aix-en-Provence, 1982.

40 P. Bon, F. Moderne and Y. Rodríguez, *La Justice constitutionnelle en Espagne*, Paris/Aix-en-Provence, 1984, p. 168.

41 Favoreu, 'Le Contrôle juridictionnel des lois et sa légitimité', p. 25.

42 L. Favoreu, 'Le Conseil Constitutionnel et l'arternance', *Revue Française de Science Politique* (La Constitution de la Cinquième République), 34 (4–5), Paris, 1984, pp. 1005–14. Cf. L. Favoreu, 'Libertés locales et libertés universitaires. Les Décisions du Conseil Constitutionnel du 20 janvier 1984', *Revue du Droit Public et de la Science Politique en France et á l'Etranger,* Paris, 1984, pp. 687–730.

43 Favoreu, 'Le Contrôle juridictionnel des lois et sa légitimité', op. cit., p. 37.

44 Kelsen, op. cit., p. 250.

45 As M. Hidén said, 'probably there are as many methods of securing the constitutionality of laws and regulations as there are countries with a written constitution': 'Constitutional Rights in the Legislative Process: the Finnish System of Advance Control of Legislation', *Scandinavian Studies in Law*, 17, Stockholm, 1973, p. 97.

## *11* *General characteristics of the diffuse system*

1 *Vanhorne's Lessee* v. *Dorrance*, (1795) 2 Dallas 304. See the text in S. I. Kutler, ed., *The Supreme Court and the Constitution. Readings in American Constitutional History*, New York, 1984, pp. 8, 29. See also *Marbury* v. *Madison* (1803)1 Cranch 137.

2 See J. Ortega Torres, ed., *Constitución política de Colombia*, Bogotá, 1985, p. 130. The origin of this norm can be traced up to Legislative Act, No. 3, Art. 40, 1910.

3 The text is the one from the 1986 *Civil Procedural Code*. With similar words it was adopted in Art. 10 of the 1897 and 1904 Codes, and Art. 7 of the 1916 Code.

4 H. Fix-Zamudio, *Los Tribunales Constitucionales y los derechos humanos*, Mexico, 1980, pp. 17, 84; A. Jiménez Blanco, 'El Tribunal Federal Suizo', *Boletín de Jurisprudencia Constitucional*, Cortes Generales, 6, Madrid, 1981, p. 477.

5 Art. 93. Fix-Zamudio, op. cit., p. 162; L. Favoreu, *Le Contrôle juridictionnel des lois et sa légitimité. Développements récents en Europe Occidentale*, International Association of Legal Sciences, Uppsala Colloquium, 1984 (mimeo), p. 14. Also published in L. Favoreu and J. A. Jolowicz, eds, *Le Contrôle juridictionnel des lois. Légitimité, effectivité et développements récents*, Paris, 1986, pp. 17–63.

6 H. Kelsen, 'La Garantie juridictionnelle de la Constitution (la justice constitutionnelle), *Revue du Droit Public et de la Science Politique en France et à l'Etranger*, Paris, 1928, p. 218. Cf. Cappelletti and Adams, op. cit., p. 1215; M. Cappelletti, *Judicial Review in the Contemporary World*, Indianapolis, 1971, p. 59. In a similar sense, M. Fromont considers that it is 'difficult to admit' the diffuse system of judicial review in countries with a Roman Law tradition. See 'Preface' in J. C. Beguin, *Le Contrôle de la Constitutionnalité des lois en République Federal d'Allemagne*, Paris, 1982, p. v.

7 Cappelletti and Adams, op. cit., p. 1215; Cappelletti, op. cit., Indianapolis, 1971, p. 58. 'since the principle of *stare decisis* is foreign to civil law judges, a system which allowed each judge to decide on the constitutionality of statutes could result in a law being disregarded as unconstitutional by some judges, while being held constitutional and applied by others. Furthermore the same judicial organ, which had one day disregarded a given law, might uphold it the next day, having changed its mind about the law's constitutional legitimacy. Differences could arise between judicial bodies of a different type or degree, for example, between ordinary courts and administrative tribunals or between the younger, more radical judges of the inferior courts and the older, more tradition conscious judges of the higher courts ... The extremely dangerous results could be a serious conflict between the judicial organs and grave uncertainty as to the law.'

8   Art. 107, Section XIII, paragraph 1 of the Constitution (amendment of 1950–1). R.D. Baker, *Judicial Review in Mexico. A Study of the Amparo Suit*, Austin, 1971, pp. 164, 250.

9   H. Fix-Zamudio, *Veinticinco años de evolución de la justicia constitucional 1940–1965*, Mexico, 1968, pp. 26, 36; J. Carpizo and H. Fix-Zamudio, 'La necisidad y la legitimidad de la revisión judicial en América Latina. Desarrollo reciente', *Boletín Mexicano de Derecho Comparado*, 52, 1985, p. 33. Also published in L. Favoreu and J. A. Jolowicz, eds., *Le Contrôle juridictionnel des lois*, pp. 119–51.

10   J.R. Vanossi and P.F. Ubertone, 'Instituciones de defensa de la Constitución en la Argentina', *La Constitución y su Defensa*, U.N.A.M., Mexico, 1984 (mimeo), p. 113.

11   E. Spiliotopoulos, 'Judicial Review of Legislative Acts in Greece', (1983) 56 *Temple Law Quarterly*, pp. 496–500.

12   J.M. García Laguardia, *La defensa de la Constitución*, Mexico, 1983, p. 52.

13   A. R. Brewer-Carías, *El control de la constitucionalidad de los actos estatales*, Caracas, 1977; L. C. Sachica, *El control de la constitucionalidad y sus mecanismos*, Bogotá, 1980.

14   E. Zellweger, 'El Tribunal Federal Suizo en calidad de Tribunal Constitucional', *Revista de la Comisión Internacional de Juristas*, 7 (1), 1966, p. 119; Fix-Zamudio, *Los Tribunales Constitucionales*, p. 84.

15   *Marbury* v. *Madison*, op. cit. See the text in Kutler, ed., op. cit., p. 29.

16   Kelsen, op. cit., p. 214.

17   *Marbury* v. *Madison*, op. cit.

18   Cf. B.O. Nwabueze, 'Judicial Control of Legislative Action and its Legitimacy – Recent Developments', *African Regional Report*, International Association of Legal Sciences, Uppsala Colloquium, 1984 (mimeo), pp. 2–3. Also published in Favoreu and Jolowicz, eds., *Le Contrôle juridictionnel des lois*, pp. 193–222.

19   Spiliotopoulos, op. cit., p. 479.

20   As B.O. Nwabueze has said: 'The fact that the duty is, and can only be performed at the instance of a person aggrieved by a violation of the law of the Constitution by government reinforces the legitimacy of the function. What this means is that, given a justiciable violation of the Constitution by the legislature, however flagrant, the court cannot, on its own initiative, intervene. It must wait until moved by someone.' Nwabueze, op. cit., p. 3. See the discussion on the matter, and the dissenting opinion in Vanossi and Ubertone, op. cit., p. 24; in G. Bidart Campos, *El derecho constitucional del poder*, Buenos Aires, Vol. 2, Ch. 29; and in J.R. Vanossi, *Teoría constitucional*, Vol. 2, Buenos Aires, 1976, pp. 318, 319.

12    *The American system of judicial review*

1    M. Cappelletti, *Judicial Review in the Contemporary World*, Indianapolis, 1971, p. 46.
2    A. de Tocqueville, *Democracy in America*, J.P. Mayer and M. Lerner, eds., London, 1968, Vol. 1, p. 120.
3    Ibid., p. 122.
4    Ibid., pp. 122, 124.
5    Ibid., p. 122.
6    Ibid., p. 124.
7    Ibid.
8    E.S. Corwin, 'Judicial Review', *Encyclopædia of the Social Sciences*, Vol. 8, London, 1932, p. 457.
9    'the responsibility for introducing the practice [of judicial review of legislative acts] as a rule for the federal courts is placed primarily on the great chief justice'. Cf. G. Haines, *The American Doctrine of Judicial Supremacy*, Berkeley, 1932, p. 122.
10    E.S. Corwin, '*Marbury* v. *Madison* and the Doctrine of Judicial Review' (1914) 12 *Michigan Law Review*, p. 538.
11    (1936) 297 U.S.
12    Corwin, 'Judicial Review', p. 457.
13    Art. 6, 2. See the comments of R. Berger, *Congress* v. *The Supreme Court*, Cambridge, Mass., 1969, pp. 223–84.
14    Cf. A. Tunc and S. Tunc, *Le Système constitutionnel des Etats Unis d'Amérique*, Paris, 1954, Vol. II, p. 272.
15    P.G. Kauper, 'Judicial Review of Constitutional Issues in the United States', in H. Mosler, ed., Max-Planck-Institut für ausländisches öffentliches Recht und Völkerrecht, *Verfassungsgerichtsbarkeit in der Gegenwart*, International Colloquium, Heidelberg, 1961, Cologne/Berlin, 1962, p. 628.
16    *Missouri* v. *Holland* (1920) 252 U.S. 346.
17    28 U.S. Code, sections 1331, 1332, 1345, 1346, 2241.
18    Cf. L. Baum, *The Supreme Court*, Washington D.C., 1981, p. 10.
19    Cf. *Marbury* v. *Madison*, op. cit.; *Muskrat* v. *United States* (1911), 219 U.S. 346.
20    Art. 3, Section 2 of the Constitution.
21    B. Schwartz, *American Constitutional Law*, Cambridge, 1955, p. 129.
22    28 U.S. Code 1254, which refers to the methods through which cases in the Court of Appeals may be reviewed by the Supreme Court.
23    28 U.S. Code, 1257.
24    28 U.S. Code, 1255, 1256.
25    28 U.S. Code, 1252.
26    28 U.S. Code, 3731.
27    28 U.S. Code, 1253, 2281, 2282, 2284.
28    See Taft, 'The Jurisdiction of the Supreme Court under the Act of February 13, 1925' (1925) 35 *Yale Law Review*, p. 2.
29    Schwartz, op. cit., p. 139.

30    28 U.S. Code, 1252.
31    28 U.S. Code, 1254, 2.
32    28 U.S. Code, 1257, 2 (cases in which a State Supreme Court has ruled an Act of Congress unconstitutional).
33    28 U.S. Code, 1257,2 (cases in which a State Supreme Court has upheld a state law against a claim that it conflicts with the Constitution or a federal law).
34    28 U.S. Code, 1253, 2281, 2282, 2284.
35    Baum, op. cit., p. 81.
36    28 U.S. Code, 1254, 1.
37    28 U.S. Code, 1255, 1.
38    28 U.S. Code, 1256.
39    28 U.S. Code, 1257,3.
40    Section 1. See Baum, op. cit., p. 86.
41    Ibid.
42    Cf. R.A. Rossum and G.A. Tarr, *American Constitutional Law*, New York, 1983, p. 28.
43    28 U.S. Code, 1254, 3.
44    Kauper, op. cit., pp. 579, 608.
45    Ibid., p. 586–7. Cf. J. A. C. Grant, 'El control jurisdiccional de la constitucionalidad de las leyes: una contribución de las Américas a la ciencia política', *Revista de la Facultad de Derecho de México*, 45, Mexico, 1962, pp. 425–9.
46    In the words of Chief Justice Stone, the Court has 'considered practice not to decide abstract, hypothetical or contingent questions': *Alabama Federation of Labor* v. *McAdory* (1945) 325 U.S. 450, 461.
47    *Frothingham* v. *Mellon* (1923) 262 U.S. 447; *Muskrat* v. *United States* (1911), 219 U.S. 346; *Ashwander* v. *Tennessee Valley Authority*, (1936) 297 U.S. 288, 345.
48    *Ashwander* v. *Tennessee Valley Authority* (1936) 297 U.S. 288, 345.
49    28 U.S. Code, Section 2201.
50    *Maryland Casualty Co.* v. *Pacific Coal and Oil Co.*, (1941) 312 U. S. 270.
51    *Nashville, C. and St. L. Ry. Co.* v. *Wallace* (1933) 288 U.S. 249.
52    28 U. S. Code, Section 2403.
53    See H.J. Abraham, *The Judicial Process*, New York, 1980, p. 373. This self-restraint has been summarized by Justice Rutledge as follows: 'Constitutional issues affecting legislation will not be determined in friendly, nonadversary proceedings; in advance of the necessity of deciding them; in broader terms than required by the precise facts to which the ruling is to be applied; if the record presents some other ground upon which the case may be disposed of; at the instance of one who fails to show that he is injured by the statute's operation, or who has availed himself of its benefits; or if a construction of the statute is fairly possible by which the question may be avoided.' *Rescue Army* v. *Municipal Court of Los Angeles* (1947), 331 U. S. 549.

54  *Frothingham* v. *Mellon*, (1923) 262 U. S. 447. See also *Ashwander* v. *Tennessee Valley Authority*, op. cit., p. 346.
55  *Frothingham* v. *Mellon*, ibid., p. 488.
56  See *Flast* v. *Cohen*, (1968) 392 U.S. 83.
57  *United States* v. *Richardson* (1974) 418 U. S. 966. Cf. *De Funis* v. *Odegaard*, (1974) 416 U.S. 312.
58  *Warth* v. *Seldin* (1975) 422 U. S. 490.
59  Cf. Baum, op. cit., pp. 74, 80, 91.
60  See *Warth* v. *Seldin*, op. cit. The action to review the constitutionality of a law in the federal courts, therefore, is clearly not the *actio popularis* that exists in certain concentrated and mixed systems of judicial review. Cf. Schwartz, op. cit., p. 151.
61  *Ogden* v. *Saunders* (1827) 12 Wheaton 213. Justice Washington said: 'it is but a decent respect due to the wisdom, integrity and patriotism of the legislative body, by which any law is passed, to presume in favour of its validity'. Also in *Cooper* v. *Telfair* (1800) 4 Dallas (4 U.S.) 14, Justice Washington said: 'The presumption indeed must always be in favour of the validity of laws, if the contrary is not clearly demonstrated.'
62  *Fletcher* v. *Peck* (1810) 6 Cranch 87.
63  *Burton* v. *United States*, 196 U.S. 283, 295 quoted in *Ashwanter* v. *Tennessee Valley Authority*, op. cit.
64  *Ex parte Randolph* (1833) 20 Fed. Cas. 242, quoted by W.J. Wagner, The *Federal States and their Judiciary*, The Hague, 1959, p. 97. See also *Ashwander* v. *Tennessee Valley Authority*, op. cit.; *Crowell* v. *Benson* (1932) 285 U.S. 22.
65  *United States* v. *Congress of Industrial Organization* (1948) 335 U.S. 106.
66  *Baker* v. *Carr* (1962) 369 U.S. 186.
67  *Ware* v. *Hylton* (1796) 3 Dallas 199.
68  *Chicago and Southern Airlines* v. *Waterman Steamship Co.* (1948) 333 U.S. 103.
69  *Luther* v. *Borden* (1849) 48 U. S. (7 Howard) 1, where the Court considered that 'decision binding on every other department of the government, and could not be questioned in a judicial tribunal'.
70  *Baker* v. *Carr*, op. cit.
71  Schwartz, op. cit., p. 157.
72  Cf. Kauper, op. cit., p. 611.
73  (1954) 347 U.S. 483.
74  (1958) 358 U.S. 1.
75  Cf. A. Tunc and S. Tunc, *Le Droit des Etats Unis d'Amérique, sources et techniques*, Paris, 1955, p. 174; Schwartz, op. cit., p. 159.
76  *Burnet* v. *Coronado Oil and Gas Co.* (1932) 285 U.S. p. 406.
77  Schwartz, *American Constitutional Law*, p. 159; B. Schwartz, *The Supreme Court. Constitutional Revolution in Retrospect*, New York, 1957, p. 345.
78  *Smith* v. *Allwright* (1944) 321 U.S. 649.
79  Cf. Kauper, op. cit., pp. 611, 617.

# Notes

80 *Vanhorne's Lessee* v. *Dorrance* (1795) 2 Dallas 304.
81 *United States* v. *Reality Co.* (1895), 163 U.S. 439; *Norton* v. *Selby County* (1886), 163 U.S. 442.
82 *Linkletter* v. *Walker* (1965), 381 U.S. 618.
83 *Chicot County Drainage District* v. *Baxter State Bank* (1940), 308 U.S. 374.
84 Ibid.
85 J.A.C. Grant, 'The Legal Effect of a Ruling that a Statute is Unconstitutional' (1978) 2 *Detroit College of Law Review*, p. 207. Cf. *Norton* v. *Selby County* (1886), 118 U.S. 425.
86 *Ex parte Siebold* (1880), 100 U. S. 371.
87 Grant, op. cit., p. 237.
88 *Marks* v. *United States* (1977), 430 U.S. 188; Cf. Grant, op. cit., p. 238.
89 *Linkletter* v. *Walker*, op. cit..
90 (1967), 388 U.S. 293.
91 Grant, op. cit., p. 237.
92 (1968), 392 U.S. 631.
93 *Adams* v. *Illinois* (1972), 405 U.S. 278.
94 (1864), 68 U.S. (1 Wall) 175.
95 *Molitor* v. *Kaneland Community Unit Dist. No. 302*, 18 Ill. 2d at 25, 162 N. E. 2d at 96. Quoted by Grant, op. cit., p. 220.
96 *State* v. *Carroll* (1871), 38 Conn. 449. Quoted by Grant, op. cit., p. 232.
97 G.H. Jaffin, 'Les Modes d'introduction du contrôle judiciaire de la constitutionnalité des lois aux Etats-Unis', in *Introduction à l'étude du droit comparé, recueil d'etudes en l'honneur d'Eduard Lambert*, Paris, 1938, Vol. II, p. 256.
98 Kauper, op. cit., p. 620.
99 28 U.S. Code 1361.

## 13 The diffuse system of judicial review in Latin America

1 The first edition of the book in Spanish was issued in 1836, one year after the French and English editions. On the influence of the de Tocqueville book on the introduction of judicial review in Latin America, see J. Carpizo and H. Fix-Zamudio, 'La necesidad y la legitimidad de la revisión judicial en América Latina. Desarrollo reciente', in *Boletín Mexicano de Derecho Comparado*, 1985, p. 33; R.D. Baker, *Judicial Review in Mexico. A Study of the Amparo Suit*, Austin, 1971, pp. 15, 33.
2 The 1844 Constitution, as well as the 1966 Constitution (Art. 46) established that all laws, decrees, resolutions, regulation or acts contrary to the Constitution would be null and void. Consequently all the courts can declare an act unconstitutional and not applicable to the

concrete case. Cf. M. Berges Chupani, 'Report', in *Memoria de la reunión de Cortes Superiores de Justicia de Ibero-América, El Caribe, España y Portugal*, Caracas, 1983, p. 380.

3   A.E. Ghigliani, *Del control jurisdiccional de constitucionalidad*, Buenos Aires, 1952, who speaks about 'North American filiation' of the judicial control of constitutionality in Argentinian law, pp. 6, 55, 115. Cf. R. Bielsa, *La protección constitucional y el recurso extraordinario. Jurisdicción de la Corte Suprema*, Buenos Aires, 1958, p. 116; J.A.C. Grant, 'El control jurisdiccional de la constitucionalidad de las leyes: una contribución de las Américas a la ciencia política', *Revista de la Facultad de Derecho de México*, 45, 1962, p. 652; C.J. Friedrich, *The Impact of American Constitutionalism Abroad*, Boston, 1967, p. 83.

4   Cf. Ghigliani, op. cit., p. 5; Bielsa, op. cit., pp. 41, 43, 179, who speaks about a 'pretorian creation' of judicial review by the Supreme Court. Cf. J.R. Vanossi and P.F. Ubertone, 'Instituciones de defensa de la Constitución en la Argentina', *La Constitución y su defensa*, U.N.A.M. Mexico, 1984, p. 91; H. Quiroga Lavie, *Derecho constitucional*, Buenos Aires, 1978, p. 481. Previously in 1863 the first Supreme Court decisions were adopted in constitutional matters, but referred to provincial and executive acts. Cf. Ghigliani, op. cit., p. 58.

5   Cf. Ghigliani, op. cit., p. 58.

6   N.P. Sagüés, *Recurso extraordinario*, Buenos Aires, 1984, Vol. I, p. 91. Vanossi and Ubertone, op. cit., p.89. See also J.R. Vanossi, *Teoría constitucional*, Vol. 2, *Supremacía y control de constitucionalidad*, Buenos Aires, 1976, p. 155.

7   In particular, regarding the unconstitutionality of treaties and the possibility of the courts controlling them, see A.G. Ghigliani, op. cit., p. 62; J.R. Vanossi, *Aspectos del recurso extraordinario de inconstitucionalidad*, Buenos Aires, 1966, p. 91, and *Teoría constitucional*, Vol. II, p. 277.

8   Cf. Bielsa, op. cit., pp. 120–48. Vanossi and Ubertone, op. cit., p. 6.

9   Cf. Vanossi and Ubertone, op. cit., p. 101; Ghigliani, op. cit., p. 76.

10  Bielsa, op. cit., p. 270; Vanossi and Ubertone, op. cit., p. 103.

11  Art. 101.

12  Cf. Bielsa, op. cit., pp. 60–1; Vanossi and Ubertone, op. cit., p. 104.

13  Ghigliani, op. cit., p. 75.

14  Ibid., p. 76.

15  Art. 100 of the Constitution; Cf. Bielsa, op. cit., pp. 213, 214; Ghigliani, op. cit., p. 75; Vanossi and Ubertone, op. cit., p. 107.

16  Cf. Bielsa, op. cit., pp. 213, 214; Ghigliani, op. cit., p. 80; Lozada, *Derecho constitucional argentino*, Buenos Aires, 1972, Vol. 1, p. 342.

17  Lozada, op. cit., p. 342; Ghigliani, op. cit., p. 82; Vanossi and Ubertone, op. cit., p. 108.

18   Bielsa, op. cit., pp. 198, 214; Quiroga Lavié, op. cit., p. 479.
19   G. Bidart Campos, *El derecho constitucional del poder*, Vol. 2, Buenos Aires, 1986, ch. 29; Vanossi, *Teoría constitucional*, Vol. II, pp. 318, 319.
20   Cf. Vanossi and Ubertone, op. cit., p. 112; Bielsa, op. cit., p. 255; Quiroga Lavié, op. cit., p. 479.
21   Ghigliani, op. cit., pp. 89, 90.
22   Ibid., p. 89; Lozada, op. cit., p. 341.
23   Quiroga Lavié, op. cit., p. 480.
24   Ghigliani, op. cit., p. 91.
25   Vanossi and Ubertone, op. cit., p. 96.
26   Cf. Ghigliani, op. cit., p. 85; Quiroga Lavié, op. cit., p. 482; Lozada, op. cit., p. 343; Vanossi and Ubertone, op. cit., pp. 96, 97.
27   Cf. Bielsa, op. cit., pp. 185, 221, 228, 245, 252, 275; Sagüés, op. cit., p. 270.
28   Bielsa, op. cit., p. 222.
29   Statute 48, Art. 14. Cf. Vanossi and Ubertone, op. cit., p. 104; Bielsa, op. cit., pp. 201, 211; Sagüés, op. cit., p. 272.
30   Cf. Vanossi and Ubertone, op. cit., p. 105.
31   Cf. Bielsa, op. cit., pp. 109, 202, 203, 204, 205, 209.
32   Ibid., p. 260.
33   Ibid., pp. 237, 238.
34   Ibid., pp. 197, 198, 345; Sagüés, op. cit., p. 156.
35   Cf. Ghigliani, op. cit., p. 95.
36   Cf. H. Quiroga Lavié, op. cit., p. 479.
37   Art. 95 of the 1949 Constitution. Cf C.A. Ayanagaray, *Efectos de la declaración de inconstitucionalidad*, Buenos Aires, 1955, p. 11; Bielsa, op. cit., p.268.
38   Cf. Vanossi and Ubertone, op. cit., p. 114.
39   Cf G.R. Carrio, *Algunos aspectos del recurso de amparo*, Buenos Aires, 1959, p. 9; Vanossi, *Teoría constitucional*, Vol. II, p. 277.
40   See Carrio, op. cit., p. 10.
41   See the *Samuel Kot Ltd.* case of 5 September 1958, S. V. Linares Quintana, *Acción de amparo*, Buenos Aires, 1960, p. 25.
42   See the *Aserradero Clipper SRL* case (1961), Vanossi, *Teoría constitucional*, Vol. II, p. 286.
43   Art. 2, d.
44   *Outon* case of 29 March 1967. Vanossi, *Teoría constitucional*, Vol. 2, p. 288.
45   G.J. Bidart Campos, *Régimen legal del Amparo*, 1969; G. J. Bidart Campos, 'El control de constitucionalidad en el juicio de amparo y la arbitrariedad o ilegalidad del acto lesivo', *Jurisprudencia Argentina*, 23, April, 1969; N. P. Sagüés, 'El juicio de Amparo y el planteo de inconstitucionalidad', *Jurisprudencia Argentina*, 20 July 1973; Vanossi, *Teoría constitucional*, Vol. II, pp. 288–92.
46   Vanossi, *Teoría constitucional*, Vol. II, p. 291.

47  The Constitution of Yucatán of 1841 adopted the institution of amparo only in relation to that state. Cf. R.D. Baker, *Judicial Review in Mexico. A Study of the Amparo Suit*, Texas, 1971, p. 17.

48  Ibid., pp. 15, 33.

49  See the text in J. Carpizo, *La Constitución mexicana de 1917*, Mexico, 1979, p. 271; Baker, op. cit., p. 23; and H. Fix-Zamudio, 'Algunos aspectos comparativos del derecho de amparo en Mexico y Venezuela', in *Libro Homenaje a la Memoria de Lorenzo Herrera Mendoza*, Caracas, 1970, Vol. II, p. 336. See also H. Fix-Zamudio, 'A Brief Introduction to the Mexican Writ of Amparo', 1977 *California Western International Law Journal*, p. 313.

50  Cf. Baker, op. cit., p. 91; J.A.C. Grant, 'El control jurisdiccional de la constitucionalidad de las leyes: una contribución de las Américas a la ciencia política', in *Revísta de la Facultad de Derecho de México*, 45, 1962, p. 657.

51  Fix-Zamudio, *El juicio de amparo*, Mexico, 1964, pp. 243, 377; H. Fix-Zamudio, 'Reflexiones sobre la naturaleza procesal de amparo', *Revista de la Facultad de Derecho de México*, 56, 1964, p. 980. Fix-Zamudio, 'Algunos aspectos comparativos del derecho de amparo en Mexico y Venezuela', p. 345; H. Fix-Zamudio, 'Lineamientos fundamentales del proceso social agrario en el derecho mexicano', in *Atti della Seconda Assemblea*. Istituto di Diritto Agrario Internazionale e Comparato, Vol. I, Milan, 1964, p. 402.

52  Cf. Baker, op. cit., p. 92.

53  Art. 107, III, V.

54  Art. 107, IV.

55  Ibid.

56  H. Fix-Zamudio, 'Algunos problemas que plantea el amparo contra leyes', *Boletín del Instituto de Derecho Comparado de México*, 37, 1960, pp. 15, 20.

57  Fix-Zamudio, 'Aspectos comparativos', pp. 358, 359; 'Algunos problemas', pp. 22, 23.

58  Art. 107, V, VI. Cf. Fix-Zamudio, 'Algunos problemas', p. 22.

59  Art. 107, IX.

60  Grant, op. cit., p. 657.

61  Ibid., pp. 657–61.

62  Art. 107, XII.

63  Fix-Zamudio, 'Algunos problemas que plantea el amparo', p. 21.

64  Art. 107, VIII,a.

65  Cf. Baker, op. cit., p. 164.

66  Self-executed statutes (*auto-aplicativas*). Cf. Baker, op. cit., p. 167; Fix-Zamudio, 'Algunos problemas que plantea el amparo', p. 24.

67  Art. 21, *Amparo Law*. Cf. Fix-Zamudio, 'Algunos problemas que plantea el amparo', p. 32. Cf. Baker, op. cit., p. 171.

68  Art. 107, II. The principle is called the *Otero* formula due to its inclusion in the 1857 Constitution under the influence of Mariano Otero. Cf. Fix-Zamudio, 'Aspectos comparativos del derecho de

amparo', p. 360; and Fix-Zamudio, 'Algunos problemas que plantea el amparo', pp. 33, 37.

69   Art. 107, XIII, 1.
70   Arts. 192, 193. See the quotations in Baker, op. cit., pp. 256, 257.
71   Art. 194. See the quotations in Baker, op. cit., p. 263.
72   Art. 107, XIII. See the comments in Baker, op. cit., p. 264.
73   Art. 107, XIII. See the comments in Grant, op. cit., p. 662.
74   Art. 107, X. See the comments in Grant, op. cit., p. 652, note 33.

*14   The diffuse system of judicial review in Europe and other civil law countries*

1    E. Spiliotopoulos, 'Judicial Review of Legislative Acts in Greece' (1983) 56 *Temple Law Quarterly*, p. 470.
2    Judgement No. 198 (1847), quoted in Spiliotopoulos, op. cit., p. 471.
3    Ibid., p. 471.
4    Judgements No. 18 (1871) and No. 23 (1897), quoted by Spiliotopoulos, op. cit., p. 472.
5    Art. 5.
6    See Spiliotopoulos, op. cit., p. 472, note 43.
7    Cf. Ibid., p. 470, note 30 and p. 474.
8    Ibid., p. 475.
9    See *Información Jurídica*, 300, Madrid, 1969, p. 103.
10   Art. 93, 4.
11   Art. 87, 3.
12   Spiliotopoulos, op. cit., p. 479. 'In the absence of a specific request, the court may itself raise the questions when a doubt regarding the constitutionality of such a statute or provision arises during the adjudication of the case.'
13   See Judgement No. 2241 (1953), quoted in Spiliotopoulos, op. cit., pp. 123, 485.
14   Cf. Spiliotopoulos, op. cit., p. 486.
15   Arts. 93–97, 1975 Constitution. Cf. Spiliotopoulos, op. cit., pp. 475–7. The Council of State, although originally created in 1835, began functioning in 1929. Cf. Spiliotopoulos, op. cit., p. 472, note 45.
16   Arts. 98–9.
17   Art. 106. See in *Información Jurídica*, pp. 99–100. Cf. the comments regarding this Tribunal in H. Fix-Zamudio, *Los Tribunales Constitucionales y los derechos humanos*, U.N.A.M., Mexico, 1980, pp. 160–1.
18   Cf. Fix-Zamudio, op. cit., p. 162.
19   Art. 100, 1, a, b, c, f.
20   Art. 100, 1, d.
21   Art. 100, 1, e.

22  Art. 100, 2.
23  Art. 48, quoted in Spiliotopoulos, op. cit., p. 497.
24  Cf. Spiliotopoulos, op. cit., p. 497.
25  Art. 51, Statute 345, quoted in Spiliotopoulos, op. cit., p. 498, note 199.
26  Spiliotopoulos, op. cit., p. 500.
27  Art. 51, Statute 345, quoted in Spiliotopoulos, op. cit., p. 499.
28  Ibid.
29  Cf. E. Smith, 'Contrôle juridictionnel de la législation et sa légitimité. Développements récents dans les cinq pays scandinaves', International Association of Legal Sciences, Uppsala Colloquium, 1984 (mimeo), pp. 2, 3, 4, 7, 50, 74. Also published in L. Favoreu and J.A. Jolowicz, eds., *Le Contrôle juridictionnel des lois. Légitimité, effectivité et développements récents*, Paris, 1986, pp. 225–82.
30  See in M. Hidén, 'Constitutional Rights in the Legislative Process: the Finnish System of Advance Control of Legislation', *Scandinavian Studies in Law*, 17, Stockholm, 1973, p. 97.
31  Ibid., p. 98. Cf. Smith, op. cit., p. 12.
32  Hidén, op. cit., p. 98. Cf. Smith, op. cit., p. 12.
33  Hidén, op. cit., p. 106.
34  Smith, op. cit., p. 12.
35  Ibid., p. 20.
36  Ibid., p. 20.
37  Ibid., pp. 10–12, 62, 67, 74.
38  Ibid., p. 16.
39  Ibid., p. 18.
40  Ibid., pp. 17, 22.
41  M. Cappelletti and J.C. Adams, 'Judicial Review of Legislation: European Antecedents and Adaptations' (1966) 79 *Harvard Law Review*, p. 1217.
42  Cf. Y. Taniguchi, 'Judicial Control of Legislation and its Legitimacy in Japan', International Association of Legal Sciences, Uppsala Colloquium, 1984 (mimeo), p. 2. Also published in Favoreu and Jolowicz, eds., op. cit., pp. 175–90.
43  Cf. Taniguchi, op. cit., p. 7; Y. Higuchi, 'Evolution récente du contrôle de la constitutionnalité sous la Constitution Japonaise de 1946', 31 (1) *Revue Internationale de Droit Comparé*, Paris, 1979, p. 22; T. Fukase and Y. Higuchi, *Le Constitutionnalisme et ses problèmes en Japon. Une approche comparative*, Paris, 1984, p. 28; J. D. Whyte, 'Judicial Review of Legislation and its Legitimacy: Developments in the Common Law World', International Association of Legal Sciences, Uppsala Colloquium, 1984 (mimeo), p. 61. Also published in Favoreu and Jolowicz, eds., op. cit., pp. 155–74.
44  See Taniguchi, op. cit., p. 2; Whyte, op. cit., p. 62.
45  Fukase and Higuchi, op. cit., p. 298.
46  Grand Bench, 8 July 1948; Keishu 2-8-801, quoted by Taniguchi, op. cit., p. 2, note 3.

47  Taniguchi, op. cit., p. 3; Whyte, op. cit., p. 64.
48  Fukase and Higuchi, op. cit., p. 299; Taniguchi, op. cit., p. 9.
49  Taniguchi, op. cit., p. 14; Fukase and Higuchi, op. cit., p. 299.
50  Taniguchi, op. cit., p. 16; Fukase and Higuchi, op. cit., p. 299.
51  Taniguchi, op. cit., pp. 16–17.
52  Ibid., p. 11.
53  Cf. Higuchi, op. cit., pp. 22, 31; Fukase and Higuchi, op. cit., pp. 300, 307; Taniguchi, op. cit., p. 17; Whyte, op. cit., p 64.
54  Taniguchi, op. cit., p. 11.
55  Ibid., p. 14; Fukase and Higuchi, op. cit., p. 301.
56  *Aizawa* v. *Japan*, 27 Sai-han Keishu 256 (1973); Grand Bench, 4 April 1973, Keishu 27-3-265 quoted in Whyte, op. cit., p. 63; Taniguchi, op. cit., p. 10, note 16; Higuchi op. cit., pp. 31, 32; Fukase and Higuchi, op. cit., p. 308.
57  *K. K. Sumiyoshi* v. *Governor of Hiroshima Prefecture*, 665 Saibansho Jiho 1 (1975), Grand Bench 30 April 1975, Minshu 29-4-572, quoted in Whyte, op. cit., p. 65; Taniguchi, op. cit., p. 10, note 17; Higuchi, op. cit., p. 32; Fukase and Higuchi, op. cit., pp. 308, 309.
58  *Kurokawa* v. *Chiba Prefecture Election Commission*, 30. Sai-han Minshu 223 (1976), Grand Bench, 14 April 1976, Minshu 30-3-223, quoted in Whyte, op. cit., p. 65; Taniguchi, op. cit., p. 11, note 19; Higuchi, op. cit., pp. 32–3; Fukase and Higuchi, op. cit., pp. 309–10.
59  Whyte, op. cit., p. 63.
60  Fukase and Higuchi, op. cit., p. 299.
61  Higuchi, op. cit., pp. 31–2.

*15  Some aspects of the diffuse system of judicial review in the Commonwealth countries*

1  Cf. J. D. Whyte, 'Judicial Review of Legislation and its Legitimacy: Developments in the Common Law World, International Association of Legal Sciences', Uppsala Colloquium, 1984 (mimeo), p. 89; also published in Favoreu and Jolowicz, eds., *Le Contrôle juridictionnel des lois. Légitimité, effectivité et développements récents*, Paris, 1986, pp. 155–74. M. Zander, *A Bill of Rights?*, London, 1985, p. 30.
2  A. Lester, 'Fundamental Rights: the United Kingdom Isolated?', *Public Law*, 1984, pp. 56–7; Whyte, op. cit., p. 96–7.
3  S.O. Gyandoh, Jr, 'Interaction of the Judicial and Legislative processes in Ghana since Independence' (1983) 56 *Temple Law Quarterly*, p. 354.
4  Cf. A.R. Carnegie, 'Judicial Review of Legislation in the West Indian Constitutions', *Public Law*, London, 1971, p. 276; Cf. Okpaluba, 'Challenging the Constitutionality of Legislative Enactment in

Nigeria: the Factor of Locus Standi', *Public Law*, London, 1982, p. 110; Gyandoh, op. cit., p. 351; E. McWhinney, *Judicial Review*, Toronto, 1969, p. 7.

5   Carnegie, op. cit., p. 276; Whyte, op. cit., p. 32.

6   Cf. Okpaluba, op. cit., p. 110.

7   See S.N. Ray, *Judicial Review and Fundamental Rights*, Calcutta, 1974, p. 270.

8   Ibid., pp. 69–70.

9   1950 A.I.R. (S.C.) 27; 1950 S.C.R. 88, 286–7, 288–90, quoted in Ray, op. cit., pp. 72–3, see the comments on pp. 259–68.

10  McWhinney, op. cit., pp. 49, 57: Gyandoh, op. cit., p. 355.

11  E. McWhinney, 'Constitutional Review in the Commonwealth', in H. Mosler, ed., Max-Planck-Institut für ausländisches öffentliches Recht und Völkerrecht, *Verfassungsgerichtsbarkeit in der Gegenwart*, Internationale Colloquium, Heidelberg, 1961, Max-Planck, Cologne/Berlin, 1962, pp. 77–8.

12  McWhinney, 'Constitutional Review', p. 78.

13  McWhinney, 'Judicial Review', pp. 58–9.

14  Ibid.

15  Ibid.,, pp. 236, 237; McWhinney, 'Constitutional Review', pp. 79, 83, 87. Regarding India, cf. Ray, op. cit., pp. 4, 72.

16  Cf. Whyte, op. cit., p. 11; McWhinney, 'Constitutional Review', p. 83.

17  C.A. Kelsick, 'Report', in *Memoria de la reunión de Presidentes de Cortes Supremas de Justicia de Iberoamerica, el Caribe, España y Portugal*, Caracas, 1983, p. 419.

18  Ibid., p. 686.

19  Art. 131. See Ray, op. cit., p. 290.

20  Art. 132, 1.

21  Art. 132, 2.

22  McWhinney, 'Constitutional Review', p. 80.

23  Arts. 18, 19. See Whyte, op. cit., p. 25. Cf. in relation to Uganda, T.M. Franck, *Comparative Constitutional Process. Cases and Materials*, London, 1968, p. 75.

24  Art. 57, 1. See J.D. Whyte, op. cit., p. 25.

25  Cf. Ray, op. cit., pp. 77–89; Okpaluba, op. cit., p. 112; McWhinney, 'Constitutional Review', pp. 83, 84.

26  McWhinney, 'Constitutional Review', p. 83.

27  Art. 143. See Ray, op. cit., p. 294.

28  See Ray, op. cit., p. 293.

29  *Bengal Immunity* v. *State of Bihar*, 1955 A. I. R. (S. C. ) 661; (1955), 2 S. C. R. 603, quoted by Ray, op. cit., p. 85. Cf. P. Trikamdas, 'El Tribunal Supremo de la India', *Revista de la Comisión Internacional de Juristas*, 8 (1) 1967, p. 106.

1   Cf. W.K. Geck, 'Judicial Review of Statutes: a Comparative Survey of Present Institutions and Practices' (1966) 51 *Cornell Law Quarterly*, p. 278.

2   Cf. M. García Pelayo, 'El "status" del Tribunal Constitucional', *Revista Española de Derecho Constitucional*, 1, Madrid, 1981, p. 19; E. García de Enterría, *La Constitución como norma y el Tribunal Constitucional*, Madrid, 1981, p. 65. In particular, in concentrated systems of judicial review, the tribunals or courts empowered with administrative justice function always have the power of acting as constitutional judge regarding administrative acts. See C. Franck, *Les Fonctions juridictionnelles du Conseil d'Etat dans l'ordre constitutionnel*, Paris, 1974.

3   Arts. 18 and 19 of the Constitution. See J.D. Whyte, 'Judicial Review of Legislation and its Legitimacy: Developments in the Common Law World', International Association of Legal Sciences, Uppsala Colloquium, 1984 (mimeo) p. 25. Also published in L. Favoreu and J. A. Jolowicz, eds., *Le Contrôle juridictionnel des lois. Légitimité, effectivité et développements récents*, Paris, 1986, pp. 155–74.

4   See T.M. Franck, *Comparative Constitutional Process. Cases and Materials*, London, 1968, pp. 75–6.

5   See S.O. Gyandoh, Jr, 'Interaction of the Judicial and Legislative Processes in Ghana since Independence' (1983) 56 *Temple Law Quarterly*, pp. 365–6, 370.

6   Ibid., p. 370.

7   Art. 2, Ibid., p. 370.

8   Ibid., p. 384.

9   *Republic* v. *Maikankan* (1971) 2 G.L.R. 473, quoted by Gyandoh, Jr. op. cit., p. 386.

10  See in relation to Ghana the comments of Gyandoh, Jr, op. cit., p. 395.

11  E. McWhinney, 'Constitutional Review in the Commonwealth', in H. Mosler, ed., Max-Planck-Institut für ausländisches öffentliches Recht und Völkerrecht, *Verfassungsgerichtsbarkeit in der Gegenwart*, International Colloquium, Heidelberg, 1961, Cologne/Berlin, 1962, p. 80.

12  Ibid., p. 80.

13  Thus the concentrated system of judicial review is known as the 'Austrian system' or the 'European system'. Cf. M. Cappelletti, *Judicial Review in the Contemporary World*, Indianapolis, 1971, p. 50; L. Favoreu, 'Actualité et légitimité du controle juridictionnel des lois en Europe occidentale', *Revue du Droit Public et de la Science Politique en France et à l'Etranger*, Paris 1985, p. 1149. Also published in Favoreu and Jolowicz, eds., op. cit., pp. 17–68.

14 Cf. Cappelletti, op. cit., p. 54; M. Cappelletti and J. C. Adams, 'Judicial Review of Legislation: European Antecedents and Adaptation' (1966) 79 *Harvard Law Review*, p. 1211.
15 H. Kelsen, 'La Garantie juridictionelle de la Constitution (la Justice constitutionnelle)', *Revue du Droit Public et le la Science Politique en France et à l'Etranger*, Paris, 1928, p. 214.
16 Ibid., pp. 201, 223.
17 Art. I.1. See in P. Cruz Villalón, 'Dos modos de regulación del control de constitucionalidad: Checoslovaquia (1920–1938) y España (1931–1936)', *Revista Española de Derecho Constitucional*, 5, Madrid, 1982, p. 119.
18 Art. I.1 states: 'All laws contrary to the Constitutional Charter and any part thereof, as well as laws that modify and complement it, are considered null and void.'
19 Art. 102 established: 'The courts can verify the validity of executive regulations, when deciding upon a specific question of laws; concerning statutes they can only verify if they have been correctly published': see P. Cruz Villalón, op. cit., p. 135.
20 It should be noted that the Romanian constitutional regime also established a system of judicial review of law in Art. 103 of the Fundamental Charter of 29 March 1923. However, it was conferred only on the Court of Cassation, and later it was eliminated by the People's Republic, under the Soviet influence, from the terms of the Fundamental Law of 1948.
21 Kelsen, op. cit., pp. 224, 226. See the comments of García de Enterría, op. cit., pp. 57, 132.
22 Kelsen, op. cit., pp. 224, 225.
23 Kelsen, op. cit., p. 223. See the comments on Kelsen's thought in García de Enterría, op. cit., pp. 57, 58, 59, 131, 132, 133. Cf. Cappelletti and Adams, op. cit., pp. 1218–9; Cappelletti, op. cit., p. 67.
24 Cappelletti, op. cit., pp. 69, 72.
25 Exceptionally, the Federal Constitutional Tribunal of Yugoslavia has *ex officio* powers to initiate a proceeding of judicial review of legislation. See Art. 4, Law of the Constitutional Court of Yugoslavia, 31 December 1963, in B.T. Blagojevic, ed., *Constitutional Judicature*, Belgrade, 1965, p. 16.

17 *The origin of the European model of judicial review and the Austrian system of the Constitutional Tribunal*

1 Exceptionally, and because of European influence, some Latin American countries have established Constitutional Tribunals although the similarities with the European model may be more in the nomenclature of these institutions rather than their power of control.

# Notes

See, in general, H. Fix-Zamudio, *Los Tribunales Constitucionales y los derechos humanos*, U.N.A.M., Mexico, 1980, H. Fix-Zamudio, *Veinticinco años de evolución de la justicia constitucional 1940–1965*, U.N.A.M, Mexico, 1968.

2 L. Favoreu, 'Actualité et légitimité en contrôle juridictionnel des lois en Europe Occidental', *Revue du Droit Public et de la Science Politique en France et à l'Etranger*, Paris, 1984, p. 1149. Also published in L. Favoreu and J.A. Jolowicz, eds., *Le Contrôle juridictionnel des lois. Légitimité, effectivité, et développements récents*, Paris, 1986, pp. 17–68.

3 M. Cappelletti, *Judicial Review in the Contemporary World*, Indianapolis, 1975, p. 46.

4 H. Kelsen, 'La Garantie juridictionnelle de la Constitution (La justice constitutionnelle)', *Revue du Droit Public et de la Science Politique en France et a l'Etranger*, Paris, 1928, pp. 197–257.

5 Art. 89.1. See E. Alonso García, 'El Tribunal Constitucional austriaco', *El Tribunal Constitucional*, Instituto de Estudios Fiscales, Madrid, 1981, Vol. I, p. 414; and in Cappelletti, op. cit., p. 72.

6 Art. 102. See P. Cruz Villalón, 'Dos modos de regulación del control de constitucionalidad: Checoslovaquia (1920–1938) y España (1931–1936)', *Revista Española de Derecho Constitucional*, 5 Madrid, 1982, p. 135.

7 Kelsen, op. cit., pp. 223, 224, 226.

8 Cruz Villalón, op. cit., pp. 129, 139.

9 P. Nikolic, 'Le Contrôle juridictionnel du lois et sa légitimité', International Association of Legal Sciences, Uppsala Colloquium, 1984, p. 46. Also published in Favoreu and J.A. Jolowicz, eds., *Le Contrôle juridictionnel des lois*, pp. 72–112.

10 Art. I, 1 of the Introductory Law of the Constitution.

11 Art. III, 2 of the Introductory Law of the Constitution.

12 Law of the Constitutional Tribunal of 9 March 1920.

13 Cf. Cruz Villalón, op. cit., p. 135.

14 Art. 121, a of the Constitution.

15 Art 9, Law of the Constitutional Tribunal.

16 Cf. Cruz Villalón, op. cit., p. 138.

17 Art. 12, Law of the Constitutional Tribunal.

18 Art. 20, Law of the Constitutional Tribunal.

19 Cf. Alonso García, op. cit., p. 413; Cappelletti, op. cit., p. 71; F. Ermacora, 'Procédures et techniques de protection des droits fondamentaux. Cours constitutionnelle autrichienne', in L. Favoreu, ed., *Cours constitutionnelles européennes et droits fondamentaux*, Aix-en-Provence, 1982, p. 189.

20 Arts. 137–148, Constitution of 1 May 1945. See a Spanish version of the Constitution in I. Mendez de Vigo, 'El Verfassungsgerichthof (Tribunal Constitucional austríaco)', *Boletín de Jurisprudencia Constitucional*, Cortes Generales, 7, Madrid, 1981, pp. 555–60.

21 Law No. 85, 1953. See T. Ohlinger, *Legge sulla Corte Costituzionale austriaca*, Florence, 1982.

22  Art. 148 of the Constitution. The Internal Regulation of the Tribunal of 1946 can be seen in Ohlinger, op. cit., p. 137.

23  See the general considerations made in this respect by Kelsen, op. cit., pp. 226–7.

24  Ermacora, op. cit., pp. 190–1.

25  Kelsen, op. cit., p. 227.

26  Art. 147.3. Cf. Kelsen, op. cit., p. 227.

27  Art. 147, 4.

28  Art. 137.

29  Cf. Alonso García, op. cit., pp. 421–2.

30  Art. 138.

31  Cf. Ermacora, op. cit., p. 191. In this case it is considered that the Constitutional Tribunal exercises a 'previous judicial review of status': W. K. Geck, 'Judicial Review of Statutes: a Comparative Survey of Present Institutions and Practices' (1966) 51 *Cornell Law Quarterly*, p. 266.

32  Art. 138, a and 15 a.

33  Art. 141.

34  Art. 141, 3.

35  Art. 142.

36  Art. 142, 4.

37  Art. 140, 1.

38  Art. 140, 1. Cf. Kelsen, op. cit., p. 232.

39  Cf. Kelsen, op. cit., pp. 228–31.

40  Ibid., p. 230.

41  Ibid., p. 233. Art. 139, 1. Cf. Alonso García, op. cit., p. 434.

42  Cf. Cappelletti, op. cit., pp. 72, 73.

43  Art. 140, 1.

44  Art. 139, 1.

45  Cf. Favoreu, op. cit., p. 1152.

46  Art. 140, a.

47  Art. 140, 1.

48  This was not recommended by Kelsen for the purpose of judicial review. Kelsen, op. cit., p. 245.

49  Cf. Favoreu, op. cit., p. 1153.

50  Art. 140, 1.

51  Art. 139, 1.

52  Art. 57, Law of the Constitutional Tribunal.

53  Cappelletti, op. cit., p. 74.

54  Arts. 139, 1 and 140, 3. Cf. Kelsen, op. cit., p. 247.

55  Art. 140, 3.

56  Art. 144.

57  Art. 144.

58  Arts. 139, 6; 140, 7.

59  Arts. 139, 4; 140, 4. Cf. Kelsen, op. cit., p. 234.

60  Kelsen, op. cit., p. 242. For instance, regarding the Austrian system, L. Adamouch stated in 1954: 'To the decision of the Constitutional Tribunal which declares the unconstitutionality of a statute, one

cannot assign a simple declarative value; it does not establish that a concrete statute has been null from its origin, whose effects are to be null *ex tunc,* that is to say, as it were an act without any juridical value from its origin; on the contrary, the decision of the Constitutional Tribunal only annuls the unconstitutional statute, that is to say, destroys *ex nunc* its juridical existence, exactly as it would have been abolished by a successive legislative act, and just as that act would have ended its juridical existence.' ('Esperienze della Corte Costituzionale della Republica Austriaca', *Revista italiana per la scienze giuridiche,* Milan, 1954.)

61  Arts. 139, 6; 140, 7.
62  Arts. 139, 5; 140, 5.
63  Art. 140, 6.
64  Art. 140, a, 1.
65  Art 140, a, 2.


*18  Judicial review in the Federal Republic of Germany: the Federal Constitutional Tribunal*


1  Art. 13 of the Constitution. Cf. the text in F. Rubio Llorente, 'El Tribunal Constitucional alemán', *Revista de la Facultad de Derecho,* UCV, 18, Caracas, 1959, p. 116; J.C. Béguin, *Le Contrôle de la constitutionnalité des lois en Republique Féderale d'Allemagne,* Paris, 1982, p. 19; F. Sainz Moreno, Tribunal Constitucional Federal Alemán, *Boletín de Jurisprudencia Constitucional, Cortes Generales,* 8, 1981, Madrid, p. 603; G. Müller, 'El Tribunal Constitucional Federal de la Republica Federal de Alemania', *Revista de la Comisión Internacional de Juristas,* 6, Geneva, 1965, p. 222.
2  Art. 19 of the Constitution.
3  Art. 59.
4  See the quotations in C. J. Friedrich, 'The Issue of Judicial Review in Germany', *Political Science Quarterly,* 43, 1928, p. 188; H. G. Rupp, 'Judicial Review in the Federal Republic of Germany' (1960) 9 *American Journal of Comparative Law,* p. 31; J. C. Béguin, op. cit., p. 15.
5  Ibid.
6  Cf. Béguin, op. cit., pp. 13–21; Rupp, op. cit., p. 32; M. Cappelletti, *Judicial Review in the Contemporary World,* Indianapolis, 1971, pp. 50, 51, 59, 64.
7  Art. 92.
8  Müller, op. cit., p. 216; Sainz Moreno, op. cit., p. 606.
9  H. G. Rupp, 'The Federal Constitutional Court and the Constitution of the Federal Republic of Germany' (1971–2) 16 *Saint Louis University Law Journal,* p. 359.

10 Art. 94, 2. The Law on the Organization and Procedure of the Federal Constitutional Tribunal (FCT Law) was published on 12 March 1951. See the whole text in Rubio Llorente, op. cit., pp. 125–67. The law has been modified in various ways: 1956, 1959, 1963, and 1970. The present text dates from 3 February 1971, modified in 1974 and 1976. Cf. Sainz Moreno, op. cit., p. 604.

11 Art. 1, 1, FCT Law.

12 Art. 30, 2, FCT Law. The interior regulation of the Tribunal was published in 1975 and reformed in 1978.

13 Art. 94, 1, Constitution.

14 The Tribunal is divided in two Chambers (*Senaten*), each one with eight judges, three of them elected from active federal judges. Art. 4, 5, FCT Law.

15 Müller, op. cit., pp. 216, 221.

16 Béguin, op. cit., p. 93.

17 Cf. Müller, op. cit., p. 233; Béguin, op. cit., pp. 69, 94.

18 Cf. Müller, op. cit., p. 234.

19 Cf. Béguin, op. cit., pp. 27, 43–6.

20 Art. 93, Constitution.

21 Art. 21, 1, Constitution.

22 Art. 21, 2, Constitution. In 1952 and 1956 respectively, the Tribunal declared a neo–Nazi party (Sozialistischen Reichspartei) and the Communist Party (Kommunistische Partei Deutschlands) unconstitutional. Cf. the reference in Sainz Moreno, op. cit., p. 622.

23 Art. 18, Constitution.

24 Arts. 36–42, FCT Law.

25 Art. 61, Constitution.

26 Art. 98, 2 Constitution.

27 Art. 93 (1) 3, Constitution.

28 Art. 93 (1) 4, Constitution.

29 Art. 93 (1) 4, b, Constitution.

30 Art. 93 (1) 1, Constitution.

31 Béguin, op. cit., p. 40.

32 Art. 41, 2, Constitution; Art. 13, 3, FCT Law.

33 Art. 29, Constitution. Cf. G. Müller, op. cit., p. 229.

34 Art. 93 (1) 4, a, Constitution.

35 Art. 100, 3, Constitution.

36 Art. 126, Constitution.

37 Art. 2, 2, Constitution.

38 Art. 100, 2, Constitution.

39 Also see Art. 76–88, FCT Law.

40 Cf. Béguin, op. cit., p. 60; Rupp, 'Judicial Review', p. 35; Müller, op. cit., p. 231.

41 Art. 76, FCT Law.

42 Art. 77, FCT Law.

43 Cf. Béguin, op. cit., p. 61; Müller, op. cit., p. 231.

44 Art. 78, FCT Law. Cf. Béguin, op. cit., p. 61; Sainz Moreno, op. cit., p. 613.

45  Cf. Béguin, op. cit., p. 61; Sainz Moreno, op. cit., p. 613.
46  Cf. Béguin, op. cit., p. 63.
47  L. Contastinesco, 'L'Introduction et le contrôle de la constitutionalité des traités et en particulier des traités européens en droit allemand', *Revue Belge de Droit International*, 2, 1969, pp. 425–59.
48  Cf. Sainz Moreno, op. cit., p. 613.
49  Art. 90, FCT Law.
50  Article 90–96. FCT Law.
51  There, the constitutional complaint is a subsidiary means of judicial protection. Art. 90, 2, FCT Law. Art 19, 4 of the Constitution establishes in general that 'Should any person's rights be violated by public authority resource to the courts shall be open to him. If jurisdiction is not specified, recourse shall be to the ordinary courts.' See also Arts. 90–6, FCT Law.
52  Art. 90, 2, FCT Law.
53  Art. 93, 1, b FCT Law.
54  Art. 32, FCT Law. Cf. Béguin, op. cit., pp. 158–63; Sainz Moreno, op. cit., p. 626.
55  See also Arts. 80–82, FCT Law.
56  Cf. Müller, op. cit., p. 233; Sainz Moreno, op. cit., p. 614.
57  Müller, op. cit., p. 232; Sainz Moreno, op. cit., p. 614; Rupp, 'Judicial Review', op. cit., p. 32.
58  Art. 80, 2, FCT Law.
59  Art. 31, 1, FCT Law.
60  Cf. Béguin, op. cit., p. 92.
61  Art. 80, 3, FCT Law.
62  Art. 81, FCT Law. Cf. Béguin, op. cit., p. 93.
63  Art. 93, 1, 4, a, FCT Law.
64  Art. 93, 1, 1, Constitution.
65  Cf. Béguin, op. cit., p. 78–81; Sainz Moreno, op. cit., p. 612.
66  See also Art. 95, 2, FCT Law.
67  Art. 31, 1, FCT Law.
68  Art. 31, 2, FCT Law.
69  R. Bocanegra Sierra, 'Cosa Juzgada, vinculación, fuerza de ley en las decisiones del Tribunal Constitucional alemán', *Revista Española de Derecho Constitucional*, 1, 1981, p. 269.
70  H. Kelsen, 'La Garantie juridictionnelle de la Constitution (la justice constitutionnelle)', *Revue de Droit Public et de la Science Politique en France et à l'Etranger*, Paris, 1928, p. 243.
71  Béguin, op. cit., pp. 209–28.
72  Cf. Sainz Moreno, op. cit., p. 624; Rupp, 'Judicial Review', op. cit., p. 37; Bocanegra Sierra, op. cit., p. 268.
73  Art. 79, 1 FCT Law.
74  Art. 79, 2 FCT Law.
75  Rupp, 'Judicial Review', op. cit., p. 38; Béguin, op. cit., p. 185.
76  Cf. Béguin, op. cit., pp. 184–207; Sainz Moreno, op. cit., p. 625.
77  Art. 32, 2 and 79 FCT Law. Cf. Béguin, op. cit., pp. 232–66; Sainz Moreno, op. cit., p. 624.

78 Cf. Béguin, op. cit., pp. 266–93; Sainz Moreno, op. cit., pp. 624–5.


*19 Judicial review in Italy: the Constitutional Court*


1 M. Cappelletti, 'La justicia constitucional en Italia', *Boletín del Instituto de Derecho Comparado de México*, 30, 1960, p. 41; M. Cappelletti, *Judicial Review in the Contemporary World*, Indianapolis, 1971, p. 50.

2 Cf. A. Pizzorusso, 'Procédures et techniques de protection des droits fondamentaux. Cours constitutionnelle italienne', in L. Favoreu, ed., *Cours constitutionnelles européennes et droits fondamentaux*, Aix-en-Provence, 1982, p. 165; J. Rodríguez-Zapata y Pérez, 'La Corte Constitucional italiana: ¿Modelo o advertencia?', in *El Tribunal Constitucional*, Instituto de Estudios Fiscales, Madrid, 1981, Vol. III, p. 2416.

3 Cf. G. Cassandro, 'The Constitutional Court of Italy' (1959) 8 *American Journal of Comparative Law*, p. 3.

4 Cf. F. Rubio Llorente, *La Corte Constitucional italiana*, Caracas, 1966, pp. 2–4.

5 Cassandro, op. cit., p. 12; Cf. Rodríguez-Zapata y Pérez, op. cit., p. 2417.

6 The Constitutional Court in decision No. 13 of 1960 defined its functions as essentially 'the exercise of a function of constitutional control, of the supreme guarantee of the observance of the Constitution ... by the Constitutional organs of the State and of the Regions' (quoted by Rubio Llorente, op. cit., p. 10, note 27); and in decision No. 15 of 1969 has defined itself as the 'highest organ for the guarantee of the republican order, to which exclusively corresponds the enforcement of the rule of the Constitution over all the other constitutional agents', quoted by Rodríguez-Zapata y Pérez, op. cit., p. 2420.

7 A. Sandulli, 'Sulla posizione della Corte Costituzionale nel sistema degli organi supremi dello Stato', *Rivista Trimestrale di Diritto Pubblico*, 1960, p. 705.

8 Art. 1, 1, Federal Law of the Federal Constitutional Tribunal (1951).

9 Art. 1, 1, Organic Law of the Constitutional Tribunal (1978).

10 Sandulli, op. cit., p. 718; Cf. Rodríguez-Zapata y Pérez, op. cit., pp. 2428–41; Cassandro, op. cit., pp. 13–14.

11 Art. 14, Statute No. 87 of 11 March 1953. Norms on the Constitution and functioning of the Constitutional Court. See the text in Rubio Llorente, op. cit., pp. 48–55.

12 Art. 135. Statute No. 87 (1953), Arts. 1–4.

13 P. Calamandrei, *La illegittimità costituzionale delle leggi nel processo civile*, 1950, p. 57; H. Fix-Zamudio, 'La aportación de Piero

Calamandrei al derecho procesal constitucional', *Revista de la Facultad de Derecho de Mexico*, 24, 1956, p. 191.

14   M. Cappelletti, *La giurisdizione costituzionale delle libertà* (Primo studio sul ricorso costituzionale con particolare riguardo agli ordinamenti tedesco, suizzero e austriaco), Milan, 1955, p. 112; Cappelletti, 'La justicia constitucional', op. cit., p. 52; Rubio Llorente, op. cit., pp. 10–13.

15   Cf. Decision No. 13, 23 March 1960. Quoted by Rubio Llorente, op. cit., p. 10.

16   Art. 134, Constitution; Art. 39, Statute No. 87.

17   Art. 38, Statute No. 87.

18   Art. 40, Statute No. 87.

19   Rubio Llorente, op. cit., p. 16.

20   Art. 37, Statute No. 87.

21   A. Sandulli, 'Die Verfassungsgerichtsbarkeit in Italia', in H. Mosler, ed., *Verfassungsgerichtsbarkeit in der Gegenwart*, Max Planck Institut für ausländisches öffentliches Recht und Völkerrecht, International Colloquium, Heidelberg, 1961, Cologne/Berlin, 1962, p. 310; quoted by Rubio Llorente, op. cit., p. 36.

22   Art. 37, Statute No. 87.

23   Art. 38, Statute No. 87.

24   Arts 90, 134, Constitution. Statute No. 20, 25 January 1962. See the text in Rubio Llorente, op. cit., pp. 55–61.

25   Arts. 74, 75 Constitution; Art. 2, Constitutional Statute No. 1, 11 March 1953. See the text in Rubio Llorente, op. cit., pp. 46–7.

26   Regarding political parties, Professor Rubio Llorente says that the Constitutional Court can decide upon their constitutionality only by indirect means when a question of constitutionality is referred to the Court regarding statutes sanctioned in accordance with Article 18 (prohibition of secret or paramilitary societies), Article 49 (freedom of association in political parties), or on the Transitory Disposition XII (prohibition of any form of re-organization of the fascist party) through which a party or a political organization could be dissolved. Rubio Llorente, op. cit., p. 16.

27   Cf. Pizzarusso, op. cit., p. 168.

28   Rubio Llorente, op. cit., pp. 4–5.

29   Ibid., pp. 5–6.

30   Art. 1, Constitutional Statute No. 1, 9 February 1948.

31   Art. 75, Constitution.

32   Art. 77, Constitution. These Decrees, issued in emergency situations, must be submitted to Parliament on the day following enactment and only when they are validated by Parliament can they be questioned on constitutional grounds.

33   Cf. Rubio Llorente, op. cit., p. 23.

34   Decision No. 1, 1956. Quoted by Rubio Llorente, op. cit., p. 35; Cf. Cassandro, op. cit., p. 5.

35   Decision No. 4, 1959. Quoted by Rubio Llorente, op. cit., p. 22.

36   Cf. Cassandro, op. cit., p. 4.

37 Cassandro, op. cit., pp. 3–4. Cf. Rubio Llorente, op. cit., p. 20.
38 The term is also used in Art. 1, Constitutional Statute No. 1, 9 February 1948; and in Arts. 23–36, Statute No. 87, 1953.
39 Compare the court decisions and the opposing doctrine on this matter in Rubio Llorente, op. cit., pp. 17–19; and G. Zagrebelski, 'Objet et portée de la protection des droits fondamentaux. Cours constitutionnelle italienne', in L. Favoreu, ed., *Cours constitutionnelles européennes et droits fondamentaux*, Aix-en-Provence, 1982, p. 330.
40 Cappelletti, 'La justicia constitucional', pp. 44, 45.
41 Arts. 23, 24, Statute No. 87, 1953.
42 Art. 25, Statute No. 87, 1953. The parties or the public official may not appeal before the Court, Art. 26. Ibid.,
43 Art. 22, Complementary Norms of the Court. Cf. Rubio Llorente, op. cit., p. 24; Cassandro, op. cit., p. 6; Pizzorusso, op. cit., p. 176.
44 Cappelletti, 'Judicial Review', p. 45.
45 See also Art. 32, Statute No. 87, 1953. The review results in fact, in a conflict of attributions between national and regional equals. Cf. Rubio Llorente, op. cit., p. 25.
46 Art. 39, Statute No. 87, 1953.
47 Art. 2; see also Art. 33, Statute No. 87, 1953.
48 Art. 25, Complementary Norms of the Court. Cf. Cassandro, op. cit., p. 8.
49 Art. 127, Constitution.
50 Art. 31, Statute No. 87, 1953.
51 Art. 128, Constitution.
52 Art. 27, Statute No. 87, 1953.
53 Art. 27, Ibid.,
54 Art. 136, Constitution; Art 30, Statute, No. 87, 1953.
55 Cf. Cassandro, op. cit., p. 6.
56 Cf. Rubio Llorente, op. cit., pp. 12, and 29–33.
57 Decision No. 3491, 1957. Quoted in Rubio Llorente, op. cit., p. 30.
58 Art. 30, Statute No. 87, 1953.
59 Decision No. 4, 1959. Quoted by Rubio Llorente, op. cit., p. 22.
60 Calamandrei, op. cit., p. 71.
61 Cf. Rubio Llorente, op. cit., pp. 32–3.
62 Cappelletti, 'La justicia constitucional', pp. 56–7.
63 Ibid., p. 57.

20 *Judicial review in Spain: the Constitutional Tribunal*

1 J.L. Melián Gil, *El Tribunal de Garantías Constitucionales de la Segunda República Española*, Madrid, 1971, pp. 16–17, 53; P. Cruz Villalón, 'Dos modos de regulación del control de constitucionalidad: Checoslovaquia (1920–1938) y España (1931–1936)', *Revista Española de Derecho Constitucional*, 5, 1982, p. 118. J.J. González

Rivas, *La Justicia Constitucional: Derecho comparado y español*, Madrid, 1985, pp. 97–109.

2  Melián Gil, op. cit., p. 9; N. González-Deleito Domingo, *Tribunales Constitucionales: organización y funcionamiento*, Madrid, 1980, p. 21.

3  Art. 121. See the text in Melián Gil, op. cit., p. 11; González-Deleito Domingo, op. cit., p. 22.

4  Art. 123, ibid.

5  Arts. 30–3, Organic Law 1933. See Melián Gil, op. cit., pp. 14, 29.

6  Art. 42, Organic Law 1933, Melián Gil, op. cit., p. 30.

7  Ibid., p. 45; N. González-Deleito Domingo, op. cit., p. 23.

8  Organic Law 2/1979. See the text in *Boletín Oficial del Estado*, No. 239, 5 October 1979.

9  G. Müller, 'El Tribunal Constitucional Federal de la República Federal de Alemania', *Revista de la Comisión Internacional de Juristas* (2), 1965, p. 221.

10  Cf. E. García de Enterría, *La Constitución como norma y el Tribunal Constitucional*, Madrid, 1981, p. 137; P. Bon, F. Moderne and Y. Rodriguez, *La Justice constitutionnelle en Espagne*, Paris, 1982, p. 41; L. Favoreu, 'Actualité et legitimité du contrôle juridictionnel des lois en Europe Occidentale', *Revue du Droit Public et de la Science Politique en France et à l'Etranger*, 5, Paris, 1984, p. 1154.

11  J. Salas, 'El Tribunal Constitucional español y su competencia desde la perspectiva de la forma de gobierno: sus relaciones con los poderes legislativo, ejecutivo y judicial', *Revista Española de Derecho Constitucional*, 6, 1982, p. 165.

12  M. García Pelayo, 'El "status" del Tribunal Constitucional, *Revista Española de Derecho Constitucional*, 1, 1981, pp. 11–34; F. Rubio Llorente, 'La relación entre Tribunal Constitucional y poder judicial en el ejercicio de la jurisdicción constitucional', *Revista Española de Derecho Constitucional*, 4, 1982, pp. 35–67. As an independent organ it also has autoregulatory powers: Art. 2, 2, Organic Law 2/1979.

13  Arts. 161, 1, c, Constitution. Arts. 60–72, Organic Law 2/1979.

14  Arts. 59, 3: 73–5, Organic Law 2/1979.

15  Art. 75, 2 Organic Law 2/1979.

16  Ibid.

17  Art. 164, 1, Constitution.

18  Art. 161, 1, b, Constitution; Art. 41, 2, Organic Law 2/1979.

19  Cf. García de Enterría, op. cit., p. 151.

20  Art. 42, Organic Law 2/1979.

21  Art. 43, 1, Organic Law 2/1979.

22  Cf. Favoreu, op. cit., pp. 1155–6.

23  Art. 55, 2, Organic Law 2/1979.

24  Art. 161, 1, a, Constitution.

25  Art. 27, 1, Organic Law 1/1979.

26  Art. 27, 2, a, b, ibid.

27  Art. 27, 2, c, ibid.

28    Art. 27, 2, d, ibid.
29    Art. 27, 2, b, ibid.
30    Art. 82, Constitution.
31    Art. 86, Constitution.
32    Art. 27, 2, f, Constitution.
33    Art. 162, 1, a, Constitution; Art. 32, 1, Organic Law 2/1979.
34    Art. 162, 1, a, Constitution; Art. 32, 2, Organic Law 2/1979.
35    Art. 33, Organic Law 2/1979.
36    S. Galeotti and B. Rossi, 'El Tribunal Constitucional en la nueva Constitución española: medios de impugnación y legitimados para actuar', *Revista de Estudios Políticos*, 7, Madrid, 1979, p. 125.
37    Art. 30, Organic Law.
38    García de Enterría, op. cit., p. 140.
39    Art. 34, Organic Law 2/1979.
40    Art. 82, 1, ibid.
41    J. González Pérez, *Derecho procesal constitucional*, Madrid, 1980, p. 101.
42    Ibid., p. 197.
43    See also Art. 35, 1, Organic Law 2/1979.
44    Art. 35, 2, ibid.
45    Ibid.
46    See J.M. Rodríguez Oliver, 'Sobre los efectos no suspensivos de la cuestion de inconstitucionalidad y la ley organica 2/79 de 3 de Octubre', in *Civitas. Revista Española de Derecho Administrativo*, 25, 1970, pp. 207–22.
47    Art. 35, 2, Organic Law 2/1979.
48    Art. 37, 2, ibid.
49    Cf. Galeotti and Rossi, op. cit., p. 134.
50    Decision No. 39/1982. Quoted in Salas, op. cit., p. 148, note 23.
51    Art. 161, 1, b, Constitution; Art. 41, 2, Organic Law 2/1979.
52    Art. 52, 2, Organic Law 2/1979.
53    Decisions 55/57/1981. Quoted in Salas, op. cit., p. 148, note 23.
54    García de Enterría, op. cit., p. 156.
55    Art. 95, Constitution.
56    M. Aragón, 'El control de constitucionalidad en la Constitución española de 1978', *Revista de Estudios Políticos*, 7, Madrid, 1979, p. 183.
57    Art. 78, 2, Organic Law 2/1979.
58    Art. 161, 1, d, Constitution.
59    Art. 79, Organic Law.
60    Art. 152, 2, Constitution.
61    Art. 93, Constitution.
62    Bon, Moderne and Rodríguez, op. cit., p. 260.
63    Art. 95, 1, Constitution.
64    Art 79, 4, b, Organic Law 2/1979.
65    Art. 79, 5, ibid.
66    Art. 39, 2, Organic Law 2/1979.
67    Art. 39, 1, ibid.

68    Art. 164, 1, Constitution.
69    Art. 38, 1; and Art. 87, 1, Organic Law 2/1979.
70    Art. 164, 1, Constitution; 38, 1, Organic Law 2/1979.
71    Art. 38, 3, Organic Law 2/1979.
72    Cf. J. Arosemena Sierra, 'El recurso de inconstitucionalidad', in *El Tribunal Constitucional*, Instituto de Estudios Fiscales, Madrid, 1981, Vol. I, p. 171.
73    Art. 161, 1, a, Constitution.
74    Art. 40, 1, Organic Law 2/1979.
75    Art. 55, 2, ibid.
76    Arts. 66; 75, 1, ibid.
77    Art. 38, 2, ibid.
78    Art. 29, 2, ibid.

*21    Constitutional justice in the socialist European countries*

1    S. Rozmaryn, 'La Constitution, loi fondamentale de l'état socialiste', in P. Biscaretti di Ruffia and S. Rozmaryn, *La Constitution comme loi fondamentale dans les états de l'Europe Occidentale et dans les états socialistes*, Turin, 1966, p. 108.
2    P. Nikolic, 'Le Contrôle juridictionnel des lois et sa légalité. Développements récents dans les pays socialistes', International Association of Legal Sciences, Uppsala Colloquium, 1984 (mimeo), p. 15. Also published in L. Favoreu and J.A. Jolowicz, eds., *Le Contrôle juridictionnel des lois. Légitimité, effectivité et développements récents*, Paris, 1986, pp. 71–115. P. Kastari, 'Le Caractère normatif et la prééminence hierarchique des constitutions', *Revue International de Droit Comparé*, Paris, 1966, p. 843.
3    Rozmaryn, op. cit., p. 99; Nikolic, op. cit., p. 7; Kastari, op. cit., p. 841.
4    H. Roussillon, 'Le Problème du contrôle de la constitutionnalité des lois dans les pays socialistes', *Revue du Droit Public et de la Science Politique en France et à l'Etranger*, Paris, 1977, p. 76; Rozmaryn, op. cit., p. 108. Cf. Nikolic, op. cit., p. 17.
5    V. Krivic, 'Foreword', in B.T. Blagojevic, ed., *Constitutional Judicature*, Belgrade, 1965, p. 6.
6    Ibid., p. 5.
7    Nikolic, op. cit., p. 21.
8    Ibid., p. 52.
9    Krivic, op. cit., p. 5
10   Law of the Constitutional Court of Yugoslavia (C.C.Y.), 31 December 1963. See the text in Blagojevic, ed., op. cit., pp. 15–36; Krivic, op. cit., p. 3.

11  Art. 1, Law C.C.Y., 1963. The Court is also authorized to 'independently adopt its Rules of Procedures and other general acts affecting its organization and operation'. Art. 16, Law C.C.Y.
12  Art. 43, Law C.C.Y., 1963.
13  Krivic, op. cit., p. 4.
14  Art. 46, Law C.C.Y., 1963.
15  Art. 44, ibid.
16  Art. 36, 1, ibid.
17  Art. 36, 3, ibid.
18  Art. 37, ibid.
19  Arts. 36, 39, ibid.
20  Art. 39, ibid.
21  Art. 2, ibid.
22  Art. 17, ibid.
23  Art. 4, ibid.
24  Art. 18, ibid.
25  Art. 3, ibid.
26  Art. 19, ibid.
27  Arts. 4, 19, ibid.
28  Art. 23, ibid.
29  Art. 4, ibid.
30  Art. 24, ibid.
31  Art. 25, ibid.
32  Art. 25, ibid.
33  Art. 25, ibid.
34  Arts. 2, 2; 72, ibid.
35  Art. 29, ibid.
36  Art. 30, ibid.
37  Art. 34, ibid.
38  Art. 29, ibid.
39  Art. 32, ibid.
40  Art. 31, 4, ibid.
41  Art. 31, 1, 2, ibid.
42  Art. 31, 1, ibid.
43  Art. 28, ibid.
44  Cf. H. Fix-Zamudio, *Los Tribunales Constitucionales y los derechos humanos*, Mexico, 1980, p. 129; Nikolic, op. cit., p. 46.
45  Art. 86, 1; Art 87, Constitutional Law. See Nikolic, op. cit., p. 48.
46  Art. 93, 90, Constitutional Law. See Nikolic, op. cit., 49.
47  Art. 92, Constitutional Law. See Fix-Zamudio, op. cit., p. 131.
48  Art. 92, Constitutional Law. See Fix-Zamudio, op. cit., p. 132.


22  *The concentrated system of judicial review in Latin America*


1  Art. 188, 1, Constitution. See in C. Quintero, 'La Jurisdicción constitucional en Panamá' in *La Jurisdicción Constitucional en*

*Iberoamérica*, Universidad Externado de Colombia, Bogotá, 1984, p. 170.

2  Art. 188, 1.
3  Art. 188, 2.
4  Art. 188, in Fine.
5  Art. 189. Cf. Quintero, op. cit., p. 173.
6  The system was originally established in 1934 and 1951. See H. Gross Espiell, 'La constitución y su defensa en Uruguay', *L a Constitución y su defensa*, U N.A.M., 1984, pp. 624, 628; 'La jurisdicción constitucional en el Uruguay', in *La jurisdicción constitucional en Iberoamérica*, pp. 71–100. The system was maintained in the 1966 Constitution, in Institutional Act No. 8 of 1977 and in the Institutional Act No. 12 of 1981. Ibid, pp. 16, 20.
7  Art. 256.
8  Art. 258. Cf. Gross Espeill, 'La constitución', pp. 645, 648; J.P. Gatto de Souza, 'Control de la constitucionalidad de las actos del poder público en Uruguay', *Memoria de la reunión de Presidentes de Cortes Supremas de Justicia de Iberoamérica, El Caribe, España y Portugal*, Caracas, 1983, pp. 661, 662.
9  Art. 258.
10  Arts. 258, 259.
11  Art. 259.
12  See Gross Espiell, 'La constitución', p. 29.
13  Ibid.
14  Arts. 200, 207.
15  L. M. Argaña, 'Control de la constitucionalidad de las leyes en Paraguay', *Memoria de la reunión de Presidentes de Cortes Supremas de Justicia de Iberoamerica, El Caribe, España y Portugal*, pp. 550, 551, 669, 671.
16  Cf. O. Tovar Tamayo, *La jurisdicción constitucional*, Caracas, 1983, p. 103. J. Tapia Valdés, 'Jurisdicción constitucional y gobiernos de facto. El caso de la Corte Suprema de Chile' in *La Jurisdicción constitucional en Iberoamérica*, p. 257.
17  See the text in H. Fix-Zamudio, *Los Tribunales Constitucionales y los derechos humanos*, Mexico, 1980, p. 143, note 251; Tapia Valdés, op. cit., p. 253.
18  E. Silva Cimma, *El Tribunal Constitucional de Chile (1917–1973)*, Caracas, 1977, pp. 12–20.
19  Silva Cimma, op. cit., p. 219; Fix-Zamudio, op. cit., p. 150.
20  H. Fix-Zamudio, 'Dos leyes orgánicas de Tribunales Constitucionales latinoamericanos: Chile y Peru', *Boletín Mexicano de Derecho Comparado*, 51, 1984, p. 943.
21  Art. 82, Constitution, 1980.
22  Fix-Zamudio, 'Dos leyes orgánicas', p. 947.
23  Art. 82, Constitution 1980. Arts 26–37, Organic Law, 1981. See the comments in Fix-Zamudio, 'Dos leyes orgánicas', p. 948.
24  Ibid., p. 949.

25 Fix-Zamudio, op. cit., pp. 148, 149; Tovar Tamayo, op. cit., pp. 132, 133.
26 Fix-Zamudio, 'Dos leyes orgánicas', pp. 949–50; Tovar Tamayo, op. cit., p. 137.
27 Art. 82. See Fix-Zamudio, 'Dos leyes orgánicas', p. 949.
28 Art. 137, Constitution of 15 January 1978.
29 Art. 138, Constitution.
30 Art 141. 1, Constitution. The Tribunal is composed of three members elected by the National Chamber of Representatives; the President of the Supreme Court of Justice; the Attorney General; the President of the Supreme Electoral Tribunal; one representative of the President of the Republic; one representative of workers; one representative of the association of employers; and two representatives of the people, elected by electoral bodies composed by the Mayors of Cantons and by the provincial authorities. Art. 140, Constitution.
31 Art. 141, 2, Constitution.
32 Art. 141, 3, Constitution.
33 G. Zambrano Palacios, 'Control de la constitucionalidad de los actos del poder público', *Memoria de la Reunión de Presidentes de Cortes Supremas de Justicia de Iberoamérica, El Caribe, España y Portugal*, pp. 667, 678.
34 Art. 138, Constitution.
35 Ibid.
36 Ibid.

23 *Preventive judicial review in France: the Constitutional Council*

1 J. Rivero, *Le Conseil Constitutionnel et les libertés*, Paris/Aix-en-Provence, 1984, p. 168.
2 L. Favoreu, 'Le Principe de constitutionnalité. Essai de definition d'après la jurisprudence du Conseil Constitutionnel', *Recueil d'etudes en hommage à Charles Eisenmann*, Paris, 1977, pp. 33–48.
3 See the comments concerning the legitimacy of the *a priori* French systems of control in a comparative perspective in L. Favoreu, 'Actualité et légitimité du contrôle juridictionnel des lois en Europe Occidentale', *Revue du Droit Public et de la Science Politique en France et à l'Etranger*, Paris, 5, 1984, pp. 1183–7. Also published in L. Favoreu and J.A. Jolowicz, eds., *Le contrôle juridictionnel des lois. Légitimité, effectivité et développements récents*, Paris, 1986, pp. 17–68.
4 Arts. 56–63, Constitution 1958.
5 Art. 61.
6 M. Cappelletti, *Judicial Review in the Contemporary World*, Indianapolis, 1971, pp. 33–5; F. Luchaire, *Le Conseil Constitutionnel*, Paris, 1980, pp. 5–6.

7    Montesquieu, *De l'Esprit des lois*, Book XI, Ch. VI, quoted by C. H. McIlwain, *The High Court of Parliament and its Supremacy*, Yale, 1910, p. 323.

8    C. Franck, *Les Functions juridictionnelles du Conseil Constitutionnel et du Conseil d'Etat dans l'ordre constitutionnel*, Paris, 1974, pp. 44–6; Luchaire, op. cit., pp. 10–11.

9    Luchaire, op. cit., p. 13.

10   The Constitutional Council is ruled by Title VII, Arts. 53 to 63 of the 1958 Constitution (*Journal Officiel*, 5 October 1958) and by Organic Law No. 58–1067 of 7 November 1958 (*Journal Officiel*, 9 November 1958). Art. 61, 2 of the Constitution was modified on 21 October 1974 by a Constitutional Reform; and the Organic Law of the Tribunal was modified by Organic Law No. 59–223 of 4 February 1959 (*Journal Officiel* 7 February 1959) and by the Organic Law of 26 December 1974 that followed the Constitutional amendment.

11   W.K. Geck, 'Judicial Review of Statutes: a Comparative Survey of Present Institutions and Practices' (1966) 51 *Cornell Law Quarterly*, pp. 256, 259.

12   A. Hauriou, *Droit constitutionnel et institutions politiques*, Paris, 1981.

13   F. Luchaire, 'Le Conseil Constitutionnel. Est-il une juridiction?', *Revue du Droit Public et de la Science Politique en France et a l'Etranger*, Paris, 1979; Luchaire, *Le Conseil Constitutionnel*, pp. 33–56.

14   T. Renoux, *Le Conseil Constitutionnel et l'autorité judiciaire. L'Elaboration d'un droit constitutionnel juridictionnel*, Paris, 1984, p. 19.

15   Art. 56, Constitution; Art 1, Organic Law 58–1067.

16   Art. 57, Constitution; Art. 4, Organic Law 58–1067.

17   Art 5, Organic Law 58–1067.

18   Art. 7, Organic Law 58–1067.

19   Art. 2, Decret, 13 January 1959; See Luchaire, *Le Conseil Constitutionnel*, p. 71.

20   Art. 7, Constitution.

21   Art. 16, Constitution.

22   Arts. 7, 11, 12, Constitution; Art. 31, Organic Law 58–1067.

23   Art. 16, Constitution; Arts. 52, 53, Organic Law 58–1067.

24   Art. 54, Organic Law 58–1067.

25   Arts. 58–60, Constitution.

26   Art. 59, Constitution.

27   Art. 41, Organic Law 58–1067.

28   Arts. 39–40, ibid.

29   Art. 30, ibid.

30   Art. 27, Organic Law 58–1067, 7 November 1958 concerning the election of the President of the Republic. *Journal Officiel*, 9 November 1958.

31   Art. 22, Organic Law 58–1067.

32   Art. 19, ibid.

33 Art. 23, ibid.
34 Art. 60, Constitution; Arts. 46, 51 Organic Law 58–1067.
35 Art. 50, Organic Law 58–1067.
36 Cf. Luchaire, *Le Conseil Constitutionnel*, p. 277.
37 Art. 50, Organic Law 58–1067.
38 In its origin, the Constitutional Council was established as the guarantor of the organic part of the Constitution and only after 1971 has it also been considered as a guarantor of the fundamental rights of the citizen against the laws. Rivero, op. cit., pp. 13–4.
39 Art. 61, Constitution; Art. 17, Organic Law 58–1067.
40 Art. 61, Constitution.
41 Art. 54, Constitution.
42 Arts. 54, 61, Constitution; Art. 18 Organic Law 58–1067.
43 Art. 61, Constitution.
44 Art. 61, Constitution.
45 Art. 20, Organic Law.
46 Art. 21, Organic Law 58–1067.
47 Art. 62, Constitution.
48 Art. 54, Constitution.
49 Art. 22, Organic Law 58–1067.
50 Art. 23, ibid.
51 Art. 62, Constitution.
52 Art. 41, Constitution.
53 Art. 27, Organic Law 58–1067.
54 Ibid.
55 Art. 37, Constitution.
56 Art. 37, Constitution.
57 See also Arts. 24–26, Organic Law 58–1067. See Franck, op. cit., p. 167.
58 Art. 34, Constitution 1946. Cf. Rivero, op. cit., p. 11; Favoreu, 'Le Principe', p. 34.
59 See L. Favoreu and L. Philip, *Les Grandes Décisions du Conseil Constitutionnel*, Paris, 1984, pp. 222–37. Rivero, op. cit., p. 140; B. Nicholas, 'Fundamental Rights and Judicial Review', *Public Law*, 1978, pp. 82–92; J. E. Beardsley, 'The Constitutional Council and Constitutional Liberties in France', *American Journal of Comparative Law*, 20, 1972, pp. 431–52; Franck, op. cit., p. 208.
60 M. Cappelletti, 'El formidable problema del control judicial y la contribución del análisis comparado', *Revista de Estudios Políticos*, 13, Madrid, 1980, p. 71. Cf. F. Luchaire, 'Procédures et techniques de protection des droits fondamentaux. Cónseil Constitutionnel français', in L. Favoreu, ed., *Cours Constitutionnelles Européennes et Droit Fondamentaux*, Paris 1982, pp. 64–73.
61 See Favoreu and Philip, op. cit., pp. 524–62. See the comments in L. Favoreu, ed., *Nationalisations et Constitution*, Aix-en-Provence, 1982; Rivero, op. cit., pp. 109–25.

62     Favoreu, 'Les Décisions du Conseil Constitutionnel dans l'affaire des nationalisations', *Revue de Droit Public et de la Science Politique en France et à l'Etranger*, Paris, 1982, p. 401.

63     See in *Recueil Sirey* (Jurisprudence), 1959, p. 392 (note R. Drago). See the comments in Franck, 'The Constitutional Council and Constitutional Liberties in France', op. cit., p. 200; Cappelletti, 'El formidable problema', p. 70.

64     See in Franck, op. cit., p. 200.

65     See in *Dalloz* (Jurisprudence), 1975, p. 497. See the comments in M. Cappelletti and W. Cohen, *Comparative Constitutional Law*, Indianapolis, 1979, pp. 156–68; Cappelletti, 'El formidable problema', p. 72.

66     In the French constitutional system, treaties have 'authority superior to statutes', Art. 55, Constitution.

67     Cf. A. Z. Drzemczewski, *European Human Rights Convention in Domestic Law. A Comparative Study*, Oxford, 1985, p. 71.

24     *The limited concentrated system of judicial review in Belgium: the Arbitration Court*

1     F. Perin, 'La Nouvelle Subdivision du royaume: les communautés et les régions', XI Congrès International du Droit Comparé, Caracas, 1982 (mimeo), p. 10. See the text in *La Constitution belge et ses lois d'application*, Cabay, Louvain-La-Neuve, 1985.

2     Art. 107, Constitution (29 July 1980). See also 'Loi portant l'organisation, la compétence et le fonctionnement de la Cour d'arbitrage', (LCA), 28 June-1983, in *La Constitution belge*, p. 105. Cf. L. Favoreu, 'Le Contrôle juridictionnel des lois et sa légitimité. Développements récents en Europe Occidentale', International Association of Legal Sciences,Uppsala Colloquium, 1984 (mimeo), p. 15. Also published as 'Actualité et légitimité du contrôle juridictionnel des lois en Europe Occidentale', *Revue du Droit Public et de la Science Politique en France et à l'Etranger*, 5, Paris, 1984, p. 1166; and also in L. Favoreu and J. A. Jolowicz, eds., *Le contrôle juridictionnel des lois. Légitimité, effectivité et développements récents*, Paris, 1986, pp. 17–68.

3     Art. 21, 22, LCA.

4     Art. 1, 1, LCA.

5     Art. 2, 1, LCA.

6     Art. 8, LCA.

7     Art. 7, LCA.

8     Favoreu, op. cit., p. 1168.

9     Art. 15, 2, LCA.

10     Favoreu, op. cit., p. 1168.

11     Art. 17, LCA.

25    *The control of the constitutionality of legislation in the Portuguese Republic*

1    Published in the *Diario da República*, 1st series, No. 227.
2    See, in general, J. Campinos, 'La constitución portuguesa de 1976 y su defensa', *La constitución y su defensa*, U.N.A.M. Mexico, 1984, p. 527; M. Gonsalo, 'Portugal, El Consejo de la Revolución, su Comisión Constitucional y los Tribunales ordinarios como órganos de control de la constitucionalidad', *Boletín de Jurisprudencia Constitucional*, Cortes Generales, 8, Madrid, 1981.
3    Art. 290 establishes material limits to constitutional revision.
4    Art. 212.
5    Art. 213, 1.
6    Art. 213, 2.
7    Art. 284.
8    Art. 280, 1, a, b.
9    Art. 280, 2.
10    Art. 280, 4.
11    Arts. 280, 3, a, b, c; 280, 4.
12    Art. 280, 5.
13    Art. 280, 6.
14    Art. 281, 2.
15    Art. 278, 1, 2.
16    Art. 279, 9.
17    Art. 279, 2.
18    Art. 279, 3.
19    Arts. 279, 2; 279, 4.
20    Art. 281, 1, a.
21    Art. 281, 1, a. The archipelagos of the Azores and Madeira have been organized within the state, as Autonomous Regions. Art. 227.
22    Art. 281, 1, b. See also Art. 281, 1, c.
23    Art. 282, 1.
24    Art. 282, 2.
25    Art. 282, 3.
26    Art. 282, 4.
27    Campinos, op. cit., p. 35.
28    Ibid., p. 42.
29    Ibid., p. 42.

26    *The limited mixed system of constitutional judicial review in Switzerland*

1    Art. 90, Constitution, 1874. See the text in W. J. Wagner, *The Federal States and their Judiciary*, The Hague, p. 104.

2   Art. 113, Constitution 1874.
3   E. Zellweger, 'El Tribunal Federal suizo en calidad de Tribunal Constitucional', *Revista de la Comision Internacional de Juristas*, 7, 1966, p. 114.
4   B. Ger. 2, 98, 105 (1876). Quoted by Wagner, op. cit., p. 105, and Zellweger, op. cit., p. 126.
5   See, for example, A. Grisel, 'Réflexions sur la juridiction constitutionnelle et administrative en Suisse', *Etudes et Documents*, 28, Conseil d'Etat, Paris, 1976, pp. 262–72.
6   Art. 114 A. See the text in Wagner, op. cit., p. 106.
7   The 1962 Federal Law on Assembly Procedures and on the Form, Publications and Validity of Legislative Acts, defines them as follows: 'Federal Laws are legislative acts of unlimited duration containing rules of law.' Legislative acts containing rules of law are all general or abstract norms 'which impose obligations on, or grant rights to individuals and corporations, or regulate the organization, jurisdiction or functions of authorities, or establish a procedure'. Federal resolutions of general and binding effect are 'legislative acts of unlimited duration containing rules of law'. See Zellweger, op. cit., p. 125.
8   Zellweger, op. cit., p. 127.
9   Ibid., p. 127.
10  Wagner, op. cit., p. 106; A. Jiménez Blanco, 'El Tribunal Federal suizo', *Boletín de Jurisprudencia Constitucional,* Cortes Generales, 6, Madrid, 1981, p. 478.
11  Zellweger, op. cit., p. 119; Jiménez Blanco, op. cit., p. 478.
12  Cf. Jiménez Blanco, op. cit., p. 479; Zellweger, op. cit., p. 119.
13  The conformity of administrative federal acts with federal law is also judged by the Federal Tribunal, but through recourse of administrative law. Cf. Grisel, op. cit., p. 255. The control of the constitutionality of Cantonal Constitutions has been excluded. Cf. Zellweger, op. cit., p. 124.
14  Art. 84, Law of Judiciary Organization. See the text in Zellweger, op. cit., p. 120.
15  Art. 85, Law of Judiciary Organization.
16  Art. 84, 2, ibid. Cf. Grisel, op. cit., p. 255; Zellweger, op. cit., p. 122; Wagner, op. cit., p. 109.
17  Art. 86, 2, Law of Judiciary Organization.
18  Art. 88, ibid.
19  Zellweger, op. cit., p. 123.
20  Ibid., p. 123.
21  Grisel, op. cit., p. 255.
22  Wagner, op. cit., p. 109.

27   *The mixed system of judicial review in Venezuela*

1   See Allan R. Brewer-Carías, *Instituciones políticas y constitucionales*, Caracas, 1985, Vol. I, p. 342.
2   See the comments regarding the mixed system of judicial review of constitutionality as a consequence of the principle of the supremacy of the Constitution, in R. Feo, *Estudios sobre el Código de Procedimiento Civil venezolano*, Caracas, 1904, Vol. I, pp. 26–35; R. Marcano Rodríguez, *Apuntaciones analíticas sobre las materias fundamentales y generales del Código de Procedimiento Civil venezolano*, Caracas, 1941, Vol. I, pp. 36–8; A. Borjas, *Comentarios al Código de Procedimiento Civil*, Caracas 1947, Vol. I, pp. 33–5.
3   Supreme Court of Justice in Pleno Court, 15 March 1962. See *Gaceta Oficial*, 760 Extra, 22 March 1962, pp. 3–7.
4   See J.G. Andueza, *La jurisdicción constitucional en el derecho venezolano*, Caracas, 1955, p. 460.
5   See, in general, Allan R. Brewer–Carías, *El control de la constitucionalidad de los actos estatales*, Caracas, 1977; also 'Algunas consideraciones sobre el control jurisdiccional de la constitucionalidad de los actos estatales en el derecho venezolano', *Revísta de Administración Pública*, 76, Madrid, 1975, pp. 419–46; and *Estado de Derecho y Control Judicial*, Madrid, 1987.
6   See Federal Court (which in 1961 was substituted by the Supreme Court of Justice), 19 June 1953, in *Gaceta Forense*, 1, 1953, pp. 77–8.
7   Art. 20 states: 'When the law whose application is demanded conflicts with any provision of the Constitution, the judges will give preference to the latter.' The text was originally adopted in the 1897 Code.
8   See Allan R. Brewer-Carías, *Las Constituciones de Venezuela*, Madrid, 1985, p. 203. Cf. H. J. La Roche, *El control jurisdiccional de la constitucionalidad en Venezuela y Estados Unidos*, Maracaibo, 1971, p. 24.
9   Art. 186. See Brewer-Carías, *Las Constituciones de Venezuela*, p. 353.
10  Art. 199. See ibid., p. 200.
11  Art. 106, 8. See the text in Brewer-Carías, *Las Constituciones de Venezuela*, p. 579.
12  See the Federal Court decision of 19 June 1953, in *Gaceta Forense*, 1, 1953, pp. 77–8.
13  Cf. Marcano Rodríguez, op. cit., Vol. I, p. 37.
14  Art. 177, 1961 Constitution.
15  Art. 215, 3, 4, 1961 Constitution.
16  Art. 106, 8. See the text in Brewer-Carías, *Las Constituciones de Venezuela*, p. 579.
17  Art. 113, 8, ibid., p. 392.
18  Art. 92, ibid., p. 422.
19  Art. 89, 9, ibid., p. 422.

20 Art. 110, 8, ibid., p. 540.
21 Art. 123, ibid., p. 541.
22 Art. 17, ibid., p. 531.
23 Art. 110, 9. Arts. 118, 119 declared those acts null, ibid., pp. 540, 541.
24 Art. 106, 8. 1901 Constitution, ibid., p. 579.
25 Arts. 34 and 120, 22, ibid., pp. 705–6.
26 Arts. 34 and 123, 11, ibid, p. 824.
27 Art. 123, 11, ibid, p. 824.
28 Brewer-Carías, *El control de la constitucionalidad*, pp. 27–9; *Estado de Derecho y Control Judicial*, pp. 209–586.
29 Art. 215, 3; 215, 4; and 215, 6..
30 Arts. 42, 1; 42, 2; 42, 3; 42, 4; 42, 11; and 42, 12 of the Organic Law of the Supreme Court of Justice (LOCSJ), 30 July 1976 in *Gaceta Oficial*, 1893 Extra, 30 July 1976.
31 Nevertheless, the Supreme Court has established in a decision of the Pleno Court of 29 April 1965 that the Laws of Approval of international treaties could not be submitted to judicial review. See the decision and critics in Brewer-Carías, *El control de la constitucionalidad*, pp. 48–52; *Estado de Derecho y Control Judicial*, pp. 71–6.
32 Art. 91, Constitution 1945. See in Brewer-Carías, *Las Constituciones de Venezuela*, p. 850. In the same sense, Art. 90, Constitution 1953, ibid, p. 947.
33 Art. 42, 2 LOCSJ attributed powers to the Court to 'decide upon the constitutionality of laws requested by the President of the Republic before its promulgation'.
34 Art. 173, 1961 Constitution.
35 Thus, in this case, Art. 175 of the Constitution, which confers on the President and Vice-President of the Congress powers to promulgate laws not promulgated by the President of the Republic within the prescribed time, does not apply.
36 See the decision of the Federal Court (C.F.) of 2 February 1960, in *Gaceta Forense*, 27, Caracas, 1960, pp. 107–8; and the decision of the Supreme Court of Justice, in Politico-Administrative Chamber (CSJ–SPA) of 3 October 1963, in *Gaceta Forense*, 42, Caracas, 1963, p. 16–20; of 6 April 1966, in *Gaceta Oficial*, 27.373 of 21 February 1964; of 30 May 1963 in *Gaceta Forense*, 52, Caracas, 1968, p. 109; and of 25 September 1973 in *Gaceta Oficial*. 1643 Extra, 21 March 1974.
37 See CSJ–SPA, 18 February 1971, *Gaceta Oficial*, 1472 Extra, 11 June 1971. CSJ–SPA, 6 February 1966, *Gaceta Oficial*, 27,373, 21 February 1964.
38 See, for example, CSJ–SPA 18, July 1971, in *Gaceta Oficial*, 1472, Extra, 11 June 1971. See Art. 121, LOCSJ.
39 Art. 112, LOCSJ.
40 Brewer-Carías, *El control de la constitucionalidad*, p. 122.

41  See decision of the Supreme Court of Justice in Pleno (CSJ–CP) of 30 June 1982, in *Revista de Derecho Público*, 11, Caracas, 1982, pp. 135–8.
42  See CSJ–SPA, 3 October 1963 in *Gaceta Forense*, 42, Caracas, 1963, pp. 20–21.
43  Art. 134, LOCSJ.
44  See CF, 12 June 1952, in *Gaceta Forense*, 1, Caracas, 1953, pp. 48–50; CF, 22 February 1961, in *Gaceta Forense*, 27, 1960, pp. 107–8; and CSJ–SPA, 25 September 1973, in *Gaceta Oficial*, 1643, Extra, 21 March 1974.
45  Art. 116, LOCSJ.
46  See CSJ–SPA, 3 October 1963, in *Gaceta Forense*, 42, 1963, pp. 19–20.
47  See Federal and Cassation Court in Politico-Administrative Chamber (CFC–SPA) 20 November 1940, in *Memoria de la Corte Federal y de Casación 1941*, pp. 264–8.
48  Art. 116, LOCSJ.
49  Art. 137, LOCSJ. Before the promulgation of the 1976 LOCSJ, see in the contrary sense CSJ–CP, 12 June 1968, in *Publicaciones del Senado*, Caracas, 1968, p. 190; and CSJ–SPA, 27 May 1970, in *Gaceta Forense*, 68, 1970, p. 111.
50  Art. 113, LOCSJ. Cf. CSJ–SPA, 23 January 1969, in *Gaceta Forense*, 63, 1969, p. 95.
51  Art. 113, LOCSJ. Cf. decision of the Federal and Cassation Court in Pleno Court (CFC–CP), 14 December 1950, in *Gaceta Forense*, 6, 1950, pp. 46–7; CSJ–SPA, 11 August 1964, in *Gaceta Forense*, 45, 1964, pp. 185–6.
52  In this respect, the Attorney General's office has indicated that 'the constitutionality of legislative acts is a matter of prime public interest. Thus, in cases in which such matters are considered, the judges' powers are not, nor can they be, limited by what is alleged or proven in the complaint'. See *Doctrina de la Procuraduría General de la República 1963*, Caracas, 1964, pp. 23–4. See also CSJ–CP, 15 March 1962. *Gaceta Oficial*, 760 Extra, 22 March 1962. In this respect, J. G. Andueza holds that the decision of the court may not contain *ultra petita*, p. 37.
53  Art. 82, LOCSJ.
54  Art. 87, LOCSJ; Cf. Andueza, op. cit., p. 37.
55  Reasons of illegality may not thus be alleged. See CSJ–SPA, 13 February 1968, in *Gaceta Forense*, 59, 1969, pp. 85–6.
56  See CSJ–CP, 12 June 1969, in *Gaceta Forense*, 65, 1969, p. 10; CSJ–SPA, 27 April 1969, in *Gaceta Forense*, 64, 1969, p. 23; and CSJ–SPA, 13 February 1968, in *Gaceta Forense*, 59, pp. 85–6.
57  See CSJ–SPA, 21 December 1967, in *Gaceta Forense*, 58, 1968, p. 68.
58  See the decision of the Federal Court, 25 March 1958, *Gaceta Forense*, 19, 1958, p. 58. On the contrary the Attorney General's office has maintained that an infraction of the 'motives' of the Constitution

cannot be the cause for the annulment of a legal text. See *Doctrina de la Procuraduría General de la República 1964*, Caracas, 1965, p. 158. Elsewhere, however, the same Attorney General's office has held that the Constitution is being violated when the law intends to achieve ends different from those proposed by the Constitution, and not only when there exists some literal contradiction between the rule in the Constitution and the legal rule. See *Doctrina de la Procuraduría General de la República 1969*, Caracas, 1970, p. 111. In general, on the various grounds for unconstitutionality of laws, see *Doctrina de la Procuraduría General de la República*, 1966, Caracas, 1967, pp. 170–4.

59  Arts. 119 and 130.
60  See CSJ–SPA, 20 January 1966, in *Gaceta Forense*, 51, 1966, p. 13. Cf. CFC–SPA, 2 December 1941, in *Memoria de la Corte Federal y de Casación 1942*, pp. 335–9, and 13 July 1942, in *Memoria de la Corte Federal y de Casación 1943*, pp. 174–5.
61  Art. 131, repeating what is expressed in Art. 119.
62  Art. 119.
63  See CSJ–CPA, 20 January 1966, in *Gaceta Forense*, 51, 1966, p. 13.
64  See Civil, Commercial and Labor Cassation Chamber of the Supreme Court of Justice (CSJ–SCCMT), 12 December 1963, in *Gaceta Forense*, 42, 1963, pp. 667–72.
65  See CSJ–SCCMT, 11 August 1971, in *Gaceta Forense*, 73, 1971, p. 477. In this respect, the Attorney General's office has described the effects of a declaration denying a popular action of unconstitutionality, in *Doctrina de la Procuraduría General de la República 1963*, Caracas, 1964, p. 199, in the following terms: 'The decision on constitutionality grounds, like any other judicial decision, produces *res judicata*. That ... obtained in objective jurisdiction, whether it be favourable or unfavourable, always produces effects *erga omnes* . Consequences of great interest, such as that of irrevocability, follow from this principle. When the Federal Court declares the action inadmissible because the state act which is challenged lacks the defects which are denounced, this decision may not be reviewed, as it enjoys all the characteristics of any decision which produces *res judicata* : it may not be discussed or changed ... In a case in which the Federal Court has denied a popular action of unconstitutionality, and nonetheless, this is brought again, for the same reasons and supported by the same constitutional provisions, the Court must disallow the new action as this is already *res judicata* . In consequence, the Court should apply *ex officio* the provious decision or decide the exception of *res judicata* filed by the Attorney General.' (J. G. Andueza, *La jurisdicción constitutional en el derecho venezolano*, Universidad Central de Venezuela, Caracas, 1954, p. 99.)
66  See CSJ–CP, 4 April 1974, in *Gaceta Oficial*, 1,657 Extra, 7 June 1974.
67  See CSJ–SPA, 17 November 1938, in *Memoria de la Corte Federal y de Casación 1939*, pp. 330–4.

68    See CFC–SPA, 21 March 1939, in *Memoria de la Corte Federal y de Casación 1940*, p. 176.

69    See CFC–SPA, 16 December 1940, in *Memoria de la Corte Federal y de Casación 1941*, p. 311.

70    See CF, June 1953, in *Gaceta Forense*, 1, 1953, pp. 77 and 78. The Supreme Court has also held in a decision of its Politico Administrative Chamber that 'the effects of the decisions issued by the Court when exercising this power only extend to the time during which the constitutional precept on which they are based continues to be valid'. See *Gaceta Forense*, 62, 1968, pp. 106–13.

71    See CSJ–SCCMT, 12 December 1963, in *Gaceta Forense*, 42, 1963, pp. 667–72.

72    Arts. 119 and 131, LOCSJ.

73    This implies the irreversibility of its decisions. See Art. 211 of the Constitution. The doctrine has, however, been established for many years by the court itself. See, for example, CFC–SPA, 17 November 1938, in *Memoria de la Corte Federal y de Casación 1939*, p. 330.

74    See CFC–SPA, 4 March 1941, in *Memoria de la Corte Federal y de Casación 1942*, pp. 128–30.

75    See CFC–SPA, 3 May 1939, in *Memoria de la Corte Federal y de Casación 1940*, p. 217; and 17 April 1941, *Memoria de la Corte Federal y de Casación 1942*, p. 182.

76    See, for exampled, the Draft Constitutional Jurisdiction Law in Public Administration Commission, *Informe sobre la Reforma de la Administración Publica Nacional*, Caracas, 1972, Vol. II, pp. 547–59. See the text also in Humberto J. La Roche, op. cit., pp. 215–38.

77    See A. and S. Tunc, *Le Système constitutionnel des Etats Unis d'Amérique*, Paris, 1954, Vol. II, pp. 294 and 295.

78    Art. 215, paragraphs 3 and 4, 1961 Constitution.

79    See Mauro Cappelletti, 'El control judicial de la constitucionalidad de las leyes en el derecho comparado', *Revista de la Facultad de Derecho de Mexico*, 61, 1966, pp. 58–9.

80    See, for example, CFC–SPA, 17 November 1938, in *Memoria de la Corte Federal y de Casación 1939*, pp. 330, 334; Cf., 19 June 1953, in *Gaceta Forense*, 1, 1953, p. 77; CSJ–CP, 29 April 1965, published by the Imprenta Nacional, Caracas, 1965, pp. 113, 116. Cf. *Doctrina de la Procuraduría General de la República 1963*, Caracas, 1964, pp. 199, 201. In other words, as Capelletti points out, 'once the decision of unconstitutionality is pronounced, the corresponding law is deprived of effects in a general manner, exactly as if it had been abrogated by a subsequent law, and *vice versa*, all the legislative provisions prior to the unconstitutional law regain their validity' (op cit., p. 59). Thus, the effects of the concentrated constitutional review system are radically different from the particular, *inter partes* effects of the diffuse constitutional review system.

81    Cf. M. Cappelletti, op. cit., pp. 63–4.

82    Art. 215, paragraphs 3 and 4.

83    In his book *La jurisdicción constitucional en el derecho venezolano*, José Guillermo Andueza has abundantly and finally demonstrated that the decision declaring nullity by reason of unconstitutionality which all acts by the Public Powers enjoy means that these produce all their legal effects until such time as they are pronounced null by the Court. Consequently, 'the Court's decision should necessarily respect the effects which the state act produced while it was in force' (p. 93), since 'it produces a change in the effects of a state act. That is to say, the sentence renders ineffective a previously valid act' (p. 94). According to Andueza himself, and following the most orthodox doctrine, 'what characterizes constitutive sentences is the absence of retroactive effects. These continue always *pro futuro, ex nunc*; that is to say, that the decision produces its effects from the day of its publication,' (p. 94). We do not then share the opinion of J. J. La Roche, *El control jurisdiccional en Venezuela y Estados Unidos*, p. 153.

84    CFC, 20 December 1940, cited by J. G. Andueza, op. cit., p. 90.

85    See CSJ–SPA, 15 February 1967, in *Gaceta Forense*, 55, 1967, p. 70.

86    Cf. CFC–SPA, 17 November 1938, in *Memoria de la Corte Federal y de Casación 1939*, p. 330; 21 March 1939, in *Memoria de la Corte Federal y de Casación 1940*, p 176; 16 December 1940, in *Memoria de la Corte Federal y de Casación 1941*, p. 311; and of the CF, 19 June 1953, in *Gaceta Forense*, 1, 1953, pp. 77 and 78.

87    See CFC–SPA, 16 December 1940, in *Memoria de la Corte Federal y de Casación 1941*, p. 311.

88    See CFC–SPA, 21 March 1939, in *Memoria de la Corte Federal y de Casación 1940*, p. 176.

89    Art. 44 of the Constitution.

90    Art. 141, 4, Constitution of Ecuador 1983. See the comments of J. G. Andueza, op. cit., p. 94.

91    Art. 18, 4, 1961 Constitution.

92    See CSJ–SPA, 18 November 1965, in *Gaceta Forense*, 50, 1967, p. 111. This was also the criterion of the former Federal and Cassation Court in Cassation Chamber when, in a decision on 27 February, 1940, it expressly decided the following: 'The decision which is appealed, to deny the action, is founded on the fact that the Municipal Ordinance which gave rise to the fine being imposed on the plaintiff for an infraction of one of its Articles, was issued by a competent authority and produced all its effects until the day it was declared null by the Federal and Cassation Court, which was the Tribunal which was competent for this purpose. The effects of the verdict of cassation cannot be made retroactive to the date that Ordinance expired, but rather they are produced from the date of that decision. As, on the other hand, the plaintiff did not appeal against the fine, he agreed to the fiscal sanction which was imposed on him, and the decision appellated concludes that there was no undue payment. The damages claimed as a consequence of that payment are thus denied. This Court considers that the grounds stated, on which the lower court based its

decision, are according to the legal principles which govern this matter. In our Administrative Law, Municipal Ordinances issued under the powers which the National Constitution grants the Municipalities 'have the character of local laws, and as such, it follows to apply to them the rule of the non-retroactivity of their provisions. As these Ordinances are the work of an administrative authority, invested with a part of the Public Power, these acts retain all their legal validity even in the case in which they suffer from defects which would make them annullable, until such time as their nullity is declared by the competent Court.' See CFC–SPA, 27 February 1940, in *Memoria de la Corte Federal y de Casación, 1941*, p. 20.

93  See CSJ–SPA, 13 February 1968, in *Gaceta Forense*, 62, 1969, p. 85.
94  See CSJ–SPA, 19 December 1968, in *Gaceta Forense*, 62, 1969, p. 112.
95  In this respect, it must be pointed out that this general principle, which is universal in comparative law and accepted by Venezuelan case law and doctrine, was followed by those who drafted the Law of Constitutional Jurisdiction when they established in Article 19 of the draft that: 'The laws which are declared unconstitutional may not be applied nor shall have any effect whatsoever, from the day following the publication in the Official Gazette or, failing such publication, as of ten days after it is signed. When a definitive criminal decision has been pronounced on the basis of these, and is being executed, it shall cease, as shall all other penal effects.' See Draft Law of Constitutional Jurisdiction drawn up by Profs. Martín-Retortillo, Rubio Llorente and Allan R. Brewer-Carías in Public Administration Commission, *Informe sobre la reforma de la administración pública nacional*, CAP, Caracas, 1972, Vol. II, p. 551.
96  See CSJ–SCCMT, 10 August 1978, in *Gaceta Forense*, 101, 1978, pp. 591–2.
97  For example, in a decision of the Politico Administrative Division of the Court on 23 February 1984 declaring the nullity by reason of unconstitutionality of an act installing the Legislative Assembly of a State of the Federation, the court provided expressly that 'this decision shall have no retroactive effects whatsoever in relation to procedures carried out in the Legislative Assembly' (consulted in original).
98  Art. 46, 1961 Constitution.
99  As pointed out by J. G. Andueza, 'the difference which exists between an act null and an annullable one should be seen in the nature of the judicial pronouncement. If the decision is solely declaratory, with retroactive effects, when the act is annulled *pro-praeterito*, we may affirm that we are in the presence of absolute nullity. By contrast, when the judges pass a constitutive judgement with effects *ex nunc*, *pro futuro*, the defect produces only the annullability of the state act': op. cit., pp. 92–3.

100 See Allan R. Brewer-Carías, *Las instituciones fundamentales del derecho administrativo y la jurisprudencia Venezolana*, Caracas, 1964, p. 62.

101 Art. 250, 1961 Constitution.

102 This has been expressly decided by the Supreme Court of Justice in a decision of 19 December 1968, in the following terms: 'It is as well to warn, moreover, that the effects of the decisions which the court passes when exercising this power only extend for the time for which the constitutional precept on which they are based continues in force. In consequence, it is possible that a legal provision which is annulled because it is contrary to the Constitution – but which in fact has continued to form part of a legal instrument which has been revoked – recovers its legal effect when a reform comes into effect repealing the Constitutional precept on which the Court rested in order to declare it null, or when the previously established regime changes radically.

Such was the situation created when – after the Federal and Cassation Court passed the verdict mentioned by the petitioner in April 1951 – the constitutional order in force at that time was reformed by the Constitutions published respectively in 1953 and 1961. In 1951, the restrictions which provided the basis for the Federal and Cassation Court to declare null the rules which the plaintiff refers to in this petition still served as a basis for the Federal and Cassation Court to deny municipal competence over the tax on industrial and trade permits, and subjected the power of local authorities to levy taxes. But when the Constitution was reformed in 1953, those restrictions were removed, and among the categories taxable by the Municipal Power were included those indicated in the current National Constitution, and, in particular, the tax on industrial and trade permits. This being the case, the Municipal Council of the Federal District was not subject to the aforementioned constitutional limitations when, in the exercise of its autonomy and of the power granted to it in the Fundamental Charter, to levy taxes it sanctioned the current Ordinance on the Permit for Industry and Trade in 1958, and if the activity of that body could not be bound by provisions, which like those of the 1936 Constitution, had already been revoked, less could it be so bound by what was decided in a decision whose effects are limited to the duration in force of the legal provisions which served as its basis." See CSJ–SPA, 19 December 1968, in *Gacenta Forense*, 62, 1968, pp. 106–13. Cf. CSJ–SPA, 29 October 1968, in *Gaceta Forense*, 62, 1968, pp. 37–9.

103 See the historical analysis of these constitutional rules in E. Agudo Freites, *Estado actual de la acción de amparo en Venezuela, Estudios sobre la Constitución*. Libro Homenaje a Rafael Caldera, Universidad Central de Venezuela, Caracas, 1979, Vol. II, pp. 659–773.

104 Art. 32, 1947 Constitution.

105 See in general H. Fix-Zamudio, *La protección procesal de los derechos humanos ante las jurisdicciones nacionales*, Madrid, 1982.

106 See the exposition of motives of the Constitution in *Revista de la Facultad de Derecho*, Universidad Central de Venezuela, Caracas, 1962, pp. 371–420, particularly pp. 380–1.

107 The right of protection (Article 49, Constitution) is thus different from the broader right to access to justice specifically regulated in Article 68 of the Constitution.

108 See Allan R. Brewer-Carías, 'El derecho de amparo y la acción de amparo', *Revista de Derecho Público*, 22, EJV, Caracas, 1985, pp. 51–61.

109 Hector Fix-Zamudio, 'Algunos aspectos comparativos del derecho de amparo en Mexico y Venezuela', *Libro homenaje a la memoria de Lorenzo Herrera Mendoza*, Universidad Central de Venezuela, Caracas, 1970, Vol. II, pp. 344–56.

110 K. Schlaich, 'Procédures et techniques de protection des droits fondamentaux. Tribunal constitutionnel Fédéral Allemand', in L. Favoreu, ed., *Cours Constitutionnelles européennes et droits fondamentaux*, Paris, 1982, pp. 105–64.

111 See J.L. García Ruiz, *Recurso de amparo en el derecho español*, Madrid, 1980; F. Castedo Alvarez, 'El recurso de amparo constitucional', Instituto de Estudios Fiscales, *El Tribunal Constitucional*, Madrid, 1981, Vol. I, pp. 179–208.

112 Cf. H. Fix-Zamudio, 'El derecho de amparo en México y en España. Su influencia recíproca', *Revista de Estudios Políticos*, 7, Madrid, 1979, pp. 254–5.

113 See *Gaceta Oficial* 31256, 14 June 1977 and 2146 Extra, 28 January 1978.

114 Fix-Zamudio, 'El derecho de amparo en México y en España. Su influencia recíproca', p. 254–5. On the contrary, the recourse of *amparo* against individual actions is accepted in Argentina. Kot case of 5 September 1958. See G.R. Carrio, *Algunos aspectos del recurso de amparo*, Buenos Aires, 1959, p. 13.

115 Allan R. Brewer-Carías, *Garantías constitucionales de los derechos del hombre*, Caracas, 1976, p. 69.

116 Art. 53, 2, Spanish Constitution 1978.

117 See the decision of the Supreme Court in Politico Administrative Chamber of 28 October 1983 in *Revista de Derecho Público*, EJV, 16, Caracas, 1983, p. 169. See the comments of René De Sola, 'Vida y vicisitudes del recurso de amparo en Venezuela', *Revista del Instituto Venezolano de Derecho Social*, 47, Caracas, 1985, p. 58

118 Allan R. Brewer-Carías, *Instituciones políticas y constitucionales*, Caracas, 1985, Vol. II, p. 491.

119 Arts. 58; 60, 3; 64, 7.

120 Art. 241, Constitution.

121 Arts. 59; 60, 4; 60, 6; 60, 8; 61; 65; 66; 67; 68; 69; 71; 76; 78; 84; 111.

122 Arts. 60, 5; 62; 63; 112.

123 Arts. 60, 1; 60, 2; 60, 9; 64; 65; 96; 99; 114; 115.

124 Arts. 68; 70; 92.

125  Allan R. Brewer-Carías, 'La reciente evolución jurisprudencial en relación a la admisibilidad del recurso de amparo', *Revista de Derecho Público*, EJV, 19, Caracas, 1984, pp. 207–18.

126  The right to protection (*amparo*) has been legally regulated in the *Ley Orgánica de Amparo sobre derechos y garantías constitucionales* of 22 January 1988, *Gaceta Oficial*, 33891, 22 January 1988.

## 28  *The mixed system of judicial review in Colombia*

1  Concerning the mixed character of the system see M. Gaona Cruz, 'El control de constitucionalidad de los actos juridicos en Colombia ante el derecho comparado' in *Archivo de Derecho Público y Ciencias de la Administración*, Vol. 7 (Derecho Público en Venezuela y Colombia), Instituto de Derecho Público, UCV, Caracas 1986, pp. 39–114; J. Vidal Perdomo, *Derecho constitucional general*, Bogotá, 1985, p. 42; D. R. Salazar, *Constitución política de Colombia*, Bogotá, 1982, p. 305; E. Sarría, *Guarda de la Constitución*, Bogotá, p. 78.

2  See L.C. Sachica, *El control de constitucionalidad y sus mecanismos*, Bogotá, 1980, pp. 59, 66; L.C. Sachica, 'La Constitución y su defensa' in *La Constitución y su defensa*, U.N.A.M., Mexico, 1984, pp. 354–5.

3  See the text in Vidal Perdomo, op. cit., p. 40; and in Sarría, op. cit., p. 77.

4  Cf. Sachica, 'La Constitución', p. 354; Sachica, *El control*, p. 73.

5  Cf. Vidal Perdomo, op. cit., pp. 47–8; Sachica, *El control*, p. 64; Sarría, op. cit., p. 77; Salazar, op. cit., p. 307; A. Copete Lizarralde, *Lecciones de derecho constitucional*, Bogotá, pp. 243–5.

6  Copete Lizarralde, op.cit., p. 246.

7  Cf. Sachica, *El control*, p. 65.

8  Through Legislative Act No. 1 of 1979 this article was reformed, and it assigned the Supreme Court the role not only to 'guard the integrity of the Constitution', but to ensure its supremacy. Cf. Sachica, *El control*, p. 142. Nevertheless, that reform became ineffective because the Supreme Court, in its decision of 3 November 1981, declared the unconstitutionality of Legislative Act No. 1 of 1979, based on defects of procedure. See the reference in Vidal Perdomo, op. cit., p. 49. The power attributed to the Supreme Court as constitutional judge has been regulated by Decree 432 of 1969. See the text in J. Ortega Torres, ed., *Constitución política de Colombia*, Bogotá, 1985, p. 148.

9  This was expressly established in the constitutional reform sanctioned by Legislative Act No. 1 of 1979. Cf. Sachica, *El control*, p. 150. The present Constitution only establishes the free intervention of any citizen when the state act impugned is a Decree of Emergency. See Art. 215, 2 and Arts. 121 and 122, Constitution; and Art. 14, Decree 432 of 1969.

10  Art. 215, 2, Constitution.

11  Copete Lizarralde, op. cit., p. 246; Sachica, *El control*, p. 106.
12  Sachica, 'La Constitución', p. 351.
13  Cf. Sachica, *El control*, pp. 73, 151.
14  Art. 76, paragraphs 11 and 12, Constitution.
15  Arts. 76, paragraph 4; 80 and 215, paragraph 2.
16  Cf. Sachica, *El control*, p. 144; Vidal Perdomo, op. cit., p. 49.
17  Cf. Sachica, *El control*, pp. 79–84. 'Clasificación de las Leyes y su control de constitucionalidad en Colombia' in *La jurisdicción constitucional en Ibero-América*, Universidad Externado de Colombia, Bogotá, 1984, pp. 24–7.
18  Cf. Sachica, *El control*, p. 80.
19  Arts. 121, 122, Constitution; Art. 13, Decree 432 of 1969.
20  Art. 215, Constitution; Art. 14, Decree 432 of 1969.
21  As was established in the constitutional reform, sanctioned by Legislative Act No. 1 of 1979, later annulled. See Sachica, *El control*, pp. 148–9.
22  Art. 215, Constitution; Art. 1, Decree 432 of 1969.
23  See the comments of H. Fix-Zamudio, *Los Tribunales Constitucionales y los derechos humanos*, Mexico, 1980, pp. 151–2. Cf. Carlos Restrepo Piedrahita, 'Tentativas para instituir en Colombia una Corte Constitucional', in *La jurisdicción constitucional en Iberoamérica*, pp. 188–240.
24  Art. 1, Decree 432 of 1969.
25  Art. 3, Decree 432 of 1969.
26  Cf. Sachica, *El control*, p. 59.
27  Decision of 1 November 1981. See in *Revista Foro Colombiano*, 151–2, 1982. See the comments in Vidal Perdomo, op. cit., p. 49.
28  Cf. Copete Lizarralde, op. cit., p. 245; Sachica, *El control*, p. 68.
29  Cf. Copete Lizarralde, op. cit., p. 246; Sachica, *El control*, p. 172.
30  Sarría, op. cit., p. 83; Sachica, *El control*, p. 68.
31  Vidal Perdomo, op. cit., p. 46.
32  Arts. 90 and 215, 1, Constitution. Art. 11, Decree 432 of 1969.
33  Art. 90, Constitution.

29  *The mixed system of judicial review in Brazil*

1  H. Fix-Zamudio and J. Carpizo, 'Amérique Latine', in L. Favoreu and J.A. Jolowicz, eds., *Le Contrôle juridictionnel des lois*, Paris, 1986, p. 121.
2  O.A. Bandeira de Mello, *A teoria das constituições rígidas*, São Paulo, 1980, p. 157; J. Alfonso da Silva, 'Sistema de defensa de la Constitución brasileña', *La Constitución y su defensa*, U.N.A.M., Mexico, 1984, p. 265; 'Da jurisdição constitucional no Brasil e na

América Latina', in *La Jurisdicción Constitucional en Iberoamérica*, p. 599.

3   Art. 59, III, 1, 1981 Constitution.

4   Art. 13, 10; Law 221 of 20 November 1984.

5   Bandeira de Mello, op. cit., pp. 158–237.

6   Art. 12, 2, 1934 Constitution.

7   Alfonso da Silva, 'Sistema', p. 265.

8   Also in Law No. 2271 of 22 July 1954.

9   Cf. Alfonso da Silva, 'Sistema', p. 267.

10  A. Buzaid, 'La acción directa de inconstitucionalidad en el derecho brasileño', *Revista de la Facultad de Derecho*, U.C.A.B., 19–22, Caracas, 1964, p. 55; Bandeira de Mello, op. cit., p. 157.

11  Cf. Alfonso da Silva, 'Sistema', pp. 265, 268; Alfonso da Silva, *Curso de direito constitucional positivo*, Sao Paolo, 1984, p. 17.

12  Art. 119, III, b, c, Constitution. Alfonso da Silva, 'Sistema', p. 276; Bandeira de Mello, op. cit., p. 215.

13  Alfonso da Silva, *Curso*, p. 18; Alfonso da Silva, 'Sistema', p. 271.

14  Alfonso da Silva, 'Sistema', pp. 299; Buzaid, op. cit., p. 91.

15  This qualified vote was first established in the 1934 Constitution (Art. 179), and is always required. See Bandeira de Mello, op. cit., p. 159.

16  Alfonso da Silva, 'Sistema', p. 276.

17  Art. 199, III, b, c, Constitution.

18  Alfonso da Silva, 'Sistema', p. 277.

19  Bandeira de Mello, op. cit., p. 218.

20  Alfonso da Silva, 'Sistema', pp. 298, 299.

21  Art. 42, VII, Federal Constitution.

22  Alfonso da Silva, 'Sistema', pp. 296, 299.

23  Cf. T.B. Cavalcanti, *Do controle de constitucionalidade*, Rio de Janeiro, 1968, p. 69.

24  Art. 7, Constitution, 1934. Bandeira de Mello, op. cit., p. 221; Alfonso da Silva, 'Sistema', p. 270.

25  Art. 10, Constitution 1934. Bandeira de Mello, op. cit., p. 170; Alfonso da Silva, 'Sistema', p. 269.

26  Art. 11, 1, Constitution; Art. 1, Law No. 2271 of 22 July 1954 and Law No. 4337 of 1 June 1964. Buzaid, op. cit., pp. 76–8.

27  Art. 11, 2, Constitution; Art. 9, Law No. 4337 of 1 June 1964; A. Buzaid, op. cit., p. 53.

28  Buzaid, op. cit., pp. 79, 97; Bandeira de Mello, op. cit., p. 222.

29  See Bandeira de Mello, op. cit., p. 212; Buzaid, op. cit., p. 95. In contrary sense see Alfonso da Silva, 'Sistema', p. 301.

30  Alfonso da Silva, 'Sistema', p. 301. For an opposite view, see Buzaid, op. cit., p. 96.

31  J. Alfonso da Silva, 'Sistema', p. 270; A. Buzaid considers this action as the only one in Brazil whose principal object is the declaration of the unconstitutionality of a law, op. cit., p. 84.

32  Art. 119, I, 1, Constitution; Law No. 4337 of 1 June 1964. Alfonso da Silva, *Curso*, p. 18.

33  Art. 42, VII, Constitution.

34 Alfonso da Silva, 'Sistema', pp. 285, 300; for an opposite view, see Bandeira de Mello, op. cit., pp. 201, 213.
35 Alfonso da Silva, 'Sistema', p. 300.
36 Bandeira de Mello, op. cit., p. 201; Buzaid, op. cit., p.96.
37 Alfonso da Silva, 'Sistema', p. 301; for an opposite view see Buzaid, op. cit., p. 95.
38 Art. 113, 33, Constitution 1934. A. Rios Espinoza, 'Presupuestos constitucionales del mandato de seguridad', *Boletín de Instituto de Derecho Comparado de México*, U.N.A.M., 46, 1963, p. 71. Also published in H. Fix-Zamudio, A. Rios Espinosa and N. Alcalá Zamora, *Tres estudios sobre el mandato de seguridad brasileño*, Mexico, 1963, pp. 71–96.
39 Art. 153, 21 Constitution.
40 Cf. Alfonso da Silva, 'Sistema', p. 279; H. Fix-Zamudio, 'Mandato de seguridad y juicio de amparo', *Boletín del Instituto de Derecho Comparado de México*, U.N.A.M.; 46, 1963, pp. 11, 17 (also published in Fix-Zamudio, Rios Espinosa, Alcalá Zamora, op. cit., pp. 3–69); Rios Espinosa, op. cit., p. 88.
41 Fix-Zamudio, op. cit., p. 16; Alfonso da Silva, 'Sistema', p. 279.
42 Bandeira de Mello, op. cit., p. 174.
43 Art. 153, 31, Constitution.
44 Alfonso da Silva, *Açao popular constitucional. Doutrina e proceso*, Sao Paulo, 1968, p. 129; Alfonso da Silva, 'Sistema', p. 280.

*30   The mixed system of judicial review in Guatemala and Peru*

1 See the comments regarding the constitutional process of Guatemala during the nineteenth century in J. M. García Laguardia, *La defensa de la Constitución*, Mexico, 1983, pp. 52–3; 'La Constitución y su defensa. Notas sobre el sistema de la República de Guatemala. Una visión historico-juridíca' in *La Constitución y su defensa*, U.N.A.M., Mexico 1984, pp. 663–7.
2 Art. 93, c, Constitution 1921.
3 See also Art. 172, Constitution, 15 September 1965.
4 García Laguardia, *La defensa*, pp. 56–7.
5 Art. 246, Constitution.
6 García Laguardia, *La defensa*, p. 58.
7 Ibid., p, 59,
8 See Fix-Zamudio, *Los Tribunales Constitucionales y los derechos humanos*, Mexico, 1980, p. 136.
9 Art. 262, Constitution. The court and the recourse of unconstitutionality are regulated in the law of *amparo, habeas corpus* and constitutionality of 3 May 1966. See the reference in Fix-Zamudio, op. cit., p. 137.
10 Art. 266, Constitution; Art. 105, Law.
11 Fix-Zamudio, op. cit., p. 138.

12    Art. 263, Constitution; Art. 106, Law.
13    Art. 264, Constitution; Art. 107, Law.
14    Fix-Zamudio, op. cit., p. 64.
15    García Laguardia, *La defensa*, p. 63.
16    Art. 263, Constitution; Art. 106, Law.
17    Art. 108, Law.
18    García Laguardia, *La defensa*, p. 67; Fix-Zamudio, op. cit., p. 140.
19    Fix-Zamudio, op. cit., p. 136; García Laguardia, 'El habeas corpus y el amparo en el derecho constitucional guatemalteco', in *La Jurisdicción Constitucional en Iberoamérica*, pp. 43–69.
20    Art. 80, 1, Constitution.
21    Art. 80, 2, Constitution.
22    García Laguardia, op. cit., p. 50; Fix-Zamudio, op. cit., p. 136.
23    See D. García Belaúde, 'La influencia española en la Constitución peruana (a propósito del Tribunal de Garantías Constitucionales)', *Revista de Derecho Político*, U.N.E.D., 16, Madrid, 1982–3, p. 201.
24    See D. García Belaúde, 'La nueva Constitución peruana', *Boletín Mexicano de Derecho Comparado*, 40, 1981.
25    See García Belaúde, 'La influencia española', pp. 205–7.
26    Ibid., p. 205.
27    Art. 296, Constitution 28 July 1980.
28    See the comments in H. Fix-Zamudio, 'Dos leyes orgánicas de Tribunales Constitucionales latinoamericanos: Chile y Perú', *Boletín Mexicano de Derecho Comparado*, 51, 1984, p. 943.
29    Art. 298, Constitution.
30    Art. 298, 1, Constitution.
31    Art. 40, Organic Law.
32    Art. 302, Constitution.
33    Art. 300, Constitution.
34    Art. 187, Constitution.
35    Art. 41, Organic Law.
36    Arts. 295; 298, 2; 305, Constitution 1980.
37    See H. Fix-Zamudio, 'Ley peruana de *habeas corpus* y amparo', *Boletín Mexicano de Derecho Comparado*, 50, 1984, p. 575.
38    Ibid, p. 579.

# INDEX